The Critical
Development
Studies
Handbook

The Critical Development Studies Handbook

Tools for Change

EDITED BY HENRY VELTMEYER

CDS Network [www.critdev.org]

PlutoPress
www.plutobooks.com
London & New York

FERNWOOD
PUBLISHING
Halifax & Winnipeg

Editing and text design: Brenda Conroy
Cover photo: Dieter Telemans/PANOS
Cover design: Anú Design (www.anu-design.ie)
Printed and bound in Canada by Hignell Book Printing

Mixed Sources
Product group from well-managed
forests and other controlled sources
www.fsc.org Cert no. SW-COC-003438
© 1996 Forest Stewardship Council
FSC

Published in Canada by Fernwood Publishing
32 Oceanvista Lane
Black Point, Nova Scotia, B0J 1B0
and 748 Broadway Avenue, Winnipeg, Manitoba, R3G 0X3
www.fernwoodpublishing.ca

Published in the rest of the world by Pluto Press
345 Archway Road, London N6 5AA and
175 Fifth Avenue, New York, NY 10010
www.plutobooks.com

Fernwood Publishing Company Limited gratefully acknowledges the financial support of the Government of Canada
through the Canada Book Fund, the Canada Council for the Arts, the Nova Scotia Department of Tourism and Culture
and the Province of Manitoba, through the Book Publishing Tax Credit, for our publishing program.

British Library Cataloguing in Publication Data
A catalogue record for this book is available from the British Library

Library of Congress Cataloging in Publication Data applied for

ISBN 9781552663806 Paperback (Fernwood)
ISBN 9781552663868 Hardback (Fernwood)
ISBN 9780745331232 Paperback (Pluto)
ISBN 9780745331249 Hardback (Pluto)

Library and Archives Canada Cataloguing in Publication

Veltmeyer, Henry
The critical development studies handbook: tools for change/ Henry Veltmeyer.

Co-published by: Pluto Press.
Includes bibliographical references.
ISBN 978-1-55266-386-8 (bound).--ISBN 978-1-55266-380-6 (pbk.)

1. Economic development. 2. Social change--Economic aspects. I. Title.

HD82.V385 2010   338.91   C2010-902966-6

Contents

Dedication

This book is dedicated to the life and work of Kari Polanyi Levitt, Canada's premier development economist; founding and on-going member of the Canadian Association for the Study of International Development and the Critical Development Studies Network; author of the seminal (and recently republished) *Silent Surrender,* the equally important recently published *Essays on the Theory of Plantation Economy* and the much-awaited but as yet unpublished *History of Development Economics*; and much-appreciated friend and colleague to many of us.

For information or to join CDS, contact us at:
www.critdev.org.
Tel. +52 (492) 998-1029 (México)
+1 (902) 420-5870 (Canada)

Acknowledgements

The editor and co-authors gratefully acknowledge the generous support of the Canadian International Development Research Centre (IDRC) for the project to create a network of scholars and practitioners concerned with advancing alternative forms of development that are socially inclusive, equitable, sustainable in terms of the environment and livelihoods, and empowering of the poor—capacitating them to act for themselves. The role of academics and activists (activist scholars, one might say) in this project, and in the interdisciplinary field of international development studies, is to promote critical thinking and substantive social change—different ways of thinking about and practising development. This publication, the project and work of the network of activist scholars, would not have been possible without the generous support of IDRC. The supportive efforts and assistance of Luc Mougeot, the project officer assigned to the project, are particularly appreciated.

On behalf of all the co-authors of this publication, the editor wishes also to acknowledge the valuable support to the project provided by so many other members of the Canadian Association for the Study of International Development (CASID) as well as the broader global CDS network. Some of these activist scholars have already committed themselves to contribute towards the production of a number of readers in diverse areas of CDS.

In addition, the editor wishes to acknowledge the valuable support of the Global Capital and Alternative Development and the Migration and Development units of the Development Studies Doctoral Program at the Universidad Autónoma de Zacatecas.

Using the CDS Handbook

The current global crisis—coming at the end of a long period of dominant market-centred development policies, which have produced considerable global instability and turmoil, especially in developing societies—cries out for a more critical, proactive approach to the study of international development. The challenge of creating and disseminating such a critical approach has become the project of a broad and increasingly global network of development scholars actively engaged in using their research to effect broad social change.

One result of this project is this Handbook, which is intended to be an important resource for all development scholars, teachers, students, researchers, activists and members of the public who share a concern for what has come to be called critical development studies (CDS). University teachers, especially, can use this Handbook for curriculum design, whether this consists of courses, seminars, workshops or lectures. There are 49 short course modules that each identify the six issues of greatest import. For each theme there is a brief discussion of the central issues as well as a list of selected references.

The Handbook is also a general resource and reference tool for determining the scope of development studies, providing a critical perspective informed by a belief in the need for substantive change for genuine, lasting progress. In short, scholars, researchers, practitioners and those actively engaged in social change—whether they work in government, nongovernmental organizations, social movements or universities—will find the Handbook an indispensable companion for guiding their research, study, teaching and practice.

Many of the essential readings referenced in the Handbook are accessible at the website critdev.org. In due course these will be updated online, with the most essential readings grouped by area and edited into a series of CDS readers, each containing the twelve most important or 'must' readings in that area.

Preface

Notwithstanding a rapidly expanding world economy, the world is by many accounts lurching towards a crisis of global proportions and multiple dimensions—financial, economic, social, environmental and political. And unless serious rethinking of the current development model occurs and corrective action is taken, the prognosis for humankind is dim. To come to terms with the forces that are propelling the world towards this crisis, it is essential that we find ways to close the growing worldwide divide between the rich and the poor—and the powerful and the powerless.

In 1970, the 'advanced countries' (IMF classification) received 68 percent of world income, while the 'rest of the world' got 32 percent. By 2000, the 'advanced countries' received or appropriated 81 percent of the world income while the 'rest of the world' received just 19 percent. In the same period the world population share of the advanced countries fell from 20 to 16 percent. Three decades of globalization, which was heralded with the promise of general prosperity, have done little to reduce the crushing poverty of much of the world's population. Several decades of concerted efforts in the direction of a more socially inclusive, equitable, participatory and sustainable development have not changed the basic structure of the economies and societies all over the world, a structure that continues to reproduce poverty. Although some U.N. organizations are reporting progress towards meeting the new millennium goals, such as eradicating absolute poverty by 2015, neither globalization nor the localization of development, neither the old nor the new development paradigm, none of the ideas, multiple and diverse strategies or actions taken by all manner of organizations over the past fifty years have managed to make much of a difference for the lives and livelihoods of the world's poor—upwards of some 2.5 billion people; fully one-third of the world population are mired in poverty and misery.

By many accounts, the world is on the threshold, if not in the throes, of a new triple crisis that will dramatically reduce the capacity of billions of people, with few resources and little income, to access potable water, nutritious food and affordable housing, sinking them further into the morass of hunger. The political consequences of such economic, political and environmental problems will also exacerbate conflicts over scarce resources, generating conditions that will lead to destabilizing violence and increased displacement of the population from the land and their communities—and even societies. In this connection, the number of migrants across the world has more than doubled over the last two decades of globalization and worldwide development, reaching a historical record of 200 million in 2008. A growing proportion of these migrants are labour migrants, forced to move from South to North to escape diverse conditions of socioeconomic exclusion and insecurity in most underdeveloped countries.

What is required is a serious rethinking of development—of the way that development is conceived, studied and practised. To this end, at the brink of a possible disaster, a number of scholars and activists have come together to collectively think through the nature of the problem and possible solutions—to search for an alternative way of thinking about development and putting it into practice. To the members of this rapidly growing network (see critdev.org), it is clear that, if the global war against poverty has not been won in over thirty years of the concerted efforts and considerable intellectual and financial resources of hundreds of thousands of policymakers, academics and practitioners, there is something seriously wrong with the development enterprise itself. Either the war on global poverty and underdevelopment is being fought with inadequate tools and weapons or, more likely, it is being fought in the wrong way—misconceived as to the nature of the problem, the best way of tackling it and the type and scope of changes required, as well as the agencies for this change.

From Zacatecas to Halifax and Back

The CDS network of scholars and consortium of institutions was formed in response to the problems that are threatening to assume the proportions of a global crisis. The first steps toward this network were taken in Mexico in 2004 in the context of a recently formed doctoral program of development studies at the Autonomous University of Zacatecas (UAZ)—the first such program in the country and one of very few in the entire region. On the basis of active collaboration with scholars in Canada, Europe and other parts of Latin America, the seeds of the idea for a global CDS network were transported to and transplanted in Halifax, Nova Scotia, in October 2006 at a gathering at Saint Mary's University that led to the formal founding of the CDS network.

At the conference an action plan was formulated to advance diverse activities designed to change the way in which development is conceived, studied and practised. The aim was to create a new centre of knowledge construction in the field of international development studies, as well as to strengthen programs of advanced or higher education in the field on the basis of (1) a deep and extensive South-North and South-South dialogue among scholars and practitioners; (2) collaborative research on critical issues of development; (3) an interdisciplinary approach towards analysis and research commensurate with the multidimensional nature of the development process; (4) a critical perspective on the existing developmental model and ways of thinking about development—oriented towards the search for substantive change designed to bring about genuine progress and a form of development that is truly equitable, participatory, socially inclusive and sustainable; and (5) the sharing of human, intellectual and institutionally based resources (bibliographic databases, etc.)—institutional partnerships as well as collaborative research and study.

CDS Summer School

One of the activities programmed by the CDS network, generously financed by the International Development Research Centre of Canada (IDRC) and constructed within the framework of an institutional partnership between UAZ and Saint Mary's University in Halifax, was the formation of a summer school in CDS. The school was designed as a graduate level course on diverse issues in several areas of CDS that would bring together graduate students from across the world, North and South. It was successfully piloted in Zacatecas in August 2008, with the participation of six faculty members and thirty-two students from Mexico and other parts of Latin America and the Caribbean, Canada, Europe and Asia (see critdev.org for the program and results).

A Study Program of Critical Development Studies

This book is the product of the collaborative work of scholars in the CDS network. It takes the form of an introductory essay on the itinerary of the development idea—a short history of diverse ideas and theories in the growing field of IDS—and a series of short course modules constructed in twelve strategic areas of CDS. The aim is to identify the most important areas of advanced study of the development process from a critical perspective and the six most important study themes in each area, as well as the most essential readings on these issues. The result is 49 short course modules constructed by leading development scholars. As such, the book serves simultaneously as a textbook for diverse course in the fields of international development studies, the policy economy of international relations, globalization and development, the sociology or politics of development and development economics, and as an alternative research agenda as well as a rich resource for independent study and research into some of the most critical issues that confront students, scholars, policymakers, practitioners and activists today.

—Raúl Delgado Wise, Universidad Autónoma de Zacatecas (Mexico)
and co-chair of the CDS Network and Consortium

—Henry Veltmeyer, Saint Mary's University (Canada),
Universidad Autónoma de Zacatecas (Mexico)
and co-chair of the CDS Network and Consortium

Section 1

Introduction

Critical development studies (CDS) entails a rethinking of development theory and practice by going back to the basics—returning to the use of concepts that describe the world as empirically given, to the assumptions and beliefs that underlie these concepts and to the creation of theories that seek to explain the realities of the current order of things, especially with respect to distortions in social equity, structural inequalities and deeply rooted social injustices. Such critical social analysis is not only *scientific* in the broadest sense of the term—reality is the baseline for theory, and theory is tested against further empirical research—it is also *critical* of systematic social narratives (ideologies) that portray the social structure in such a way as to make the 'losers' in the social enterprise accomplices in their own exploitation through the socialized acceptance of the superiority of the 'winners.' It is part of critical development studies both to expose the social purpose of such narratives and to reveal the basic untruths about social reality that lie at their heart.[1]

The first module in this handbook reviews the evolution of development theory, with a focus on basic concepts and the key ideas advanced over the years in regard to the process of change and development—to assess and evaluate their meaning and use in analysis and practice. The meaning given to these concepts and the use made of the associated ideas are crucial in that they profoundly shape our perception of the development problematic, the appropriate form of analysis and ultimately the social action that we see as possible or even desirable. However, it is too often the case that these concepts and ideas are derived not from some scientific process of data-theory dialogue but from an ideology created with the purpose of explaining away the ascendency and domination of one social class or group by another, clearing the way for the appropriation of resources by the entitled class or group and explaining away the structural disentitlement of the subaltern classes or groups.

See the box, 'The Tao of Neoconservatism: George Mankiw,' for an illustration of this point. This insert exemplifies the power of ideology in development analysis, in this case furnished by one of the most celebrated economists of our time. The profound ignorance of the actual empirical state of affairs, especially in the 'real world' of developing societies, evidenced in this excerpt on Mankiw would be astonishing were it not perfectly understandable in terms of the ideology that governs his thinking. In reality, the overall effect, perhaps more uncharitably, the aim, of this ideology is to throw a veil of untruth over the real state of affairs in the world—by purveying a social fable, if you will—in order to justify social arrangements, policies and actions that on a closer, critical analysis prove to be just those social actions and policy regimes that serve the interests of the few, the rich and the powerful, at the expense of the many, the poor and the powerless.

This theme is elaborated by Anthony O'Malley in Module 27, where he looks at the different basic ways of thinking about development and carrying out analysis from a critical standpoint. In his construction, the central issue has to do with the concepts of *social structure* and *social action* (or 'agency'). 'Structure' refers to the way society is organized, including the institutional practices that give form to social behaviour and provide the boundary conditions for consciously directed individual actions or social strategies. Although 'development' can be viewed as the outcome of *social actions* taken within the 'pathways' of the *social and institutional structure*, analysts or scholars tend to emphasize one or the other.

It is possible to approach analysis from a *strategic* perspective (to view development as the outcome of consciously directed actions pursued by an actor or agency, a matter of goal, means and agency), or from a *structural* perspective (to view development as the outcome of forces beyond the individual's control, generated by the social and institutional structures of the system). Theories that emphasize individual purposiveness, actions and strategies focus on goal-oriented behaviour and the individual or small group instruments created to realize these goals. This is what is meant by social action or agency. The emphasis is on social action, on actors as creators of social organization through a combination of individual desires and purposes in a context of other wilful individual actors. Analysis in this form and theories in this tradition usually play down the overarching presence and the determining or conditioning features of a given social structure and generally put the analysis in the service of human liberty, desire, will, individual goals and purposes. This picture of humans acting in society is often termed *voluntarism*.

Armed with a critical perspective, the authors in this Handbook are concerned with serious, rigorous thinking about the complex and incredibly dynamic interaction of individual and society, agency and structure. However, as *critical* analysts of the development process they are compelled to emphasize over and over again the importance of the conditioning and, in varying senses according to each thinker, the determining aspects of the social structure (and associated processes of change and development) in given times and places. Only in this way can they address what evidence clearly suggests are structured inequalities in the relations of production and power that underpin and shape the experiences of most people, determining their life chances and opportunities—who gets what. A structural analysis is the only instrument for tackling the very clear existence of a global structure in which people in all countries of the world find themselves and which, to an important extent, delimits and conditions the possible pathways for collective or self-development.

'The Tao of Neoconservatism': George Mankiw by Gilles Raveaud

You might not have heard of Gregory Mankiw. The Harvard economics professor and former advisor to George W. Bush is touted as one of the most gifted economists of our generation. He is also one of the most effective and talented propagandists of our times. His target: young economics students. His field of operation: the world's universities. His weapon: the best selling textbook in the world. It includes 36 chapters and 800 pages of nice colours, graphs, captivating stories and interesting asides.

What is most worrisome is that Mankiw's text presents economics as a unified discipline, entirely committed to the agenda of what has been called ... 'neoliberalism.' Mankiw believes that markets are the solutions to everything .... If a problem persists, it is can only be for one of two reasons: the market is imperfect or it is non-existent. ...

For ... Mankiw, if unemployment exists it is only because of ... unemployment benefits, trade unions and minimum wages. Indeed, such 'protective' social instruments actually help *cause* unemployment. Mankiw presents this view as consensual among economists. In fact, quite a few economists admit that the labour market is a very special 'market'; indeed, the price of the labour commodity involved—the wage—is not set the same way as the price of other 'goods,'... by the competitive forces of supply and demand.

Pollution is another example of market imperfections, or in some cases of non-existent markets. Mankiw admits that in some cases markets do not ensure that the environment is kept clean, the result being excessive pollution (what economists call technically a 'negative externality'). But what is the solution? According to Mankiw, it is to define the right to pollute as a form of property that can then be traded—in effect commodifying pollution and setting up an exchange for its trading. Public authorities issue 'pollution permits' to polluting companies (who then cannot pollute more than the amount covered by the permits they hold). Companies buy and sell these permits on the market, depending on how much they will pollute in a year. The fewer the permits, the higher their price and the higher the incentives for firms to reduce pollution... But the problem is that Mankiw... downplays government regulation as a way to regulate production which produces pollution, a way to diminish consumption or manage waste. Nor does he bring up the possibility of using renewable sources of energy. He even insists that we are not running out of resources because if that were the case, the price of oil would be much higher than it is. Climate change is a critical issue, caused by ever-growing economic activity but it does not even merit an index entry.

In Mankiw's chapter on growth, the only two factors of production are capital and labour. [No mention is made of knowledge or technology as forces of production?] Workers and firms do not use land or electricity, gas or coal.... As natural resources and energy are absent in Mankiw's model, they cannot become a problem—for economists, that is.

... Since markets are a good way to organize economic activity, supply and demand is just about all you need to know in economics. Whatever you desire, you can pay for in the market: tomatoes, healthcare, housing, a car. That is demand. On the other side... firms compete to supply the consumers with the latest in clothes, or mobile phones or housing. That is supply. When supply is higher than demand the price falls.... When demand is higher than supply the price rises (e.g., a war in the Ivory Coast reduces the supply of cocoa)....

Mankiw accustoms his readers to the centrality of the idea of individual choices and preferences. The words 'poor' and 'rich' are rarely used. But, more surprisingly, there is also no mention of the power of corporations.... This is because Mankiw's world is a world of small firms operating on perfectly competitive markets...

Mankiw downplays inequality, even if the growing gap between rich and poor over the last decade has commanded the attention of more and more economists, even within mainstream economic thinking.... It is clear... that Mankiw's real interest, rather than training students in the complexities of economics is to shape the minds... of citizens and future leaders around the world. A metatheorem running throughout the textbook is a voluntarist one: there is really no such thing as an overarching, conditioning social structure. Rather, the world is made up of isolated individuals, agents of their own destiny, driven by their desires, all of which are *sui generis*. In this... fantastical world, fairness and equity prevail: everyone gets what they deserve and are free to choose with equal opportunity. It is also a world where, thanks to the magic of markets, private enterprise and property rights, standards of living rise constantly. 'It's a wonderful world.' If only it existed.

Module 1

The Evolution of an Idea
Critical Development Studies

Jane Parpart
Dalhousie University, Canada; University of the West Indies, Jamaica

Henry Veltmeyer
Saint Mary's University, Canada; Autonomous University of Zacatecas, Mexico

Wolfgang Sachs (1992) argues that the idea of 'development' was invented as part of a geopolitical project to lure countries liberated from the yoke of colonial rule away from communism, to steer them along a capitalist path already traced out by the democracies of Western Europe and North America. In this context Tucker (1999) writes of 'development' as a form of cultural imperialism, the imposition of an idea advanced in the interests of imperial rule. In any case, it is possible to identify six 'development decades'—from 1948, when President Truman launched his Point-4 Program, to the present. This module traces the evolution of ideas associated with the development project over these decades in terms of the changing contexts that shaped these ideas and gave rise to identifiable shifts in thought and practice. (See Veltmeyer & Parpart 2004) for a full-length essay on this theme.)

1. Launching the development idea: Theory in the 1950s and 1960s

As a field of study and as a geopolitical project taken up by governments and international organizations, 'development' can be traced back to the late 1940s in two strands. Scholars such as Walter Rostow (1960) and Sir Arthur Lewis (1954), concerned with 'economic development' *within* the capitalist system, dominated the study and practice of 'development.' However, Marxist political economists, such as Paul Baran (1957), and 'Latin American structuralists,' such as Raúl Prebisch and Fernando Cardoso, while less influential in development circles, laid the groundwork for critiques that would emerge in the 1970s (see Modules 5–7).

   In addition to the anti-colonial movements and associated nationalisms and the emergence of an East-West ideological struggle and the Cold War, the context for this evolution in development theory was provided by a secular path of unprecedented economic growth within the institutional framework of the Bretton Woods 'world economic order.' French historians wrote of 'the thirty glorious years' while others celebrated 'the golden age of capitalism' (Marglin and Schor 1990).

   In this geopolitical context and institutional framework, 'development' was conceived in conditional terms as relative *progress* in per capita *economic growth* and in structural terms as *industrialization* and *modernization*. So conceived, 'development' entails the following feature: (1) an increase in the rate of savings and investment—the accumulation of physical and financial capital; (2) investment of this capital in industry (each unit of capital invested in industry, in theory generating up to five times the rate of return on investment in agriculture, with strong

4

multiplier effects on both incomes and employment); (3) in the absence of a strong endogenous capitalist class, the state assumes the basic 'functions of capital'—investment, entrepreneurship and management; (4) the nationalization of economic enterprises in strategic industries and sectors[2]; (5) an inward orientation of production, which, together with a secular increase in wages and salaries, will expand the domestic market; (6) regulation of domestic and other markets and the protection and subsidized support of the firms that produce for the market, insulating them from the competitive pressures of the world economy; and (7) modernization of the production apparatus, the state and social institutions, reorienting them towards values and norms that are functional for economic growth.

2. Saving capitalism from itself: A decade of reform

In the 1970s, under the conditions of a system-wide production crisis, the development project came under serious question, challenged from the left with proposals of revolutionary change and the right with proposals to reverse the gains made by workers and small-scale producers or peasants at the expense of capital and the propertied class. At the same time, some scholars and activists began to call for a participatory, people-centred approach to development problems in the Third World (Hollnsteiner 1977; Rahman 1991).

On the left there emerged a sidestream of development thought oriented towards a belief in the need for radical change. Those who subscribed to this belief turned towards both Marxism and Latin American 'structuralism' to construct what came to be known as 'dependency theory' (see Module 6). Within the framework of a centre-periphery model, dependency theory argued that development and underdevelopment were two sides of the same coin—that a country's socioeconomic conditions were inextricably linked to the position it occupied in the 'world capitalist system.' In the 1970s, dependency theory in its diverse formulations achieved a relative consensus in academia but no such consensus existed in policymaking circles. Voices of dissent from the political right questioned state-centred solutions to developmental problems and began to argue for global free trade as the engine of economic growth (Bauer 1982; Lal 1983). Pressure to consider poverty from a people-centred perspective intensified as well. A growing number of scholars and activists argued that development could only address the problems of the poor if it engaged the poor as agents of their own development (Cohen and Uphoff 1977).

In the face of conflicting demands, the mainstream development project was reconstructed in the direction of liberal reform—to stave off pressures for more radical change, or social revolution, as well as calls to abandon the field. The essential features of this new policy agenda included an enhanced role for the state regarding (1) programs that would establish the social conditions of development (education, health, social welfare); (2) a poverty-oriented strategy designed to meet the basic needs of the poor; (3) reforms designed to improve the poor's access to society's productive resources (e.g., land reform); (4) redistributive 'growth with equity' policies, e.g., taxation, to redistribute more equitably market-generated incomes; and (5) an integrated program of rural development that corrected for the urban bias of government policies and the neglect of agriculture.

In the 1970s, this model ('growth with equity,' or basic human needs approach) was advanced in the context of an extensive, at times heated, debate on the role of inequality in the growth and development process and policy priorities and trade-offs—'growth with efficiency' versus 'growth with equity.' Simon Kuznets (1953), a pioneer of the theory of economic growth, maintained that inequalities in poor countries would inevitably widen with economic growth before levelling out. Another pioneer of economic development, Caribbean economist Sir Arthur Lewis (1963 [1954]), advanced a similar argument that widening inequality was the unavoidable price that poor countries would have to pay for the economic development and prosperity that would eventually ensue.[3]

3. Capitalist development as neoliberal globalization

In the absence of or with a weak capitalist class in many developing countries, the state became the primary agent of development, taking on the role assigned in economic theory to the 'private sector.'[4] However, by the 1980s, in the context of a system-wide production crisis, a looming fiscal crisis and a decade of reforms with negligible results in terms of development, the liberal reformers abandoned the field, providing theoretical—and political—space for the emergence of a 'counter-revolution' in mainstream development thinking and practice. This counter-revolution was supported by a neoconservative ideology and associated political regimes—Reaganism and Thatcherism. In economic terms, it was based on a neoliberal model of the 'world market,' freed from the regulatory constraints of the welfare-developmental interventionist state, as the engine of growth. The private sector (i.e., the capitalist class and multinational corporations in this sector) took over the responsibility of driving this engine, while the 'forces of freedom'—the freedom of individuals to pursue their self-interest, accumulate capital and profit from their investments—fuelled the economic growth process. Development was relegated to an incidental by-product of this process.

The economists at the World Bank assumed responsibility for designing the 'new economic model' to promote capitalist development (Bulmer-Thomas 1986). This model was based on the idea of 'globalization'—the insertion of all national economies into the system of global capitalism, a 'new world economic order' (Ostry 1990). The Bank's series of structural reforms was intended to facilitate this integration into the new (neoliberal) world order of free market capitalism (see Modules 9, 14–15).

Seven major components comprised this model, which was 'imposed' by the International Monetary Fund (IMF): (1) a *realistic* rate of currency exchange (devaluation) and measures to *stabilize* the economy (tight fiscal and monetary policies); (2) *privatization* of the means of production and state enterprises, reversing the nationalization of strategic industry; (3) *liberalization* of capital markets and trade, reversing the policy of state protection and opening up domestic firms to free competition and market prices; (4) *deregulation* of private economic activity, reducing the impact of government regulations on the operations of market forces; (5) *labour market reform*—reduced regulation and employment protection, erosion of minimum wages, restrictions on collective bargaining and reduced public expenditures; and (6) *downsizing* of the state apparatus, *modernizing* it and *decentralizing* decisionmaking powers to provincial and local levels of government, allowing for a more democratic and participatory form of top-down development. The last in these 'steps to hell'—to quote Joseph Stiglitz (2002), former chief economist at the World Bank but now a major critic of the IMF's neoliberal policies—is (7) a free market in both capital and tradable goods and services, first regionally and then worldwide.

Throughout the 1980s World Bank economists clung to the idea that stabilization and structural adjustment policies (SAPs) provided a necessary framework of 'good policy' and 'good governance' (Stiglitz 2002). The 'Washington Consensus' (see Williamson 1990) was that these measures provided the required ingredients to stimulate economic growth, a belief repeated in all of the World Bank's annual reports. Countries such as Zimbabwe were constrained to adopt SAPs with promises of guaranteed economic growth and as a condition of receiving foreign aid (see Modules 9, 15–16). However, few SAPs delivered the promised growth, leading some economists and Bank officials to recognize the need for further reform—to give structural adjustment and the neoliberal agenda a 'human face.'

A decade 'lost to development' (no progress whatsoever in Latin America and Sub-Saharan Africa) and the emergence of huge disparities in the distribution of productive resources, wealth and income—and widespread dissent and resistance—led to a new policy agenda and the search for a more sustainable form of structural adjustment. The resulting 'post-Washington Consensus' (PWC) included (1) a 'new social policy' (NSP) targeting the poor; (2) a decentralized form of governance, to bring government closer to 'the people'—to create a more participatory and empowering form of local or community-based development based on the accumulation of 'social capital,' exploiting the one asset that the poor were deemed to have in abundance (on the dynamics of this new paradigm, see Module 24); and (3) the 'strengthening of civil society' as a strategic partner in the development process, using the nongovernmental organizations (NGOs) in this 'third sector' as a means of delivering 'assistance'—as a strategic partner in the development process.

4. The search for 'another development'

Pressures for reform dominated mainstream development thought and practice in the 1970s. These pressures inspired many to search for an alternative form of development (Goulet 1989; Rahman, 1991). While the impetus for this alternative approach can be found in the early to mid 1970s, it was well into the 1980s before a broad shift towards a new paradigm could be discerned (Chopra, Kadekodi & Murty 1990; Veltmeyer & O'Malley 2001). Advocates of reform began to patch together a new model based on the ideas advanced in the search for 'alternative development' (AD)—initiated 'from within and below' rather than 'from above' (by government) or 'the outside' (international organizations or 'overseas development associations' [ODAs])—and development was conceived as socially inclusive, equitable, human in form and scale, sustainable in terms of both the environment and livelihoods and above all, predicated on community or popular participation. This approach draws on the ideas of Paulo Freire (1970), feminists writing about empowerment (Antrobus 1995; Kabeer 1994; Moser 1993) and community-based research and practice (Chambers 1987).

Some advocates called for an alternative model that would restore the role of the state in regulating economic activity in the public interest. This model aimed to improve access of the poor to society's productive resources, such as land, technology and capital in the form of credit, and to redistribute equitably these resources and the fruits of development. Others, however, focused on 'the local.' These scholars and activists were sceptical about the transformative capacities of the weak and often corrupt states that are all too common in parts of the developing world, particularly in Sub-Saharan Africa (Parpart, Rai and Staudt 2002: Chap. 1).

Another form of so-called 'alternative development'—currently much in favour in certain circles within academia and the U.N. system)—is based on the notion of 'sustainable livelihoods' (see Module 25). What distinguishes a sustainable livelihoods approach (SLA) is a concern with the *social* assets of the rural poor—what in the literature is conceived of as 'social capital,' bound up and accumulated in the capacity of the poor to network, to cooperate productively and to work together (Woolcock & Narayan 2000). Unlike natural, physical or financial forms of capital, *social capital* requires neither land reform nor other redistributive policies nor radical structural reforms, but taps into a resource that is abundantly given to the poor. The process involved is *social empowerment*—capacitating individuals and groups to actively participate in making decisions that affect their livelihoods. Like the 'people-first' or 'people-centred' approach of Chambers (1987) and Korten & Klaus (1984), and the gender and empowerment approach of Moser (1993) and feminists such as Kabeer (1994) and Antrobus (1995), advocates of this approach emphasize the resources and knowledge of the poor as well as their active role in the process of social transformation and development.

From a CDS perspective (see Akram-Lodhi in Module 33), the SLA is not an 'alternative' form of development at all. By placing each of five identified types of 'assets' on an equal footing, the SLA suggests that the poor can do better simply by 'reallocating' their portfolio of assets. But, as Akram-Lodhi notes, this is nothing more than suggesting that the poor pull themselves up by their own bootstraps! Also, this approach does not address in the least the issue of a fundamental inequality in access to and the distribution of resources, including 'power.' To suggest that all assets are fundamentally of equal value and that one can simply focus one's efforts and concern with assets such as 'social capital,' to which the poor have ready access, is absurd. Also, by stressing the ways in which poor households can do things for themselves and by not stressing the social and structural foundations of poverty, the SLA entails methodological individualism, or, in Terry Byres' phrase, 'neoclassical neopopulism.'

One of the strengths of the SLA (see Module 25) is precisely this focus on social empowerment of the poor through participation in their own development. However, the question of power is also its Achilles' heel. The weakest component of this approach, and this point applies to all forms of 'alternative development,' has to do with *political power*, that is, the capacity to make decisions (and determine government policy) related to society as a whole in the 'authoritative allocation of society's productive resources.' Proponents of alternative development assume that dominant groups and classes in society are willing to surrender their power—or to share it, particularly with the poor.

This assumption, as it turns out, is the nub of the problem (as recognized, interestingly, by the UNDP in its 2002 *Human Development Report*). Indeed, it is the Achilles' heel of most development efforts to date. Unlike social capital, the accumulation of political capital (decisionmaking power) and other forms of capital (financial, natural, physical) by the poor requires radical structural change. It requires a direct confrontation with the power structure—with those who hold the levers of economic and political power and reap a disproportionate share of society's productive resources. However, the rich and powerful, as noted, will not easily surrender either their wealth or their power. Power sharing to them means what it does to the World Bank: to let the poor participate in local decisions while leaving broader power structures intact.

Amalric 1998; Chambers 1987; Helmore & Singh 2001; Liamzon et al. 1996; Veltmeyer & O'Malley 2001.

5. Postdevelopment: A new way of thinking or the end of development?

In the 1980s, the structuralist approach came under attack from a variety of standpoints, leading to the assertion that development theory was at an impasse. Critiques drew heavily from post-structuralist epistemology and methodology and the theoretical perspectives of postmodernism. Critics of development theory, such as Frans Schuurman (1993) and Michael Edwards (1993), drew on postmodern analysis of structural notions of linear progress and modernity to denounce prevailing forms of development theory and practice. Development was viewed as a Western project, oblivious to 'relations of difference' and the complex dynamics of cultural diversity, used to pressure nations and peoples around the world to fit Western notions of 'progress.'

This critique also drew on poststructuralist concerns with language and discourse, which looked at the need to deconstruct language to find hidden transcripts and acknowledged the power of discourse to shape thought and practice (Escobar 1995). The tendency of Western development practitioners and theorists to ignore the voices of marginalized peoples in the South (as well as the North) was seen as a key element in the development project. The silencing of subaltern peoples was thus a major concern (Mallon 1994). The writings of Foucault, particularly his analytic focus on the capillary nature of power, its pervasiveness and relational character, also influenced these critics, who argued that a more nuanced analysis would reveal the power of marginalized peoples, particularly women (Mallon 1994; Parpart, Rai and Staudt 2002; Ferguson 1991). While the utility of poststructuralist and postmodernist thought for development is a matter of continuing debate, it has led to two different strands of poststructuralist/postdevelopment thought: anti-development and critical alternative development.

Some scholars concerned with the development impasse concluded that the ideas surrounding the development project and process were deeply flawed. Even worse—from the standpoint of most theorists of development at the time—they called into question the development project itself. Some, like Wolfgang Sachs and his associates in 'grassroots postmodernism' (Esteva and Prakash 1998) or 'postdevelopment' (Rahnema & Bawtree 1998), conceived of development in this intellectual context as a misbegotten enterprise.

From this perspective, the overarching ideologies and metatheories constructed to explain the process of historical change—and to fuel one project of social transformation after another—had lost their relevance. Systemic forces were regarded as uniformly negative, and development came to be seen as simply an attempt to force Western institutions, assumptions and practices on hapless people in the impoverished nations of the South. As one of the key proponents of anti-development, Escobar (1997: 85) argues that development functions as a discourse that 'created a space in which only certain things could be said and even imagined.' Development discourse shaped social reality in ways that reflected the understandings and meanings of those who crafted that discourse, namely development experts from the North (and some sympathetic Southerners, often trained in Northern institutions). Escobar (1997: 88–93) concludes that development as discourse and practice cannot emancipate people in the South because it erases social/cultural contexts and seeks (sometimes unconsciously) to appropriate local institutions and beliefs, replacing them with a vision of a globalizing world based on the Western model of 'normality.' Escobar argues that development as currently practised can never bring about social transformation. In fact, he and others maintain that development should be abandoned—that development discourse and practice is a seductive dead end and that marginalized people should depend on themselves in that they have the capacity, the need and the opportunity to construct their own futures from the fabric of their own political imagination and cultural resources (Esteva and Prakash 1998; Rahnema & Bawtree 1998).

This anti-development position has been equated with postdevelopment thinking but it is only one strand. Others, while sympathetic to Escobar's argument, recognize that development problems cannot simply be wished away. This alternative or populist wing of postdevelopment thinking is deeply critical of the top-down, hegemonic character of most mainstream development discourse and practice. It calls for more of a bottom-up, participatory approach where development 'experts' become or give way to facilitators who work with the poor rather than simply directing them from a position of expert knowledge (Munck 1999a). Development from this perspective cannot be simply 'given' to the poor. It requires attention to local knowledge and accumulated wisdom, respectful partnership and participatory practices. This will empower the poor by allowing them to define their own development problems, goals and solutions (Friedmann 1992; Parpart 2002). Thus, participation and empowerment came to be the essential building blocks for a grassroots, people-oriented transformative form of development. At least this is the theory.

While raising important issues and providing new ways of thinking about the way power and empowerment play out in even the most marginal of communities, anti-development and critical alternative development approaches have been criticized for romanticizing the local and the possibility that marginalized people can bring about transformation in a world increasingly stacked against them. Another criticism is that these approaches ignore relations and structures of economic and political power, particularly those based on the state and transnational corporations.

Griesgaber & Bernard Gunter 1996; Munck & O'Hearn 1999; Schuurman 1993.

6. Towards Critical Development Studies

After some six decades, whither development theory? The wellspring of development thought has not yet dried up; it continues to generate ideas that fuel public policy and direct the actions of diverse agents in a broad and complex field. At the same time, many of these ideas do not translate into action but serve as fodder for a number of unresolved and ongoing scholarly debates in the academy. In this regard at least, development theory in its diverse forms and dimensions has shown itself to be resilient, refusing to be cast into one mould.

Within the framework of several paradigms, it is possible to identify eight schools of thought, each of which places 'development' in a distinct theoretical perspective and provides a toolbox of useful ideas that can be used to orient policy and inform public action. They can be tagged as follows: (1) theories of growth and modernization, with classical, current and new formulations— 'new growth theory' (Hounie, Pittaluga, Porcile & Scatolin 1999); (2) 'neostructuralism' (Sunkel 1993); (3) sustainable human development and community-based forms of local development within the framework of the 'new paradigm' (Cornia, Jolly & Stewart 1987; UNDP 1990, 1996, 2002); (4) the political economy of development and underdevelopment—neo-Marxist dependency theory reformulated as 'world systems theory' (Wallerstein 1979); (5) the 'new political economy,' based on the neoclassical paradigm of the free world market and a rational choice model of economic and political behaviour (Krueger 1974; Bates 1981); (6) 'international political economy,' in diverse theoretical forms (crisis theory, regulationism, governance and transformation, et cetera); (7) 'alternative development,' in diverse forms but initiated 'from below' and 'people-centred,' socially inclusive in terms of gender, ethnicity and the poor, human in scale, participatory and sustainable in terms of the environment and livelihoods (Antrobus 1995; Chambers 1987, 1995); and (8) postdevelopment and 'grassroots postmodernism' (Esteva and Prakash 1998); Escobar 1997; Parpart, Rai and Staudt 2002; Munck 1999a).

Considering the range of ideas offered by these diverse schools of thought, it seems that international development studies is alive and well. At the same time the world appears to be in the throes of a systemwide or global crisis whose explanation constitutes a major challenge to development theory. This challenge has been met by some but there remains the need for more innovative thinking about the development implications of this crisis. Failure to respond to this challenge could jeopardize the project in which development scholars and practitioners are generally engaged.

In the wake of the effervescence of revolutionary ferment and the last great offensive of labour against capital in 1968, there emerged a powerful belief in the possibility and necessity of substantive change, not just incremental reform. But today, after the collapse of the Soviet Union, representing 'actually existing' socialism, and the apparent triumph of capitalism, this impetus has waned. Not even widespread opposition to capitalism, in the form of neoliberal globaliza-tion, and a virtual consensus on the need to move beyond or away from it, has reactivated the revolutionary impulse, the ability to re-imagine an alternative future—and act on it.

The end of the last millennium saw a global anti-globalization movement as well as heightened resistance in many forms against the dominant neoliberal model. But the first decade of the new millennium dampened this movement led by peasants and indigenous communities in the Global South. The conclusion is clear. Development studies needs a more critical edge. It needs to be reoriented towards substantive change and social transformation and more sharply focused on the needs and interests of the excluded, the oppressed and exploited. It needs to move beyond policy to implementation, translating fine words and policies into progressive and liberating change. What we need is a more critical approach towards development—critical development studies—and action informed by these studies.

Munck & O'Hearn 2009; Parpart & Veltmeyer 2004.

Notes

1. Bibliographical note on the language of the suggested readings: In every part of this course, many es-sential readings are originally published in languages other than English. The editors find the absence of such original readings regrettable, but felt that matters of expediency for the first edition dictated that the book be prepared for the English-language reader, that is, for those able to speak, write and read in the language of what has become the imperial *lingua franca* of the world. In subsequent edi-tions, efforts will be made to correct this absence. However, for better or worse, it is a fact that many contemporary scholars in the South are writing in English, or in many cases their best writings have been translated into English.
2. Not all development economists at the time, whose thinking was generally based on theories of eco-nomic growth and modernization, shared this nationalist concern for the developmental state in the absence or weakness of an indigenous capitalist class. Some mainstream thinkers on this tradition, such as Sir Arthur Lewis and Walt Rostow, continued to pin their hopes and expectations in regard to 'an expansion of the capitalist nucleus' on the 'private sector.'
3. The Lewis model would serve as an analytical tool for several generations of policymakers.
4. See Evans (1995), Weiss (2000) and Woo-Cumings (1999) on the 'developmental state.'

Section 2

Bringing History Back In

In recent years there has been a large increase of enrolment in undergraduate courses in international development studies (IDS). IDS attracts some of the best and brightest students, many of them as joint majors with another social science discipline. They are predominantly female, with a significant number originating in families from Asia, Africa and Latin America. Many of the students wish to work in NGOs or governmental organizations, national or international. They are strongly motivated and idealistic, and they want to make a difference. However, with some exceptions, the IDS programs on offer do not do justice to the quality of the students or the complexity of the subject.

Undergraduate programs vary in content according to the interests of the professors who design them and the resources of their respective universities. There is generally an interdisciplinary introductory course and required courses on the politics, sociology and economics of development. Theories of development, including modernization, dependency, Marxism and institutional and ecological approaches, are surveyed. These theories are usually presented at a high level of abstraction, without historical or geographic context of the circumstances that gave rise to them. Moreover, as postmodernism has devalued metanarratives and 'development' has largely been reduced to a matter of poverty alleviation, course content tends to be topical, with emphasis on globalization and critiques of international institutions such as the IMF, the World Bank and the World Trade Organization (WTO).

At the micro-level there is a general emphasis on development projects, including those providing microcredit targeted at the empowerment of women, connecting health issues including HIV/AIDS and more generally, fostering community economic development as preparation for 'doing development.' The development discourse is thus largely limited to issues of social policy including education and health, formalized in the Millennium Development Goals of the U.N. In summary, the central concern appears to be the effective delivery of development assistance whether by official or nongovernmental agencies. Development assistance however is now marginal compared with the large volume of private capital flows, both portfolio and foreign direct investment (FDI). Also marginal are the financial resources of the U.N. system. In the food crisis of 2008, for example, the U.N. World Food Program had difficulty in raising $500 million,[1] whereas profits of the first quarter of a single mega-corporation dealing in grains was $1.3 billion.[2]

None of the above addresses the basic problem of development defined in terms of the ability of society to mobilize its human and natural resources to increase productive capacity. Development in a meaningful sense implies a social and economic transformation to eradicate injustices of the past whether of imperialist or traditional origin. Development is a process from within. It cannot be programmed or externally imposed. It is a creative social process, and the matrix that nourishes it is located in the cultural sphere—the way of life of the ordinary people. Development is ultimately not a matter of physical capital or access to foreign exchange or markets, but of the capacity of a society to tap the root of popular creativity, to free up and empower people to exercise their intelligence and collective wisdom. The diversity of cultures that nourish human creativity is as precious an inheritance as the diversity of plant and animal life. It is the repository of collective wisdom from which springs the capacity of individuals and societies to survive adversity and renew the commitment to future generations.

As for the historical dimension of critical development studies this section of the Handbook takes the form of three modules. In Module 2 Kari Levitt provides a masterful review of the historical landscape of development—'rolling back the canvas of time' as she puts it. The following two modules, by Isaac Saney and Alain Gresh, bring into focus some of the most critical issues regarding the 'history of development' and the way that this 'history' has been constructed. Module 3 emphasizes the importance and development dynamics of imperialism—the projection of state power in the efforts of some people or states to dominate others and to subordinate their development path to the national interests of the dominant state. While Module 3 focuses on the historical dynamics of imperialism associated with the development of capitalism, Module 9 is concerned with the contemporary dynamics of this process. Module 4, on the other hand, conceives of imperialism in very different terms—as what some critical theorists view as false historical consciousness: constructing 'history' from the ideological vantage point of the dominant power. In these terms Module 4 seeks to correct a fundamental dominant 'Western' bias in historical scholarship. In the vortex of this bias, not only are 'subaltern voices' and the historical perspective of the oppressed repressed or lost, but the extraordinarily important 'history' of the orient vis-à-vis development is entirely ignored. In this context, there is a need—as André Gunder Frank put it—to 'reorient history' (and, we might add, development studies).

Module 2

Rolling Back the Canvas of Time

Kari Polanyi Levitt
McGill University, Canada

Neither foreign assistance nor projects at the grassroots can substitute for a national developmental state acting in the public interest of the majority population. Only an effective national government can assure the framework for the provision of the basic amenities of modern life to its citizens, including a supply of potable water to every household, a comprehensive system of public transportation, free primary and secondary education and universal access to health services.

Liberal policies of economic globalization were and are aimed at creating a 'borderless world' for capital—but not for labour. Global capital has no address, no country and no social responsibility. By contrast, people live in societies with specific geographic, historical and cultural characteristics and support systems that enable them to survive adversity and exercise collective solidarities to improve their lives. There is no such thing as global society. 'Think globally, act locally' is the motto of development and environmentalist activists, but the problem with this

approach is that at the global level, power lies with capital. At the community level, social movements cannot secure their objectives without a government able to defend society against the
destructive capacities of the global market to invade, reorganize and exploit human and natural
resources. Where countries are too small, this calls for regional cooperation.

1. Origins of the development agenda

Development came on the agenda before the end of World War II in anticipation of the decolonization of Asia and Africa. Leaders of struggles to free the colonial world from imperialist
control and refugee economists from continental Europe gathered in London, Cambridge and
Oxford. The early literature on development economics was produced by independent-minded
scholars. A remarkable number originated from Scandinavia (Frisch, Myrdal, Nurkse), Western
Europe (Hirschman, Mandelbaum, Perroux, Singer, Tinbergen) and Central and Eastern Europe
(Bauer, Georgescu-Roegen, Kaldor, Kalecki, Rosenstein-Roden, Streeten, Schumacher). Others
came from Britain (D. Seers), Russia (Gerschenkron, Kuznets, Leontieff), India (V.K.R.V Rao,
Chakravarty, Mahalanobis), Burma (Myint), Argentina (Prebisch), Egypt (S. Amin), Brazil
(Furtado), the West Indies (W.A. Lewis) and the U.S. (Chenery, Rostow). The early U.N. pro-
vided a supportive environment, and important conferences were held in New Delhi, Rio de
Janeiro and Cairo.

In 1945 the U.S. and the Soviet Union emerged as the two most important world powers.
Both enjoyed respect and influence in Europe and Asia, but neither was initially concerned
with the development of underdeveloped regions. The primary concern of the U.S. in the early
postwar years was the threat of communism in Europe and Asia. A secondary objective was the
dissolution of British and also French preferential economic spheres of influence and currency
blocs. The Marshall Plan, a large volume of unconditional economic assistance, was successful in
limiting Soviet influence to the satellite states of Eastern Europe, where communist governments
were installed in 1948 after a brief period of democratic multiparty regimes. In Asia, following
the defeat of Japan in 1945, U.S. hegemony was challenged by the victory of Mao's communist
revolution in 1949. The remnants of Chiang Kai-Shek's forces retreated to Taiwan. For the next
thirty years, the U.S. recognized the Nationalists in Taiwan as the legitimate government of China
with a veto in the Security Council in the U.N. A major war in Korea pitted a U.S.-led U.N. force
against China, resulting in the division of the country between North and South, with 30,000
troops on the border to this day. The U.S. Seventh Fleet is permanently deployed in the waters
of Japan, Korea and Taiwan.

A rising tide of anti-imperialist forces in Southeast Asia were engaged in struggles to free
the region from Japanese occupation and attain political independence from British, French
and Dutch colonialism. British India gained independence in 1947, tragically by the division
of the subcontinent into India and Pakistan. India established friendly relations with the Soviet
Union while Pakistan drifted into the U.S. sphere of influence. In 1956 Egyptian president Nasser
nationalized the Suez Canal, and the U.S. refused to support British and French intervention.

In 1955, President Sukarno of Indonesia, joined by Nehru of India, Nasser of Egypt and
Nkrumah of Ghana, convened a conference of Asian and African non-aligned states in Bandung.
China's premier and foreign minister Zhou Enlai headed the Chinese delegation. By this time
China's relations with Russia had chilled, and Tito's role in the Non-Aligned Movement, formal-

ized in Belgrade in 1961, was evidence that the Bandung initiative sought independence from Moscow as well as Washington.

The U.S. used every means at its disposal in efforts to replace secular national leftwing governments, including assistance to religious fundamentalist extremists, as in Afghanistan in the 1980s. From the overthrow of Mossadegh and the installation of the Shah in Iran, to the massacre of a million supporters of the Sukarno regime in Indonesia by General Suharto in 1965, to the war in Vietnam from 1965 to 1975, and massive support for the Marcos regime in the Philippines, which hosted a principal U.S. military base, Asia was the prize, and official development assistance was directed toward securing the gains.

2. The development project takes shape

In the course of the 1950s, development studies was institutionalized, and the U.S. State Department engaged the services of leading U.S. universities to fashion programs of economic development. India was assigned to Harvard, and Indonesia to MIT, and the University of Chicago played the leading role in Latin American studies. MIT professor W.W. Rostow's *Stages of Economic Growth*, subtitled *A Non-Communist Manifesto*, suggested that any country could engage in an aeronautical assent from 'takeoff' to self-sustaining growth and mass consumption, provided cultural and historical obstacles to modern business practice were overcome. The model was appealing, and the modernization approach dominated development studies in political science and sociology.

In the 1950s, Latin American states were firmly locked into friendly relationships with the U.S., which could at all times count on their votes in the U.N. It is important to note, however, that the U.S. did not pressure these governments to comply with free trade treaties. Brazil was particularly successful in implementing policies of industrialization. The U.S. responded to the Cuban Revolution of 1959 by launching the Alliance for Progress. The U.S. also imposed a trade embargo and made a number of unsuccessful attempts at regime change in the island. In 1962, Cuba was suspended from the Organization of American States (OAS); only Mexico and Canada maintained diplomatic relations. With the end of easy import substitution, political tensions mounted. In 1964, a military government took control of Brazil and exiled thousands of intellectuals and other opponents of the regime. In 1973, the democratically elected government of Allende in Chile was overthrown by a U.S.-supported military coup. Murderous military dictatorships were also established in Argentina and Uruguay, in 1976. Strong economic growth in the 1970s was driven by favourable markets for primary products, and Latin America attracted large inflows of capital from U.S. commercial banks seeking returns higher than could be obtained domestically. The foundations of the debt crisis of the 1980s were laid.

As an increasing number of African and Caribbean countries acceded to political independence, the U.N. established the Conference on Trade and Development (UNCTAD) in 1964 under the direction of Raúl Prebisch to address the problems of export dependent peripheries. But it was the Organization of Petroleum Exporting Countries (OPEC) in the Middle East, with participation of Venezuela, that was effective in exercising commodity power.

In the 1970s, the General Assembly of the U.N. adopted the Action Plan for a New International Economic Order. Many international conferences were held, but no meaningful concessions were made by the North. It marked the end of an era in which the U.N. could effectively give voice to the aspirations of the developing world. In his Nobel prize lecture of 1979, renowned development economist W. Arthur Lewis noted that there will be no new international economic order until the nations of the Global South develop their own resources, individually and collectively, to increase food production and employ their populations in productive industries and services. He noted that the 'engines of growth' of industrialized countries were slowing down and that continued dependence on exports to these countries would ensure that they remain poor. A more equitable international economic order would have to await the rising power of the Global South. With the accession of Prime Minister Thatcher (in 1979) and President Reagan (in 1980), an economic regime change was instituted in Britain and the U.S. The objective was to restore the discipline of capital over labour in the industrialized world and reduce the powers of government in the developing world. A doctrinal coup at the World Bank dismissed liberal-minded economists including Streeten and Ul Haq, who had introduced a basic needs approach to development, and installed a team of hard-nosed neoliberals including several trade economists. Policies of domestic industrialization, which had achieved growth rates in the South equalling those of the industrialized countries from 1950 to 1980, were now deemed to be inefficient and contrary to principles of comparative advantage in international trade. Export oriented development became the new panacea. The early pioneers of development economics were demonized as 'structuralist,' a heresy bordering on socialism.

3. The right to development

There was no longer a need for development economics because, in the new order, the laws of economics had universal validity without regard for structural or historical difference. Two prominent pioneers of development economics, Albert Hirschman and Dudley Seers, wrote eulogies with titles such as 'The Rise and Decline ...' and 'The Birth, Life and Death of Development Economics.'

The declaration of the Right to Development by the U.N. in 1986 was a defensive action intended to confirm the right of developing countries to engage in national strategies of social and economic transformation. However, under the influence of the rising tide of neoliberalism, the U.N. Universal Declaration of Human Rights of 1948, which included social and economic rights, was reinterpreted as a doctrine of individual human rights, which effectively excluded the collective right to development. Twenty-five years of structural adjustment policies imposed on African and Latin American debtor countries has systematically limited the exercise of sovereign states to achieve the goals of human development for their citizens. Development was replaced by macroeconomic and structural adjustment to demands of private and official creditors. The Washington Consensus of deregulation, liberalization and privatization became the universal prescription. The authors of the *U.N. Contribution to Development Thinking and Practice,* the official history of the U.N., acknowledged that in the 1980s intellectual and policy initiative regarding development passed to the IMF and the World Bank. The U.N. found itself 'unable to come forward with a new agenda that offered the prospect of coping with the new problems while preserving the social and human development goals it had been advocating' (Jolly, Emmerij, Ghai & Lapeire 2004: 150). The U.N. became increasingly impotent.

An extreme rise in interest rates at the opening of the 1980s plunged Latin American countries into a decade-long debt crisis. Over-exposed commercial banks were rescued by the IMF and the U.S. Treasury. Private debt was socialized and added to public debt. The blame for the debt crisis and the entire cost of adjustment was placed on the debtor countries and borne by their populations.

Africa became a gigantic laboratory for experiments in economic liberalization, as scores of countries came under the tutelage of the IMF and the World Bank. Subsidies to farmers were eliminated, and domestic food production declined as scarce resources including water were reserved for the production of exotic products, such as strawberries and flowers, for European markets. Where tropical agricultural commodities competed with U.S. products, as in the case of cotton, African exports were effectively embargoed. Few economists in Africa believed in these policies, but desperation elicited compliance.

By contrast, in the 1970s and 1980s, Korea had embarked on industrial policies that combined import substitution with export promotion guided by large and effective planning agencies with the full support and direct participation of political authorities. The corporatist business organization of Korea was modelled on Japan, with close association between large productive enterprise and domestic development banks. Foreign direct investment was restricted. In Taiwan, medium sized enterprises were favoured. The success of the so-called Tiger economies owed nothing to the World Bank or the IMF but benefited from the geopolitical interests of the U.S., which permitted them to engage in active industrial policies that violated neoliberal doctrine. With variations, such as the encouragement of FDI, policies combining domestic industrialization with export of manufactures were followed by Malaysia, Thailand, Indonesia and later also Vietnam. In all these cases, nationally owned enterprises were critical to successful economic development. In the late 1970s, China launched a program of economic reform combining private with state enterprise in a unique model of a socialist market economy. This yielded unprecedented high rates of growth, based on very high rates of domestic and foreign investment, the latter principally from overseas Chinese capital from North and South East Asia. External markets for manufactured exports in North America and Europe were complemented by a dense network of China-centred regional trade relations. In the early 1990s, China, and to a lesser degree India, emerged as new growth poles of the world economy.

4. The nation-state in development

As in the earlier case of the late industrializers of the nineteenth century—Germany, the U.S., Russia and others—no country has ever achieved economic development without the construction of an effective modern nation-state, and no country has established a viable industrial base without protecting its industries from the unrestricted import of goods and capital. In all cases of late industrialization, economic development was a political project requiring a state with authority and legitimacy to negotiate conflicting interests of classes and regions.

Following the victory of the West in the Cold War and the implosion of the Soviet Union, social democratic governments in Europe embraced Anglo-American doctrines and policies of privatization. Socialism was in ideological retreat, and the social welfare state on the defensive. In Russia a new oligarchy of former Soviet officials acquired state assets at fire sale prices. Huge fortunes were made in this chaotic condition of wild capitalism, while millions descended into poverty and average life expectancy plummeted. Similar policies transformed the countries of East Europe from Soviet satellites to economic and political clients of the Western powers. NATO military installations were shifted from West to East Europe, and control over the Balkans was secured by dismantling the former Yugoslavia. In 1991, the U.S. launched the first Gulf War against Iraq, which it had previously supported in its war with Iran.

In the rest of the world, the projection of Western economic power was aimed at securing access to markets and natural resources and, most importantly, protection of foreign investments from regulation and control by host national governments. The first attempt at a treaty designed to privilege investor rights over the sovereign rights of national governments, was the Multilateral Agreement on Investment (MAI) drafted by the Organisation for Economic Co-operation and Development (OECD). This was blocked by a campaign of international NGOs. The arrangements governing mutually negotiated trade agreements under the GATT (General Agreement on Tariffs and Trade) was converted to the WTO, with binding rules and mechanisms of enforcement of all member countries; now extended to include services, intellectual property and so-called trade-related intellectual measures (TRIMS). Although disadvantaged in negotiations, developing countries were able to use their votes to block agreement on further extensions to include investment, government procurement and competition aimed at entrenching the privileges of the transnational corporations and proposals granting foreign investors extended rights under enhanced free trade agreements (FTAs) such as the North America Free Trade Agreement (NAFTA). Signed in 1994, the NAFTA served as a template for the proposed Free Trade Agreement of the Americas (FTAA) and all subsequent FTAs. Commitments made by countries signing FTAs with the U.S. or Economic Partnership Agreements (EPA) with the European Community go far beyond what is required of member countries of the WTO. In the early 1990s, a word was lifted from the literature of communications and presented as describing an irreversible historical trend toward a borderless global economy: 'globalization.' For developing countries, there appeared to be no alternative to deeper integration into circuits of trade and capital flows. As Latin America emerged from the debt crisis of the 1980s, governments advised by U.S.-trained economists installed in central banks and ministries of finance instituted neoliberal reforms—most radically in Argentina. In Africa, debt relief failed to reverse the excess of the outflow of debt service over the inflow of official development assistance. This so-called TINA (There Is No Alternative) effect was accompanied by extravagant claims for the beneficial results of 'globalization.'

The World Development Report of 1995, entitled *Workers in an Integrating World*, suggested that globalization promised a return to the 'golden age' of 1870–1914, which could bring untold prosperity to developing countries provided they opened their economies to unrestricted imports and capital flows. The title of the report suggests that workers could be the principal beneficiaries of globalization. The authors of this flagship publication of the World Bank seem to have forgotten the fact that 1870–1914 was the Age of Empire, when European imperialist expansion engulfed all of Africa and most of Asia. Throughout this period, colonial labour exploited in the mines and plantations of Africa and Asia contributed to the accumulation of capital in the industrialized countries, on impoverishing and deteriorating terms of trade. Colonial possessions became captive markets for British and other European textiles and their traditional agricultural economies were transformed to supply cotton, rubber, palm oil, jute, indigo and other agricultural and mineral commodities to the metropoles.

When Adam Smith published *The Wealth of Nations* in 1776, the living standard of an Indian peasant was no lower than that of an English agricultural labourer, and China was regarded as a model of a prosperous and stable civilization. From the Conquest of Bengal by the East India

Company and throughout the nineteenth and early twentieth centuries British India regressed from a viable agricultural economy to an impoverished underdeveloped country. In the late 1870s and again in the late 1890s, the failure of monsoon rains produced the greatest famines in recorded history in India and also in Northern China. British authorities failed to provide famine relief and continued to ship large quantities of grains to London on railways whose costs were charged to the colonial government of India. Because colonial authorities neglected to maintain traditional management of water resources of canals, wells and storage tanks to provide for drought, many millions perished unnecessarily from hunger and disease. In China, social disintegration due to the introduction of opium by the British East India Company earlier in the nineteenth century had weakened the capacity of the government to come to the aid of the victims of the famine in Northern China, which claimed between eight and twenty million lives. Both in India and in China the forced opening of the country to 'world markets' by British imperial policies turned devastating droughts into human disasters (Davis 2002a).

It is difficult to understand how an agency mandated to serve 'development' could have advocated a return to the globalization of the nineteenth century as a prescription for development for the twenty-first century. Moreover, the World Development Report of 1995 cannot be dismissed as a lapse of memory, because the World Bank continues to urge countries to increase exports, encourage imports to compete with domestic firms to improve efficiency, open up to unrestricted flows of capital and generally to deepen integration into the world economy.

5. The financialization of development and the global crisis

The most serious crisis since the Great Depression has most heavily affected precisely those countries that are most deeply integrated into the financial networks of capitalism. The epicentre of the crisis is in the U.S., and the countries most vulnerable include the U.K., Australia, Switzerland, the Eurozone, Eastern Europe and the OECD country of Korea. Among the least vulnerable are the large developing countries, including China, Indonesia and Nigeria. For the first time since the 1970s, the IMF has extended rescue packages to European countries, including Iceland ($12 billion), Hungary ($20 billion), Latvia and other Baltic countries indebted to Western banks. By contrast, in the developing world, only Pakistan and Turkey requested IMF assistance.

The 1990s witnessed more frequent and more severe financial crises than those of the 1930s, not yet in the heartlands of capitalism, but in Mexico, Turkey, Brazil, Argentina, Russia and most importantly in East Asia. In some of these crises, incomes plunged not by 2 or 5 percent but by 20 or even 30 percent at a time. The IMF intervened to save major international banks from losses in East Asia in 1997–98 and facilitated the transfer of ownership of industrial enterprises from domestic to foreign capital. Following the rescue by the U.S. Federal Reserve of a very large New York hedge fund, which threatened to bring down the world financial system, there was talk of the need for a new architecture to oversee and control global financial markets. The panic soon passed, and in 1999 legislation enacted during the Great Depression, which had prohibited deposit-taking commercial banks from engaging in the sale of stocks, bonds and insurance and issue of mortgages, was repealed by the Clinton administration at the urging of Wall Street. The firewall separating commercial from investment banks was thereby removed. For the next ten years, an inverted pyramid of financial assets and claims was constructed on the base of the savings of millions of people in pension funds, mutual funds, insurance premiums, equities and investment in real estate, whose value appeared to be forever rising. During the Bush administration, all remaining restrictions on financial transactions were removed.

Since the mid 1980s, the returns on portfolio investments and the opportunities for capital gains have exceeded profits from investment in non-financial enterprise. Corporations moved assets from production to distribution and finance. They engaged in downsizing, subcontracting and outsourcing to cheaper labour locations to boost shareholder value and compete on stock markets with financial service industries. Some 40 percent of total corporate profit accrued to financial enterprise. The contribution of finance, insurance and real estate now amounts to 20 percent of GDP in the U.S. and Britain whereas manufacturing has declined to levels of 13 and 11 percent respectively. There has been no increase in median wage and salary earnings in the past twenty-five years.

Millions of people were employed in the unproductive activity of transferring ownership of paper claims. Billions of dollars were made by promoters, traders and insiders of this virtual casino of exotic financial products that transfer resources from producers and taxpayers to owners of legal claims to a portion of the output of the real economy. Both at the domestic and international levels it has been an engine of inequality and instability.

Ten years after the Asian crisis, the inevitable crash finally hit the heartlands of this predatory Anglo-American variety of capitalism. The epicentre was the U.S. and Britain, but the damage extended to Europe and to financial institutions in many other countries. The permissive condition of the extraordinary accumulation of public and private debt was the inflow of capital from the Rest of the World to cover a 6 percent external current account deficit in the U.S. Since 1971, when the U.S. abandoned gold convertibility, the U.S. dollar has served as the principal reserve currency of the world, and banks have been able to create dollar liabilities unconstrained by official reserve ratios.

Keynes's greatest fear was that finance would destroy capitalism. By this he surely meant that the unrestricted power of financial capital could corrupt the capitalism that organized the production of useful goods and services and applied technology to improve living standards of the people. Western governments are pouring billions into the bottomless coffers of banks to save a rapacious form of capitalism that has demonstrably failed to deliver on its promises. The ideologues and institutions that preach their doctrines of 'reform' designed and serving to subordinate societies and nations to the global republic of capital have lost all legitimacy. Henceforth, the crisis must present an opportunity to regain political and economic control of governments by the majority population in the developing world.

Globalization, it has often been said, provides challenges and opportunities, winners and losers. But history has surprises. The advocates of globalization did not imagine that the principal beneficiary of the liberalization of trade would be communist China. Nor did they anticipate that the failures of liberalization policies in Latin America would result in the election of a new generation of left-leaning political leaders. They certainly did not expect that the deregulation of powerful financial institutions would unleash the most serious financial and economic crisis since the Great Depression.

Evidence of the failure of the established authorities to comprehend the consequences of the financialization of the major capitalist economies is provided by the drastic downward revision of IMF estimates of growth for 2009 for All Advanced Countries (from -0.3 to -2.0 percent); for the U.S. (-0.7 to -1.6%); the U.K. (-1.3 to -2.0%); Eurozone (-0.5 to -2.0%); and Japan (-0.2 to

-2.6%). Downward revisions from positive to negative growth were also made for Russia (3.5 to -0.7%); Central and East Europe (2.2 to -0.4%); Canada (0.3 to -1.5%) and Korea and other Newly Advanced Countries of Asia (2.1 to -3.9%). Revised projections for 2010 expect the recovery of All Advanced Countries to positive growth of 1.1%. This may be excessively optimistic.

In contrast to declining output in the 'advanced capitalist countries' and also in the 'emerging market economies' of Russia and East Europe, IMF revisions for the developing world showed reduced but significant growth in Asia (China, from 8.5 to 6.7%; India, from 6.3 to 5.1%; ASEAN, from 4.2 to 2.7%), Middle East (from 5.4 to 3.9%) and Africa (from 4.8 to 3.4%). In Latin America (from 2.5 to 1.1%), growth projected for Brazil is 1.8% (reduced from 3.0%), while negative growth for Mexico at -0.3% (reduced from 0.9%) accords with negative projections for its NAFTA partners. In all regions of the developing world, reduced export earnings and cancellation of investment projects substantially reduced growth rates from levels attained in 2007, but the engines of growth have not shut down. World growth of 0.5% is now sustained by the developing world.

For a hundred years or more, growth in the commodity supplying peripheries was dependent on growth in the major industrial centres. This relationship of dependence is undergoing a significant change as countries and regions of the developing world are generating a measure of self-sustaining growth. The divergent growth rates projected for 2009 reveal the lesser vulnerability of the Global South to the unfolding economic crisis, although this point is arguable. As noted earlier, the most vulnerable economies are those that are most closely integrated into metropolitan circuits of international commerce and finance. Export dependent countries with diversified external (and regional) markets, such as the ASEAN countries, are less vulnerable than the countries of Latin America. The contrast of the poor performance of Mexico, which is economically integrated with the U.S. and Canada, and Brazil, with a strong industrial base and diversified external markets in Europe, Japan and North America, is instructive. Developing Asia, which accounts for roughly a third of world output is currently the growth point of the world economy at the impressive rate of 5.5%.

What is interesting here is why Latin America, which in 1950 had GDP per capita levels approximating those of Southern Europe, accounted for half the trade of the developing world and averaged 6.1% growth from 1960–80, lost a decade of growth in the 1980s and failed to recover growth momentum in the 1990s. The most striking difference between East Asia and Latin America is the extreme inequality of land ownership and of income in the latter. In Japan, Korea and Taiwan, America instituted a thoroughgoing land reform after the end of World War II. In China, the communist revolution dispossessed landowners and reorganized agriculture, while maintaining state ownership of land. It is important to note that it is not only in China and former colonies of Japan that rural producers have been able to share in the economic growth of the country, but equality of assets and income is also far higher in Indonesia, Malaysia and Thailand than in Latin America. Only in the Philippines has the legacy of Spanish and U.S. colonialism resulted in inequalities of land ownership approximating those of Latin America. The deep cleavages of class and ethnicity in Latin America have their origin in the conquest and dispossession of aboriginal peoples 500 years ago and the legacy of the slave trade, which brought African labour to work the plantations of Brazil and the Caribbean, and the subsequent settlement of European populations on stolen lands. Since the beginning of the nineteenth century, landed oligarchies controlled and profited from the export of primary commodities, more recently accompanied by industrialization by import substitution for a domestic market that was restricted to the middle and upper levels of a highly skewed distribution of income. With the exception of Brazil, Latin American business classes did not develop manufacturing industries capable of competing in international markets; they preferred to place their savings in overseas financial institutions in Miami, New York or Toronto. There is an absence of national cohesion. Elites effectively do not pay taxes, nor can they be collected from the large informal economy in which the majority of the population is engaged. The state is in perpetual fiscal shortfall. Governments, which have largely been controlled by business interests, have welcomed multinational corporations and have been quick to sell off the national patrimony of state enterprises, in some cases merely to meet payroll. Privatization in Latin America has been more far-reaching than in East Asia or in India (we remind the reader that Korea was closed to FDI prior to the Asian crisis of 1997–98). The frequency of political and economic crises in Latin America and the temptation of populist governments to deal with distributional conflict by printing money is ultimately due to the unresolved legacies of the origins of Latin American society. The recent political assertion of indigenous peoples of the Andean region constitute a break with the past and hold out the promise that the long suppressed cultural practices and institutions of indigenous peoples of the Americas may contribute to novel forms of democratic governance and organization of economic life.

6. From global crisis to a reconfiguration of international power relations

It is evident that the economic crisis that was triggered by the implosion of financial institutions in 2008 will have transformative consequences of power relations within the world economic order. The U.S. will continue to play an important but no longer a hegemonic role, and the U.S. dollar will lose primacy as countries diversify their holdings of official reserves. It may prove difficult to revive the U.S. economy because three decades of neoliberal policies have significantly reduced the share of wage and salary income in U.S. GDP from levels of the 1960s and 1970s. The American economy is driven by the growth of consumption expenditure, but since the end of the 1990s, consumption expenditure has increased only by the annual increase in the volume of household debt, which has now reached levels of 140 percent of household income. Consumption expenditure will now decline, as will domestic investment. As long as other economies remain in recession, the prospect for exports is dim. Only massive government expenditures can lift the economy out of the slump, but who is going to cover the fiscal deficit, which will now be very much larger? Will foreigners wish to continue to purchase U.S. securities, whose value will decline with a weaker dollar?

For years the U.S. market has driven the export-led growth of developing Asia, Africa and Latin America, and access to this market has been the principal bargaining chip in negotiations for enhanced FTAS or EPAS. Will declining export earnings encourage production for domestic use? Will developing countries concerned with food security assist domestic agriculture to meet a larger share of the food bill? Will developing countries engage in managed non-market trade? Will they now create regional institutions of mutual financial assistance? These are some of the possibilities arising from the crisis.

We do not know what the future holds, but it is clear that the world has become both more diverse and more interdependent. We live on one planet, which is seriously threatened by climate change and environmental degradation of the rivers, seas and earth that sustain our lives. There is agreement that the predatory mode of capitalism, which has dominated international trade and finance, has failed. But there is no agreement, indeed there cannot be, on any one alternative mode of economic organization. All modern economies are mixed economies, with some combination of state enterprise, at national, regional or municipal levels, private sector, cooperative, community or social economy, non-profit associations and work performed within the household. But all societies require an effective state with the authority and legitimacy to negotiate conflicting domestic interests. Just as there are many forms of organizing an economy, there are many forms of democratic governance, and representational government by political parties is not necessarily the most appropriate for any particular society. The economic crisis invites innovation in the regions of political and social organization in accordance with the specific historical and cultural heritage of the varied peoples of the world. This much more interesting approach to the study of international development challenges its students to explore the history and the culture of the diverse societies of the world.

Module 3

History from a Critical Development Perspective

Isaac Saney
Dalhousie University, Canada

That's one of the great problems of the modern world... Forgetting. The victim *never* forgets. Ask an Irishman what the English did to him in 1920 and he'll tell you the day of the month and the time and the name of every man they killed. Ask an Iranian what the English did to him in 1953 and he'll tell you. His child will tell you. His grandchild will tell you. And when he has one, his great-grandchild will tell you too. But ask an Englishman... if he ever knew, he has forgotten. *Move on!* You tell us. *Move on! Forget what we've done to you. Tomorrow's another day!* But it isn't.... *Tomorrow* was created yesterday, you see.... And by the day *before* yesterday, too. To ignore history is to ignore the wolf at the door. (John Le Carré, *A Most Wanted Man*, 279–80)

1. Viewing history with a critical mind

The basic feature of a critical development perspective on history is the need to not only 'learn from history' but to 'relearn history,' particularly in terms of the logic and dynamics involved in the inexorable expansion of capitalism. History, of course, can be traced back millennia. But this module is concerned primarily with the modern history of capitalist development, a relatively short period of some 500 years from the mid-fifteenth century, a time that also saw European 'civilization' into the 'new world' and the dynamics of colonialism. During this period of 'primitive [original] accumulation' (see Marx 1976), communities of indigenous agricultural producers were dispossessed from their land and means of production, expropriated usually by means of brutal violence but also legislation, and in some contexts enslaved or colonized if not subjected to physical or cultural genocide.

From this inauspicious beginning, historians have traced out patterns of seismic change associated with the process of capitalist development and globalization (Wallerstein 1979), which can be roughly periodized as follows:

1450–1800: a period of primitive accumulation, violent expropriation, piracy and large-scale theft and colonialism dominated by merchant capital—European-based crown chartered commercial companies;

1800–1870: a period characterized by the rise of industrial capitalism in Western Europe, including an 'industrial revolution,' the consolidation of the nation-state, a social and political revolution that displaced the landed oligarchy from power and the formation of an economic structure based on the class relation of capital to labour;

1870–1914: a period characterized by 'globalization'—a large-scale international movement of both capital and labour—and imperialism, in which large areas of what we now term the Global South were dominated, colonized and subjected to a process of capitalist development (productive and social transformation);

1914–1944, a thirty-year interwar period that featured a major involution in the capitalist system and a process of state-led social reform—the 'taming of capitalism' in the words of Surendra Patel (2007);

1944–1970: the 'golden age of capitalism' (another twenty-five to thirty years), characterized by a system-wide rapid economic growth within the framework of a liberal capitalist world order, the undisputed economic supremacy of the Pax Americana, an East-West cold war between a U.S.-led capitalist system and a U.S.S.R.-led socialist system, a process of decolonization and nation-building and the launching of a project of international cooperation for (capitalist) development;

1970-–1982: a period of transition from state-led national development to a new world order of neoliberal globalization; and

1983–2007: a new world order characterized by several cycles of structural or policy reform, increasing integration into a system-wide globalization process, the collapse of the socialist bloc, the decline of U.S. hegemony and a growing development divide.[3]

Hallward 2007; Rist 2002; Kothari 2005; Harman 2008; Mallon 1994; Parker & Rathborne 2007; Rolph-Trouillot 1995: Chap. 1; Wallerstein 2006: Chap 1.

2. In the interstices of colonialism and imperialism: Dynamics of 'primitive accumulation'

In the 1980s, there was a robust debate among Marxists and world system theorists (dependency theorists, at the time) about the nature and origins of capitalism. At issue in this debate were the defining characteristics and dynamics of the market economy, which for world system theorists defined capitalism, and the formation of the social relations of production, which for Marxists was critical. Nonetheless, there was agreement on the importance of the period 1500–1900, dominated as it was by 'mercantile capital' (merchant houses that financed the commercial operations of crown-chartered companies in what we might today term the 'Global South.' These operations, in what Marx himself labelled 'the capitalistic era… of primitive accumulation,' entailed not only commerce and piracy but as Marx, in *Capital* Vol. 1 (Part V III, Chap. 26), described so eloquently, the violent expropriation of the direct producers from their means of production, rape, 'commerce' and outright theft, enslavement and genocide, the massacre of entire peoples (Wright 1993). Under these conditions of 'primitive [original] accumulation,' Marx argued, capitalism was formed on the basis of an exchange of labour power, provided by the 'proletariat' (the class available for hire), for a living wage: *the capital-labour relation.*

Goody 2006; Marx 1976: 459–515; Perelman 2000.

3. Conquest, slavery and genocide

The rise of Europe within a process of primitive accumulation and capitalist development has raised a number of questions about and research into the dynamics of colonialism and what has been termed the 'colonial model of development.' At issue in this model are conditions that would lead to and generate the 'development' of a number of countries in the North, resulting in a global divide and the 'underdevelopment' of many countries in the South. André Gunder Frank (1967) was heavily criticized for his theoretical representation of this unequal and polarized development as the 'development of underdevelopment,' but he highlight an important dimension of capitalist development. The global dynamics of slavery and colonialism, the 'colonizers' model of development,' captured other critically important dimensions of the process of capital accumulation. Williams (1944) and Rodney (1973) establish the magnitude and crucial importance of slavery and the slave trade in creating conditions of underdevelopment.

Blackburn 1998; Rodney 1973: Chaps. 2–4; Williams 1944; Wright 1993.

4. The 'great transformation'

This theme engages a review of the ideas used to periodize the process of social and capitalist development—to identify the major stages or phases in this development. The importance of this process is that it provides the context for the analysis of social change: (1) the structurally determined, and objectively given, conditions of capitalist development; (2) the subjective-political conditions of this development, namely forms of social consciousness or ideas; and (3) conditions that are historically specific and conjunctural, and thus not possible to determine theoretically, requiring in fact a concrete analysis of historically specific situations.

Desai 2000; Mayhew 2000; Hall & Chase-Dunn 2006; Polanyi 1944 [1957, 1968].

5. From Pax Britannica to Pax Americana: The long century (1890–1990)

The era of imperialism related to the process of capitalist development can be divided into two phases: (1) British imperialism (expropriation and dispossession), including resistance and colonization of the Global South; and (2) U.S. economic dominion, cultural domination and ideological hegemony—from colonialism (in the context of U.S. hegemony and the Cold War) to neocolonialism (as some see it, the 'end of history' in the conjuncture of a new world order).

Leys 1975; Nkrumah 1965; Rodney 1973: Chaps. 5–6; Amin 1973; Amin 1999: 17–31.

6. A short history of the last decade of the twentieth century: The era of neoliberal globalization

The critical issues are complex and many but they include questions and topics such as: (1) how can the 1990s best be viewed—as the 'end of history' (the triumph of the idea of freedom in the form of liberal democracy) or a new conjuncture of imperial power (and U.S. hegemony)? (2) What is the nature of capitalist development in the era of neoliberal globalization and the new imperialism? (3) The post Cold War conjuncture: in the vortex of the 'new imperialism': Ideological constructions of 'the enemy' and strategy ('counterinsurgency'—from international communism to terrorism; (4) From Vietnam to Iraq: lessons of U.S. imperialism—over-extension or a giant with feet of clay? (5) U.S. hegemony and the neoconservative imperial dream of U.S. hegemony—the Project of the 'American Century'; (6) The White House Gang of Five and the dynamics of global American power; (7) The new world of uni-polar state power: from multilateralism and diplomacy to unilateralism and war. On the nature of imperialism in the current era see in particular the interpretations by Ellen Meiosis Wood and David Harvey, reviewed in a most interesting and useful commentary by Bob Sutcliffe (2006).

A revealing microcosm of contemporary history from a critical development perspective, i.e., with a critical eye on the 'imperial savagery and heroic resistance' that marks capitalist development over the past 500 years and more, is provided by the case of Haiti—by the efforts of the poor in the poorest country in the hemisphere to advance their heroic if desperate struggle for dignity and the forces, hiding behind the banner of freedom, that have stymied this struggle. Peter Hallward's brilliant and well-research account of this struggle, *Damning the Flood*, is a must read for all students of history and all those interested in the theory and practice of 'international development.'

Hallward 2007; Harvey 2005: 64–86; Federici 1992, 2002; Sutcliffe 2006.

Module 4

Reorienting History

Alain Gresh
Le Monde Diplomatique, France

Shortly after World War I, the French literary critic and historian Henri Massis (1886–1970) preached a crusade against the dangers threatening European values and thought—largely identified with those of France, in his mind. He was not entirely misguided: across the world, colonized nations were in revolt. He wrote:

> The future of western civilization, of humanity itself, is now under threat…. Every traveller, every foreigner who has spent any time in the Far East agrees that the way in which the population thinks has changed more in the last 10 years than it did over 10 centuries. The old, easy-going submissiveness has given way to blind hostility—sometimes genuine hatred,

just waiting for the right moment to act. From Calcutta to Shanghai, from the steppes of Mongolia to the plains of Anatolia, the whole of Asia trembles with a blind desire for freedom. These people no longer recognize the supremacy that the West has taken for granted since John Sobieski conclusively stemmed the Turkish and Tartar invasions beneath the walls of Vienna. Instead they aspire to rebuild their unity against the white man, whose overthrow they proclaim. (Gresh 2009)

1. Resurfacing fears

These fears are resurfacing today in a very different context, marked by a series of cataclysmic events: the end of the Cold War, 9/11, the wars in Iraq and Afghanistan and above all the restructuring of the global order in favour of new powers, such as China and India. Various authors, many of them highly regarded, have picked up on the Manichean view of history as an eternal confrontation between civilization and barbarism as they excavate the roots of what Anthony Pagden calls the '2,500-year struggle' now bathing the world in blood.

Pagden has taught in some of the world's most prestigious universities, including Oxford, Cambridge and Harvard. The picture he paints of world history is crude:

A flame had been lit in Troy which would burn steadily down the centuries, as the Trojans were succeeded by the Persians, the Persians by the Phoenicians, the Phoenicians by Parthians, the Parthians by the Sassanids, the Sassanids by the Arabs, and the Arabs by the Ottoman Turks.... The battle lines have shifted over time, and the identities of the antagonists have changed. But both sides' broader understanding of what it is that separates them has remained, drawing, as do all such perceptions, on accumulated historical memories, some reasonably accurate, some entirely false. (Gresh 2009)

Despite this minor reservation about 'entirely false' memories, Pagden's vision is a binary one whose founding event was the confrontation between the Greeks and Persians as described by the Greek historian Herodotus.

What [Herodotus] is concerned to show is that what divided the Persians from the Greeks or the Asians from the Europeans was something more profound than petty political differences. It was a view of the world, an understanding of what it was to be, and to live like, a human being....

And while the cities of Greece, and of 'Europe' more widely, were possessed of very different personalities and had created sometimes very different kinds of societies, and were all too happy to betray each other if it suited them, they nevertheless all shared the common elements of that view. They could all distinguish freedom from slavery, and they were all committed broadly to what we today would identify as an individualistic view of humanity.

2. The battle that changed the world

Paul Cartledge, Professor of Greek history at Cambridge University, takes a similar view of 'the battle that changed the world': Thermopylae (480BCE). 'This clash between the Spartans and other Greeks on one side, and the Persian horde (including Greeks), on the other, was a clash between freedom and slavery, and was perceived as such by the Greeks both at the time and subsequently.... The battle of Thermopylae, in short, was a turning-point not only in the history of Classical Greece, but in the world's history, eastern as well as western' (Gresh 2009). Cartledge notes that, in the mid-nineteenth century, economist John Stuart Mill described the battle of Marathon, fought some ten years earlier, as 'more important than the battle of Hastings, even as an event in English history.'

In his preface, Cartledge makes no secret of his ideological perspective: 'The events of 9/11 in New York City and now 7/7 in London have given this project [understanding the significance of Thermopylae] a renewed urgency and importance within the wider framework of East-West cultural encounter.' Not so much an encounter as a clash between despotism and freedom, in Cartledge's view.

A popularized version of this academic view is presented in 300, a film depicting the battle, directed by Zack Snyder and based upon the graphic novel of the same name by Frank Miller and Lynn Varley. The two-hour film, which was a hit at the U.S. box office, resembles a video game in which chiselled musclemen, high on amphetamines, square off against effeminate barbarians (black or Middle Eastern in appearance) whose deaths nobody would regret. 'No prisoners!' shouts the hero, King Leonidas of Sparta, who has already killed the Persian ambassador at the beginning of the film: savages are excluded from humanity's most sacred laws.

So basically civilization means exterminating barbarians. As early as 1898, the German political scientist Heinrich von Treischke stated what many of his contemporaries would have regarded as the obvious: 'International law becomes meaningless when any attempt is made to apply its principles equally to barbarian nations. The only way to punish a black tribe is to burn their villages; it is the only sort of example they understand. For the German empire to apply international law in cases like this would not be either humanity or justice; it would be a shameful weakness.' The Germans showed no 'weakness' between 1904 and 1907 when they exterminated the Herero in Namibia. This first genocide of the twentieth century was one of a series of colonial policies that served as model and precursor to the Nazi genocide against the Jews.

According to Cartledge, there is no Persian source—no native Herodotus—for the Greco-Persian wars. But we now know enough about the Persian Empire to modify traditional views. Touraj Daryaee, professor of ancient history at California State University, Fullerton, points out that slavery, widely practised in Greece, was rare among the Persians, whose women enjoyed higher status than their Greek counterparts. He also reminds us of the Cyrus cylinder, a document that the U.N. translated into all its official languages in 1971; this first known charter of human rights was granted by Cyrus the Great in the 6th century BCE and called for religious tolerance, the abolition of slavery, the freedom to decide one's profession and so on.

3. 'The true religion of democracy'

It is unsurprising that the Greeks—particularly Herodotus, who, to be fair, was less of a caricature than his literary heirs—should have presented their victory as a triumph over barbarism. As long as wars have been fought, the protagonists have draped themselves in idealistic principles. U.S. leaders have similarly depicted their campaigns in Iraq and Afghanistan as wars of Good against Evil. But it may be worth asking why, 4,500 years later, we remain so obsessed by the Greeks.

According to Marcel Detienne of Johns Hopkins University in Baltimore: In his *Instructions*, Ernest Lavisse (1842–1922), an important influence on the teaching of history in late nineteenth-century France, declared that what secondary-school pupils need to be taught, without their realizing it, is that:

> Our [French] history begins with the Greeks, who invented liberty and democracy and who introduced us to *the beautiful* and a taste for *the universal*. We are heirs to the only civilization that has offered the world 'a perfect and as it were ideal expression of justice and liberty.' That is why our history begins—has to begin—with the Greeks.
>
> This belief was then compounded by another every bit as powerful: 'The Greeks are not like others.' After all, how could they be, given that they were right at the beginning of our history? Those were two propositions that were essential for the creation of a national mythology that was the sole concern of traditional humanists and historians, all obsessed with nationhood. (Gresh 2009)

Detienne continues:

> It is commonly believed not only that both the abstract notion of politics and concrete politics one fine day fell from the heavens, landing on *classical* Athens in the miraculous and authenticated form of Democracy (with a capital D), but also that a divinely linear history has led us by the hand from the American Revolution, passing by way of the *French Revolution*, all the way to our own western societies that are so blithely convinced that their mission is to convert all peoples to the true religion of democracy.'

4. Marginalization of the East

A number of Anglo-Saxon writers, not persuaded of Europe's 'uniqueness,' have questioned the idea of a direct line of descent from classical antiquity via the 'Renaissance'—a term invented by the historian Jules Michelet during the nineteenth century—to contemporary Europe. Their message has rarely reached French shores.

John Hobson, of Sheffield University (2004), has shown that it is impossible to understand world history without recognizing the crucial importance of the East:

> This marginalisation of the East constitutes a highly significant silence because it conceals three major points. First, the East actively pioneered its own substantial economic development after about 500. Second, the East actively created and maintained the global economy after 500. Third, and above all, the East has significantly and actively contributed to the rise of the West by pioneering and delivering many advanced 'resources portfolios' (e.g., technologies, institutions and ideas) to Europe. (Gresh 2009)

How many of us are aware that the first industrial revolution began in the eleventh century, in Song dynasty China? This dynasty produced 125,000 tonnes of iron in 1078, seven centuries before Britain managed to produce 76,000. The Chinese mastered advanced technologies like iron casting and substituted coke for charcoal to prevent deforestation. During the same period they revolutionized transport, energy (the water mill), taxation, trade and urban development. Their green revolution attained levels of agricultural production that Europe did not match until the twentieth century.

Until 1800, China remained the leading player in a global economy that some described as Sinocentric; India, too, was of enormous importance. Many Chinese technologies, ideas and institutions spread to Europe and helped bring about the rise of modern capitalism. The British industrial revolution would have been impossible without China's contribution. And the same is true of the contributions of the great Muslim empires [see #6—Hobson, 'Rational and Progressive'].

According to John Hobson (2004):

Eurocentrism errs by asking wrong questions at the outset. All Eurocentric scholars (either explicitly or implicitly) begin by asking two interrelated questions: 'What was it about the West that enabled its breakthrough to capitalist modernity?' and 'What was it about the East that prevented it from making the breakthrough?' (Gresh 1009).

But these questions assume that Western dominance was inevitable and lead historians to scour the past for the factors that explain it. 'The rise of the West is understood through a logic of immanence: that it can only be accounted for by factors that are strictly endogenous to Europe.' East and West come to be regarded as distinct entities separated by a cultural Great Wall of China, which protects us from barbarian invasion.

5. Fear of barbarians

But who are these barbarians? Tzvetan Todorov, in *The Fear of Barbarians* (2008), questions the definition by famous French anthropologist Claude Levi-Strauss of the barbarian as 'the man who believes in barbarism' and suggests that 'it is someone who believes that a population or an individual is not fully human and therefore merits treatment that he would resolutely refuse to apply to himself' (Gresh 2009). In *The Fear of Barbarians*, Todorov develops an argument he presented in earlier works such as *On Human Diversity*, a thought-provoking book that deserves to be far more widely read (1998). 'The fear of barbarians,' he writes now, 'is what is in danger of turning us into barbarians. And the evil that we do will far exceed what we initially fear' (Gresh 2009).

Only the individual who fully recognizes the humanity of others can be called civilized. 'For a long time,' Todorov continues,

the ideas of the Enlightenment served as a source of inspiration for a liberal, reformist tendency that fought conservatism in the name of universalism and equal respect for all. Things have changed now, and the conservative defenders of the superiority of western thought claim to be the heirs of the Enlightenment, battling against the *relativism* that they associate with the Romantic reaction of the early nineteenth century. But they can only achieve this by renouncing the true Enlightenment tradition with its articulation of universal values and cultural pluralism.

We must go beyond the clichés: Enlightenment thought should not be confused either with dogmatism (my culture must be imposed upon all) or nihilism (all cultures are equally valid). To use it to denigrate others, as an excuse to subject or destroy them, is simply to hijack the Enlightenment. (Gresh 2009)

But was the Enlightenment really hijacked, or did it go along willingly? Hobson argues that the construction of eighteenth- and nineteenth-century European identity allowed the affirmation of an 'exceptionalism' that no other civilization has ever asserted. 'Ultimately, the Europeans did not seek to remake the world simply because "they could" (as in materialist explanations). They sought to remake the world because they believed they should. That is, their actions were significantly guided by their identity that deemed imperialism to be a morally appropriate policy.'

Many European supporters of the anti-colonialist struggle and the Third World rejected this vision, often in the name of the Enlightenment. The debate will no doubt continue.

6. Rational and Progressive

Let us suppose we were living back in, say, 900CE. The Islamic Middle East/North Africa was at that time the cradle of civilization. Not only was it the most economically advanced region in the world, standing at the centre of the global economy but it enjoyed considerable economic growth and perhaps even per capita income growth—the alleged sine qua non of modern capitalism. Were we to set up a university at that time and enquire into the causes of Islamic economic progress we might come up with the following answer. The Middle East/North Africa was progressive because it enjoyed a unique set of rational and progressive institutions.

First, it was a pacified region in which towns sprang up and capitalists engaged in long-distance global trade. Second, Islamic merchants were not just traders but rational capitalist investors who traded, invested and speculated in global capitalist activities for profit-maximizing ends. Third, a sufficiently rational set of institutions was created including a clearing system, banks engaging in currency exchange, deposits and lending at interest, a special type of double-entry bookkeeping, partnerships and contract law, all of which presupposed a strong element of trust. Fourth, scientific thought developed rapidly after about 800. And fifth, Islam was especially important in stimulating capitalism on a global scale. Certainly no one would have entertained the prospect of writing a book entitled *The Christian Ethic and the Spirit of Capitalism*, which would dismiss Islam as growth-repressive.

More likely, someone would have written a book called *The Islamic Ethic and the Spirit of Capitalism*, which would definitively demonstrate why only Islam was capable of significant economic progress and why Christian Europe would be forever mired in agrarian stagnation. Or we might subscribe to the claim made by the contemporary Sa'id al-Andalusi (later followed by Ibn Khaldun): that Europe's occupation of a cold temperate zone meant that its people were ignorant, lacked scientific curiosity and would remain backward (Hobson, quoted in Gresh 2009).

Jabu-Lughod 1991; Goody 2006; Frank 1998; Hobson 2004; Pomeranz 2000.

Notes

1. "Press Conference by World Food Programme executive director on Food Price Crisis," April 24, 2008, <http://www.un.org/News/briefings/docs/2008/080424_WFP.doc.htm>.
2. "Cargill Reports Third-quarter Fiscal 2008 Earnings," Lisa Clemens, April 14, 2008, <http://www.cargill.com/news-center/news-releases/2008/NA3007634.jsp>.
3. There are diverse permutations of this periodization, each identifying or emphasizing different patterns. As to which patterns are taken to represent or characterize the development process in each period is largely a matter of theoretical perspective. See for example, Desai (2000).

Section 3

Thinking Critically about Development

Whether conceived of in structural terms as a process, or in strategic terms as a project, development connotes substantive improvements in the human condition for an ever larger part of the world's population and the institutional and structural change needed to bring about these improvements—what has been termed 'genuine progress.' Critical factors and important principles in this development process are *social inclusion* and *equity*, a matter of extending these improvements in the human condition to those who are still mired in conditions of underdevelopment and poverty, to include the hitherto excluded. In this connection, it is estimated that close to two billion people on the 'South' of the global development divide—speaking metaphorically rather than geographically—are still, after five decades of 'development' efforts, unable to meet their basic physical and spiritual needs, deprived of the resources and opportunities needed for them to live and work collectively in dignity and justice and to flourish as social beings. The problem then—the fundamental problematic of critical development studies—is how to escape this state of underdevelopment and to bring about genuine progress, 'another world,' in the lexicon of critical development studies.

Over the years, development thinking and practice have tended to concentrate on the economic, on the dynamic forces of growth in economic production (development of the forces of production) and the associated pattern of consumption. Development theory, in this connection was mainly concerned with identifying (and analyzing the associated dynamics) of (1) the basic factors of economic production and growth (capital, labour, land and technology); (2) the role and agency of the state and the market; and (3) the historical context in which these agencies functioned, responding to changing conditions.

Over the years, however, other dimensions of the development process were brought into focus—the social, cultural, ecological and political—within the framework of several paradigmatic shifts, i.e., changes in the way development is envisioned, theorized and analyzed, and put into practice. Each of the three modules in this section of the handbook focuses on a critical dimension of this problematic—thinking critically about of development.

Module 5 briefly reviews the major theories that have been constructed over the years to identify and explain the changing dynamics of the development process—its driving forces, enabling or facilitative factors, the elements of the 'structure' (the institutionalized practices) that work to either inhibit or facilitate advances in the process, and the most appropriate agencies and effective strategies of social change.

Module 6 makes more specific reference to the significant contributions of Latin American social science to the production of knowledge in this area—the corpus of ideas (development theory) that defines the field of international development studies.

Module 7 makes a distinction between the body of ideas constructed in this field on the mainstream of international development thought and practice, and the body of ideas (development knowledge) constructed on the margins and in various sidestreams of development theory.

As Ronaldo Munck reconstructs it, this growing corpus of 'critical development theory' provides a critically important toolbox of ideas for revisioning and rethinking development—for bringing about social change, genuine progress and 'another world' of real development.

Module 5

Theories of Development

A Critical Economic Perspective

James Cypher
Universidad Autónoma de Zacatecas, Mexico

Since the late 1970s mainstream or orthodox analysis and perspectives on economic development have come to dominate policy both within international financial institutions (IFIS) and governments of the 'developed' industrialized nations as well as some nations on the South of the growing global divide. This orthodox focus, conventionally labelled 'neoliberalism'—an economic doctrine based on the ideology of free market capitalism—constitutes, at least in part, a return to formulations extant prior to World War II. At that time the economies of many nations in the Global South were colonized and structured to export primary products without regard to any internal coherence between the small export sector and the domestic economy. Under conditions of this 'dualism' the economic structure of the non-industrialized nations of the so-called 'Third World' were disarticulated and rendered incapable of capturing the impulses of the dynamic export sector.

As in earlier times, the concern of neoliberals is to expand the potential for exports, regarded as the fundamental engine of economic growth. Neoliberalism in theory operates within the confines of 'monoeconomics,' which assumes that there are no structural distinctions between those nations termed 'developed' and those termed 'developing.' Neoliberal analysis thus operates within a historical vacuum, which avoids examination of the development policy methods and strategies used by the industrialized nations to achieve their 'developed' status (Chang 2007). It also denies the historical impacts of colonial and neocolonial economic structures in the 'developing' regions.

With few exceptions, the emergence of 'development economics' after World War II marked the rise of 'heterodox' interdisciplinary theoretical formulations. Outliers could be found among the Chicago School—such as Arnold Harberger, Harry G. Johnson and Theodore Shultz—who commenced a 'war against developmentalism' in the 1950s. 'Developmentalism' captures a range of perspectives including those that would later be termed 'heterodox,' such as post-Keynesianism, structuralism, dependency theory and neo-Marxism. During the 'developmentalist' era, it could be difficult to determine where each variant of the developmentalist or heterodox perspective began and ended, with those operating within this broad framework frequently borrowing elements from other orientations.

Uniting all—at least to some degree—against what would become 'neoliberalism' was a deep suspicion of economic doctrines resting on the guiding but 'invisible hand' of autonomous unregulated market forces. Without doubt, the historical moment that gave birth to 'development economics'—conditioned as it was by the triple disasters of World War I, the Great Depression and World War II—led the early practitioners and analysts of development to varying permutations of critical engagement with economic formulations resting upon 'free' market forces. This included the most famous of all neoclassical (or liberal) formulations—Ricardo's 'law' of comparative advantage, which had been used as policy bludgeon to annihilate opposition to the 'trade is development' approach until the onset of the Great Depression.

With the Depression foreclosing the export market numerous 'developing' nations—particularly in Latin America—began, in earnest, to re-jig their economies. Extroverted, export-led economies being impossible to consider, introverted economies relying to varying degrees on the mass internal market flourished. Unfortunately, the term for this policy shift—import substitution industrialization (ISI)—suggested much less than the actual approach taken. What has too often been overlooked or intentionally distorted regarding this policy shift is the crucial role played by the state in creating a new industrial base (Amsden 2007). This project went far beyond merely 'substituting' domestic production for goods formerly imported. On the whole, as Alice Amsden has documented, this mislabelled 'ISI era' was remarkably successful—so successful it only 'ended' in Africa, the Middle East and Latin America in the early 1980s. In Asia, however, the ISI era—more correctly labelled 'industrial policy'—has not waned in the least. The ISI era has also been understood, due to the research of Robert Wade, as one of 'governing the market.' Nonetheless, neoliberalism has focused its opposition on the idea of the activist state, viewed by all those within the heterodox perspective as *the* crucial variable of economic development.

This course module is designed to both revisit and reinterpret the neoliberal critique of developmentalist/heterodox perspectives and to engage with those contemporary analysts who are forging a new critical theory of development. It does so through an examination of six fundamental, interrelated themes of profound current importance for the advance of CDS.

1. Origins of a critical perspective in development economics

As a point of departure, the first subject will be an intensive examination of some of the classic economic formulations of critical development theory. The objective is to present a set of common core of elements that were influential in many, but certainly not all, attempts to advance a developmental strategy throughout the 'developing world' in the 1950s and 1960s. Given the extensive outpouring of analyses during this crucial period it is not possible to examine even the majority of influential perspectives. The function of the lecture will be to broaden the scope of the material under examination. The focus of this theme will be on: (1) the CEPAL structuralists, particularly Raúl Prebisch; (2) dependency theory, particularly the neo-Marxist version; and (3) the original institutionalist perspective.

Alavi 1982: 289–307; Kay 2005: 1201–07; Sunkel 1990: 29–40.

2. Situating the state in the developmental process

Frequently disparaged, dismissed or disappeared in orthodox analyses of economic development, the state can and has served as a major agent of change in numerous Third World nations both in the past and the present.

Cypher & Dietz 2008b; Chang 2003b: 41-60; Chang 2007b: 1–18.

3. Industrial policy or 'free trade': Beyond import substitution industrialization

The neoliberal attack on the welfare-development state was based in part on the market-distorting effects of government intervention. Other arguments included the excessive costs of welfare and development vis-à-vis government revenues and the negative developmental consequences of an import-substitution industrialization (ISI) strategy and an inward oriented approach to development. This strategy, the argument went, resulted in undue protection of inefficient firms, a major obstacle to the implementation of an effective development strategy. This theory of the presumed exhaustion of a strategy that had worked well in earlier but different circumstances in turn led to a series of as yet-unsettled debates about the pros and cons of globalization and the policy conditions of integrating into the 'new world order.'

Amsden 2007: 71–133; Rodrik 2007: 99–152; Chang 2007a: 1–17; Shaik 2005: 41–49).

4. The new development economics: An emerging post-Washington Consensus?

Dissatisfaction with the Washington Consensus formulations has led to marginal changes at the IFIs and the 'higher circles' of development economic policymaking, highlighted by the interventions of Joseph Stiglitz (2002, 2005, 2006) and the construction of a new model of 'sustainable human development and good governance' (UNDP 1997a, 1997d). In academic circles, post-Washington Consensus formulations of the way forward can be put into seven categories:

1. Proposals for a 'more inclusive neoliberalism' based on (i) a new social policy that targets the poor; (ii) local institutions for poverty alleviation and (iii) specific policies for, and fiscal expenditures on, health and education services designed for social inclusion equity (i.e., equal opportunity) and capacitation for self-help;
2. A 'decentred but capable state' with a 'joined-up decentralized governance' (Craig & Porter 2006);
3. A new development paradigm based on decentralized governance, the accumulation of social capital and local development, empowering the poor to act for themselves (Atria et al. 2004);
4. A call for 'more balance between the state and the market' (Ocampo 2007);
5. Institution of a 'social democratic regime' capable of 'reconciling... growth through globalized markets with extensions of political, social and economic rights' (Sandbrook, Edelman, Heller & Teichman 2007: 3);
6. An overarching comprehensive development framework (CDF) and, within this framework,

construction of a new policy tool—the poverty reduction strategy paper (PRSP)—introduced to the 'development community' in 1999 at the G8 Summit; and

7. Empowerment of the poor—capacitating them to act for themselves, converting them into the fundamental agency for development.

In this 'consensus,' the CDF represents the realization that 'developing countries need to develop their own mix of policies to reduce poverty, reflecting national priorities and local realities' (World Bank 2000/2001: 7). In this context, PRSPs, linked to debt relief, are designed to provide an incentive for developing countries to buy into macroeconomic 'structural reforms' set out in the PRSP *Sourcebook*. The role of the state is restricted to the provision of an appropriate facilitating institutional and policy framework. The fundamental responsibility for development is shifted to the poor themselves—to have them 'own' their development.

Stiglitz 2005: 14–32; Ocampo 1998: 7–28; Van Waeyenberge 2006: 21–45; World Bank 2007: 39–42; Craig & Porter 2006: Chaps. 3–4; Fine 2006: 1–20; Ocampo 2007: 1–31.

5. What role does globalization play in the development problematic?

Globalization has become a term used in so many contexts with such varied meaning that the term has no implicit content. Nonetheless, there is considerable evidence pointing to a new context for world production with highly mobile international flows of capital and increasing interdependence if not actual integration among different national economies on both sides of the development divide. There are diverse theoretical perspectives on this globalization phenomenon, from those who view it as an extension of the long-term economic development process (Nayyar 2006) to those who see it as a new form of imperialism (Federici 2002; Petras & Veltmeyer 2001, 2003).

Nayyar 2006: 71–99; Keping 2007: 44–60; Cypher & Delgado Wise 2007: 27–43; Amsden 2005: 216–32; Cypher & Dietz 2008b.

6. Latin America at the crossroads: A new development paradigm in the making?

In rapid succession in the new millennium, left-of-centre governments (broadly defined) have achieved political power throughout Latin America, including in Argentina, Brazil, Chile, Ecuador, Nicaragua, Paraguay, Uruguay and Venezuela. Does this left turn in the tide of national regime politics offer new lessons for economic development? Does it imply a new development paradigm, a new model of national development that reached beyond the theoretical consensus aschieved in a post-Washngton consensus on a development paradigm and policy agenda between proponents of neoliberalism and neostructuralism?

Developments in Venezuela, Bolivia and Ecuador, advanced in terms of the 'Bolivarian Revolution' and the construction of an entirely new alternative arrangement for regional trade (ALBA), are seen by some scholars and activists (Girvan 2009, for example) as auguring an entirely new development path and model, 'another world' based not on reform of neoliberalism but on a fundamental break with it—the 'socialism of the twenty-first century,' in the conception of

Hugo Chávez, the president of Venezuela. Clearly this is matter of debate and controversy—and further study from a critical development perspective. Some guideposts and further readings for such as study are given in Modules 48 and 49.

Girvan 2009; Kay 2002: 1173–02; Cypher 2007: 31–61; Rocha 2007: 132–61.

Module 6

Development Theory from a Latin American Perspective

Cristóbal Kay
Institute for Social Studies, The Netherlands

Development studies emerged as a field of study, research and policy after World War II. It has grown enormously as an academic subject ever since, as can be gauged by the growing number of students following courses in development studies (or international development studies) and the significant rise in the number of articles published in this field in an ever increasing number of journals. Like in other disciplines, contending schools of thought have emerged in development studies. In six sessions it is impossible to do justice to the richness of this field of enquiry even if the priority is only on critical or heterodox development studies. This module thus focuses on the Latin American contribution to development studies, which has largely been critical of orthodox development theories. For CDS, this contribution is an important resource a major repository of ideas for rethinking development.

1. Introduction: An overview of development theories

IDS as an interdisciplinary approach was the product of the 1970s and 1980s, an analytical response to the inadequacies of single-discipline based approaches such as 'development economics.' The theoretical perspectives and diverse meanings of development that emerged at this point need to be understood in their historical context, particularly the 1959 Cuban Revolution and the concern of governments, international organizations and financial institutions that the demand for revolutionary change might spread. In this context the 1970s development effort in theory and practice was dominated by the ideology of liberal reform, i.e., reforming the capitalist system rather than changing the system). The readings in this unit explore the key development issues and controversies involved in this process. Beyond these development issues, the key political issue, as formulated by James Petras (Petras & Zeitlin 1968), was: *'reform or revolution?'*

Leftwich 2000: 40–70; Pieterse 2000: 197–214; Hettne 1995: 21–66.

2. The structuralist school of development

The major challenge to orthodox theories of development was presented by proponents of several theories constructed within the framework of a 'centre-periphery' model of the world capitalist system and in the context of a call in the General Assembly of the U.N. for a 'new international economic order.' This model and the theories constructed with it constituted what would become a new development paradigm: the centre-periphery paradigm, common to both 'Latin American structuralism' (a school of thought associated with CEPAL, the Economic Commission of Latin America, or ECLA, or later, with the addition of the Caribbean, ECLAC) and 'dependency theory,' an approach with its roots in both neo-Marxism and CEPALism. This course unit or class focuses on the key theoretical and policy debates conducted within the framework of this paradigm—on the terms of trade between the centre and periphery of the world system, an inward-directed development strategy and the policy of import substitution industrialization.

Kay 1989: 1–57; Rodríguez 1977: 195–239; Furtado 1964; Love 1980: 45–72.

3. Internal colonialism and marginality

Latin American structuralism (LAS) and dependency theory (DT) shared a focus on and concern with conditions of 'underdevelopment' or 'dependent capitalist development,' generated by the centre-periphery structure of the world capitalist system. In this concern and emphasis on the 'external' and a consequent relative neglect of 'internal' conditions and relations of economic exploitation and dependency, LAS and DT theorists were widely criticized. However, some dependency theorists, armed with a more sociological rather than structural-economic perspective, argued the need to apply the principles and concepts of 'dependency' to 'inside' relations and conditions—as in the concepts of 'internal colonialism,' 'redundant or surplus labour' and 'marginality.' This unit reviews the relevant debates on these and other such issues.

Kay 1989: 58–124; Stavenhagen 1965: 53–77; Stavenhagen 1968: 13–31.

4. Structuralist approaches to dependency

Latin American theories of development and underdevelopment can be sorted into two schools: LAS and DT. The central proposition of LAS is that the centre-periphery structure of world trade (the export of raw materials and primary commodities in exchange for manufactured goods) works against countries on the periphery because of the monopoly structure of trade in manufacturing and a resulting tendency towards deterioration in the terms of trade for exporters on the periphery. The solution to this problem, argued Raúl Prebisch, the founder of LAS, was a policy of import substitution industrialization, to break thereby a dependent pattern of consumption and create the conditions of self-reliant economic growth. The proponents of LAS dominated one side of the debate in development economics, from the late 1950s to the late 1980s, between economic liberals and structuralists, particularly in regard to the relative weight to be accorded the state and the market. In 1990 and subsequently (see Sunkel 1993), ECLAC published a series of important studies that reflected what Sunkel (1990) saw as 'an exploration of common ground and disparities' as well as an emerging post-Washington Consensus on the need for a 'better balance between the state and the market' (regarding the recognition, by World Bank economists, that they had 'gone too far' in the direction of the free market). On the part of ECLAC, this meant a departure from its structuralist opposition to liberalism and some theoretical convergence towards neoliberalism at the level of macroeconomic policy.

The basic argument advanced by dependency or 'world system' theorists was that the centre-periphery structure of the world system inhibited the capitalist development of economies on the periphery, resulting in an 'underdevelopment' of these economies, including a disarticulated structure of capitalist production, a deepening of social inequalities worldwide and a growing social divide between the wealthy few (within the transnational capitalist class) and the many poor (the direct producers and the working class). The basic theory was that the system of global capitalist production worked to the advantage of countries at the centre and to the disadvantage of those on the periphery; that, in effect, the critical structural factor explaining the development of some economies and the underdevelopment of others was location in the world capitalist system.

Kay 1989: 125–39; Sunkel 1990: 29–39.

5. Neo-Marxist approaches to dependency

The major difference between LAS and neo-Marxist dependency theory is that the latter views the economic (centre-periphery) structure of world capitalism as a relation of economic exploitation, allowing capitalists at the centre of the system to extract surplus value or an economic surplus from the direct producers and workers on the periphery. Essentially, it is argued, neither wages nor prices for goods received on the world market reflect the true value produced (products are sold and labour is remunerated at levels of exploitation, and even 'super-exploitation' (i.e., prices and wages do not even reflect the costs of production).

Within a relation of 'unequal exchange' and under conditions of 'dependency'—the mechanisms of which include trade, capital investment in various forms (even 'aid' according to Teresa Hayter)—'development' in the centre (the advanced capitalist countries) means at one and the same time 'underdevelopment' (Gunder Frank) or 'associated dependent development' (Cardoso) on the periphery (the countries in the Third World or Global South).

This theory in its different permutations and in its diverse Latin American and Caribbean formulations (see Kay 1989; Palma 1978)[1] came under heavy attack in the 1970s and 1980s from both an orthodox Marxist perspective (capitalism as a progressive as well as a destructive force) as well as from a more mainstream economic development perspective on the emergence of a group of 'newly industrializing countries' on the periphery of the world capitalist system— a serious 'reality test' for dependency theory, which in the 1980s led to various reformulations (basically as world systems theory).

Kay 1989: 139–96; Palma 1978: 881–924; Munck 1999b: 56–74.

6. Moving forward—theoretically?

In the early 1980s the conservative offensive against the progressive reforms and advances in development achieved in the 1970s (on this see Toye 1987) helped to bring about a new world order in which the development project was displaced by another entirely different project (the reactivation of the capital accumulation and economic growth process), even though this project was presented by the economists at the World Bank as a 'development project,' a means of improving the lives of the world's poor by mortgaging their future and hitching their livelihood opportunities on the fortunes of the rich and powerful.

In a radically changed context of an exploding external debt, fiscal and continuing production crisis and structural readjustment to the 'new world order,' development theory reached an 'impasse,' requiring and resulting in a serious rethinking of the entire development project—reflections that moved beyond or reformulated diverse main- and side-stream approaches. In this context of theoretical renewal, a major way forward ('neostructuralism'), and what can be regarded as a 'renewal of development studies,' was based on a rethinking of different Latin American and Caribbean theories of development and underdevelopment.

Kay & Gwynne 2000: 49–69; Kay 1993: 691–702; Ramos & Sunkel 1993: 5–19; Bernstein 2005: 111–37; Girvan 2006: 327–50; Kay 1989: 197–227; Levitt 2005: 355–68; Levitt 2009; Nixson 2006: 967–81; Schuurman 2000: 7–20.

Module 7

Critical Development Theory

Ronaldo Munck
Dublin City University, Ireland

Critical theory, in its broadest or ecumenical sense, could be said to start with Karl Marx, and via the Frankfurt School and then Michel Foucault to reach the present in the shape of feminism, ecology and postcolonialism amongst other liberating impulses. Critical theory is, in essence, concerned with the critique of modernity. In its Frankfurt School variant critical theory can be distinguished from traditional theory according to its specific and practical purpose. A social theory is critical insofar as it seeks human emancipation, that is 'to liberate human beings from the circumstances that enslave' (Horkheimer). Such theories seek to explain the circumstances that enslave human beings and provide the normative bases for social enquiry that will decrease domination and increase freedom in all their aspects. Following on from Horkheimer, I take 'critical development theory' to refer to those approaches that explain what is wrong with the current social order, identify the agents for social change and provide practical goals for social transformation. This module takes up critical development theory through six distinct themes.

1. Modernity and development

While critical dependency theory became somewhat codified and simplified in the North through the prolific polemics of André Gunder Frank, in Latin American social science it produced undoubted advances in our understanding of the original path capitalist development took in the periphery. The influence of external vulnerability on development, the foreign debt burden, financial and technological dependence and the rise of marginality and the informal sector are all debates springing from dependency debates. In the Cardoso-Faletto (1979) version, there was even a sustained engagement with the interaction between capital accumulation, the development of social classes and the political process.

From a present day critical development theory perspective, the dependency approach seems severely flawed (Palma 1981). Most visions or perspectives (although not all) were economistic and neglected the role of social classes and political struggle. The precise mechanisms of dependent development were underspecified to say the least. For most of these writers the choice was stark—underdevelopment or revolution—and thus the great leap forward by the newly industrializing countries (NICs) in the 1970s set them back severely. The intuition that backward capitalism would not follow the progressive path charted for it by Marx seemed simply disproven.

In an era when the dependency theory of the 1960s seems as remote to present day development debates as the Soviet industrialization debates of the 1920s, what might remain relevant to the contemporary (re)construction of a critical development theory? First of all, since around 2000 the theories of imperialism are making a comeback, albeit under conservative and postmodern guises. To understand the precise dynamics of the globalization processes we urgently need a robust renewed theory of imperialism. As to Latin American 'structuralism' and 'dependency,' they have been resuscitated as 'neostructuralism' (Sunkel 1993; Leiva 2008). But rather than contesting the hegemonic neoliberal paradigm it has converged with it. If we turn to mainstream development, we find for example that in the U.N. Millennium Project and its widely disseminated goals, the underlying dominant modernization paradigm is tempered by an explicit recognition of the 'structural constraints' to development, the exogenous roots of development problems and the growing gap between rich and poor countries, all once dependency theory staples.

Cardoso & Faletto 1979; Palma 1981.

2. The 'greening' of development theory

The greening of development theory took a sometimes parallel path to its engendering (see Adams 1990 for a useful overview) although its acceptance by the mainstream was much more marked. The critique of mainstream environmentalism centred on its innate conservatism, which would leave social structures untouched. During the 1970s the desirability of growth from an ecological point of view was consistently questioned albeit in very different ways. While radical strands on the ground stressed grassroots development and empowerment, the mainstream 'development machine' took up a bland 'sustainable development' as its leitmotif. A foundational statement of intent was *Our Common Future,* which followed in the steps of the global Keynesianism of the *Brandt Report.* Sustainable development would address both the environmental and poverty-related causes of the perceived environmental crisis through a strategy designed to meet 'basic needs' and by recognizing the 'environmental limits' set by technology and social organization.

There are many strands of critical ecology theories within CDS. Many theorists in the radical tradition tried to bridge the gap between ecology and modernist socialism. Thus, Michael Redclift (1984) argued that the growing concern with the environmental crisis of the South in the 1970s was not matched by an understanding of global economic relations and the uneven share of resources obtained by different social groups across the world. This could be called a green/red synthesis in a way. For others, such as Sachs (1999), the greening of development theory and planning needs to go far beyond a concern with the environment to take up the politics of development and the need for the empowerment of the poor to determine the future of their own environment. Beyond this scenario lie the 'deep ecologists' with their ecocentrism and biocentrism development models posing a fundamental, not to mention fundamentalist, critique of utilitarian, reformist and managerial conceptions of the environment.

Adams 1990; Redclift 1984; Sachs 1999.

3. The 'gendering' of development theory

One strand of the gender and development approach has focused most clearly on the domain of patriarchy, capital accumulation and work. There was an intense focus on the sexual division of labour and on the household as locus of unequal gender relations. The early studies all rejected the notion that if only women had equal access to the market—in terms of jobs, equal pay, childcare provisions—women's subordinate position in capitalist society would end. In the dialectic between class and gender oppression, the latter was, at the end of the day, seen as more determinant. There was later (see Bakker 1994) a concentrated focus on the gendered nature of macroeconomic policy and on the impact of the 1980s structural adjustment programs. The main element in the feminist engagement with development discourse and practice in the 1990s was a much greater emphasis on the practical policies that the likes of the World Bank needed to adopt for gender planning in development. Here an advance in terms of engendered policies was a certain domestication of once radical policies (Rai 2005).

An arguably distinct element in destabilizing dominant theory was what Chandra Mohanty referred to as the 1990s challenges posed by Black and Third World feminists that can point the way towards a more precise, transformational feminist politics. The feminist critique of mainstream development theory took various forms including the Third World Marxist feminism challenge to orthodoxy (Sen & Grown 1988), the poststructuralist feminist critique of global capitalism's totalizing project and the imaginative (re)integration of the productive, reproductive and virtual elements of global political economy.

Bakker 1994; Rai 2005; Sen & Grown 1988.

4. Culture and development

Culture in the 1980s became a key element in the management of development while it could also be seen as part of the contestation of mainstream development notions. Peter Worsley's challenge to develop the 'missing concept' of culture was taken up by many theorists and practitioners (Tucker 1997). Vincent Tucker pursued this task on the basis of his argument that 'development thinking must be underpinned by a conceptualization of culture as a dynamic and conflictual process' (1999: 17). It is perhaps best to see this shift in terms of bringing cultural politics into critical development theory, in other words, to advance a cultural critique of development. It is at this juncture that the cultural critique of development joins the terrain of social movement theory and its rich understanding of the 'culture of politics and the politics of culture' (Alvarez, Dagnino & Escobar 1998).

A fundamental critique of mainstream development came through the Foucault-inspired 'turn to language' and the radical deconstruction of the very concept of development. The linguistic turn in cultural studies directed our attention to the crucial importance of language through an emphasis on discursivity and textuality. Escobar argued that 'Critical thought should help recognize the pervasive character and functioning of development as a paradigm of self-definition' (1995: 215). From this perspective flowed the critique of development as discourse with very different results from the critique of development as political economy. The discourse of development from the nineteenth century onwards and particularly following World War II is seen to create the object of development and its others in the shape of 'underdevelopment,' the 'poor,' the 'landless,' 'Third World women' and all those shaped and marked by the totalizing gaze of development.

Alvarez, Dagnino, & Escobar 1998; Escobar 1995; Tucker 1997.

5. Postdevelopment theory

If the 'culture turn' opened up development as discourse to options beyond modernity, the explicit adoption of a 'postdevelopment' perspective in the 1990s took this shift one stage further. Gustavo Esteva puts this hypercritical perspective most clearly when he states:

> If you live in Mexico City today, you are either rich or dumb if you fail to notice that development stinks... the three 'development decades' were a huge, irresponsible experiment that, in the experience of a world-majority, failed miserably. (Esteva 1987: 138)

We could argue that people living in China and India today would testify instead to the dynamism and 'creative destruction' that is still capitalism's *modus operandi* with all the contradictory effects that implies. Even in Latin America after the 'lost decade' of the 1980s, development in terms of capitalist accumulation has proceeded apace. Certainly this development process has been uneven and has, in its unfolding, created great levels of social exclusion. Development may 'stink' but it is far from dead or just kept alive by the clever discourse of the World Bank.

So where do the critical social theorists of postdevelopment take us with their critique of mainstream development? There are very distinct strands in the postdevelopment literature. Some versions or modalities of postdevelopment are in many respects a reprise of classic anti-modernist or romantic critiques of modernity. It is entirely understandable that after half a century of 'development' not delivering on its original optimistic promises, critics may well wish to turn for inspiration to a pre-development era. But apart from producing a warm glow there is very little that this particular perspective might add to current debates on globalization and how oppositional social networks might in practice counter its negative effects. It certainly does not offer a plausible alternative development strategy (see Pieterse 2001 for a critique of postdevelopment thinking).

However, modalities of postdevelopment thinking, such as the one articulated by Gilbert Rist, by no means can be understood as an anti-modernist, romantic-conservative critique. Rist (2002) in particular provides a critical postdevelopment perspective that warrants close reading. He reconstructs the itinerary of this idea from its origins and conditions in the seventeenth and eighteenth centuries, and the enterprise or industry that has surrounded it ever since the reinvention or social construction of the development idea in the post World War II context. In Rist's reconstruction of development as an idea and practice it has its origins in an attempt to commodify nature and labour, the transposition of the laws that govern nature (Newtonian physics) onto social relations and the colonization of the minds of people living in the not-yet-developed world in order to justify interventions designed to benefit primarily the North rather than the South.

A more conventional (critical- rather than postdevelopment) but equally sceptical and trenchant critique of development by Adam Fforde (2009) is based on a penetrating unpacking of the basic—and largely false—default assumptions that underlie development thinking and practice.

Crush 1995; Esteva 1992; Fforde 2009; Pieterse 2001.

6. The politics of development theory

The challenge of critical development theory cannot be met by moving beyond or giving up on development. Rather, the challenge is to imagine and practise development differently. It is Eurocentrism that is probably what stands in our way most decisively and the need is thus to develop an epistemology of the South to put it in spatial or geographical terms. Boa Santos points acutely to the powerful obstacle of Enlightenment thinking through what he calls its monoculture of knowledge, of classification and of linear time, which produces the 'non-existent' pre-modern or underdeveloped vis-à-vis the declared objective of modernity. A new critical social theory of absences would focus on the alternatives to hegemonic Eurocentric practices and articulate the concrete ways in which another world is indeed possible.

We need to bring politics and even ideology back into critical development theory (see Saul 2006 for a passionate statement in this regard) if there is to be an effective alternative to actually existing world capitalism. *Politics is the art of responding to the demands and advancing the interests of those who one proposes to represent.* The problem in regard to the politics of development is to determine whose interests are advanced by means of development. If we are, indeed, as argued by Saul, now moving beyond the 'easy' stage of globalization, which in the 1990s foresaw economic homogenization and political democratization spreading smoothly across the world, then might there be room for a revival of a critical development approach? And whose interests would be so represented? There is little question, as argued by Petras in his various writings (see also Module 9), that globalization is the ideology and represents the interests of the 'global ruling class.' By the same token anti-globalization is in the interest of the classes subordinate to this class.

We could argue that the only alternative to neoliberalism or 'actually existing globalization' is not some vague utopian era of postdevelopment but rather a *critical development approach* to globalization. This is the space where *critical development studies* meets *critical globalization studies* (see Module 10). It takes us beyond methodological nationalism and an emphasis on national development to the new challenges of development in an emerging era. This implies not neoliberal globalization or postdevelopment but critical globalization and critical development.

Corbridge 2007: 179–211; Munck & O'Hearn 1999; Kothari & Minogue 2002; Saul 2006.

Note

1. One of the clearest expositions of this neo-Marxist dependency theory was by Che Guevara (1970: 524) in the following: 'The IMF acts as a custodian of the dollar for the capitalist world. The International Reconstruction and Agricultural Bank is an instrument that is used to penetrate into underdeveloped countries, and the IDB fulfils this sad role in the American continent. The laws and principles that these organizations are governed by appear to be, on the surface, acting in the interests of the people they are supposedly there to help. They are promoted as safeguarding equity and reciprocity within the area of international economic relations. However, in reality they are merely subtle instruments used to perpetuate exploitation and backwardness.'

Section 4

A System in Crisis

From a critical development perspective, the most significant patterns of economic and political development over the past four decades derive from a fundamental built-in propensity of the operating world capitalist system towards crisis. Once (prior to the 1990s) there were two operating systems, capitalist and socialist, and three worlds of development based on these systems (Worsley 1984). But for a number of as yet not well explained reasons the socialist system succumbed to a structural and political crisis, which led to an economic and political restructuring process in which a number of 'actually existing' forms of socialism collapsed—in the U.S.S.R. and Eastern Europe but also China and other parts of Asia. As it turned out, socialism in Africa never was more than an idea; the conditions for its implementation were not available. Cuba, a victim of the forces deriving from this collapse as well, managed to survive the crisis by means of a radical restructuring of the socialist model.

The other countries in the region and the world, under the sway of a restructured worldwide capitalist system, have been subject in their national development to the diverse forces generated by a process of crisis and economic restructuring that can be traced back to the 1970s. The production crisis of the early 1970s unleashed a lengthy multifaceted restructuring process that entailed: (1) a technological revolution, leading to a process of productive transformation and a major technological conversion of the production apparatus; (2) a spatial or geographical displacement of capital and production, resulting in a new international division of labour and the appearance of the NICs in the Global South; (3) a restructuring of macroeconomic policy to renovate the world capitalist system, releasing the forces of economic freedom from the regulatory constraints of the welfare-developmental state; and (4) a corresponding political restructuring— a neoconservative counter-revolution that diminished the power of the centralized state and organized labour vis-à-vis capital, resulting in a process of decentralization and what a number of scholars in the 1980s defined as 'redemocratization.'

This multidimensional restructuring process can be traced out in close to four decades of developments that were dominated by the turn from a welfare-developmental state to a neoliberal state and a neoliberal world order: a 'short history of neoliberalism' in the conception of David Harvey (2005) and others. This short history can be traced out in the following four development cycles:

1. An initial round (in the 1970s) of 'neoliberal' (free market) policies engineered by a new generation of 'Chicago-trained' economists, implemented under Chile's military regime led by Augusto Pinochet;
2. A second round of policy reform (in the 1980s) in response to a call for a 'new world order' in which neoconservatives (Thatcher, Reagan, etc.) turned to a program of structural reforms in national policy designed by the economists at the World Bank on the model of the Chile experience and under the Washington Consensus;

3. a third round of structural reform (in the 1990s) under the post-Washington Consensus on the need for a more inclusive, sustainable and governable form of neoliberalism based on achieving a better balance between the state and the market in the development process; and

4. a pragmatic neoliberal policy program (in the new millennium) under conditions of an initial production crisis, the financialization of production, a primary commodities boom (2003–08) led by the demand in China end India for energy and natural resources and the emergence of a global financial and production crisis.

The discussion and readings in this section elaborate on the development dynamics of this crisis and restructuring process. Module 8 theorizes the basic dynamics of capitalist development in the context of what has become known as the 'new world order.' Today, after more than two decades of development, this 'order' is better described as 'neoliberal globalization.' Module 9 elaborates on the development dynamics of globalization and imperialism within this 'world order,' which refers to the set of rules established for 'international relations' among the major 'actors' on the world stage (on these 'actors' and the political dynamics of 'international relations' see the next section, 'The International Dimension'). Module 10 brings into a sharper focus the dynamics of development from a 'critical globalization studies' perspective. Barry Gills, the author of this module, is a major theorist of this perspective. Module 11 by Walden Bello analyzes the crisis dynamics of the globalization process.

Module 8

Contemporary Capitalism

Development in an Era of Neoliberal Globalization

Guillermo Foladori, Raúl Delgado Wise
Universidad Autónoma de Zacatecas, Mexico

The political economy of capitalist development should be studied with reference to, and in the context of, its different phases. To this purpose several scholars in the tradition of radical political economy have constructed a periodization framework to facilitate analysis of the capitalist development process. See Module 3, theme 1 for an elaboration of these seven phases from the period of original accumulation (1450–1800) to the era of neoliberal globalization (1983–2007).

It is also possible, and in fact essential (on this see Petras and Veltmeyer 2007b), to break down the neoliberal era into three sub-phases. First, an initial phase of structural reform under the Washington Consensus (1983–89) witnessed the retreat of the state from the economy; a two-level process of democratization (the restoration of the 'rule of law' and elected civilian regimes, administrative decentralization coupled with a strengthening of civil society); and a 'decade lost to development,' resulting from the absence of productive investment under conditions of debt repayment, which absorbed well over 50 percent of export revenues generated in the forced 'opening' to the global economy. This phase was followed by a decade of uneven development (a large inflow of foreign direct investment attracted more by the opportunity to acquire the privatized assets of lucrative public enterprises than any 'emerging market'); a mild recovery of economic growth; and then the onset of financial crisis followed by a deep production crisis); and an extension, and deepening, of structural reform under the new policy agenda of the post-Washington Consensus.

The decade also saw the emergence of powerful movements, led by the landless rural workers in some contexts (Brazil) and peasant farmers and indigenous communities in others (Chiapas, Bolivia, Ecuador). These movements actively mobilized resistance, succeeding not in reversing but at least in halting or slowing down the neoliberal agenda of most governments in the region (Petras & Veltmeyer 2005). The dynamism of these movements ebbed somewhat with the new millennium, in part the result of a shift on the left from a reliance on social mobilizations and political opposition to the use of the electoral apparatus of the political class on the centre-left (Petras &Veltmeyer 2009).

The first decade of the new millennium has been described by some as a postneoliberal era, characterized by widespread disenchantment with and the demise of neoliberalism and the achievement of state power by the centre-left riding the wave of anti-neoliberal sentiment in the context of a primary commodities boom (2002–08). This phase appears to be drawing to a close with the onset of a global financial crisis with serious ramifications in the real economy. The crisis has unsettled the existing structure of institutionalized practices, generating new forces of resistance, mobilized against the coup makers in Honduras as well as the continuing neoliberal policies of some governments in the region (Peru, Colombia, Mexico). The unsettling effects of the crisis have also expanded an opening towards alternative forms of regional integration and what Chávez has termed the 'socialism of the twenty-first century.' In the context also of diverse political responses by governments and international organizations to save capitalism from itself and restore a more socially inclusive form of neoliberalism, the neoliberal era appears to becoming to an end in the vortex of the global financial crisis (see Module 11 on the dynamics of this crisis).

1. The great transformation

Capitalist development has been conceived as a process of productive and social transformation—the 'great transformation' as Karl Polanyi (1944) conceived of it—from a precapitalist, traditional and agrarian society into a modern industrial and capitalist system. As for the dynamics of this process of capitalist development it is a matter of theoretical perspective. As noted in Module 27, economic historians and sociologists have formulated three basic metatheories of this development based on alternative sets of ideas about 'modernization,' 'industrialization' and 'capitalist development' (conversion of the direct agricultural small producer or peasant into a proletariat or working class). In addition Karl Polanyi (1944) analyzed this historic process as the evolution of a market economy in its detachment ('liberation') from the social and political institutions within which it had been embedded.

Desai 2000; Harvey 2005; Sachs 1999a, 1999b: 90–101.

2. The capitalist world-system:
Marx's theory of the capitalist laws of development

Capitalism is by definition a wage-labour system of commodity production driven by the implacable search for private profit, a system that nowadays operates on a global scale and thus is constituted as a world system. As a system, capitalism is essentially constituted by four fundamental institutions: (1) private property in the means of production, a legal institution incorporated into the capitalist state; (2) the social relation of wage labour, an institution that defines two basic classes—the owners of the means of production or the capitalist class (the bourgeoisie) and the proletariat: the workers who own nothing but their capacity to labour, which they are compelled to exchange against capital for a living wage; (3) the state, a complex of institutions designed to create the necessary conditions of capital accumulation, including minimally (other institutions can be added as needed) the provision of an economic and social infrastructure for the capital accumulation process and for reproducing the system, legitimating its basic arrangements; a legislature, an institution for law-making; the government of the day with an administrative apparatus; and a repressive apparatus, designed to reconcile conflict over property and preserve order; and (4) the market, an institution of economic exchange, serving as a mechanism for the authoritative allocation of society's resources and distribute income; it can be free or, more often than not, regulated by the state.

The dynamics of capitalist development can be explained by reference to, and in terms of, various 'laws' that specify patterns of fact or tendencies (what is tends to occur under specified objectively given conditions). There are various available theories of capitalist development but none as important or useful to understand and study as that constructed by Karl Marx. This theory has four major propositions:

1. capitalism is a system of commodity production and that the value of a commodity (reflected in its market price) is equivalent to the socially necessary labour time used in producing it;
2. capitalist development is based on the exploitation of labour—the worker does not receive the full value generated by his/her labour, and that surplus value (in excess of that required to maintain the worker and his/her family) is the source of the capitalist's profit (the theory of surplus value);
3. migration of capital from one sector to another creates an average system-wide rate of profit, and this rate tends to fall over time—the theory of the law for a falling rate of profit;
4. capitalist development is governed by a 'general law of capital accumulation,' which specifies a twofold tendency—on the one hand, for capital (pools of investment funds) to concentrate and assume a corporate and monopoly, and on the other, for the direct producers to be separated from their means of production—the 'original accumulation of capital'—leading to the 'multiplication of the proletariat' or the conversion of small-scale agricultural peasant producers into a working class, and at the same time, as the organic composition of capital rises, a growing part of labour becomes surplus to the requirement of capital, resulting in the growth of an 'industrial reserve army' of unemployed workers.

To the degree that these and other laws have begun to operate on a global scale we can conceive of capitalism as Immanuel Wallerstein (1979) and other world system theorists do: as a 'world system.'

Amin 1972; Lenin 1969; Mandel 2002; Wood 1994: 14–40.

3. The capitalist system

To define the economic and social system as 'capitalism' is to define it in terms of the underlying mode of production: a particular combination of society's 'productive forces' (at a certain stage of their historic development) and the corresponding 'relations of production,' relations that all members of society necessarily enter into and form in the process of organizing production. The totality of these relations, according to Marx in his historical materialist conception of society, constitute the economic structure of society, the foundation on which is constructed an ideological superstructure and a state apparatus.

From a critical development perspective, it is important to move as soon as possible from a reading of capitalism in the abstract, as defined in a purely theoretical discourse (see, for example, the excellent introduction to Marxist economic theory provided by Mandel), towards a class analysis of the dynamics of capitalist development in a contemporary and current context. A reading of Berberoglu, Osorio, Regalado and Saad-Filho are useful entry points into these dynamics.

Berberoglu 2003, 2005, 2007, 2009; Regalado 2007; Saad-Filho 2003.

4. Capital accumulation and economic development

The driving force of capitalist development is the accumulation of capital based on the extraction of surplus value out of its direct producers. The starting point of this accumulation process, what Marx defined as 'primitive accumulation,' is the separation of the direct producers from the means of production, a process of dispossession and proletarianization (the conversion of a society of small-scale 'peasant' producers into a working class). The endpoint of this accumulation process is in the productive investment of capital and the financing of productive activity or 'development'—which is 'productive' when capital in money form (it can also take physical, natural and human forms) is invested in new technologies that increase the productivity of labour (growth in output per unit of labour power expended and money invested), leading to the development of the forces of production.

Development finance or 'financial capital' is accumulated and invested through a variety of institutional mechanisms such as banking and stock markets. In its relation to economic development and the revolutionary advances in information technology, 'development finance' or 'capital' is highly mobile, predominantly in the form of 'private capital' or 'international resource flows' (managed by a range of international financial institutions) from country to country, and across each country and the world, seeking profitable outlets or returns on investments. The development and globalization dynamics of these financial resource flows are analyzed from a critical development perspective in the readings.

Saxe-Fernández & Núñez 2001; Petras & Veltmeyer 2004, 2009.

5. Structural and policy dynamics in the era of neoliberal globalization

The internationalization (or globalization) of capital has been characterized by a dominant power in economic relations. The ideological expression of this is the idea of globalization presented in neoliberal form, i.e., in terms of the defined need for countries to adjust their policies to the requirements of a new world order in which the 'forces of economic freedom' (the market, private property, capitalism) are liberated from the restrictions of the welfare-developmental or socialist state. Such neoliberal policy prescriptions include: (1) balance national payments and fiscal accounts, and control inflation; (2) 'get prices right' by reduced government intervention and interference with the market; (3) privatization of the means of production and state enterprises; (4) deregulation of capital, product and labour markets; (5) liberalize trade and the movement of investment capital; (6) democratize the state-civil society relation and decentralize government, creating thereby conditions for participatory development and good governance.

To legitimate these policies, set as conditionalities of aid and access to global capital markets, and to ensure governability of these societies, these policies are justified and legitimated by reference to the idea of 'globalization' as inevitable and desirable, the best, indeed only, path to 'general prosperity.' Together, neoliberalism and globalization constitute the fundamental policy dynamics of capitalist development in the 1980s and the 1990s, providing for development and facilitating environmental and institutional frameworks. Neoliberal 'structural reforms' were implemented in sequence, generating several cycles, each with its own social and political dynamics, each generating forces of resistance (Petras & Veltmeyer 2005a).

The social policies of neoliberalism and their dynamics constitute a critical area of CDS. Key issues in this area—the policy dynamics of the post-Washington Consensus include: (1) the expectation and promise of economic growth and the alleviation of poverty; (2) associated or resulting structural change and social transformation that constitute and open up various pathways out of poverty—labour, migration, farming (World Bank 2008); (3) a decentralized form of local governance and development; and (4) an overarching comprehensive development framework, and within it a new policy tool—the Poverty Reduction Strategy Paper—introduced to the 'development community' in 1999 at the G-8 Summit of that year.

Amin 1997; Chase-Dunn & Gills 2005; Hahnel 2008: 11–28.

Module 9

Globalization, Imperialism and Development

James Petras
Saint Mary's University, Canada

It has become fashionable to use the term 'globalization' as a description of the international economy and international political relations. Globalization is meant to have taken over from imperialism, when a handful of large states openly and directly ran most of the world. *The Economist* in July 1998 ran a major article called 'The New Geopolitics,' which described this supposed transformation: 'The imperial age was a time when countries A, B and C took over the governments of countries X, Y and Z.' But, it continues, 'the aim now is to make it possible for the peoples of X, Y and Z to govern themselves, freeing them from the local toughs who deny them that right.'

Many on the left have critically adapted this description of the 'new world order.' The central idea is that the growth of multinational corporations (MNCs) means that the age of imperialism has been replaced by a more abstract but equally powerful rule by capital not tied to any state: an empire of corporate capital (see Hardt & Negri 2000). Petras and Veltmeyer (2003, 2007b) among others, however, debunk this idea, demonstrating that the state is anything but dead and that imperialism, the state-led project of world domination, is very much alive and well—behind the drive of corporate capital in the advanced countries to dominate the world economy in the name of freedom.

These scholars have found that imperialism, backed by state military power, today takes a number of forms: cultural hegemony of the ideology of neoliberalism and globalization and the imposition of structural adjustment and policy reform leading to privatization and denationalization—direct multinational corporate investment and multinational operations leading to resource pillage and enormous profits (Petras & Veltmeyer 2007b). This is development as the soft glove to draw attention away from the iron fist in the form of military force led by the U.S. state.

The U.S. neoconservative regime, led by George W. Bush, advanced the Project for the New American Century—to unilaterally project state power by any means, including military force, needed to restore U.S. hegemony. Neoconservatives themselves, as well as a growing number of U.S. foreign policy analysts, term this policy the 'new imperialism.' Petras and Veltmeyer (2003), among other critics, term it 'military imperialism.'

1. Globalization, imperialism and development

'Globalization is a cover for American imperialism, but the beneficiaries are not the American people at the expense of foreigners but corporate executives at the expense of working class and poor people wherever they may be' (Johnson 2004).

By many accounts—and diverse theoretical perspectives—the 1980s saw the advent of a new neoliberal world order in which the 'forces of freedom' (markets, the private sector) were liberated from the constraints of the welfare-development state and advanced by the trimmed down and supposedly hollowed out neoliberal state. This 'development' (globalization) was facilitated by a neoliberal program of 'structural reforms' in national policy (the 'structural adjustment program' or SAP), designed according to the Washington Consensus (Williamson 1990). The 1990s, however, saw the advent of a contradictory development: on the one hand, the further liberalization of international financial and commodity markets, together with the fall of communism, unleashed a new golden age for free-wheeling and -dealing capitalism; on the other, the emergence of powerful forces of resistance and serious concerns with the sustainability of the neoliberal economic model led to diverse efforts to move beyond the Washington Consensus in the re-design of a more sustainable and governable form of globalization based on a new 'development paradigm' (see, for example, Ocampo 2007).

By several accounts (Petras and Veltmeyer 2001, for example) globalization is an ideological cover for U.S. imperialism. Presented by the World Bank and others as a program of economic development, poverty alleviation and general prosperity, globalization is better understood as a tool for legitimating the neoliberal reforms of the structural adjustment program.

Kiely 2007; Ocampo 2007: 1–31.

2. Toward a new world order:
From the development state to the neoliberal state

The transition from the Bretton Woods liberal world order based on the agency of a development state into a new world order based on the agency of a neoliberal state and the 'private sector' (i.e., the capitalist class within the sector) freed from the regulatory constraints and state interventions took place in the 1970s and early 1980s in a context of crisis (a global production crisis, a widespread fiscal crisis and an emerging debt crisis in the Global South). The resulting dynamics of neoliberal globalization are critical to an understanding of development over the past two decades. As for the academic literature on these dynamics, the website *Globalization & War texts & analysis* <www.agp.org> provides access to a broad range of studies that place the war-globalization relation in a critical theoretical perspective. The website is an excellent source of study for critical review.

3. Multinational corporations: Agents of development?
Maldevelopment? Or empire?

There is no question that the world economy is dominated by the operations of multi- or transnational corporations (MNCs or TNCs), most of which are based in the U.S. and Western Europe but a growing number of which have their headquarters in Japan and other parts of Asia. The question that remains unsettled is the economic power of these corporations relative to the nation-state, hitherto the dominant player in international relations regarding the world economy. Some see the MNCs as the leading players in a new global 'empire' that has essentially displaced the imperialism of the nation-state system (Hardt & Negri 2000). Others, however, see the MNCs and the imperial state-system working hand in glove, both under control and instruments of the 'new global ruling class'—the 'new rulers of the world' (Pilger 2002).

Nonetheless, the most important issue is whether MNCs contribute to, or should be seen as, agents of 'development' or 'underdevelopment': Can the MNCs contribute to development (that is, can they be usefully incorporated into the development process, as the international financial institutions and the U.N. have been attempting to do since 1989)? Or, as Petras and Veltmeyer (2001, 2003, 2007b) argue, should they be understood as the operating units of the world capitalist system and as such a major mechanism of economic exploitation and surplus transfer—sucking resources and surplus value (potential capital) out of the periphery for the benefit of capital accumulation at the centre?

Chang 1998; Petras & Veltmeyer 2004: 31–52; Cypher & Dietz 2008b.

4. Social dynamics of neoliberal globalization:
A calculus of inequality

A voluminous literature considers whether globalization, as promised by its advocates, generates economic growth and prosperity, or whether, as charged by critics, it dramatically increases social inequalities to the extremes of highly concentrated wealth on the one pole and widespread immiseration on the other. While the debate continues to rage, it is important to examine the specific but diverse forms of neoliberal policies and to determine their outcomes and social impacts in different contexts. In this connection it is evident that development in any form or policy has a differential impact, benefiting some and harming others. In other words, there are always, as neoliberals often assert, winners and losers—at least, if as is normally the case in capitalism, the system is set up in the form of a competitive race and, moreover, the race is rigged to the advantage of some. Thus, it is important from a critical perspective to identify not only the supposed 'targets' of the any development policy but the actual beneficiaries. This is especially the case in regard to neoliberalism, whose programs purport to be development oriented but are anything but. It has been argued by critics that the war on poverty waged by the World Bank with so much effort and fanfare and so many resources is in actuality a war on the poor. Notwithstanding arguments and protestations to the contrary, 'pro-growth' is generally not 'pro-poor.'

Petras & Veltmeyer 2007a: 180–209; Benn & Hall 2000; Grandin 2006; Jomo & Baudot 2007.

5. The new imperialism: The tyranny of neoliberalism

Imperialism refers to attempts by some states and the dominant class in these states to dominate the world and impose their will on others. As such, it is based on the projection of diverse forms of state power, including economic and ideological, which is ultimately backed up by military force. In the Pax Britannica (the British-led empire of the 1880s to World War II), as in earlier eras of empire, imperialism meant dictation of government policy from the imperial centre and direct colonial rule through surrogates and client states. It also meant imperial control over an international division of labour that locked countries on the periphery of the system into supplying goods, mainly natural resources, needed by the empire. With important changes, especially in the locus of imperial power and the immemorial dream of world domination, this form of imperialism continued in the post World War II period. It was so maintained by means of what the theorist Gramsci termed 'hegemony' (cultural or ideological dominance)—convincing the rest of the world that its exercise of state power is well-intentioned and in the common interest of humankind. However, in the new world order of neoliberal globalization and postmodern society, imperialism has taken what some see as a 'new' form (hence the 'neoimperialism' of the 1980s and the 'new imperialism' of the 1990s).

There are diverse theoretical and political perspectives and a growing body of studies on this 'new imperialism,' but what characterizes it above all is a reversion to military force, projected unilaterally by the one remaining superpower—the U.S. state. The hegemony of U.S. power, hitherto based on the idea of 'freedom' embodied in the belief in globalization and democracy, had been eroded and weakened if not entirely lost, forcing the neoconservative regime in state power to advance its imperial 'Project for a New American Century,' as well as the 'national interest,' by any and all means, including military force (Petras & Veltmeyer 2003: Chap. 11).

Cammack 2006: 229–60; Petras & Veltmeyer 2003; Biel 2000; Veltmeyer 2008; Petras & Veltmeyer 2005; Saad-Filho & Johnston 2005.

6. The politics of development in the new world order

The shift from the Keynesian welfare state (instituted in the 1930s, in the North) and the development state (instituted in the 1950s, in the South) towards liberalism and the neoliberal state (in the 1980s) not only entailed a counter-revolution in development thought and practice (Toye 1987) but a turn into a 'new world order' and a fundamental change in the agency of development. Hitherto (from the 1950s on) the main agency of change and development was the state. But the 'new world order' meant the relative retreat of the state from the 'function of capital' (ownership, investment, entrepreneurship and enterprise management, i.e., the responsibility for capital accumulation and economic growth). It also meant a retreat from the responsibility for the 'development function.' This role was reassigned, or rather, shared by the state with 'civil society'—a host of nongovernmental organizations. The state itself was viewed not as responsible for the fiscal crisis that afflicted virtually every government in the system and the failure to close the North-South development gap, but as inherently rentierist and subject to corruption. Thus, civil society was engaged and strengthened as a means of ensuring the transparency of public policy and a partner in the development process—as a catalyst and change agent. This was under the Washington Consensus on the need for 'structural reform' in the direction of free market capitalism—to liberate the forces of 'economic freedom' from the regulatory constraints of the welfare-development state.

The 1990s, however, brought about a shift in policy based on a 'post-Washington Consensus' (PWC) on the need to 'bring the state back in' and to establish a 'better balance between the state and market' (Ocampo 2007) via a 'new social policy' that would ensure that the 'pro-growth' policies of the government are 'pro-poor' (see Module 5).

Petras & Veltmeyer 2003: Chap.10; Veltmeyer 2007a: Chap. 4; Bebbington, Hickey & Mitlin 2008; Kothari & Minogue 2001: Chap. 7; Ocampo 2007: 1–31.

Module 10

Critical Globalization Studies

Barry K. Gills
Newcastle University, United Kingdom

Globalization, a concept increasingly seen as central to social science and economic thinking, invites a significant range of uses and interpretations. To some it is already a 'dominant' or 'dominating' paradigm. Some argue that globalization is a single, overarching process. Others contend that there is a plurality of processes, which may be called 'globalizations.' Some challenge the idea that globalization is an 'it' and argue that globalization is merely a 'space' for debate and conceptualization. Is globalization all-inclusive, i.e., does it represent some type of 'comprehensive' concept? In the nineteenth century, there were numerous attempts to formulate a 'grand theory' or a theory of all social change and development. Is modern 'globalization' another attempt to create a 'totalizing notion' that can encompass all types of social action? Can there ever truly be a single theory of globalization? Or is it wiser to recognize that no such consensus could realistically be expected to result from the debate?

Does globalization represent a sharp break in continuity with past social and economic history, i.e., a radical historic discontinuity, or does it represent some fundamental continuities, e.g., in the development of capitalism, 'modernity' and urban civilization? Are globalization processes merely 'intensifications' of already existing tendencies or historical and evolutionary logics? Some scholars see a danger in ascribing to globalization attributes that render it historically determinist or that propose a 'law of history,' inevitability or even teleological aspects. Others contend that globalization is a historically open process or processes, not pre-determined but rather socially contested. In this latter view, the 'outcomes' of globalization remain unpredictable and the prospect of even radical transformation is possible, given what social agency may or may not bring about in the future.

There is a long–standing analysis of the 'transnationalization' of class and of capital, on which some analysts of globalization have built new arguments about the future social structure of the world. Analyses of both a transnational capitalist class and the transnationalization of labour have proliferated. Transnational civil society, or alternatively 'global civil society' and 'transnational social movements' have likewise occupied increasing theoretical and empirical attention, reflecting important changes in global politics.

To some, globalization is seen as an ideology, particularly of the elite, sometimes related closely to neoliberalism and to U.S. global and/or corporate hegemony. Such 'hegemonic globalization' is also met with many forms of 'resistance,' both intellectual and political. Hegemonic (neoliberal) globalization is viewed by radical critics as representing not only private corporate interests and the ideology of 'free market economics' but also an economistic and apolitical mode of thinking. The idea that such forces are bringing the entire world into a form of homogenized economic and social order is promoted by some but fiercely resisted by others. Alternatively, we can see that the complex set of processes we call globalizations contain elements of both homogenizations and the opposite tendencies, i.e., to greater differentiations, fragmentation and 'heterogenization' or 'hybridization.'

Another line of argument contends that globalization is a form of historical consciousness and represents a specific type of 'historical globality' of the present era of global history. Some therefore argue that globalization is fundamentally about global governance and about the historical and evolutionary developments that may contribute to the emergence of global polity formation in one form or another. For a time, the argument that 'globalization' was a set of forces that undermined or 'weakened' the national state took centre stage in international political economy. However, critics of this approach argued in reply that states are not simply passive receivers of globalization but active shapers of its tendencies, and states themselves are not coming to their historic 'end' but rather have been 'rearticulated' both internally and externally in specific ways, which may in future be subject to further change.

The recent reversals of mainstream thinking and policy on such central issues as the regulation of finance and domestic fiscal and monetary policy remind us of how intellectual fashion changes. Suddenly the pendulum has swung again, and state interventionism and international regulation are very much back on the agenda in the context of the current global financial crisis. The question as to whether past mainstream ideas and economic policies of 'globalization' have in fact led to the present crisis and to its systemic 'disequilibrium' is central to address today. The future of globalization is still very much a matter of on-going debate and political contestation around the world.

1. Globalization and international political economy: A critical introduction

The concept of 'globalization' has generated considerable controversy and a deluge of scholarship, both supportive and critical of its meaning and uses. These readings can be used to sort through from a critical perspective the issues involved.

Bowles 2008; *Cambridge Review of International Affairs* 2000
(articles by Desai, Gen, Sklair, Lal, Petras & Veltmeyer); Rodrik 2002.

2. The trajectory and dynamics of neoliberal globalization: Empire versus cosmopolis

How the U.S. hegemon and the European states have pursued their economic interests via the multilateral organizations is the central issue of this class meeting. Other critical issues include the evolution of the new world order, the transition from a development state to a neoliberal state, a reconfiguration of economic and political power and changes in the form of global governance.

Bowles et al. (2007) contains twenty-four essays by country and regional specialists on national and regional forms of 'globalizations,' highlighting the fact that globalization, like capitalism, takes multiple forms and must be understood in its complexity as well as generalities.

Gills, Rocamora & Wilson 1993; Gills 2008; Chomsky 2003; Kiely 2005; Bowles et al. 2007.

3. A system in crisis: The search for global governance

Chase-Dunn (2007) describes the evolution of global governance over the past several centuries and puts contemporary proposals and movements that are seeking to democratize global governance in world historical perspective. Global governance has evolved toward world state formation and some democratization has emerged. The abolition of large-scale slavery and formal colonialism, the proclamation of a global human rights regime and the spread of more democratic national governments constitute an overall trend towards democratic global governance. But, despite continuing contestation and uses of it as an ideological cover for the persistent push for world domination and U.S. imperialism, the ideal of democracy has become increasingly adopted by people across the world at a rate that has outpaced the democratization of global governance.

In this context, as Chase-Dunn (2007) observes, the contemporary institutions of global governance fare badly by comparison to even the most tepid definitions of democracy. Most people have little say over the existing global institutions of governance, which are generally dominated by what has been termed the 'global power elite.' This 'super class' manages international relations and secures the stability of the world system: world governance, which, despite the banner of 'democracy and freedom' that it hides behind, is decidedly undemocratic.

Although a laudable goal, democracy within nation-states does not add up to global democracy. Existing global-level governance institutions reflect the outcome of World War II. These badly need to be reformed or replaced by legitimately democratic global institutions that can help the peoples of the world deal with the new challenges that are emerging in the twenty-first century, which result from the propensity of capitalism towards a crisis of global proportions and multiple dimensions.

Chase-Dunn 2007; Bello 2008a, Chap. 5; O'Brien, Goetz, Scholte & Williams 2000.

4. Globalization and the labour movement

Up to a decade ago many labour movement strategists and analysts would probably have thought they were witnessing the beginning of the end of labour as a major political voice. 'There is no alternative' was not just a slogan of the political right but a palpable feeling in the general atmosphere. But by the turn of the century the mood began to shift as the labour movement regained some ground after the long neoliberal onslaught. Maybe we were now at the 'end of the beginning' of a new era where the workers and their organizations would begin to impact on the new global order they had helped to create. That is the premise of this unit. It is not, however, a falsely triumphal vision, but rather a realistic appraisal of the challenges of globalization and possible responses by the labour movement. (Munck 2008)

Munck 2002, 2007.

5. The globalization of capital and the ecological crisis

The world capitalist system is in serious crisis, a crisis of multiple dimensions—financial, production, ecological, social and political. In its financial dimension, the crisis not only threatens the savings and investments of individuals and households in the upper and middle classes of societies all over the developed world but the livelihoods and development prospects of people all over the South, even in the most remote and marginalized localities and communities of the world's rural and urban poor. The possibility that the spreading financial crisis will lead to a broader and deeper production crisis has raised questions about the fundamental dynamics of capitalist development as well as the strategic and political responses to the forces generated by these dynamics. The reading on this theme (Bello 2008) explores some of the dynamics in the current context.

6. Anti-capitalism and anti-globalization: Mobilizing the resistance

Aside from the long-term process of productive and social transformation, its dynamic tendency towards uneven development and social polarization and its propensity towards crisis, a significant feature of capitalist development is that each advance generates forces of resistance. The readings in this unit make reference to, and analyze the dynamics of, the resistance to capitalist development in its most recent phase of neoliberal globalization.

Gills 1999; Munck 2007; Veltmeyer 2008
(in particular, essays by Chomsky, Teivainen & Veltmeyer).

Module 11

The Global Collapse

Walden Bello
Focus on the Global South, Thailand

1. The fundamental crisis

Orthodox economics has long ceased to be of any help in understanding the current world financial crisis. Non-orthodox economics, on the other hand, provides extraordinarily powerful insights into its causes and dynamics. From the progressive perspective, what we are seeing is the intensification of one of the central crises or 'contradictions' of global capitalism: the *crisis of overproduction*, also known as overaccumulation or overcapacity. This is the tendency for capitalism to build up, in the context of heightened inter-capitalist competition, tremendous productive capacity, which outruns the population's capacity to consume owing to income inequalities that limit popular purchasing power. The result is an erosion of profitability, leading to an economic downspin.

To understand the current collapse, we must go back in time to the so-called 'golden age' of contemporary capitalism—from 1945 to 1975 (Marglin & Schor 1990). This was a period of rapid growth both in the centre economies and in the underdeveloped economies—growth that was partly triggered by the massive reconstruction of Europe and East Asia after the devastation of World War II and partly by the new socioeconomic arrangements and instruments based on a historic class accord between capital and labour, institutionalized within the new Keynesian state.

This period of high growth came to an end in the mid 1970s, when the centre economies were seized by stagflation, meaning the coexistence of low growth with high inflation, which was not supposed to happen under the theories of neoclassical economics. Stagflation, however, was but a symptom of a deeper problem. The reconstruction of Germany and Japan and the rapid growth of industrializing economies like Brazil, Taiwan and South Korea added tremendous productive capacity and increased global competition, while income inequality within countries and between countries limited purchasing power and demand, thus eroding profitability. This was aggravated by the massive oil price rises of the seventies.

The most painful expression of the crisis of overproduction before the current collapse was the global recession of the early 1980s, the most serious to overtake the international economy since the Great Depression.

Foster & Magdoff 2008; McNally 2008.

2. Escape routes from the crisis of overproduction

Capitalism tried three escape routes from the conundrum of overproduction: *neoliberal restructuring, globalization* and *financialization*.

Neoliberal restructuring took the form of Reaganism and Thatcherism in the North and structural adjustment in the South. The aim was to invigorate capital accumulation, and this was to be done by (1) removing state constraints on the growth, use and flow of capital and wealth and (2) redistributing income from the poor and middle classes to the rich, on the theory that the rich would then be motivated to invest and reignite economic growth. The problem with this formula was that redistributing income to the rich meant gutting the incomes of the poor and middle classes, thus restricting demand, while not necessarily inducing the rich to invest more in production. As a result, neoliberal restructuring, which was generalized in the North and South during the eighties and nineties, had a poor growth record. Global growth averaged 1.1 percent in the 1990s and 1.4 percent in the 1980s, compared with 3.5 percent in the 1960s and 2.4 percent in the 1970s, when state interventionist policies were dominant.

The second escape route global capital took to counter stagnation was 'extensive accumulation,' or *globalization*: the rapid integration of semi-capitalist, non-capitalist and precapitalist areas into the global market economy. Rosa Luxemburg, the famous German radical economist, saw this long ago in her classic *The Accumulation of Capital* as necessary to shore up the rate of profit in the metropolitan economies. How? By gaining access to cheap labour, by gaining new, albeit limited, markets, by gaining new sources of cheap agricultural and raw material products and by bringing into being new areas for investment in infrastructure. Integration is accomplished via trade liberalization, removing barriers to the mobility of global capital, and abolishing barriers to foreign investment. China is, of course, the most prominent case of a non-capitalist area to be integrated into the global capitalist economy over the last twenty-five years. By the middle of the first decade of the twenty-first century, roughly 40–50 percent of the profits of U.S. corporations came from their operations and sales abroad, especially in China.

The problem with this escape route from stagnation is that it exacerbates the problem of overproduction because it adds to productive capacity. A tremendous amount of manufacturing capacity has been added in China, and this has had a depressing effect on prices and profits. Not surprisingly, by around 1997, the profits of U.S. corporations stopped growing. According to one calculation, the profit rate of the Fortune 500 companies went from 7.15 in 1960–69 to 5.30 in 1980–90 to 2.29 in 1990-99 to 1.32 in 2000–02. By the end of the 1990s, with excess capacity in almost every industry, the gap between productive capacity and sales was the largest since the Great Depression.

Given the limited gains in countering the depressive impact of overproduction via neoliberal restructuring and globalization, the third escape route—*financialization*—became very critical for maintaining and raising profitability. With investment in industry and agriculture yielding low profits owing to overcapacity, large amounts of surplus funds have been circulating in or invested and reinvested in the financial sector—i.e., the financial sector is turning on itself.

The result is an increased bifurcation between a hyperactive financial economy and a stagnant real economy. As one financial executive noted in the *Financial Times*, 'there has been an increasing disconnection between the real and financial economies in the last few years. The real economy has grown… but nothing like that of the financial economy—until it imploded' (Bello 2009). What this observer does not tell us is that the disconnect between the real and the financial economy is not accidental: the financial economy exploded precisely to make up for the stagnation owing to overproduction of the real economy.

One indicator of the super-profitability of the financial sector is that while profits in the U.S. manufacturing sector came to 1 percent of U.S. GDP, profits in the financial sector came to 2 percent. Another is that 40 percent of the total profits of U.S. financial and non-financial corporations is accounted for by the financial sector although it is responsible for only 5 percent of U.S. GDP (and that is likely an overestimate).

The problem with investing in financial sector operations is that it is tantamount to squeezing value out of already created value. It may create profit but it does not create new value; only industry, agriculture, trade and services create new value. Because profit is not based on value that is created, investment operations become very volatile, and prices of stocks, bonds and other forms of investment can depart very radically from their real value. For instance, the stock of Internet startups may keep rising to heights unknown, driven mainly by upwardly spiraling financial valuations. Profits then depend on taking advantage of upward price departures from the value of commodities, then selling before reality enforces a 'correction,' that is, a crash back to real values. The radical rise of prices of an asset far beyond real values is what is called a 'bubble'—and what can become a 'balloon.'

Profitability being dependent on speculative coups, it is not surprising that the finance sector lurches from one bubble to another. Because it is driven by speculative mania, finance-driven capitalism has experienced about 100 financial crises since capital markets were deregulated and liberalized in the 1980s, the most serious before the current crisis being the Asian financial crisis of 1997.

Bello 2006: 1345–68.

3. The 'subprime implosion' and the collapse of the real economy

The current Wall Street collapse has its roots in the technology bubble of the late 1990s, when the price of the stocks of Internet startups skyrocketed, then collapsed, resulting in the loss of $7 trillion worth of assets and the recession of 2001–02. The loose money policies of the U.S. Treasury under Alan Greenspan had encouraged the technology bubble. When it collapsed into a recession, Greenspan cut the prime rate to a 45-year low of 1.0 percent in June 2003 and kept it there for over a year, which had the effect of encouraging another bubble—the real estate bubble or 'subprime crisis,' which broke in the summer of 2007. This crisis was not a case of supply outrunning real demand. The 'demand' was fabricated by speculative mania on the part of developers and financiers who wanted to (and did) make enormous profits from their access to foreign money, much of it Asian and Chinese in origin, that flooded the U.S. in the last decade.

The 'cause' of the financial and subsequent production crisis was the speculative ventures and unchecked avarice—unchecked because of the deregulation of the financial system under the neoliberal model—of capital ('investors'). The idea was to make a sale quickly, get your money upfront and make a tidy profit, while foisting the risk on the suckers down the line—the hundreds of thousands of institutions and individual investors that bought the mortgage-tied securities. This was called 'spreading the risk,' and it was actually seen as a good thing because it lightened the balance sheet of financial institutions, enabling them to engage in other lending activities.

The banks and other financial institutions all played into the speculative mania. Instead of performing their primordial task of lending to facilitate productive activity, the banks are holding on to their cash or buying up rivals to strengthen their financial base. Not surprisingly, with global capitalism's circulatory system seizing up, it was only a matter of time before the real economy would contract, as it has with frightening speed. Woolworth, a retail icon, folded in Britain, the U.S. auto industry is on emergency care, and even mighty Toyota has suffered an unprecedented decline in its profits. With American consumer demand plummeting, China and East Asia have seen their goods rotting on the docks, bringing about a sharp contraction of their economies and massive layoffs.

Ironically, 'globalization' ensured that economies that went up together in the boom would also go down together, with unparalleled speed, in the bust.

Bello 2008a; Foster & Magdoff 2008; Hanieh 2009; McNally 2008.

4. Dimensions of the crisis in the Global South

There is a clear propensity of capitalism towards crisis although the occurrence of the virus seems to be on the increase decade by decade. A financial crisis need not necessarily provoke a production crisis, but it has done so when severe enough and deeply entrenched in the real economy as in the current conjuncture. The financial crisis has provoked not only a deep recession in the U.S. and the major countries at the centre of the system but has undermined the livelihoods and economic development prospects of people all over the developing world. One manifestation of this financial-production crisis is the incapacity of working peoples and especially the poor, those that have been impoverished by the same process that generated so much grossly concentrated wealth over the past two decades of laissez-faire capitalism, to meet their basic needs, especially for food, which has become thoroughly 'commodified.' The dynamics of this global food crisis have become an issue of major concern for critical development studies. Another dimension of the system-wide crisis is the ecological crisis—the incapacity of the ecological foundation of the global production system and indeed life itself to sustain the current and projected level of economic growth driven ever forward by the incessant impulse of capitalists to accumulate capital. Modules 8-11 address the resulting dynamics of this crisis.

Several studies have highlighted different causes for the global food crisis but they all relate to the economic, environmental and political dynamics of global capitalist production. One particularly salient factor is the use of biotechnology to convert food resources into agro-fuel. In this connection William Engdahl, author of "Seeds of Destruction" (2007) and the best-selling book on oil and geopolitics, *A Century of War: Anglo-American Politics and the New World Order*, has brought to light a secret World Bank report that proves that agro-fuel production is a major cause of the food scarcity and higher prices for staple food products. The report estimates that the doubling and tripling of world food prices in the past three years have forced an added 100 million people below the poverty line, triggering food riots from Bangladesh and Egypt to Haiti.

The study demonstrates that production of agro-fuels has distorted food markets in three main ways. First, it has diverted grain away from food for fuel, with over a third of U.S. corn now used to produce ethanol and about half of vegetable oils in the E.U. going to production of bio-diesel. Second, farmers have been encouraged to set land aside for agro-fuel production. Third, it has sparked financial speculation in grains, driving prices up higher. Engdahl notes that this report and the study behind it is the first to include all three factors. However, he also notes the absence of the longer-term geopolitical agenda behind the present global food and energy crises: 'the long term agenda of powerful leading circles in the West … represented in tax exempt private foundations such as the Rockefeller, Ford and Gates foundations and the private wealth behind them ... population reduction in the interests of the global economic and financial elites' (2008).

Engdahl 2008; Hanieh 2009; Paul & Wahlberg 2008.

5. Strategic responses to the crisis: Saving the world or saving capitalism?

There are diverse forces built into the system and generated by the process of capital accumulation that tend towards crisis. Structural responses (those that do not result from consciously designed or planned activities) to the crisis include 'technological conversion or 'productive transforma-tion' and spatial relocation of the production apparatus, creating a 'new international division of labour' (NIDOL). There is, of course, a conscious acting component to these and other forms of restructuring, but as with the NIDOL it emerges from a multitude of individual decisions made by thousands of corporate CEOs, each concerned with the 'bottom line' of their corporation rather than the survival of the overall system. That is, it is non-strategic thinking and action.

In the current conjuncture of global crisis, however, there is no end of diverse and at times frantic attempts to *think* and *plan* a way out of the crisis. Strategic responses to the crisis include 'deglobalization,' an attempt to derail the neoliberal agenda that has facilitated the crisis (Bello 2004). But the main strategy or proposal is to seek a solution to the crisis within the capitalist system—to re-establish a regulatory framework for the flow of capital—capital controls on the basis of a new 'global financial architecture' or a new form of global governance. At issue is not only the agency and organizational form of such regulatory constraint but how to ensure the democratization of decisionmaking regarding the necessary international agreements. The pres-ent international institutions designed for the purpose are notoriously undemocratic, leading to a struggle and even a global movement in the direction of 'good' (i.e., democratic) governance.

In the context of the efforts by organizations and governments in the North to seek a way out of the crisis by once again restructuring the *capital-labour relation*—reducing the capacity of labour to share in the proceeds of global production and weakening its capacity to organize and resist the solutions proposed by capital in its strategic response to the crisis. Organizations in the popular sector of an emerging global civil society are also beginning to organize—and in concert with other anti-capitalist forces—to seek a systemic alternative to neoliberalism and the current crisis. In this connection, developments in the social movement sector of Latin American politics are particularly instructive and worthy of careful study from a CDS perspective. On this, see the discussion and readings (Abya Yala 2009, etc.) given in module 49.

Abya Yala 2009; Bello 2008a; Oakland Institute 2009; Petras & Veltmeyer 2009.

Section 5

The International Dimension

The fundamental dynamics of the development process and its major agencies can be identified and analyzed at four distinct levels: (1) international or global; (2) regional; (3) national; (4) subnational—regional and local. The major agency for advancing development has always been the state ... conceived of in relation to the market, a major institution of capitalist form of development. However, as evidenced by Modules 2–4 (Bringing History Back In), there has always been an international dimension to development, with references to conditions that arise from the structure of the global economy and its changing development dynamics.

In this area of critical development studies, the critical factors are: (1) the nature and dynamics of the economic and political relations among the nation -states that make up and operate within the world order ('international relations,' as conceived of by the political scientists within this field, and reviewed in Module 12; (2) the organizations formed within the system of these international relations—'international organizations' in the lexicon of development studies, and addressed in Modules 12, 13 and 14; (3) the policy and institutional framework for advancing international development, the critical issues of which are conceptualized in Module 15; and (4) the dynamic and changing conditions of aid, debt and trade that arise within this institutional and policy framework, addressed in Module 16.

Module 12

International Relations in Development

Timothy Shaw
University of the West Indies, Trinidad

Henry Veltmeyer
Universidad Autónoma de Zacatecas, Mexico

A good question is whether, or to what extent ... [the] North-South divide will predominate in twenty-first century international relations [in the way that] the East-West divide preoccupied the second half of the twentieth century. (Reuveny & Thompson 2007: 557)

Historically, knowledge domination has been an integral part of North-South relations.... Knowledge renovation serves to interpret contradictions and changing realities, responding to challenges to the hegemonic discourse in ways that maintain existing hierarchies of power. The devices used include linguistic cooptation, conceptual/theoretical innovation and revision of policy agendas. (Girvan 2007: 6–7)

As the global political economy approaches the end of the first decade of the twenty-first century, the study of international relations (IR) is in flux, reflecting conditions of considerable world disorder and uncertainty as to how to theoretically represent the facts of the Iraq and Afghanistan wars, the financial turmoil of the last decade, the apparent demise of 'globalization' in its dominant neoliberal form, the dynamics and apparent eclipse of U.S. hegemony and the proliferation of conditions that give rise to international relations of conflict. The state of flux in the study of IR and the world political economy is also reflected in the emergence of developments and events that are not easily reconciled or explained within the dominant paradigm in the study of IR. This has led to several lines of revisionist interpretation by analysts as different in their perspective as Collier, Duffield, Klein, Naim, Soros, Stiglitz and others such as those IR scholars published in the Routledge Global Institutions Series <www.tandf.co.uk> and Palgrave Macmillan's International Political Economy Series <www.palgrave.com>.

Studies in this revisionist tradition—see also the fourth edition of Baylis, Smith & Owens (2008), which includes an online resource centre—can be placed into the following six categories of concern/critical issues.

1. The political economy of international relations: Theoretical perspectives

Apart from crosscutting differences in the study of IR based on epistemological issues (realism, etc.) it is useful to sort IR studies into three ideological categories: (1) *liberal reformist* in terms of an overriding concern with individual freedom from social and political constraint; (2) *radical* in terms an orientation towards a fundamental concern for social equality and the belief in the need for fundamental change in the structure of IR and the underlying political system; and (3) *conservative* in the sense of a fundamental concern with order, viewing change as neither progressive nor liberating but as disruptive of order.

Consonant with, although to some extent overriding this ideological division, it is also possible to identify three contemporary schools of thought, each with different currents, variants and forms of analysis: (1) a liberal reformist or social democratic approach, based on the separation of politics and economics and a relative devalorization of the role of power in determining the structure and dynamics of international relations (Soros, Stiglitz); (2) radical political economics, an approach based on a critical class analysis, a Gramscian analysis of hegemony or world systems analysis, of the political dynamics of IR and world development (Gil, Petras, Robinson); and (3) the 'new political economy,' the political adjunct to neoclassical economics in terms of the belief that society is composed of individuals who rationally calculate and act on their self or class interest, and that the basic repository of political power that can be exercised or wielded by individuals if in a position to do so, the state, is structured accordingly.

From the perspective of reformism in its contemporary form (social liberalism) the development problems generated by the structure of international relations are amenable to and can be resolved by means of democratic reform—consummating the marriage between capitalism and democracy, democratizing the society-state relation and strengthening civil society in its capacity to participate in the political and development process. The assumption shared by some libertarian analysts in this tradition is that the state is essentially a predatory device used by those in power to further their own interests, giving rise to rentierism, corruption and bad governance (World Bank 1994).

From a radical political economy perspective the fundamental issue in the study of IR is the concentration of political and economic power exercised in the interest of what in the contemporary context has been alternatively defined as 'the rulers of the world' (Pilger 2002), 'the transnational capitalist class' (Robinson, Sklair), the 'brain trust of the new world order' (Salbuchi 2000) and the 'global ruling class' (Petras 2007). The context of this political economic analysis—a new form of 'transnational studies' based on a new 'model of Third World transitions'—is an understanding of the global economy in terms of the dialectics of globalization and the nation-state (Robinson 2003).

As for political conservatism in its current 'neocon form,' it closely if somewhat paradoxically adheres to a fundamentalist form of liberal individualism at the level of economic doctrine, and it finds expression in the theory and policy of the 'new imperialism'—the belief in the right and need for the U.S. state to exercise its prerogative of state power unilaterally, by means of force if necessary.

Baylis, Smith & Owens 2008; Reuveny & Thompson 2007: 556–64; Robinson 2003.

2. China-India-Asia: World development and the 'new regionalisms'

The global economy is undergoing a profound and momentous shift. The first half of the twenty-first century will undoubtedly be dominated by the consequences of a new Asian dynamism. China is likely to become the second biggest economy in the world by 2016, and India the third largest by 2035. The rise of China and India as global economic and political powers is one of the most important transformative processes of our time…. A cluster of other countries in the Asian region is also growing rapidly. We refer to these dynamic Asian economies collectively as the 'Asian drivers of global change (Kaplinsky & Messner 2008: 197).

> There is a historic shift taking place on the global stage. Economies across Asia are being transformed from passengers to co-drivers of globalization. In 2000, Indian companies made 50 acquisitions worth a total of U.S.$957 million. In 2006, they made over 146 acquisitions worth a total of U.S.$20.2 billion. Chinese companies bought 27 foreign firms in 20000 worth a total of $1.8 billion. In 2006, they bought 85 companies worth U.S.$15.5 billion. (*Economist* 2008: 58)

'America and China,' according to the *Economist* (*The World in 2008*), 'will be prime players in the matters that will concentrate minds around the world in 2008.' One of these matters is the world economy, which will no longer depend on the U.S. economy as the engine of economic growth. Rather, the driver will be the Chinese economy, which has been growing at an annual rate of over 10 percent for well over a decade, leading to a major social transformation within China and an immense realignment of the global economy, with a significant impact on countries in the South and the structure of international relations—and thus the study of IR. As Humphrey & Messner (2006: 108) assert: 'The emergence of China & India as powerful actors in global governance arenas and global politics poses a series of questions for development policy and the future of global governance.'

Kaplinsky & Messner 2008: 197–344; Soderbaum 2004; Breslin 2007;
Humphrey & Messner 2006: 107–14; Schmitz 2007: 51–58.

3. The security syndrome: Dynamics of geopolitical risk and insecurity

Insecurity or political disorder is one of the most critical issues in the study of international relations, with reference to problems that most often arise from diverse relations of conflict and geopolitical risk. Relations of conflict arise from the projection of power, power imbalances and the search for advantage in international relations, the dream of some states for hegemony or world domination; they also derive from relations of ethnic or religious conflict—cultural wars—or class struggles over scarce or desired resources, or the grossly unequal allocation or distribution of these resources and wealth; and there are geopolitical conditions of insecurity.

Students of IR have been traditionally concerned with issues of geopolitical risk and security—issues that relate to and derive from contradictory forces generated by the prevailing structure of international relations. In the current context, one of the major issues of geopolitical risk of concern to policymakers and students of both IR and world development has to with U.S.-Iran relations over the nuclear ambitions of Iran's government. Another example of a high geopolitical risk factor, raising the spectre of international conflict, even war, and necessitating diplomacy or negotiated management, is a movement towards independence in Taiwan. Neither of these issues, however, has a direct developmental impact. In the case of Iran there would be an indirect development issue were nuclear technology to be applied to the generation of electrical power, a condition of economic development.

Other risk issues with security and more obvious developmental implications can be found, and are widely studied, in areas such as the global environment and unequal access to the means of food production, decent work and adequately remunerated jobs, and public services designed to meet the basic needs of the population. Worldwide, the numbers of people who are at risk and made insecure in regard to one or more basic needs as a result of natural or 'man-made' disasters, conflict over scarce resources, unequal opportunities and social exclusions of one sort or another are staggering. The precise and variable contextualized dynamics of the forces and conditions involved, be they structural, natural or politically induced, constitute a major subject matter of 'international' as well as 'critical' development studies.

Isaak 2005; Karl 2000: 149–56.

4. Managing conflict and global governance: Saving capitalism and making globalization work

In regard to developmental implications, political economic studies of IR are generally if not primarily concerned with the management of forces generated by the structure of global production and international relations. That is, the focus of concern is not with the system as such—with its basic institutional structure and the pillars of this structure—but with the possibilities of improving the socioeconomic conditions experienced by a country as a whole, a matter of the position that the country occupies in the international division of labour and in the structure of international relations. In the current context of neoliberal globalization, the success of a country in increasing its level of national development, measured conventionally by annual increases in overall output or GNP per capita, is also presumed to depend on the ability of the government to insert the economy and society into the globalization process—enabling the country to take advantage of the presumed benefits of global integration.

Whether or not globalization in its neoliberal economic form leads to overall development or the prosperity of all countries in the system, or whether it results in grossly uneven development—a world of a few winners and many losers—is heavily debated by scholars. But an area of considerable consensus is the importance of establishing the global architecture of institutional arrangements and agreements (global governance) needed to preserve 'order'— an orderly way of managing international relations. On this there are least two theoretical (and ideological) perspectives. One is that 'order' or 'governance' should be democratic, i.e., based on international relations of relative equality, a relation among equals regardless of the country's size, importance in the global economy and state power. In this perspective, there is an emphasis on multilateralism as an institutional mechanism for maintaining order and the inclusion of non-state actors (international organizations, multinational corporations, global civil society organizations) in the responsibility of 'governance.' The other 'realist' or *realpolitik* perspective emphasizes the importance of hierarchy and power in international relations—the formation of power blocs and strategic alliances among leading states, as well as policy forums and summit meetings among officials and leading representatives of these states, with less emphasis on the U.N. and multilateralism.

This liberal reform perspective and technocratic concern for the 'management' of international relations are represented in studies of [1] conflict resolution; [2] response to the diverse crises that beset the system from time to time—be these crises production, fiscal, debt or political; [3] studies of how economic growth policies are, or can be, implemented under conditions of sustainable development—green technologies and conservation practice—secured through international agreements and global forums; and [4] proposals for corporate and global good governance—maintaining order at the global level not by means of world government but by means of an architecture of arrangements and agreements inclusive of diverse international 'actors,' including corporations and a global civil society.

One of the most critical issues on this agenda of international cooperation and the search for consensus is economic insecurity based on climate change, the focus and title of the UNDP's 2007/08 *Human Development Report*. Other issues relate to the 'modern diasporas' of forced migration including refugees from natural disasters, climate change, conflict over scarce resources and war; the uneven social and development dynamics of globalization in its neoliberal form; and the class conflicts that arise from the growing divide of the rich and the poor.

In regard to the latter it is clear from evidence on its social dynamics that neoliberal globalization is profoundly exclusive, rewarding the few—the rich and powerful, as it unsurprisingly turns out—and excluding the many; and thus it is unsustainable, generating widespread forces of social discontent and political resistance (Karl 2000; Kapstein 1996). A study and report commissioned by the U.K. Ministry of Defence is eloquent in pointing out the profound political implications of the global divide in wealth and development that continues to breed 'forces of resistance' and will likely lead to a 'resurgence of not only anti-capitalist ideologies… but also to populism and the revival of Marxism' (2007: 3).

The development implications and dimensions of these governance issues—the unilateral projection of state power/the imperialist ambition of world domination, climate change, the modern diasporas, social inequities in the neoliberal world order and the destabilizing effects of 'the shock doctrine' espoused by neoconservatives—are explored in other units of this course as well as by Klein (2007), Mittelman and Othman (2000) and Stiglitz (1998, 2006) among others.

As for the structure of 'international relations' and the conditions and forces of change associated with it, the following readings explore some of the issues from a political economy perspective.

Cavanagh & Mander 2004a; Stiglitz 1998.

5. Political dynamics of conflict and war

Among the key issues in the study of international relations are the conditions that lead to conflict among states and other players in the arena of world development (Module 20). Scholars in the tradition of radical political economy tend to be primarily concerned with the social and development conditions and dynamics of this conflict, which assume diverse forms from fights over scarce resources, class struggles and tribal and ethnic communal conflicts, to inter-state or cultural wars and imperialist ventures, which often complicate other sources of conflict. On the other hand, the concern of political scientists and policymakers in the field seems to be with means of resolution of conflicts regardless of the conditions that give rise to them or the forms taken.

The peaceful end of the Cold War with the abrupt collapse of the Soviet bloc and the U.S.S.R. ignited numerous re-assessments of world politics and strategy in relation to development and other issues The perceived revolution in the structure of the international system is one of the sources of new ideas about the nature of conflict and war in the new world order and how they impinge on development.

IR and development dynamics of conflict assume diverse forms in different parts of the world and temporal contexts. Currently, one of the major concerns of IR specialists in this area is with what Samuel Huntington (1993) dubbed 'the clash of civilizations' but that others view through the lens of the 'new imperialism,' that is, the effort of the current U.S. administration, in the context of 9/11, the war against 'international terrorism' waged in Afghanistan and Iraq, and the Palestine Question in the Middle East, to advance the national interests of the U.S. (control the 'big game' for oil in the Gulf region and beyond in Eurasia), restore its dominance and spread 'democracy' all over the world. As suggested by the literature in this as in so many other areas things are often other than what they seem. A significant contribution of CDS is not only to disclose the development dynamics that underlie the structure of international relations but also to penetrate the fog of rhetoric and the ideological veil cast over developments and events in the area.

The 'clash of civilizations,' the 'cultural wars' and the emergence and political dynamics of religious fundamentalisms, which can be both politicized and criminalized (in U.S. anti-terrorist legislation if not in international law) define issues that are the subject of a growing number of studies in the field of IR and what might be termed 'the political economy of globalization.' The connection of these dynamics with the development process in the South is an issue of critical importance in these studies, especially as regards the channelling of 'overseas development assistance' and achieving the U.N.'s 'millennium development goals.'

Duffield 2001; Kaldor 1999; Karl 2000: 149–56.

6. Reconfigurations of power in the neoliberal world (dis)order

The paradigmatic concern of IR scholars who take a political economy or developmental perspective is with power—the structure of power embedded in the international relations among different groupings of nation-states. However, the new world order is characterized by a major restructuring of these relations, leading to a downsizing in the role of states in the world system and a diminution in their capacity to secure development within the political space of their sovereign power. Globalization in certain forms has led to the surrender by the state of some power and prerogatives to international organizations and agreements, and at a different level, to civil society organizations that have come to assume some of the functions formerly exercised by the state. The state, in effect, has been restructured, hollowed out and downsized, at least in regard to its economic development and social welfare functions.

The corollary of this political development is that other actors have emerged to occupy the space previously held by the state, with developmental impacts that have yet to be fully determined—requiring more study, from a critical perspective. From the vantage point of several recent studies, the new actors in this space range from international organizations/financial institutions and multinational corporations to a multitude of civil society organizations, constituting what has been termed a 'global civil society.' Most of these intergovernmental and nongovernmental organizations are engaged in an active search for a more human form of capitalism, a more ethical form of globalization, a more equitable form of 'development—'another world' it is claimed. They have also been incorporated into the development process and the system of international relations in the search for a sustainable form of global governance. The importance of this issue for scholars in the fields of IR and global political economy is suggested by the eighth edition of the annual *Global Civil Society;* the work of institutions such as the Centre for Civil Society at the London School of Economics; and the Routledge series on Global Institutions <www.tandf.co.uk>. The global governance dimension of this issue is explored by the range of studies from diverse perspectives (Welch and Nuru 2006; World Bank 1994).

The precise role of non-state actors in the arena of international relations, and the institutional agreements/arrangements and North-South relations of economic and state power they have to navigate, are by no means clear. This is another area of CDS, which can be conceived in two broad categories: (1) critically supportive of the many concerted efforts to reform, humanize and save capitalism—to bring about a more equitable form of capitalist development and a more ethical form of globalization; and (2) disposed to the view that capitalism cannot solve the problems that it generates; they are endemic to the system and require for their solution a fundamental restructuring if not abandonment of the system—rejection of capitalism, imperialism, neoliberalism.

Each cycle of neoliberal reforms to macroeconomic policy led to diverse forms of resistance (Petras & Veltmeyer 2005b, 2009; Mittelman and Othman 2000). However, in the third cycle of neoliberal policy reform the forces of resistance by some accounts were transnationalized in the formation of a broad coalition of popular and middle class organizations and construction of a broad 'anti-globalization movement.' The complex IR dynamics of these forces of resistance and this anti-globalization movement are the subject of a number of studies.

Bello 2008a; Cox 2001: 3–28.

Module 13

The United Nations and Development

Krishna Ahooja-Patel

Institute on Equity and Development, India

The preamble of the U.N. Charter, constructed in the immediate wake of World War II by the assembled representatives of fifty nations concerned with issues of collective security and development, began with 'We the People ....' It was the first step in a move to advance the concept of a 'family of nations,' a system of multilateral conflict resolution and a more equitable world order. The charter was conceived as a people's charter, expressing the 'common aims' of humankind. One of its main objectives was to apply multilateral negotiation mechanisms for the promotion of economic and social advancement of all peoples. To this end, topics such as decolonization, disarmament, economic and social progress, world trade, debt and the environment, industry and labour, science and technology, finance and foreign exchange, gender and development, and more recently peacekeeping were placed on the agenda of diverse organizations within the U.N. system. More than half a million civil servants from over 170 nations serve this agenda.

In the last decade of the old millennium, a series of U.N. world conferences, all designed to advance the development process, were held on the environment, population, human rights and women. At the same time governments both in the North and South were moving on an uncharted course to reconstruct the world order in the direction of a more equitable form of development within the current world order. In this context the U.N. in December 2000 organized the Millennium Summit to establish global targets to achieve minimum standards of 'development' and to secure a 'compact among nations to end human poverty' (UNDP 2003b).

At this historic juncture of concerted effort to redesign the world order, achieve the millennium development goals and establish the institutions of a new more democratic form of global governance, an amalgam of economic and social structures have emerged on the international arena. However, the currently dominant lexicon of 'freedom and democracy,' 'development,' 'globalization,' 'equity' and 'good governance' presumes 'another world,' an alternative system to neoliberal globalization, in place since the early 1980s. This alternative vision points towards a genuinely progressive and 'new' world order that reaches well beyond the social structures and institutions of the neoliberal world order towards urgent actions that need to be taken to both achieve the millennium goals and bring about a new world of genuine progress.

This readings in this module review and analyze the diverse efforts in this direction taken by key organizations within the U.N. system, particularly the United Nations Conference on Trade and Development (UNCTAD) and the United Nations Development Programme (UNDP). The role of the U.N. Economic Commission for Latin America and the Caribbean (ECLAC) in generating an important school and body of applied development knowledge is explored in Module 6.

The U.N. is the most important coordinating body of organizations engaged in the international development 'project.' From a CDS perspective, a critical understanding of these efforts is imperative.

1. The agency and development role of the United Nations

Development, as an idea and as a project for bringing about a better form of society in the direction of progress, freedom and equality, can be traced back to the eighteenth-century 'Enlightenment' in Europe (France and Scotland in particular). But to all intents and purposes (at least those of the contributors to this Handbook) the development *project* dates back to the post World War II period—to 1944, in the construction of a world order designed to reactivate the capital accumulation process based on relatively free international trade. This new world order included a set of rules, established and agreed to at a meeting in Bretton Woods of the U.S. and its European allies, for governing international relations; and the institution of the International Monetary Fund (to assist countries cope with any temporary balance of payment deficits), the World Bank—originally the International Bank for Economic Recovery and Reconstruction—(to assist countries in their nation-building and economic development efforts) and a free trade negotiating forum (GATT—General Agreement on Tariffs and Trade).[1]

On the heels of this system (see Module 15 as its policy dynamics), 1945 also saw the creation of a system of international organizations designed to keep the peace (via a United Nations security apparatus) and to assist the economically backward countries in what was later conceived of as the 'Third World' (unaligned with either the capitalist or socialist bloc). In the same year the U.N. Charter of Human Rights (twenty-nine of them) with its statutes, a Magna Carta of collective rights and responsibilities, designed to prevent unilateral action by any one nation on its own 'national interest,' was formally ratified by a majority of governments represented at the initial U.N. conference.[2]

It needs to be understood that at the beginning, the United Nations system of international organizations did not provide a framework to bring about 'progress' or advance the 'development' of the growing number of nation-states seeking national independence. The concern for economic development was initially overshadowed by greater concerns for global security—to regulate the efforts of different countries to advance the national interest and ensure that any conflicts in the process be settled on a multilateral basis. It was not until the 1960s with the establishment of UNCTAD that the United Nations took an active role in the development process. There are different narratives on this process, but the most valuable, from a CDS perspective, is undoubtedly the history of the United Nations coordinated and written in part by Richard Jolly et al. (2004).

Jolly, Emmerij, Ghai & Lapeire 2004.

2. UNCTAD, the group of 77 and the regulation of capitalism

UNCTAD was officially formed in 1964 as an instrument of policy research on issues of trade and development, to represent a system-wide project of national development but in particular the interests and development concerns of the 'group of 77.' In fact, UNCTAD is the only U.N. institution that reports directly to the General Assembly, in regard to development oriented research and policy prescriptions for governments in the Global South. In this sense it can been as the counterpart to the Organisation for Economic Co-operation and Development (OECD), formed in 1961 to advance the interests initially of some twenty-seven countries, constituting what was regarded as the 'club of rich nations'—the capitalist democracies of North America, Western Europe and Japan. UNCTAD's first director was Raúl Prebisch, who had been the first director of ECLA (later ECLAC) and actively involved in the institution of UNCTAD.

In the 1980s, UNCTAD, particularly its operational agency, the U.N. Centre of Transnational Corporations (UNCTC), came under attack by proponents of a 'new world order.' In fact, in the Heritage Foundation's five-plank program for installing this new world order, the second was 'elimination of the UNCTC —viewed as an enemy of the 'forces of freedom,' providing as it did policy advice to governments in the Global South as to how best to regulate multinational corporations and other 'international financial institutions' (IFIs) as well as the flow of FDI, etc. The concern of UNCTAD was to help these governments ensure the protection of their workers and communities and to gain some benefits from these operations. From the perspective of the architects and guardians of the new world order, however, such policy prescription and government regulation—as well as UNCTAD's call for a 'new international economic order'—was a direct and intolerable interference in the forces of the free market, damaging vital economic interests. UNESCO and its call for a 'new international information order' were viewed in a similar light and similarly attacked by the U.S. government as hijacked by 'special interests' operating within the U.N.

As it turned out, the U.S. government, with the support of the Heritage Foundation and other such Washington-based neoconservative thinktanks and policy forums, was successful in decapitating (and decapacitating) the UNCTC—and marginalizing UNCTAD, essentially displacing it in 1994 with the institution of the WTO, an international organization instituted to advance the 'forces of economic freedom.'

Jolly, Emmerij, Ghai & Lapeire 2004; Patel 2007.

3. The U.N. in the development process: Development with a human face

In addition to the institution of UNCTAD in the 1960s the United Nations established an array of organizations to operationalize the idea of 'development.' They include in particular UNRISD (U.N. Research Institute for Social Development), INSTRAW (the Institute for Research on the Advancement of Women), UNEP (U.N. Environment Program), UNESCO (U.N. Educational, Scientific and Cultural Organization), the WHO (World Health Organization), the FAO (Food and Agriculture Organization) and most importantly, from a development perspective, the UNDP (the U.N. Development Programme).

The UNDP pioneered the concept of 'human development' and an index (HDI) to measure it and rank countries in its first annual *Human Development Report* (HDR), launched in 1990. Unlike the *World Development Report*, the concept of development is defined not just in terms of economic growth, measured by annual changes in GNP (total income) per capita, but with reference to social and political conditions such as health, education and participation, which provide individuals with the resources and capacity to realize their full human potential and live rich, meaningful lives. Module 26 delves into the theory and practice of human development (HD), the dimensions of which are explored in the UNDP's HDRs and the readings set for this topic. The UNDP, like the World Bank and ECLAC, has established useful databases on development issues. One of them <http://hdrstats.undp.org/buildtables> also provides a useful tool that allows students to readily access HD data in regard to any country and construct their own tables. As for the critical issues and diverse dimensions of the human development problematic, they can be traced out via a review of the HDRs published annually since 1990.

Annan 2000; Krasno 2004; ILO 1994, 2003; UNDP 1990, 1996, 2002, 2003a; UNRISD 1995.

4. The U.N. on gender and development

Since the declaration of International Women's Day in 1975, which was later implemented as the U.N. Decade for Women (1976–1985), methodologies have been compiled to determine and measure progress of women worldwide. Four U.N. world conferences, held in 1975, 1980, 1985 and 1995, recorded and analyzed women's social status and their contribution to the economy. In September 2000, the U.N. General Assembly held a special session to review and assess globally the advancement of women.

In 1985, when the Nairobi Forward Looking Strategies were adopted during the Third International Women's Conference, a political debate emerged regarding the proposal of a one-word change, from 'women' to 'gender.' Since then a large number of resolutions have substituted the word 'gender' wherever 'women' appeared. Opponents consider that the use of 'gender' in policies and legislation blurs the reality of women's lives. Those who are in favour of retaining gender advocate that this sociological term refers to relationships between men and women. The study of 'gender and development' therefore requires an analysis of 'relationships' at all levels, from the community and its linkages to social groups, to national participation and international relations.

Ten years later, bringing gender issues into the mainstream of society was clearly established as a global strategy for promoting equality in the Platform for Action adopted in the U.N. Fourth World Conference on Women in 1995. According to the UNDP (2003a: 8) 'the term gender arose as an analytical tool from an increasing awareness of inequalities due to institutional structures.' The 'ultimate goal,' this report adds, 'is the advancement of the status of women in society with gender equality….'

Development indicators (trends and data) published by the U.N. and other organizations in 2000 covered all aspects of the condition of women in almost all parts of the world. On the basis of these data, statistical profiles of different regions can be constructed to provide insight into the processes of policy change and legislation. From this global information, the following areas are particularly relevant for research: population, health, education, employment, politics, women and men in households and women's human rights.

The first point to note is that the transformation of economic and social status of women in the twentieth century was brought about by women themselves, through protests and struggle as an integral part of national women's movements mostly after the two world wars. The political struggle for independence in Asia, Africa and Latin America is clearly linked to the economic struggle for equality and emerging place of women in the world of work. Empirical evidence clearly shows that without the active participation of women and the incorporation of women's perspectives at all levels of decisionmaking, the millennium goals set by the international community in 2000 will not be achieved. A remarkable feature of the change in the last century has been that women's economic activity rates have increased all over the world, which in turn has transformed women's lives permanently.

Ahooja-Patel 2007.

5. The inequality predicament:
Social and human development without social change?

The development idea, according to Wolfgang Sachs and his associates in postdevelopment theory (1992), was 'invented' as a reformulation of the notion of 'progress' but in a strictly economic sense and to the purpose of controlling the actions and responses of the people in the economically 'backward areas' of the world. They also termed the project of advancing this idea as 'imperialism,' colonizing the mind and subjugation. However, the United Nations system of international organizations conceived of development in a very different way, as genuine progress based on respecting the fundamental human rights of each person in every society, and stressing the social dimensions of this development. From this perspective, the fundamental barrier to human or social development is a social structure and a system in which some, by virtue of their power and greater access to resources, are able to appropriate the lion's share of the national and global output, the wealth of nations (as Adam Smith phrased it). In its 1996 HDR, the UNDP reported that a roomful of people, fewer than 400, disposed of as much wealth and income as the world's poor, some 40 percent of the total population. In its 2005 Report, the U.N. documented, and to some extent analyzed, the international and national dimensions of this 'inequality predicament'—this 'grotesque situation' in which so few have appropriated so much, generating a development gap of such proportions as to condemn up to 1.7 billion people, mostly in societies marginalized in the development process, to poverty, unable to meet their basic needs let alone live meaningful lives.

The diagnosis is clear. But what is the prescription for dealing with the predicament? And what is the institutional response of the U.N.? With the lens provided by CDS, the 'inequality predicament' implicates not just a deficient government policy and model used by governments to make public policy, but the operative economic system and the social structure of that system maintained by relations of economic and political power. The question is: is this the perspective of the economists and sociologists working at and for the U.N. and its operational development agencies? And if not, why not? And what is it?

U.N. 1995, 2000, 2005; UNDP 2003a, 2006; UNRISD 1995.

6. The U.N. in the new millennium: Capitalism versus development

In addition to its social dimension, the idea of development is conceptualized and institutionalized by the U.N. in its political dimension, which is to say, in regard to (1) a fundamental commitment to the need to respect universal human rights (the U.N. Charter, 1945) and (2) agency and participation in decisionmaking and policy construction regarding 'development'—implicating and inclusive of diverse 'stakeholders,' who need to be not only consulted but to actively participate in the development process.

In the 1990s, the UNDP substantially advanced its understanding of the political dimension of human development in the form of reports on the need for democratic governance as a fundamental part of its model for sustainable human development. Conditions of this 'democratic governance' include levelling the playing field for individual self-advancement, greater social inclusion in education and other public services, empowerment of the poor (enabling them to act for themselves), the strengthening of civil society and a mechanism of popular participation in public decisionmaking and development efforts. In effect, the 'solution' of the UNDP to the 'inequality predicament' and the 'human development problematic' (how to remove existing barriers to the capacity of each and every person to realize their full potential and live meaningful lives) is to rebuild and humanize the workings of the operative capitalist system—to create a more inclusive, equitable and participatory form of capitalist development (Solimano, Sunkel & Blejer 1983). This 'solution,' to 'rebuild capitalism' from within needs to be carefully deconstructed—from a critical development perspective.

Esping-Anderson 1994; Solimano, Sunkel & Blejer 1993;
UNDP 1996, 1997a, 1997b, 1997c, 1997d.

Module 14

Multilateral Organizations in the New (Neoliberal) World Order

Walden Bello
Focus on the Global South, Thailand

This module looks at the structure and dynamics of the system of multilateral global governance from its origins in 1944 to the current period. The focus is on the economic pillars of the multilateral system of international relations, i.e., the International Monetary Fund (IMF), World Bank, World Trade Organization (WTO) and the G-8. The U.N. system (Module 13) is largely excluded from this module, and insofar as there is a discussion relating to it, this is in relation to the United Nations Conference on Trade and Development (UNCTAD) and the United Nations Development Programme (UNDP).

The module situates the multilateral system with the system of global capitalism dominated by one hegemon—the U.S. How the U.S. and the European states have pursued their economic interests via the multilateral organizations is a key question. The clash of competing interests, especially between the North and the South, is a major concern, especially as it has contributed to the weakening of the legitimacy of these institutions, a process that is most marked in the IMF. The divergent approaches of the Clinton and Bush administrations towards the multilateral organizations and multilateralism is studied, as are the postures of the European Union and the other G-8 countries.

The module concludes with a discussion of alternatives to hegemonic multilateralism that are being proposed by different parties. The discussion includes the question of how people in different parts of the world can contribute to the creation of a just multilateral system.

1. From Bretton Woods to neoliberal globalization:
Divergent perspectives

The institutional pillars of the multilateral system of international relations within the world capitalist system are the International Monetary Fund (IMF) and the World Bank, both formed at Bretton Woods in 1944, and the World Trade Organization (WTO), initially formed as a trade negotiations forum (the General Agreement on Tariffs and Tariffs—GATT) but not actually instituted until 1994, and coterminous with the initiation of the North American Trade Agreement (NAFTA). The institution of this Bretton Woods system is presented and analyzed from diverse theoretical perspectives in the following readings.

Ellwood 2001: Chap. 2; Frieden 2006: 253–300; Gowan 1999: 8–18.

2. The IMF, the World Bank and the WTO: Dynamics of international organization and multilateral action

The Bretton Woods institutions arguably served as an institutional framework for the process of capital accumulation and economic growth that unfolded from the late 1940s in what historians have dubbed 'the golden age of capitalism.' However, the engine of economic growth and capitalist development began to stall towards the end of the 1960s and into the 1970s as the entire system went into crisis—a serious production crisis that led to a series of strategies designed to restructure and renovate the system, to find a way out of the crisis.

These strategies included (1) the export of bank capital in the form of loans to governments to finance their development programs, and inter alia, to simultaneously relieve the crisis of overproduction and underconsumption (the saturation of the markets in the North for manufactured goods, the incapacity of countries in the Global South to purchase these goods) and excess liquidity (petrodollars); (2) relocation of industry overseas closer to sources of cheaper labour, creating as an unintended consequence, a 'new international division of labour'; (3) a technological conversion of the global production apparatus based on a new mode of labour regulation (postfordism); and (4) a 'new world order' of neoliberal globalization in which the market and the 'forces of economic freedom' are liberated from the constraints of the development state.

The World Bank, in tandem with the IMF and later with the WTO, assumed primary responsibility for advancing the globalization agenda. In this connection see, in particular, the World Bank's 1995 World Development Report: *Workers in an Integrating World*. This report can be read as a capitalist manifesto on the need, unavoidability and desirability of globalization as the only pathway to general prosperity and on 'structural adjustment' as the policy framework for ensuring entry into the new world order.

Bello 2005: 101–28; Stiglitz 2002: 89–179; Woods 2006: 39–64, 84–103, 141–78.

3. Policy dynamics of structural adjustment: Securing the 'new world order'

The globalization agenda in the mid 1980s replaced the earlier call for a 'new world order' by the Heritage Foundation and other Washington-based foundations, policy forums and financial institutions. It served as an ideological cover for the World Bank's policy reform agenda—to justify foisting 'structural reforms' on governments as financial aid conditionalities, as the price of admission into the new world order. In 1983, the stabilization policy agenda of the IMF was combined with the structural reform agenda of the World Bank (privatization, deregulation, financial/trade liberalization, decentralization and so on) as part of the Washington Consensus (see Williamson 1990).

Bienefeld 2000: 27–43; Stiglitz 1998: 1–32.

4. Crisis of the neoliberal world order

One of the most salient dynamic features of capitalist development is its propensity towards crisis, threatening not only the livelihoods and development prospects of people all over the world but the system itself.

Currently the world is in the grips of another such serious crisis, of multiple dimensions—financial, production, ecological, social and political. In its financial dimensions the crisis not only threatens the savings of individuals and households in the upper and middle classes of societies all over the developed world but the livelihoods and development prospects of people all over the world. The possibility, if not the prospect, that the spreading financial crisis will lead to a broader and deeper production crisis has raised questions about the fundamental dynamics of capitalist development as well as the strategic and political responses to the forces generated by these dynamics.

Bello 2006: 1345–68; Onis 2006: 239–63.

5. Liberal reform, system-supportive alternatives: The search for 'global governance'

The liberal world order established in 1944 was based on the multilateral institutional frame-work of the Bretton Woods system, the U.N. system and a western trilateral alliance of states in North America, Europe and Japan (the OECD) and a balance of state power. At the base of this system was the sovereign nation-state. The new world order, however, is structured differently. First, it is based on the integration of national economies into one global economy, forcing the nation-states in the system, including the most powerful—reluctantly, as it turns out, in regard to the U.S.—to concede some of their powers to transnational institutions within the state sector and what might be termed 'global civil society.' Order in this system is maintained not by world government or a supra-national state but by a global form of 'governance,' which by definition includes non-state as well as state actors. However, the central question remains the same: is 'order' maintained by means of a relation of unequal power among the state players in the system or can the architecture of the system be established in more democratic terms? For some, Stiglitz, for example, it is a matter of 'making globalization work.' For others, the issue is democracy in the exercise of power—to democratize decisionmaking power in transnational institutions such as the IMF and the World Bank. In the absence of internal democracy, and democracy in both accountability and representation, these institutions are merely adjuncts to state power, even the handmaidens of imperial ambition.

Held 2004: 94–116; Stiglitz 2006: 3–102, 245–92.

6. Radical systemic alternatives: Deglobalization, anti-imperialism and social transformation

From a CDS perspective, the current world order raises questions that go well beyond good governance or reform of the system of power relations, and this is because—not to put too fine a point on it—the system is designed to benefit certain powerful interests vested in property and wealth (private ownership of the means of global production); and, to maintain the grossly unequal structure of these benefits, the rich and powerful have a disproportionate capacity to 'govern' the entire system, constituting themselves as the 'new rulers of the world' (Pilger 2002). There are diverse mechanisms of control by this global ruling class over the neoliberal globalization process, one being control of the state apparatus in the most powerful countries, such as the U.S. In the context of this state power, particularly when supported by and combined with corporate economic power, many analysts speak and write of 'imperialism' and 'hegemony,' a system of economic, political and ideological domination (Petras & Veltmeyer 2001, 2005).

From this angle of imperial power, or the efforts of some states to achieve or maintain hegemony, the concern is not to democratize or humanize the system but to overthrow it or transform it into something radically new and different. The fundamental agency of change in this connection—a radical alternative to economic (i.e., neoliberal) globalization—is an anti- or deglobalization movement that brings together the North-South forces of resistance. One element of this movement is the emergence of a 'global civil society' in the North. Another is the popular movement in the South, raising questions as to how, under what conditions and where these two forces of resistance can combine so as to bring about 'another world.'

Cavanagh & Mander 2004: 30132; Bello 2004.

Module 15

The International Policy Framework

Manfred Bienefeld
Carleton University, Canada

This module provides students with a broad understanding of the evolution of the main features of the international policy framework that governs the ways in which national markets, production systems and financial systems are linked to the 'outside world.' Of course, the international policy framework evolves within certain political parameters, which also have to be understood. To this end, the first and last lectures specifically address the political parameters that help to determine the trajectory of the international policy framework, even as they are shaped by that evolving framework.

The module is concerned with the period since the end of World War II, which can be broken down into three more or less distinct phases. The first, roughly from 1945 to 1973, was a relatively nationalist 'Keynesian' phase that we label Bretton Woods I (BW-I). The next, from 1973 to 1994, was a neoliberal, internationalist phase, dubbed Bretton Woods II (BW-II). While this new system retained and even strengthened the same Bretton Woods institutions established in 1944, these nominally unchanged institutions were actually radically transformed in the process. The third phase, BW-III, began in 1994 but is known and generally referred to as the new world order (neoliberalism, globalization). This latest phase, in effect, represents a logical extension of BW-II in that it has more deeply entrenched a neoliberal world order by expanding the power and responsibility of international institutions relative to those of nation-states. The discussion ends by reflecting on the most recent developments in which the coordinating powers of those international institutions are increasingly being transferred to 'the markets.'

The module identifies the main characteristics and consequences of each international policy framework (IPF) phase and examines alternative ways of understanding their evolution and results, paying particular attention to the question of whether, and in what sense, these shifts enhance global prosperity and stability, as their supporters contend, or whether they are reviving the chronic instability and conflict that characterized the twenties and thirties.

1. Erosion of national sovereignty

The rise of capitalism was closely associated with the rise of the modern nation-state. And a world of nation-states needs an international policy framework to manage the inevitable tension between the national and the international. Nation-states must have sovereign powers if they are to be able to allow their citizens to build the societies of their choosing. But they must also be prepared to relinquish a degree of that sovereignty in order to live in peace with one another and to benefit from mutually advantageous relationships. Ultimately it is the shifting balance between these conflicting objectives that defines the central character of any IPF. And since the end of World War II, that balance has steadily shifted in the direction of the international and away from the national, to the delight of some and the growing despair of others. Readings in this theme explore different interpretations of these developments. Some authors believe in the rationality of markets over the nation-state, while others bemoan the loss of sovereignty and the weakening of the state. Bienefeld sees no alternative but to seek some way to rebuild national sovereignties, difficult though that has become. Gill thinks that such 'national' options are no longer available, so that attention must focus on building more effective international political movements. Helleiner concludes that nation-states retain more control than is often thought; he is impressed that the erosion of sovereignty has proceeded unevenly and that nation-states themselves have entered into agreements to constrain their sovereignty. Panitch, in reviewing the debate, reminds us that any real alternative must challenge the inner logic of neoliberal globalization and this could never be done by one state in isolation. And this takes us full circle. Just as James celebrates the attempt to establish a quasi-legal system of international cooperation based on 'neoliberal' economic principles, so Panitch and, in their way, the other authors, all see a need to embark on that same task, but on the basis of a different set of principles. But which principles? The essentially 'social democratic' principles enshrined in the original Bretton Woods agreement? Or some other 'internationalist' or 'socialist' set of principles?

Bienefeld 1988: 332–50; Gill 1995: 65–99; Panitch 1994: 9–43.

2. The Bretton Woods system

This theme examines the Bretton Woods system's first years of operation, when the relatively cautious and pragmatic BW-I turned out to be too 'liberal' to deal with the challenges of West European reconstruction and the even more pragmatic and more 'generous' Marshall Plan had to step into the breach. This led Milward (1984) to argue that it is simply wrong to suggest that economic liberalization can be credited with the unexpected economic successes of the postwar reconstruction. In fact, he shows that European reconstruction was based on highly nationalist and interventionist policies because BW-I, despite its pragmatism, would have required an unacceptable degree of liberalization in a politically precarious postwar Europe. The Marshall Plan provided extensive aid without demanding the abandonment of successful interventionist development strategies. These pragmatic nationalist and interventionist growth strategies paradoxically laid the foundations for eventual European integration—and even for economic liberalization—because they allowed the process to proceed in a form, and at a pace, that was sufficiently responsive to the social and political circumstances of the time. The story serves as a reminder that in the world of public policy, the shortest distance between two points is often not a straight line.

World War II left the world economy in a precarious state. Many countries had suffered enormous losses and economic imbalances, and political tensions were high throughout much of the world. The balance of opinion expected a dangerously volatile and unstable postwar world to emerge out of these conditions. But this is not what happened. Instead, between 1948 and 1973, the world experienced a quarter century of unprecedented growth and stability during which the lives of working people in the industrial world were radically transformed for the better, and even in the developing world, solid foundations for development were laid. While it is not possible to claim that this was simply the result of BW-I, these achievements did materialize during the BW-I era, and they began to be eroded as soon as the safeguards that had been the defining characteristics of that regime were effectively dismantled.

Helleiner 1994: 51–77, 81–100; Bienefeld 1991: 3–28.

3. Bretton Woods II: Managing the chaos

When BW-I was being dismantled, the advocates of neoliberal reform claimed that a move to flexible exchange rates would increase stability because 'real' exchange rates would become more stable once nominal rates were free to adjust to changing economic fundamentals. But in the real world these dreams were not fulfilled. Instead the collapse of BW-I led to a period of chaotic instability, with lower growth and investment and with higher rates of unemployment and inflation. Efforts to recreate a new cooperatively managed IPF failed in the face of U.S. and corporate opposition, leaving a chaotic market-driven system to emerge, essentially by default. BW-II was never negotiated or agreed, and although the same institutions remained at its centre and although it was still known as the Bretton Woods system, its essential features had been transformed. Whereas BW-I was clearly designed to protect the international economy from financial instability, BW-II empowered the very market mechanisms that were widely thought to promote that volatility. In a fundamental sense, the world had come full circle. The new neoliberal BW-II embodied everything that the original architects of BW had feared. From their perspective, it was a recipe for disaster.

Of course BW-II, having dramatically deregulated and empowered financial markets, was now charged with the task of regulating those same deregulated markets to contain their well-known potential for volatility. But this has proven a very challenging task as short-term capital flows have continued to grow, as 'financial innovation' has continued to increase the complexity of financial instruments and transactions, and as the power wielded by financial and corporate interests has continued to increase. Under these conditions, the official response to volatility has focused mainly on enhancing the quality of information available to market players, increasing the transparency of transactions and promoting the better regulation of banks. But the problem persists.

Bienefeld 1993b: 347–70; Duménil & Lévy 2002: 245–74; UNCTAD 1998: 83–110.

4. Reviving the ITO: The birth of the WTO

The third Bretton Woods institution designed in the 1940s was the International Trade Organization, but it never came into existence as such but rather as the World Trade Organization (WTO). However, the international regulation of trade raised insurmountable concerns about sovereignty in the U.S., so the agreement could not be ratified by Congress and the world was forced to 'make do' with a much more relaxed, less intrusive and voluntary structure to promote more liberal trade in the shape of the General Agreement on Tariffs and Trade (GATT). By the 1980s, the increasing international integration of investment, production and trade (Hart), and the increasing power of corporate entities, led to growing demands for a stronger, more effective institution that could harmonize trade related policies globally. This eventually led to the creation of the WTO, which came into existence on January 1, 1995, and whose operation is closely harmonized with that of the IMF and the World Bank.

Gowan 2003: 295–321; IMF 1994: 1–26.

5, The policy dynamics of neoliberal globalization: The pros and cons of structural adjustment

This section looks at a number of readings from the Citizens' Challenge to Structural Adjustment [www.saprin.org] that provide critical perspectives on the World Bank's vaunted 'structural adjustment' policies. These critiques question the standard arguments in favour of neoliberal adjustment and argue that the impact of these policies has been deeply problematic in that they have often (though not always) proven to be destructive and destabilizing. Students are asked to weigh the arguments and the evidence on both sides of this debate in order to work towards an 'on balance' conclusion that they are able to defend.

Agarwala & Schwartz 1994: 1–32; Easterly 2002: 88–103; Rodrik 1990: 933–47;
SAPRIN 2001: Weisbrot et al. 2000.

6. Where do we go from here?

This final section looks back at the debates and reflects on the options that now confront the global system. It returns the discussion to the question of the future role of the nation-state as a mechanism for facilitating the politically transparent and legitimate construction of the frameworks within which market forces must operate if they are to function in the public, and the human, interest. The tension is between the need for local sovereignty to make the necessary choices and the simultaneous need for international integration and harmonization. Some of the central questions that remain include: What is to be taken as given when we think about alternatives? What is reversible and what is irreversible? At what cost? What are the risks and costs of simply accepting the current trajectory?

Bienefeld 1994: 44–79; Wade 2002.

Module 16

Aid, Debt and Trade

In the Vortex of Capitalist Development

Luciano Vasapollo
Università di Roma 'La Sapienza,' Italy

1. The policy framework of the neoliberal world order

What is the policy and institutional (multilateral and bilateral) framework for the delivery of foreign aid? What is the rationale for a policy of foreign aid and how does this policy connect to international cooperation for international development and to the foreign policy of donor states? Multilateral and bilateral channels? What is the role of nongovernmental organizations in the development process? In the 1980s, the new world order was brought about by Washington-designed policies of structural adjustment—privatization; financial and commodity trade liberalization; deregulation of commodity, capital and labour markets; administrative decentralization and the incorporation of civil society in the responsibility for development and democratic politics. By the end of the decade, it was evident that these policies were economically dysfunctional and unsustainable socially or politically, leading to diverse efforts to reconstruct a new post-Washington Consensus (Saad-Fihlo 2005).

> Chang 2006; Dasgupta 1998; Stiglitz 1998; Ocampo 2007: Saad-Fihlo 2005: 113–19.

2. The development dynamics of foreign aid

What are the pros and cons of foreign aid in regard to its 'development' form (a large part is not developmental but designed only to provide humanitarian or disaster relief)? Why do donors 'give' and why do recipient countries 'seek' aid? Is foreign aid a catalyst of growth or an agency of imperialism? How effective is it? Who benefits from it?

On these questions there is a large and growing literature and some continuing debate from a variety of theoretical perspectives. Some, like economist Jeffrey Sachs (2005), an architect of Bolivia's pioneering stabilization measures and structural adjustment program in the 1980s, argue that notwithstanding its problems foreign aid in the form of financial and technical 'assistance' can be a catalyst for development, as it was in India's Green Revolution and as it is in much of Sub-Saharan Africa: an indispensable source of development-inducing 'international resources transfers.' The contrary position, articulated, for example, by William Easterly (2006), professor of economics at New York University, author of *The White Man's Burden* and former research economist at the World Bank, and Kenyan economist James Shikwati, is that aid breeds corruption and relations of dependence and has serious deleterious effects on the economies and societies of the recipient countries by distorting incentives or foisting on these countries conditionalities that inhibit rather than facilitate development. Theresa Hayter (1971), and more recently Petras and Veltmeyer (2002), go as far as to argue that aid is designed and functions as a mechanism of imperialist exploitation and as such serves as a catalyst of regression rather than development, not only providing more benefits to the donors than the recipient countries but presenting a major obstacle to economic and social development.

Petras & Veltmeyer 2002, 2005: Pilger 2005: 5–30.

3. Structural and policy dynamics of Third World debt

What are the root causes—structural, economic and political—of Third World external debt? What are its economic, social and political dynamics? The explosive size and weight of the external debt experienced by many countries in the Global South and the negative impact of debt payments on these countries are major issues. However, relatively little attention has been paid to the way that debt serves as a lever of power and dependence—debt peonage or imperialism, according to some. The U.N. Security Council mechanism, by which the major powers control the U.N. and hence military intervention, is well known. However, what is not so widely realized are the similar mechanisms that exist by which—without resorting to arms—the major imperial powers, the U.S. in particular, can control the world economy. Once this is revealed the idea of globalization appears as little more than a cheap card trick, designed to disguise and take attention away from the imperialist domination of the world.

The massive debt owed by Third World countries is one aspect of this economic control and has received a lot of public if not academic attention, even if indirectly, through the Jubilee 2000 campaign, which demanded that 'unpayable' debt be abolished. The campaign did in fact have considerable success in mobilizing tens of thousands on demonstrations in support of this demand. Some 800,000 people in Ireland alone signed the petition for the abolition of the debt. But what is seldom mentioned is the central part debt plays for the Western powers in dictating how Third World economies are organized. In fact, the debt crisis of the early 1980s proved an ideal leverage for the West (through the World Bank and the IMF, both essentially adjuncts of the world's most powerful governments) to force 'free trade' on the Third World. This occurred when countries in the Global South were faced with the scissor-squeeze of falling incomes and rising interest rates, both beyond their control, defaulted on their loans. Before this many countries had followed a policy of 'import substitution,' which meant that they tried to manufacture goods they had previously imported. Without suggesting this sort of policy offered a positive alternative, it did have one big disadvantage for the imperialist powers in that it tended to deny them both markets and cheap raw materials. What the imperialist powers wanted, and what they essentially won, was a system where the Third World provided cheap raw materials and labour and acted as a market to consume the products of companies with their bases in the imperialist countries—in the name of the widely touted or assumed 'failure' of import substitution, protectionism, government interference and state-led development. But for obvious reasons this was not a popular policy for the people of those countries, except perhaps the few who received a share of the profits for administering the system. The readings explore some of the dynamics of the debt trap and its underdevelopment consequences.

Buckley 2002/03; Focus on the South 2004; George 1998: 47–57, 119–40; Langdon 1999.

4. Aid versus trade

By many accounts, 'foreign aid' is more of a development trap than a catalyst for development. First, at least half of all 'foreign aid' that is provided in the project of international cooperation has no 'development function'; its purpose is humanitarian assistance, which is of critical importance and needs to be extended further as required. As for the aid that does have a development function, several scholars and practitioners continue to argue that in the form of technical assistance and supplementary finance it can serve as a 'catalyst' to jump-start a development process and under certain conditions can make a significant contribution. However, the critical scholarship on 'foreign aid' has identified a number of serious issues that makes it more likely that aid serves as an obstacle to development, a catalyst of 'regression' (Petras & Veltmeyer 2002).

Issues with aid include the fact that it generally takes the form of a loan rather than a grant, and the conditions attached to the loan are designed to provide more benefits to the donor than the recipient. Conditions include (1) the requirement that the recipient purchases good and services from the donor country ('tied aid') and (2) the implementation of specific 'structural reforms,' such as liberalization, privatization and deregulation, that weaken the capacity of the government to pursue a strategy of choice or to make public policy. In this context, some authors view aid as a form of 'dependency' or 'imperialism,' a means of establishing a relation of power or dominance over the recipient country. Taking into account these and other such criticisms leads many scholars to the conclusion (see Chang 2006) that the costs of aid exceed its presumed benefits and that trade would be a much more effective and preferable development strategy.

Chang 2006; Petras & Veltmeyer 2002.

5. Free trade versus fair trade

Many policy analysts and development theorists argue that the solution to underdevelopment is trade rather than aid, but not trade under prevailing conditions—nor under proposed 'free trade' regimes because such trade invariably rewards or benefits the better positioned or more powerful. What is needed is fair trade—trade governed by rules of a different world order that provides equality of opportunity. At present, world trade is conducted on an unlevel playing field, and when a developing country has a comparative advantage in terms of the price at which it can export its products—as in agriculture generally—countries like the U.S. erect protective barriers against them, insisting that their own exports be freed from control while their own producers are protected from competitive imports.

Of course, this does not apply to China, whose insatiable demand for all sorts of natural resources, energy and primary commodities, and the enormous size of both its domestic industry and market puts it in a very different position in world trade. But most developing country exporters do not have the leverage or economic power of China, nor do they have their governments behind them as China does and the imperialist powers do.

The readings for this theme explore the issues that surround this problem, as well as the policy and systemic dynamics of free trade versus fair trade, which is essentially an issue of protecting small producers and indigenous communities in the Third World from the rapacious practices and market power of the multinational corporations that dominate world trade, As Fridell (2007) points out, this is a matter of how production is socially organized—cooperatively—and the producer being able to deal directly with the consumer, without all sorts of business operators appropriating an undue share of the proceeds.

The idea of cooperative production and fair trade raises serious questions about the possibilities and limits of reform within capitalism, but it is simple to organize small coffee farmers into co-operatives and build their capacity to produce, transport, process and export their high quality coffee at a fair price. This would allow them to escape the clutches of 'coyotes' or inter-mediaries and give them dignity, control and hope for a better future.

Chang 2008; Daviron & Ponte 2005; Fridell 2007; Saguier 2007: 251–65.

Notes

1. The original idea was to create an international trade organization, but protectionist pressures on and within the U.S. government prevented its institution. It was finally established fifty years later, in 1994, in the form of the World Trade Organization (WTO)—implicitly designed as a bulwark against UNCTAD (see discussion below), viewed by many U.S. policymakers, advisors and politicians as an instrument of 'international communism' (i.e., as a restriction on the freedom of economic enterprise).
2. The U.S. Congress did not ratify the U.N. Charter because it implied that decent jobs (or meaningful and well- remunerated work) and housing, as well as health and education, were fundamental *human* rights that the state had the responsibility to project and ensure, rather than leaving them to the 'forces of economic freedom' (the market, private enterprise, etc.).

Section 6

Class, State and Development

Although economics in the liberal tradition originated in a political economy approach (an integrated focus on market economics and public policy or the state), economics and politics in this tradition are generally studied separately. However, in CDS as with the radical tradition of social thought, economics and politics are not only analyzed from an integrated 'political economy' perspective but with what C.W. Mills termed a 'sociological imagination,' which is to view what happens to the individual as part of a larger pattern defined by the individual's social relations under conditions shared with others in the same social position or belonging to the same social group or class. From this 'sociological perspective' (see Module 27), critical development studies in regard to 'politics' (essentially a system set up for determining or deciding 'who gets what' in the distribution of the product of collective activity—the social product) takes two fundamental forms: *state-centric* or *class-based* analysis.

Berch Berberoglu (Module 17) argues both for the centrality of class in the critical study of development and the pivotal role of the capitalist state in the twentieth century as the fundamental agency for development in the postcolonial era of the Bretton Woods world order. He contends that development must be understood in class terms: 'Which *classes* benefit from the development process evolving in a particular direction? How is the nature of the development path pursued affected by the *class character of the state*? What are the particular *class forces* that initiate and/or take part in the development process, and what are the results of that process in terms of *which classes benefit and which classes lose*?' It is in this context of class domination of society that the state must be situated to give meaning to developments taking place in a particular country.

The state has taken different forms over the centuries, but in the form of the nation-state it is coterminous with and fundamental to the process of capitalist development. In theory, the state is assigned responsibility for providing (1) legal security to each person and their property (to secure private property in the means of production); (2) basic infrastructure for economic growth (the capital accumulation function); (3) law-making and administration ('government'); and (4) political order (internal and external security). In addition, the state is responsible for determining 'who gets what' (allocating appropriate returns to diverse factors of production), a role that is subject to continuing debate.

In practice, this role is shared between the market and the state, with neoliberals privileging the free market, and Keynesians (liberals but proponents of market regulation and an activist interventionist state) pushing to expand the role of the state. In addition to the above 'functions' the state can also assume different degrees of responsibility for the provision of 'welfare' (education, health, social security and other 'basic needs'). By the 1950s, the weight of this responsibility in the capitalist states of Europe had become so great that the state as such could be defined in terms of its 'welfare function.'

As for the countries in the Global South, the relative weakness of market institutions and a capitalist class prepared to assume its theoretically defined function of capital accumulation led theorists of economic development to turn to the state, giving rise to what would become known as the 'developmental state.' The development state, like the welfare state, was systematically dismantled in the 1980s, stripped of both its welfare and development functions. As noted by Petras (Module 18) in his summary review of the development dynamics of the state in the era of neoliberal globalization, these functions in the 1980s and 1990s would be either taken over by or shared with 'civil society' (in a neoliberal model of participatory development, in which the poor are empowered to act for themselves, converted into 'actors' or 'subjects,' the active agents of the development process). In his analysis of the 'politics of empire' and the 'imperial state,' which encompasses both the developmental state of the 1950–1970s and the neoliberal state of the 1980–1990s, Petras elaborates on Berberoglu's class analysis of the capitalist state in the latest and current phase of capitalist development, that of neoliberal globalization.

The state is not the only site of political struggle or *politics*, which, at the most general level, can be defined either as a means of determining who gets what or the art of exercising power. Power here is the capacity to make decisions on behalf of a group (or, as Weber saw it, to either 'exert one's will against resistance' or 'issue commands with the probability that they will be obeyed'). So defined, politics is not necessarily a matter of class or the state but—as John Harriss in Module 19 describes it—a matter of the relationship between democracy and development. In the context of this relationship, Harriss focuses on the political dimension of the development process, with particular emphasis on 'democracy and processes of democratization, and ... contemporary discourse in regard to good government or ... governance in relation to development.' As Harriss constructs it, the shift in development discourse in recent years from 'government' to 'governance' reflects 'a concern to broaden the social base of decision- and policymaking from the political class and political actors to non-state actors, and the concern to incorporate civil society.'

As both Berberoglu and Petras have it, the state is both a site of class struggle and a fundamental source of class power, a multi-functional instrument wielded by the ruling class in its own interest as a means of maintaining order and reconciling different forms of social conflict. As a means of maintaining order, the state is able to use diverse instruments, including the legal system, to administer law and 'justice,' and what political theorists have conceptualized as a 'repressive apparatus'—the police and the armed forces, by which the state maintains a monopoly on the use of violence as means of settling conflicts. In Module 20 Michael Clow elaborates on the use of violence and armed force by the state as a means of prosecuting and settling a certain form of conflict—war. As Clow defines it, 'wars are armed struggles in which organized groups attempt to use violence for political purposes.' Needless to say, warfare (politics as violence or armed struggle) can, and does, take diverse forms—from civil war and class war to wars among nations. Clow's module explores the complexities and the simplicities of the war-development nexus—what we might term the development dynamics of war.

Module 17

The Centrality of Class in Critical Development Studies

Berch Berberoglu
University of Nevada, United States

Until recently, most social scientists engaged in development studies have utilized institutional, crossnational, cultural and other similar approaches compatible with modernization theory in studying development in the Third World. Neglecting the class dynamics of development and change arising from the political economy of a global system that has been evolving since the eighteenth century, these development specialists have focused on the surface manifestations of inter-state relations in an institutional framework, missing the crucial social relationships based on class and class conflict, which have shaped much of the history of the developing world over the course of the past several centuries.

This module addresses the central issues in critical development studies through the adoption of a class analysis approach informed by a critical understanding of the development process and its contradictions. Such an approach (also see Module 27) elucidates the underlying class dynamics of development and provides a fresh look at development studies in a critical way.

1. Approaches to analysis

Mainstream economists often focus on macroeconomic institutional processes such as imports, exports, balance of trade and payments, GNP, growth of output, manufacturing, level of industrialization and other indicators of economic performance, without any serious regard to social classes and class relations. In their preoccupation to record national accounts statistics, they lose sight of which classes benefit and which classes lose from these processes. What is the relationship of social classes to the state and to power relations in society? What is the nature of struggles between different class forces vis-à-vis the state? Such questions are viewed by mainstream economists as irrelevant, having no apparent bearing on the structure and dynamics of society and social life in the global political economy.

Other mainstream social scientists, such as anthropologists, sociologists, historians and political scientists, are also not exempt from this neglect of class analysis. Sociologists and anthropologists often focus on cultural and societal phenomena in terms of values, beliefs, religion, nationalism and other superstructural institutional forms to explain social life in divergent states in the Third World. Political scientists are almost exclusively preoccupied with forms of the state and bureaucracy, the role of the army, political factionalism as a result of superpower rivalry and more recently, forms of terrorism, including state terrorism, to explain the nature of states and their social/political orientation. Finally, academic historians have contributed not much more than a chronicle of events in recent decades with their primary focus on the history of nation-states as such, and within this they limit their studies to particular regimes and leaders, not classes and class struggles.

Such approaches do not contribute much to our understanding of the *real* forces at work in conflicts and crises affecting many countries in the Third World. For example, while abstract institutional analyses of trade patterns, import-export structure, indebtedness to Western banks, balance of payments crises and other such aggregate data help us catalogue the economic performance of states and their position relative to others on some specific variables, they *do not* tell us much about the nature of the political crises, the balance of class forces, national and international alliances, social/political movements and other forces at work in shaping the societal landscape—forces that are ultimately based on the nature of *social classes* and *class struggles.*

Berberoglu 1992; Callinicos 1987.

2. Critical development studies and class analysis

To provide answers to these and related questions now confronting the Third World, we must adopt a class analysis approach based on relations of production and their attendant superstructure, expressed first and foremost by the *state.* Thus, as class relations, class struggles and the role of the state constitute crucial elements of the study of power and power struggles in society, societies in the Third World—especially at this critical juncture of crises and conflicts—are not exempt from this requirement of informed scientific analysis in critical development studies.

Critical social scientists informed by the principles of Marxist political economy have always argued that abstract notions of modernization, development and underdevelopment, colonialism and imperialism, conflicts between nation-states and between states and national movements, and other such phenomena that have affected the world historical process, cannot be fully understood without the analysis of their *class* character. It is in this context that we can raise such questions as: Which *classes* benefit from the development process evolving in a particular direction? How is the nature of the development path pursued affected by the *class character of the state?* What are the particular *class forces* that initiate and/or take part in the development process, and what are the results of that process in terms of *which classes benefit and which classes lose?* What are the *class-driven* dynamics of colonial and imperialist expansion throughout the world over the centuries, how have these changed in accordance with historical changes in the *class structure* of the colonial and imperial centres, what has been the impact of the interaction of these colonial centres with the colonies in *class* terms, and which classes or groups have benefited or suffered from such interaction, *both* in the colonial/imperial centres *and* in the colonies and neocolonies? Finally, what is the *class content* of relations between different states—what is the nature of the *class forces in control of the state apparatus in the dominant, imperialist states* and what is their *class-motivated* position toward national liberation movements led by classes (or alliance of classes) whose interests are antagonistic to and in fact threaten the interests of the dominant classes within the dominant imperial states and in the neocolonies?

Burris 1988; Wright 2005; Zweig 2004.

3. The theoretical and methodological tools of historical materialism

Avoiding careful discussion of questions such as these, as most development theorists and area specialists have done, seriously hampers our understanding of the nature and contradictions of the development process and greatly distorts the history of social development and societal transformations now underway throughout the world. This module contains a critical examination of mainstream and radical theories of development and an alternative conceptualization of the development process through the utilization of the theoretical and methodological tools of the historical materialist approach—an approach that is based on the analysis of class relations and class struggles. Such an approach can be applied to explain the historical and contemporary structures of development in different regions and states on a global scale. It is within this framework of the study of the internal class structure of states and societies around the world that one can understand the nature and impact of relations with colonial and imperialist states and assess the net effect of these relations on the prospects for change and development in the Third World.

Berberoglu 2005; So 1990; Veltmeyer 2010; Tabb 2004.

4. A new challenge for development theory

Development theory now faces a new challenge: it can either cling to old, worn-out analyses and remedies of mid-twentieth century developmentalism, which are now thoroughly discredited in the minds of intellectuals and the masses the world over, adopt an 'enlightened' liberal reformulation of the dependency problematic for intellectual consumption around the North-South debate *or*, as we suggest, help clear the way for the paradigmatic consolidation of class theory informed by the materialist conception of history.

With the growing conflicts and struggles throughout the Third World, as well as the actions of the state, assuming more and more a *class* character, it is becoming increasingly clear that if development theory is to become a viable tool to explain these changes convincingly, it too must move forward and adopt a critical class analysis approach to development that is both concrete and historically specific.

Applying this approach to the study of particular states and societies around the world, we must then delineate their nature, dynamics and contradictions in class terms and place them within the broader context of relations with the imperialist states in the development process. Thus, while studying the dynamics of colonialism and imperialism in the formerly dominated states of the Third World and determining the nature and structure of these states, it is imperative that we examine the internal class structure and class relations of these societies so that the class nature of the state and its future course of development can be clearly understood.

Beams 1998; Chilcote 1982; Howe 1982.

5. Class and class struggle in the development context of neocolonialism and imperialism

In the context of a class analysis methodology, the continued reliance and collaboration of the less developed capitalist states with imperial states can be conceptualized within the framework of a theory of neocolonialism. The development process seen in these terms can help us locate the internal class agents of neocolonial domination imposed by imperialism to facilitate the neoliberal globalization agenda of transnational capital and capitalist imperialism over the less developed societies. A class analysis approach to sort out these entangled relationships is imperative if we are to develop a clear and concise understanding of the development process.

This is also the case when attempting to understand the role of major national and global institutions that appear to be neutral but in fact serve class ends. The military, political and economic institutions of society may be presented as serving the interests of the 'nation' as a whole, but a military dictatorship in power in a Third World state may in fact serve the interests of certain dominant class forces (capitalist, landowning, etc.), which use military powers to crush opposition political parties and organizations linked to a rival social class vying for state power. While this is clearly the case in the struggle between opposing class forces, it may also be the case with rival factions within a single class, representing sectional or fractional class interests that nonetheless conflict with the policies of ruling elites tied to the military or other political and legal institutions that legitimize the class rule of one or another fraction of a ruling class.

Chandra 1975; Petras 1978, 1981.

6. Neoliberal globalization and capitalist development

Like national institutions, major global institutions, such as the World Bank, the International Monetary Fund and the World Trade Organization, may appear to be neutral development agencies with a set of policies that (correctly or incorrectly) facilitate the development process through funding projects and regulating trade. In reality they may well serve the long-term interests of a particular system that benefits a particular class. Hence they may impose policies that are at odds with the interests of those who become the victims of this process of unequal and uneven development. Such policies facilitate the accumulation of capital for a small minority of the world's population, which directly benefits from the neoliberal globalization project overseen by these very same institutions, designed to protect imperial ends.

A class analysis approach confronts these realities, takes on these institutions and exposes them for what they are. They may go a long way in explaining the problems encountered in the development process and set the stage for a better understanding of the reasons for the failure of states in the Third World to overcome the myriad problems they confront in fighting mass poverty and other consequences of the neoliberal global capitalist system into which they have become integrated.

An analysis of classes and class struggle at the national and global levels is indispensable, not only from a sociological perspective that is informed by the principles and precepts of historical materialism through the Marxist conceptualization of society and social relations, but also in understanding economic, political and ideological questions that constitute the very basis of critical development studies. It is hoped that this module will help frame the central issues that are vital for the study of the nature, dynamics and contradictions of the development process, thus providing a useful tool for the critical analysis of the process of development at the national and global level.

Berberoglu 1987, 2003, 2009.

Module 18

Power and Development

The Politics of Empire

James Petras
Saint Mary's University, Canada

1. Imperialism and development:
From the welfare-development state to the neoliberal state

In the 1930s, in the wake of the 'Great Depression,' the state in the Global North assumed responsibility for what economists conceptualized as the 'welfare function' (e.g., health, education, social security, unemployment insurance, public housing). Prior to that, the state's basic functions were seen as protecting the property and person of each citizen, providing legal security to private property in the means of production; making and administration of law; provision of economic infrastructure for the growth of economic production, the responsibility for which was left to the market and the capitalist class within the private sector; and maintenance of political 'order,' by force if necessary.

In the 1960s, the role of the state was expanded to include responsibility for 'development'—improvement in the physical quality of life on the basis of economic growth and structural transformation of a traditional, precapitalist form of agrarian society into a modern industrial capitalist system. The resulting 'state-led development' included the traditional functions of the capitalist state but in the Global South also the following: (1) policies designed to improve access of the poor to productive resources such as land, credit (capital) and technical assistance (technology); (2) nationalization of the strategic sectors of the economy and the institution of state enterprises where capital was weak (non-functioning markets and the lack of a class disposed to invest its capital productively); (3) protection of domestic producers from the forces of the world market; (4) redistribution of market-generated growth in the form of social and development programs that transferred income from the rich to the poor to ensure that basic needs were met; and (5) responsibility for social infrastructure—to ensure a process of social or integrated 'development.'

In the 1980s, the welfare-development state was systematically dismantled under the aegis of the architects and guardians of the new neoliberal order. The state retreated from its responsibility for the growth of economic production (and capital accumulation), turning it over to the 'forces of economic freedom' (to quote from George W. Bush's 2002 National Security doctrine). The 'welfare' and 'development' functions were decentralized, reassigned to local governments under conditions that allowed for 'popular participation,' shared responsibility with 'civil society.' The development role of the state was restricted to providing an appropriate and facilitating institutional and policy framework. The responsibility for and the agency of development shifted from the state to grassroots or community-based social organizations, empowering the poor to act for themselves.

Bienefeld 1993b; Petras & Veltmeyer 2005a; Saul 2006; Veltmeyer 2005a: 89–106.

2. Globalization, Development and Imperialism

The new economic model (NEM) was advanced by the World Bank in the early 1980s as a form of development, i.e., a means of promoting 'pro-growth.' More generally, however, it was used to promote globalization, a fundamental aspect of the new world order. However, a closer look at the dynamics of social change and development associated with the NEM, more popularly known as 'neoliberalism,' suggests that rather than a way of improving the socioeconomic conditions of the population, it is much better understood as a means of advancing the interests of a globally dominant transnational capitalist class and the nation-states that dominate the world system. Neoliberal policies of structural adjustment to the requirements of the new world order, especially when as they generally were imposed on governments, are better understood as a form of imperialism.

Imperialism refers to a project of world domination pursued earlier by various European states led by Great Britain during the time of nineteenth-century global capitalism. Since the end of the World War II, however, the U.S. has taken over the lead in this project. In the late 1940s, the U.S. commanded a lion's share of the world's productive resources and industrial production capacity—having 50 percent of development finance (gold and monetary reserves) and 38 percent of industrial production. Since then, U.S. administrations have been possessed of the imperial dream—a belief in the right to global rule, rooted in a sense of superiority and an ideology of a 'manifest destiny,' a mission supported by an all too clear awareness of the *economic and political power commanded by the state* (Chomsky 1998; Petras and Veltmeyer 2005b).

However, this imperial dream had to contend with pressure to avoid the fate of the declining British Empire and a widespread concern among allied capitalist states to prevent world domination by a unilateral projection of power. This latter concern resulted in the formation of the U.N. and a system of multilateral organizations designed to prevent any one state from seeking and establishing hegemony over the world system. The U.S. was a party to the negotiations involved in setting up this system, but foreign policy documents and subsequent events show that the U.S. state actually never abandoned the imperial dream of Pax Americana and the political project to realize it. Indeed, foreign policy by successive U.S. regimes has been geared toward securing a world order designed to support their own national interest.

Chomsky 1998; Egan & Chorbajian 2005; Little & Smith 2005;
Petras & Veltmeyer 2001, 2003, 2005a; Pilger 2002.

3. Imperialism in the new world order

According to Woflgang Sachs and his associates in postdevelopment theory (1992), the idea of 'development' was invented as a means by which the West, i.e., the complex of nation-states that emerged victorious from World War II, could impose their will on the economically 'backward' countries emerging from European colonial rule and to make sure that these countries would take a capitalist path towards national development.

Similarly, it could be argued (see Veltmeyer and Petras 2005a) that the project of international cooperation for integrated rural development in the 1960s, particularly in Latin America, was designed as a means of ensuring that there would be not be another Cuba, which, in 1950, succumbed to the demand by the people and the forces for revolutionary change. The aim of 'development' in this context, implemented by means of a strategic alliance among Western capitalist states, was to lure the rural poor away from the revolutionary social movements that were emerging at the time and to turn them towards the virtues of reform and capitalism—towards a politics of dialogue and negotiations rather than violent confrontation, towards the free market and local development rather than the conquest of state power.

In this new political context, which could be encapsulated in the formula, '*Reform or Revolution*,' imperialism took diverse new forms, which include the following:

- international cooperation for development—a project of multilateral and bilateral 'assistance,' ostensibly oriented towards the improvement of socio-economic conditions and a process of nation-building and capitalist development for those countries seeking to escape economic backwardness and European colonialism;
- support for U.S. multinational banks and corporations in their search of profit and opportunities for capital accumulation overseas;
- foreign aid in the form of humanitarian assistance, disaster relief and funds for local self-development, designed (with the strategic assistance of private voluntary and nongovernmental organizations contracted by the U.S. government) to help subdue the fires of revolutionary ferment in the Latin American countryside;
- policies (via the World Bank and other IFIs controlled or dominated by the U.S.) designed to adjust the economies of developing societies to the requirements of the Washington-designed new world order;
- policies to secure the subservience of a series of satellite or client states, able and willing to protect U.S. economic and political interests; and
- where and whenever necessary, as in the Gulf Coast region, Iraq and Afghanistan, the use of military force.

Veltmeyer & Petras 2005a; Petras &Veltmeyer 2003, 2005a; Sachs 1992.

4. Natural resource wars: The political economy of global pillage

The history of capitalist development is predicated on a process of 'primitive [original] accumulation,' the separation of the direct producers from their means of production—or in broader more systemic terms, the enclosure and privatization of the global commons, the world's repository of natural and productive resources. The capital accumulation process entails the pillage and privatization of these resources and the institution of the rights and prerogatives of private property to capacitate the owners of the means of production to dispose of the social product, to extract by diverse means (wage labour, etc.) an economic surplus from the direct producer. However, the capital accumulation process is fraught with class conflict, resulting in different types of class war (on this see Module 20), including (in the current context of neoliberal globalization) what Maude Barlow (2007) terms the 'coming battle for the right to water.'

In this connection Brecher and Costello (1994), as so many others on the left, argue the need to articulate diverse forms of resistance and organization in the struggle against neoliberal globalization—against the 'global pillage.'

Brecher & Costello 1994; Barlow 2007.

5. Civil society, the state and the new world order: Democratizing development and good governance

The process of structural adjustment and globalization associated with the short history of neo-liberalism since the early 1980s generated new forms of social exclusion, poverty and inequality, which in turn, generated new forms of political resistance that threatened the existing political order and that made many societies and economies difficult to govern or ungovernable. In a strategic response to this problem, the guardians of the new world order have sought to establish new forms of 'governance' as a means of restoring order. Since 'government' in the neoliberal worldview and model is viewed as 'bad,' responsible for economic downturn and the failure of societies across the world to develop their forces of production, the search for 'good governance' was directed towards strengthening 'civil society'—democratizing its relation to the state and actively engaging the social or civil organizations in a process of participatory development and politics. The readings in this unit reconstruct the thinking behind this process.

The essence of the post-Washington Consensus, constructed in the 1990s as a response to the evident dysfunctionality and politically destabilizing effects of market-led capitalist develop-ment or neoliberalism, was to engage 'civil society' in the responsibility for social and political development—a policy of 'sustainable human development' based on 'good governance' and initiatives 'from below and within' and that is participatory, equitable and empowering of the poor.

Veltmeyer 2007a, 2007b.

6. Paving the way for change: The dynamics of electoral politics, social movements and local development

A report commissioned by the U.K. Ministry of Defence (2007) raised the alarm about a problem that had the potential to derail the entire system of global capitalism. According to the Report, which echoed similar analysis made by a growing number of critics of globalization in its neoliberal and corporate form, the excessive inequalities in the distribution of wealth and income produced by the process was generating forces of resistance and opposition that were placing the entire system at risk of collapse or overthrow. As the authors of the report argued, the global divide in wealth and development was breeding 'forces of resistance' and likely to lead to a 'resurgence of not only anti-capitalist ideologies … but also of populism and the revival of Marxism' (2007: 3).

The readings in this theme focus on the strategic and political responses of groups, classes and organizations in the popular sector of society to the dynamics of neoliberal globalization and the contestation of class power. These responses, it can be argued (with particular reference to modalities of social change and political developments in Latin America), can be put into three main categories.

One is *electoral politics*: the pursuit of political power within the institutional framework and trappings of liberal democracy. Another takes the form of social movements: *mass mobilization* of the forces of resistance against government policies and the underlying system. Unlike politi-cal parties, social movements are not organized to capture state power as such, but nevertheless the state tends to be the major object of their confrontational politics. A third way of 'doing politics' or bringing about social change is *local development* with social capital, i.e., networks of cooperation constructed on the basis of a culture of solidarity and relations of reciprocal exchange This particular modality of change, conceptualized by Holloway (2002) as the 'no-power' approach ('bringing about change without state power') and by others as 'a new way of doing politics,' seeks to make improvements in the lives of people ('development') by means of local or community-based development, empowering the poor to act for themselves in their localities and communities.

In this approach, the politics of social change is based on the accumulation of 'social capital' rather than a direct confrontation with the holders of political power. 'Social capital' in this context is defined as 'a person's or group's concern, caring, regard, respect, or sense of obligation for the well-being of another person or group that may produce a potential benefit, advantage, and preferential treatment for another person or group beyond that which might be expected in an [economic] exchange relationship' (Atria et al. 2004: 14). This type of capital is embodied in, and accumulated through, social networks that are constructed around norms of reciprocity and relations of trust, solidarity and social exchange—conceptualized by some (Razeto 1993) as 'the economics of solidarity' and by others, more recently, as the 'social economy.' At issue in this form of development is changing how people feel about themselves, empowering them to act on their own behalf, to participate in their own development.

While the electoral approach of democratic politics dictates conformity to the rules of 'political class,' and the 'no power' approach to social change relies on local development, social movements take a more confrontational approach towards change in the mobilization of the forces of resistance and opposition. The permutations this approach can be traced out in the recent political history of several countries in Latin America, particularly in Brazil, Bolivia and Ecuador, in the Andean highlands and in parts of Mexico. Political developments in these countries over the past decade, formed in resistance against government policies in the neoliberal mould, are not that different from earlier waves of social movements in the region. But what *is* 'new' is the particular context of objective and subjective conditions and, as a result, the particular developmental and political dynamics involved. The readings in this unit elucidate some of these dynamics.

Petras & Veltmeyer 2005b; Veltmeyer 2007b.

Module 19

The Politics of Development

John Harriss
Simon Fraser University, Canada

This module focuses on the political dimension of the development process, with particular emphasis on democracy and processes of democratization, and—not unrelated—on the contemporary discourse in regard to 'good governance' in relation to development. The shift in development discourse from 'government' to 'governance' reflects a concern to broaden the social base of decisionmaking and policymaking from the political class and political actors to non-state actors, to incorporate civil society, which refers to the gamut of social organizations and non-state institutions, into the policymaking process related to the allocation of society's productive resources and decisions as to 'who gets what.'

Normally, these issues have to do with the state, the strictly political sphere of collective decisionmaking, and the market, an institution formed by the aggregate of decisions made by individuals on economic matters. However, good governance is deemed to be a matter of democracy—engaging stakeholder organizations in civil society in the responsibility of maintaining order.

1. What is democracy? How does it work in developing countries?

Democracy in recent development discourse has two points of reference. One dimensions refers to the institutional arrangements that allow citizens to participate in the electoral process leading to the formation of a constitutional government. These arrangements are based on the principles of *participation, representation* and *accountability*. The second is about engaging people in more active forms of participation in the process of collective and authoritative decisionmaking and policymaking. This process (social and economic rather than political) is predicated on a policy of decentralization—the devolution of government responsibility, decisionmaking and program administration to lower levels (regional and local) of government (Rondinelli 1989; Rondinelli, McCullough and Johnson, 1989).

Carrothers 1999; Khan 2005: 704–24; Rueschemeyer et al. 1992: Chap. 3;
Bratton & Can de Walle 1997; Patomäki & Teivainen 2004; Rondinelli 1989: 181–207;
Rondinelli, McCullough & Johnson 1989: 57–87; Welch & Nuru 2006.

2. Democracy and development: Connections and disconnections

From the outset of development thought (in the 1940s) until the onset of the new world order (in the 1980s), the prevailing idea was that authoritarian, non-democratic forms of government provided more favourable conditions for economic development. This was the case whether development was capitalist or socialist in form.

The new thinking in the 1980s, however, was that democracy or political liberalism would lead to economic freedom, and vice versa. This thinking gave way to the neoliberal notion that democracy and capitalism are intrinsically connected and that the marriage between capitalism and democracy was the best way of promoting development. 'Capitalism' was understood in terms of the market, freed from the regulatory constraints of the welfare-developmental state, and the private sector (especially the capitalist class), in command of the economy. Democracy, on the other hand, was understood as both constitutional government (free elections) and the strengthening of civil society, engaging it in both the development and the political process.

The issues involved in this relation between democracy and development are well reviewed by Chan (2001) from a liberal democratic or mainstream political science perspective. Petras and Veltmeyer (2001) and Veltmeyer (2007) review the same issues from a more critical prescriptive.

Bardhan 1993: 40-86; Chan 2001; Sen 1999b: Chap. 6;
Petras & Veltmeyer 2001; Veltmeyer 2007a: Chap. 4.

3. When and what states are 'developmental'?

The notion of a 'development state' relates primarily to the responsibilities assumed by the state in the South in the post World War II context of a weak or absent market and a social class available and disposed to assume the 'development function.' This role included (1) ownership in the form of public or state enterprises, or nationalization of firms in strategic sectors; (2) provision of economic and social infrastructure for production; (3) productive investment, particularly in industry; (4) protection of domestic firms and producers from the forces of the global market; (5) regulation of product, capital and labour markets; and (6) a secondary distribution of market-generated incomes, via a progressive taxation policy, to finance the welfare and development functions (social and development programs).

Doner et al. 2005: 327–61; Evans 1992, 1995; Bardhan 2005: Chap. 1;
Kohli 2004; Woo-Cumings 1999.

4. Does a 'vibrant civil society' give rise to a responsive democratic polity?

One of the fundamental shifts in political development in the 1980s was the connection made between economic and political liberalization and a twofold democratization process—in the form of (1) reinstating the rule of law and democratic elections; and (2) democratizing the state—civil society relation: strengthening civil society in the form of enhanced political participation in decisionmaking and its capacity to ensure the transparency of public policy—'good governance.'

Chatterjee 2004: Chaps. 2–3. Fernandes 2006; Harriss 2007: 2716–24.

5. Spaces for change? Prospects for participatory governance?

The policy of administrative decentralization, widely adopted in the 1980s, was designed to bring about the engagement of civil society in the development process and in the responsibility for maintaining order. In theory this was designed to open up and expand spaces for popular participation in the formulation of public policy and the transparency of decisionmaking. The dynamics of theory and practice related to this idea are discussed in these readings from different angles and standpoints but generally from a critical perspective.

Fung & Wright 2003 (Chaps by Baiocchi, Heller & Isaac); Heller 2001: 131–63; Baiocchi 2005;
Veltmeyer 1997a; Weber 2002.

6. Government or governance: What makes it 'good'?

In political discourse related to 'development,' the 1980s saw a fundamental shift from 'government' to 'governance.' A part of this shift was the negative conception of government from the optics of the 'new political economy' (Kreuger, Bates), which saw the state much as Adam Smith saw it—predatory, given to rentierism and vulnerable to corruption. From this perspective, the notion of 'good governance' was introduced in the form of engaging civil society in the responsibility of designing the rules governing international and national relations, providing a regulatory framework for democratic participation in decisionmaking in diverse institutional contexts.

In *Good Government in the Tropics*, Judith Tendler questions widely prevailing views about why governments so often perform poorly and about what causes them to improve. Drawing on a

101

set of four cases involving public bureaucracies at work under the direction of an innovative state government in Brazil, Tendler reviews findings of significance to current debates about organization of the public-sector workplace, public service delivery, decentralization and the interaction between government and civil society. The case studies represent four different sectors, each traditionally spoken for by its distinct experts, literatures and public agencies: rural preventive health, small enterprise development, agricultural extension for small farmers and employment-generating public works construction and drought relief. Tendler also raises questions about the policy advice proffered by the international donor community. She shifts the debate away from mistrust of government toward understanding the circumstances in which public servants become truly committed to their work and public service can significantly improve.

Moore 2001; Tendler 1997: Introduction, Chap. 6; World Bank 1994.

Module 20

War and Development

Michael Clow
St. Thomas University, Canada

Wars are armed struggles in which organized groups use violence for political purposes. Political violence between nation-states is termed *international war*; warfare between organized political groups within one state is *civil war*. International wars tend to be studied by political scientists, while sociologists are preoccupied with civil wars between organized movements representing class, ethnic or tribal groups seeking state power.

In practice many wars straddle these two categories. Some civil wars concern the seizure of state power (to determine which domestic political group will rule the country); others are secessionist wars, seeking to splinter the existing state into several smaller states. *Wars of national liberation* were fought within the colonial territories of international empires between armed supporters of national independence movements on one side and imperial armed forces and colonial supporters of the empire on the other. Nation-states have also been known to spark or support civil wars as a means of gaining influence over other states (for example, the U.S.-backed Contras waged war against the revolutionary government of the Sandinistas in Nicaragua in the 1980s, seeking thereby to restore the power of the capitalist class in Nicaragua and return the country to its pre-revolutionary place in the American empire). International wars can also unintentionally trigger civil wars—for example, the religious and ethnic fighting in Iraq following the U.S. invasion and the disintegration of Somalia into warring factions in the wake of the Ethiopia-Somalia wars.

This module considers theoretical and empirical studies that relate war to development, i.e., that examine the dynamics of this relation. These studies have been categorized into major themes, each problematizing the war-development relation, each raising questions to be studied critically.

1. War as a social institution

Underlying the varying purposes and boundaries of specific wars in all their complexity is the *institution of war and warfare*. Warfare is not conducted because it is natural. War is the deliberate activation of an established, highly destructive social practice by the leadership of nations or 'political' organizations in relations of conflict. Warfare is so familiar that we fail to see it as an invention, a very particular way to conduct politics. It has been used to settle disputes of every kind over the course of history, but it is a destructive and unpredictable means to do so.

Violence—the use of force and the threat of force—plays an important role in many human affairs. Violence can be deployed at many levels of organization, between individuals, small groups or whole societies. Force or the threat of force in this context is normally about political power: the ability to dictate to others the terms and conditions of the relationship between them. There is no 'argument' stronger than violence, which is why agreements coerced from others are not legally binding in civil law. Political violence is a means to persuade others to bend to your will or a sanction for refusing to do so (Caringella-MacDonald & Humphries 1991). Once violence comes into play, force must be met if not settled with force to dispute those willing to resort to violence. Often there is a gross imbalance in the access of different groups or countries to the instruments of armed force. The state, for example, normally has a monopoly on the authoritative use of force to settle disputes in relations of conflict.

A major aim of the state is to set the rules by which disputes between political factions, classes, ethnic communities and regions will be settled. An important aspect of this effort is the attempt of the state to maintain a monopoly over the use of political violence to settle internal disputes, via established political and judicial processes of the regime. Civil wars represent a breakdown of this state structure and the use of violence to achieve political goals outside of established national political institutions.

Internationally, the world is in anarchy. There is no form of world governance to effectively settle disputes among nations. In the absence of the constraint of an effective global police with a monopoly over political violence, state officials are free to use force—go to war—and take their chances with their military strength in disputes with other states. In the anarchy of 'international' affairs, sovereign states can resolve their disputes with other nations only through negotiation (diplomacy) or violence (war). International wars are not a breakdown of the anarchic social order of the world; they are the utilization of one of the fundamental institutions available to 'structure' international relations.

As Dyer points out in *Future Tense*, a major goal in the formation of the U.N. after World War II was to curb the right of nations to engage freely in warfare as a means of imposing their will or for the ruling classes to act out any dreams they might have of world domination. A major concern of the U.N. as a system has been to discourage the attempt of any one nation to seek hegemony over the whole system via the unilateral projection of armed force. Not surprisingly this concern has been focused on the possibility of warfare between the major, nuclear-armed powers. Another concern has been to create a rough level playing field in the international arena of conflicting economic and political interests. The Security Council might be seen as an institutional response to this concern. Another response was the construction of diverse institutions, such as UNCTAD and the UNDP, to promote a more equitable sharing of the world's productive and financial resources. This reflects the belief that the global development divide not only means that over a billion people are unable to meet even their basic needs, but this 'inequality predicament' is major source of existing and potential violent conflict among groups and nations. Development, in other words, is a matter of security as much as poverty alleviation, protection of the environment and sustainable livelihoods, social welfare and the freedom of individuals to choose and lead meaningful lives.

Dyer 2004.

2. War and development

It is easy enough to pose the question: 'What is the relationship of war and development?' But it is not so easy to answer it. The notion of 'development' is freighted with political judgments and commitments that cannot be avoided. Above all, 'development' as a concept can be traced to the need to explain Europe's explosive economic growth in the modern era and the successes and failures of repeating that historically unprecedented process elsewhere in the world.

Mainstream liberal development theory is supportive of the existing social, political and economic arrangements. In this tradition, 'development' means economic growth in 'free market' economies. The outcome of development is 'progress'—a continuing expansion of production, growing abundance of material goods of increasing variety and technological innovation. Economic progress, it is argued, is accompanied by the emergence of liberal democratic political institutions, urbanization and secularization in an essentially harmonious society. In this vision, war and political violence are interlopers in the process of development. War does not flow out of the development process; warfare impedes the development process.

In contrast, Marxists understand development as a process growing out of class and international struggles—class war and wars of national liberation. Civil wars and repressions, conquests, occupations and incorporation into the capitalist system, wars of national liberation and struggles between the capitalists of different imperial nations have all provided the circumstances for resort to war. Put another other way, warfare has been a not infrequent means by which the political struggles of capitalist development have been fought out. But there is no clear, singular and universal relationship between warfare and economic development. Wars and warfare have played a complex and historically contingent role in the political struggles of the global and national development process.

The complexity of the relation of war and development can be thought of in at least three ways: (1) the use of warfare in struggles over the course of development; (2) the effects of development on the use of warfare; and (3) the unintended effects on development of warfare. The role of warfare in shaping the world economic system can be illustrated along these lines with a few examples. We begin with the use of warfare to impose particular lines of development.

The most obvious way in which warfare has been used to set the direction of development is that the world economy we see today began in about 1500 with the European conquest of the rest of the world's peoples and their forcible inclusion as colonial economies with European empires. In Europe itself, a proletariat was produced by forcible expulsions of agriculturalists from the land. The repression of workers' resistance to the conditions of the new factory system was integral to the emergence of expansive capitalist industry.

These uses of large-scale political violence continue. The U.S. invaded, subverted and sponsored military coups in so many countries of the South to secure the interests of capital that it became the basis of its foreign relations. Repressions and civil wars in the South are often directly connected with the struggle to expropriate land and resources (for example, oil in Nigeria and farmland in Central America in the 1970s). By contrast, the wars of liberation that helped speed decolonization and resist imperialism were attempts to create a space for autonomous development. Revolutionary civil wars, like that in Cuba under Fidel Castro or the Sandinistas in Nicaragua, sometimes have opened new possibilities for more egalitarian forms of economic and social development.

Wars have also been used to decide the outcome of European rivalries in the scramble for what we would now call 'development.' Military conflict between European powers clearly connected with the emergence of capitalism begins with the piracy and privateering, by which Britain and France first get in on the wealth plundered by the Spanish in the New World. Wars helped 'settle' the competition for territory, resources, labour and markets of the world between the European mercantilist empires of the sixteenth to eighteenth centuries.

The processes of war and other political violence engendered by the international struggle to accumulate capital have continued. Both world wars in the twentieth century grew out of the competitive struggle of national monopoly capitalists for growth, cheap colonial resources and captive markets. They so weakened European society that the U.S. became the global capitalist superpower. The defeat of European countries and the absorption of much of their Asian colonies by the Japanese shattered the myth of European superiority. This weakening of European states emboldened nationalists in their colonies to press successfully for the formal decolonization of the Third World, ushering in the U.S. empire and its neocolonialism.

There is no clear, singular and universal relationship between warfare and economic development, but there has indeed been a close and complex relationship between the two. In the following sections we examine several of these connections in greater depth.

Caringella-MacDonald & Humphries 1991; Dyer 2004; Pearce 1981.

3. Conflict: Midwife of social change or a development trap?

In Marxist social theory, class conflict is generally seen as an agency for change, a means of resolving the contradictions of development processes in class divided societies. In development theory, however, conflict normally is not conceptualized as a development issue; nor, until recently, has it been theorized. Diverse forms of conflict, such as resource war, class war, imperialist war, cultural war and the war on terror, are seen as a political rather than a development issue, and left for specialists in the study of international relations or social conflict. Even so, conflict and associated conditions have entered the consciousness of some development theorists and many practitioners, who frequently have to come to terms with the effect of relations of conflict on their interventions. Links between development and conflict stress the difficulties of development aid (and humanitarian relief) provision under conditions of violent conflict. Peacebuilding interventions in or after situations of violent conflict address the same concerns as development interventions. Development is at the core of post-conflict interventions, where the economic and social infrastructure has been seriously damaged if not destroyed. The way forward, according to Collier (2004), is to break out of the 'conflict trap.'

A part of the problem is the lack of any systematic analysis of the structural and political sources of the conflict—and of the almost certain contributing factor of the state itself, too often responsive to pressures from the international community to implement policies that exacerbate rather than alleviate the problems that make development impossible. This is evidenced by the UNDP's 2003 *Human Development Report*, which reflects a deep concern with armed, violent and military conflicts such as inter-state and civil war, but does not consider that such conflicts can preclude the achievement of development goals. This has begun to change, however, as indicated by the World Bank's *Comprehensive Development Framework and Conflict-Affected Countries* (Von Meijenfeldt 2001), which examines the possibility of development under conditions of unresolved conflict. In any case, as the UNDP noted (1996: 37) the connection between conflict and human development runs both ways... in terms of creating a disabling environment and conditions for 'capacity and income poverty.' Another study that weighs in on this issue is John Overton's *Development in Chaos* (2000).

Collier 2004: 1125–45; Overton 2000; Andersen 2000; Collier 2003; Von Meijenfeldt 2001.

4. Globalization and war: Imperialism and wars for national liberation and social justice

First came the foreign bankers eager to lend at extortionate rates; then the financial controllers to see that the interest was paid; then the thousands of foreign advisors taking their cut. Finally, when the country was bankrupt and helpless, it was time for the foreign troops to 'rescue' the ruler from his 'rebellious' people. One last gulp and the country had gone. (Pakenham 1992: 126)

Globalization & War texts & analysis <www.nadir.org/nadir/initiativ/agp/free/9-11/indexauthorc.html> provides access to a broad range of studies that place the war-globalization relation in a critical theoretical perspective. The website is an excellent source of study for critical review.

As the proliferation of conflicts in Africa, Asia and the Middle East and the zest of the U.S. for military intervention throughout the 1980s and 1990s demonstrate,[1] war is on the global agenda. Silvia Federici (2002) argues that this is because the new phase of capitalist expansionism requires 'the destruction of any economic activity not subordinated to the logic of accumulation, which is necessarily a violent process.' Corporate capital, she adds, 'cannot extend its reach over the planet's resources—from the seas to the forests to people's labour, to our very genetic pools—without generating an intense resistance worldwide.' Moreover, 'it is in the nature of the present capitalist crisis that... that development planning in the Third World give way to war.'[2]

That the connection between globalization (integration in the global economy) and war is not generally made is because 'globalization today, while in essence continuing the late nineteenth-century colonial project, presents itself primarily as an economic [development] program' (Federici 2002). 'Its first and most visible weapons,' Federici notes, 'are structural adjustment programs, trade liberalization, privatization, and intellectual property rights.' These policies, she adds, 'are responsible for an immense transfer of wealth from the Third World to the metropoles, but they do not require territorial conquest, and thus are assumed to work by purely peaceful means.'[3]

Military interventions in the era of neoliberal globalization are also taking new forms, often appearing under the guise of benevolent initiatives, such as 'food aid' and 'humanitarian relief,' or, in Latin America, the 'war against drugs.' A further reason why the marriage between war and globalization—the form that imperialism takes today—is not more evident is that most of the new 'globalization wars' have been fought on the African continent, whose current history is systematically distorted by the media, which blame every crisis in it on the Africans' alleged 'backwardness,' 'tribalism and incapacity to achieve democratic institutions.

Federici 1992, 2002; Globalization & War <www.agp.org/> <www.all4all.org>;
Johnson 2001; Le Billon 2001: 561–84.

5. War and peace: gender, development and social dimensions

Most scholars in this area assume that conflict in the form of civil, inter-ethnic or class war inhibits development—that development requires the resolution of conflict (i.e., 'peace') as a precondition of post-conflict reconstruction and the resumption of development aid. As Bereket Selassie (2001) notes, 'It is customary to consider peace as the normal, and war as the abnormal, condition, because most societies experience war as the aberrant event, disturbing normalcy in human relations. And although there have been instances in history in which war acted as the spur to technical innovation, for the most part, peace has been an essential precondition for human progress.' The reasons for this, she notes, include the fact that 'all people who act, as agents of human progress need peace to concentrate on their work' and 'conflict situations draw resources away from development.'

Moe Espen (2006) argues that war can sometimes actually create conditions for development—that it 'will aid the process of structural change, and lead to an accelerated rate of growth once the war is over.' The conditions in question are summarized under the heading of 'political consensus and social cohesion.' Under such conditions, Espen argues, 'the war becomes a force for change not only in the long-term international system, but the economic system as well.' Espen constructs this argument in terms of a theoretical framework that combines ideas from Mancur Olson and Joseph Schumpeter, allowing him to predict that the only wars where such an outcome should be expected are those that have occurred in conjunction with economic structural change.

While the link between conflict and development is a relatively new field, in recent years a number of international organizations and government agencies have begun to argue the importance of both studying it further and prioritizing it in order to improve development outcomes among the poorest of the poor, usually the most vulnerable. Preventing and ending conflicts, it is argued, will do more to create a climate for poverty reduction than any amount of costly aid programs.

Bessell 2001; Byrne 1996; Espen 2006; Kumar 2000; Manchanda 2001;
Moser 2001; Tsjeard, Frerks & Bannon 2005; UNDP 2003a.

6. The development dynamics of national liberation and class war

The evolution of capitalism is based not so much on the working of what for the sake of analysis have been treated as 'laws of capitalist development' as on class struggle, a struggle based on the relation of conflict between two basic classes—the bourgeoisie or the capitalist class and the proletariat or the working class. In some contexts, as in the period post-1968, this struggle assumes the scope and shape of a war—a class war, in effect. Jeffrey Faux (2005)[4] has written about this war as it is unfolding inside the U.S. at the centre of the world capitalist system, home to the key agencies of the 'new rulers of the world,' including the state apparatus of the hegemon. As for the diverse forms that this class war is taking in the 'new world order' of globalization, students of CDS can do no better than to turn to the archives 'War & Peace,' which provides access to a broad range of studies on globalization and class wars in the era of neoliberal globalization.

Broad 2008; Collier 2003; War & Globalization <www.nadir.org/nadir/initiativ/agp/free/9-11/ indexauthor.html> or <http://www.nadir.org/nadir/initiativ/agp/en/index.html>.

Notes

1   There were seventy-five countries experiencing some form of war in 1999; thirty-three of them are to be found in Africa's forty-three continental nations. This is the 'Fourth World War' against the world's poor that Subcomandante Marcos often writes about (Federici's note).

2   For a description of this new phase of capitalism that emphasizes the disappearance of interclass mediations, see Federici (2002), who notes that the phrase 'new enclosures' is used to indicate that 'the thrust of contemporary capitalism is to annihilate any guarantees of subsistence that were recognized by socialist, postcolonial or Keynesian states in the 1950s and 1960s.' This process, she adds, 'must be violent in order to succeed.'

3   The immense existing literature on structural adjustment, globalization and neoliberalism has amply described this transfer of wealth. See: Brecher & Costello 1994; and Federici 1992.

4   Founder of the Economic Policy Institute, Faux (2005) critiques both Democrats and Republicans for protecting MNCs 'while abandoning the rest of us to an unregulated, and therefore brutal and merciless, global market.' He describes how free trade and globalization have encouraged businesses to become nationless enterprises detached from the economic well-being of any single country to the detriment of all but transnational elites.

Section 7

The Poverty Problematic

Since the discovery by the World Bank under Robert McNamara's presidency in 1968 that two out of every five of the world's population were unable to meet their basic needs, development has been primarily a matter of poverty reduction/alleviation. And it has been the World Bank that has led the war on poverty ever since, which raises a number of questions as to how it is possible that after thirty-five years, having dedicated so many human and financial resources in the prosecution of this war, so little has been achieved. By the World Bank's very conservative poverty line measure ($2 a day or $1 for indigence) the percentage of the world population suffering from conditions of material deprivation and poverty is virtually unchanged, which of course means many more millions—up to three billion (1.4 billion in a state of extreme poverty). To all intents and purposes, the poverty problematic is as entrenched in the economic and social structures of society and critical in its human dimensions today as it ever was.

As for the complex—albeit in some ways rather simple—issues involved in understanding poverty at the level of theory and redressing it in practice, Modules 21–23 review and dissect them from a critical development perspective. A key issue vis-à-vis both theory and practice is the level (and diverse forms) of social inequality in the distribution of wealth and income. The 'inequality predicament,' as the U.N. in its 2005 study phrases it, is manifest at different levels—international and national—but its most dramatic appearance is in the North-South development gap, in which the inequities in wealth and poverty reach extraordinary extremes. From the perspective of both neoclassical economic theory and structural-functional sociological theory, the condition of social inequality is a device used by 'society' (or the market) to reward effort, an incentive to motivate the most resourceful and talented individuals to undertake the effort needed to expand production and generate wealth. From this perspective social equality is neither liberating nor progressive, just an utopian ideal; and social inequalities in the distribution of wealth and income are indispensable to the proper functioning of society's economic institutions. From a critical development perspective, however, this view is far from scientific; it is rather an ideology, a self-serving belief reassigned to obfuscate the socioeconomic interests at play and justify the appropriation by the powerful few of the wealth generated cooperatively by the many—the direct producers and the working classes.

The three modules in this area explore the most critical dimensions of the poverty problematic. Module 21 brings into focus the World Bank as an ideological apparatus, responsible for constructing a theoretical and policy discourse for cultural hegemony—selling the idea of globalization as inevitable and desirable, the only road to 'general prosperity,' and as such a means of justifying both the unpalatable program of 'structural' (neoliberal) reforms, presenting them as 'pro-growth,' and the gross inequalities between the rich and the poor brought about by these 'reforms.' Module 22 elaborates on the 'inequality predicament': whether to push for and implement policies that provide material incentives for productive investment (promoting thereby the 'entrepreneurial spirit') but that are known to generate and exacerbate existing social inequalities. Module 23 explores the policy dynamics of the development project and the war on poverty.

Module 21

The World Bank

Development, Poverty, Hegemony

David Moore
University of KwaZulu-Natal, South Africa

[We must] take into account the fact that international relations intertwine with those internal relations of nation-states, creating new, unique and historically concrete combinations. A particular ideology, for instance, born in a highly developed country, is disseminated in less developed countries, impinging upon the local interplay of combinations. (Gramsci 1971: 182)

The book edited by David Moore (2007b) on the World Bank deconstructs the dominant ideology of neoliberal globalization and provides a Gramscian constructivist interpretation of how this ideology was manufactured and used to establish global hegemony by 'the power that is' (the 'new rulers of the world,' to borrow a phrase from John Pilger). The aim of the diverse studies collected in this volume is to deconstruct the dominant ideology so as to help dismantle the project of hegemony—to level the resulting understanding against 'the power that is' in the hopes that the 'power that is coming' will be 'more responsive to its subjects' (16). The working of this ideology is so critical and the role of the World Bank's organic intellectuals in its construction—in manufacturing, disseminating and imposing this ideology in the form of ideas about capitalist development and globalization—is so central as to warrant an entire course module on the World Bank.

1. The World Bank and the 'Gramsci effect': Construction of an ideology and hegemonic discourse

In Chapter 1, Moore (2007) deconstructs the hegemonic discourse of the World Bank with reference to a framework established by Antonio Gramsci. In Chapter 13 he elaborates on the constructivist strategies pursued by the Bank to attain 'the Gramsci effect' of its ideological discourse. Chapter 7 reconstructs the elements of the neoliberal 'project' behind this discourse.

At the centre of this Gramscian framework is the concept of 'hegemony,' used by Gramsci as a means of understanding both the successes and the failures of socialism on a global scale, and of elaborating a feasible program for the realization of a socialist vision within the actually existing conditions that prevailed in the world at the time. Among these conditions were the rise and triumph of fascism and the disarray on the left that had ensued as a result of that triumph. Also pertinent, both theoretically and practically, were such terms as 'organic intellectual' and 'historical bloc,' which acquired radically new and original implications in his writings and inspired generations of Marxist scholars in their analysis of the dynamic forces of resistance to capitalist development in its various forms and stages, and the struggle over ideological hegemony (as the leader of the 'free world'—the 'forces of freedom') and cultural dominion (the superiority of the 'American way of life') as well as the dynamics of ideological power analyzed by Moore.[1]

Moore 2007a: 27–62; Moore 2007b: 387–412, Module 24.

2. Constructing the economic space: Homo economicus, the market and the state

Williams' and Fine's chapters establish the underpinnings of development discourse in the liberal notion of *homo economicus,* a theoretically defined 'individual' who rationally calculates the costs and benefits involved in each 'action' and decision in the pursuit of self-interest. This notion is the ideological core of the Bank's conception of development and its current strategy of empowering the poor to act for themselves, to mobilize the one asset that they have in abundance ('social capital'), converting them into active agents of their own development. Ben Fine establishes the use of this ideology as a means of depoliticizing the poor—turning them away from a confrontational politics of direct collective action. On the dynamics of this 'new development paradigm' see Module 24.

Williams 2007: 95–120; Fine 2007: 121–44.

3. The construction of the poor and the war on poverty

In the chapters by MacWilliam, Pithouse and Schech and vas Dev, the book turns a spotlight on the World Bank's self-proclaimed 'war on poverty,' showing it to be, if anything, more of a 'war on the poor' themselves. A key weapon in this war is the social construction of 'poverty,' creating thereby conditions that allow and lead the poor to see themselves as such and to justify outside intervention. This social construction of a 'development' discourse, deeply embedded in both development theory and practice, is 'deconstructed' by Wolfgang Sachs and his co-authors (1992) from a critical postdevelopment perspective.

MacWilliam 2007: 63–94; Pithouse 2007: 413–52; Schech & vas Dev 2007: 63–94.

4. Greenspeak: The power of knowledge, 'sustaindevelopment' and the 'agrarian question'

In these chapters Wanner and Bernstein explore and deconstruct the World Bank's discourse on 'sustainable development' (economic growth facilitated by scientific research, a technological fix and better resource management) and its conception of the available pathways out of rural poverty: labour, migration and farming (on this also see the World Bank's 2008 *World Development Report: Agriculture for Development*). In a nutshell, the solution is the capitalist development of agriculture: to accelerate an ongoing process of productive and social transformation, converting some of the peasantry into capitalist entrepreneurs, others into rural emigrants.

Wanner 2007; 145–70; Bernstein 2007: 343–68.

5. The World Bank on globalization, development and governance: A capitalist manifesto

David Moore deconstructs the Bank's ideological discourse on 'globalization' and 'good governance' as necessary conditions of 'development' in Africa. For an alternative formulation of this ideology, in the form of what might be termed a 'neoliberal manifesto,' see the World Bank's 1995 *World Development Report: Workers in an Integrating World*.

Moore 2007: 227–66; Harrison 2007: 369–86; World Bank 1995.

6. The art (and science) of paradigm maintenance, and the construction of a counter-hegemonic discourse

In the chapters by Wade, Berger and Beeson, and Bond, the book explores the art and science of paradigm maintenance in the face of an evident propensity of capitalism towards crisis, the Asian development model and the counter-hegemonic discourse constructed by proponents of a global civil society.

Wade 2007: 267–316; Berger & Beeson 2007: 317–42; Bond 2007: 479–506.

Module 22

The Inequality Predicament

Henry Veltmeyer
Universidad Autónoma de Zacatecas, Mexico; Saint Mary's University, Canada

The neoliberal counter-revolution in development thought and practice in the 1980s deepened the global income and wealth divide but, as shown in the U.N.'s 2005 report, the *Inequality Predicament*, it also deepened inequalities *within* countries in both the North and the South. Moreover this report shows that income inequality has grown comparably faster in countries that embraced the neoliberal doctrine than in countries that did not. In these countries, particularly in the U.S., analysts have documented the growing gap between the very rich and the very poor, with a rapidly shrinking middle class (Chang and Grabel 2001: 21).

The pattern of a growing income gap within countries and the connection between this pattern and the strategic turn towards neoliberalism also show up in other contexts. For example, data provided by the *World Income Inequality Database* shows that within-country income inequality decreased during the 1950–1970s in most developed, developing and centrally planned economies, but since the 1980s this decline levelled off, and within many countries income inequality has risen, in some cases dramatically so. Cornia and Kiiski (2001) discovered that in the countries that once constituted the socialist bloc, as the direct result of the dismantling of the state, income inequality from 1989 to 1996 rose by an average of 10 to 20 Gini points and the number of people living in poverty jumped from 14 million to 147 million.

The readings in this module explore the policy and political dynamics of these social inequalities—their connection to the process of capital accumulation under conditions of neoliberal globalization.

1. The sociology of development: Theoretical perspectives on social inequality

A sociological perspective on social change is based on the social organization of individuals in society, i.e., the social relationship of individuals to others who belong to the same social groups or who occupy different class positions in the organization of production. Within capitalist societies, the social structure revolves around the capital-labour relation, which defines two basic social classes: the owners of the means of social production (the capitalist class) and those who are dispossessed from their means of production except for their labour power, which they are therefore compelled to sell in exchange for a living wage. Of course there are also several classes and groups of individuals that are not positioned within the structure of this social relation. However, the assumption is that the labour-capital relation is the dominant feature of the social structure in capitalist societies and that it explains more than any other factor what goes on in these societies.

A central concern of sociological analysis is with the relations and conditions of social inequality, particularly in regard to the distribution of wealth and income, the output of collective or cooperative economic activity. According to Nancy Birdsall, former chief economist at the World Bank and now executive vice president of the Inter-American Development Bank, the most critical factor in the development process and the poverty problematic is the unequal distribution and unequal access to society's productive assets such as land and education, which creates a 'vicious circle' in which 'high initial asset inequality inhibits asset accumulation which traps the poor in poverty and, by limiting aggregate growth, reduces society's capacity to help the poor [and for the poor to help themselves, she might have added]' (Birdsall 1997).

Chossudovsky 1997; Munck 2005; Rapley 2004.

2. The inequality predicament: The distribution of wealth and income

Reflecting a long series of as yet unsettled debates among economists on the relationship between social inequalities and development, Nancy Birdsall (1997) argues that 'income distribution per se is not the fundamental issue.' The critical issue, she argues, is 'something more fundamental: the distribution of assets and opportunities, especially as it affects the poor.' To argue this point she raises the question as to 'why growth been consistently higher and poverty reduction so much greater in East Asia compared to Latin America.' Her explanation: 'destructive inequality' in the case of Latin America and in cases of rapid growth and the so-called 'Asian miracle,' it is a matter of 'growth from below; i.e., growth fueled by increasing productivity of the poor... where the distribution of opportunities [i]s relatively equal.' She elaborates: 'With East Asia's distribution of assets—land and education—in 1960, Latin America [today] would have half the number of people living in poverty [that it has].' She also notes that 'in the context of Latin America, the multilateral development banks have long decried populist transfers ... [but] there is an alternative: to focus on programs that put productive assets in the hands of the poor.' This means 'focusing not only on expanding education but on its distribution ....' It means 'seeking other mechanisms beyond education to increase the access of the poor to productive assets: land reform, reform of legal systems, credit, and fair competition.' All of these, she adds can create opportunities in previously unequal societies, eliminating the hidden privileges in asset markets historically enjoyed by the rich' and that, she implies, are indirectly if not directly responsible for the high level and incidence of poverty and the relative absence or low level of development.

The poverty problematic, as Birdsall understands it, concerns and is a matter of social inequalities in access to society's productive resources and in the distribution of the social product (i.e., wealth and income)—what the U.N. in a 2005 study terms the 'inequality predicament.' This predicament, as the U.N. constructs it, can be identified (and needs to be analyzed) at different levels—within and among countries, and along a North-South global divide, the central focus of CDS.

In terms of this global divide, there are a number of studies in the mainstream of development thought and a growing number of international conference reports that point towards a trend toward income convergence and a reduction in the global divide in wealth and income and the associated development gap. On the other hand, when China and India are not factored into the analysis, available data show a rise in worldwide income inequality—that the income gap between the richest and poorest countries has widened over the course of the neoliberal era of globalizing capital and neoimperialism.

The data in these studies (see Petras and Veltmeyer 2007b) reveal a trend towards increasing international disparities in income distribution and a connection between this trend and the turn towards neoliberal policies. In the *Atlas of Social Exclusion* (Pochman et al. 2004) constructed by Pochman and colleagues over the past two decades, twenty-eight countries improved their standing on an index of social inequalities and exclusion; these countries, all found in the developed centre of the global economy, represent 14 percent of world population but account for 52 percent of world annual income (and, of course, a much larger percentage of wealth, most of which is neither earned nor measured in available statistics). Sixty countries, representing 36 percent of world population, account for only 11 percent of world income.

Milanovic 2004; Birdsall 1997; Bulmer-Thomas 1986; Collins, Hartman & Sklar 1999.

3. Inequality and the North-South divide: Income distribution among nations

At issue in this theme is a process of growing disparities in the international distribution of productive resources and incomes—inequalities among and within regions and countries in the world capitalist system. Although the key issue (whether global incomes are diverging or converging in the globalization context of neoliberal policies over the past two decades) is heavily debated (see Jomo 2007: xvii–xxv, 1–98), the evidence is clear enough: neoliberal policies of structural adjustment to the requirements of the new world order have brought about a dramatic increase in these and other forms of social inequality, and with this 'development' a growing global divide in wealth and new forms of poverty, deprivation and social exclusion. In 2005, three major publications focused on issues of global, inter-regional, North-South and intra-country inequalities in the distribution of income. In mid-year the U.N. Secretariat issued its 2005 report on the *World Social Situation: The Inequality Predicament* (UNESCO 2005), to critical acclaim. Not long thereafter, the UNDP considered the same issues in its annual *2005*

Human Development Report, just before the September summit to consider progress towards achieving the millennium development goals. And in quick succession the World Bank issued what is considered by some as its best ever *World Development Report* (World Bank 2006) on *Equity and Development.* The various contributors to K.S. Jomo's 2007 edited publication on the same issues provide a range of incredibly important critical studies into the political economic and policy dynamics of global income distribution. From a CDS perspective, they constitute the most essential readings on issues of critical importance to an understanding of the dynamics of global development and underdevelopment. They warrant very careful study.

Jomo, with Baudot 2007: Chaps. 1–5, 10–15; Berry & Serioux 2004;
Petras & Veltmeyer 2007b: Chap. 4.

4. Social dimensions of inequality: Class, gender and race matters

Social inequalities in the distribution of wealth and income take diverse forms and are correlated with membership in different social groups and different social characteristics, particularly those based on relations of class, gender and race. The readings in this theme review the facts surrounding these social distributions (an inequality of social conditions related to wealth, income and power) and explore the social dynamics involved.

Ahooja-Patel 2007; Portes & Hoffman 2003.

5. Bridging the divide: From social exclusion to development with equity

A central issue in a longstanding debate among development economists is whether a general improvement in the human condition of people in the Global South is advanced more effectively by market-led 'pro-growth' policies that leave everyone free to pursue their self-interest or whether governments should intervene in the allocation of productive resources and a redistribution of income in the interest of equity. The readings on this theme explore the theoretical and political permutations of this problematic: growth and distribution—whether it constitutes a trade off (for example, does a concern for equity and income redistribution inhibit economic growth?) or whether the optimum results are achieved by a 'growth with equity' approach? The readings also serve as a means of critical examination of recent debates on this issue as well as the thinking and practice associated with economic development models constructed over the years by organizations such as ECLAC, the World Bank, the UNDP and UNICEF.

Deininger & Squire 1998: 259–87; Ferreira, & Walton 2005: 34–37.

6. The poverty of development: Reports of a failure

For over three decades, the World Bank has led a coalition of powerful international development organizations in the war against poverty in the less-developed countries (LDCs). And yet the problem of poverty in the LDCs remains as entrenched as ever, arguably even more so now than in the past if we disaggregate the Bank's figures on growth and inspect more closely the effects of Bank-led programs on the poorest sectors of LDC populations. The reality of poverty in fact has defeated all the efforts that the Bank and this 'world community' of concerned organizations, governments and individuals—backed up by truly enormous financial and human resources—have dedicated to the progressive eradication of what is the central problem of developing societies. Even sympathetic observers have been caught reflecting ruefully that the decades-long campaign has been a measurable failure. The readings in this theme explore the dynamics of this failure.

O'Malley & Veltmeyer 2006; Petras & Veltmeyer 2007a: 180–209; Burkett 1990: 20–31.

Module 23

The Policy Dynamics of the War on Poverty
John Harriss
Simon Fraser University, Canada

The model of knowledge underlying most poverty research aims to build scientific knowledge of the nature and causes of poverty and implicitly or explicitly asserts that sound policy should be based on such scientific knowledge. This model presupposes that it is possible to come up with a definitive answer to a question such as whether India's economic reforms have been instrumental in reducing poverty. It is a model of knowledge that leads to dismissal of (or offering of the faintest of praise towards) the value of context sensitive case study research, because such research does not give rise to generalization.

This module follows the assertion by Bent Flyvberg (2001—although Flyvberg is not the only scholar to have developed this argument) that the attempt to emulate the natural sciences in the study of society is doomed to disappointment. The lack of accumulation of knowledge in the social sciences is one marker of this. Specifically in regard to poverty knowledge, normal science encourages a focus on measurement and has led to defining poverty in terms of the characteristics of individuals or the households in which they live. Even recent attempts at studying 'poverty dynamics' generally retain a focus on the characteristics of individuals and households and do not concern themselves with the structural processes that give rise to the factors that are identified as proximate causes of (or associations with) movements in and out of poverty.

Among several examples of the limitations of normal science in regard to poverty, we may take the case of poverty measurement in Vietnam. The successive household living standards surveys conducted for that country bolster the story that poverty has been significantly reduced in the context of Vietnam's integration into the global economy. Pincus and Sender do not dispute that there have been improvements but do point out that the surveys systematically exclude large numbers of migrant workers, because the sampling frames are based on lists of registered households and many migrants are not registered. A pilot survey revealed large numbers of poor migrant workers even in a part of the country that is supposed not to hold many poor people at all. Given that it is well known in Vietnam that migrants are liable to be missed from the survey, Pincus and Sender argue that there is intent in the survey design. Further, 'normal science' poverty research in Vietnam associates poverty with geography, household size, ethnicity and education and gives rise to recommendations about the encouragement of household-based private enterprise, improved targeting of basic services and giving voice to members of ethnic minorities. It is remarkable, especially in the context of a country that is experiencing rapid industrialization and urbanization, that no attention is given at all to the finding of much research that the most effective route out of poverty is secure wage employment—and that there is not more research going on into labour market dynamics.

Poverty profiles can probably be built up more economically and effectively by means other than the preferred instrument of household livelihood surveys. Numerous studies highlight the significance of the following factors in explaining the incidence of poverty and movements in and out of it: household characteristics (especially dependency ratios and female headship); holdings of assets of different kinds, including education; the nature of occupations (regular waged employment amongst household members whether resident or working outside is often found to be crucial in movements out of poverty, partly because it helps to provide insurance against conjunctural factors such as, notably, episodes of ill-health); and sometimes ethnicity and/or geography (that amongst other significant factors influence access to public goods). How many more studies are needed to describe the proximate factors influencing the economic well-being of individuals and households? Such research has been encouraged by development agencies and by the research institutions dependent upon them or upon a small number of foundations because of the belief in the possibility of deriving policy from such supposedly value 'neutral' scientific knowledge. The effect, even if not necessarily the intention, has been to depoliticize the problem of poverty and to discourage attempts to understand processes of political economy, which are the processes of accumulation under capitalism, which continually create poverty as well as wealth. An earlier body of research on agrarian political economy not only describes in detail the portfolios of activities through which households in different social classes reproduce themselves but also explains the relationships of these different groups of households and the political economy underpinning them. But research of this kind has not been encouraged, presumably because it is not seen as being the sort of value-neutral science that is required for sound policy formulation.

This module shows that the effects of mainstream poverty analysis, translated into policy, are to set up approaches that make for the management of poverty and the disciplining of the poor (Flyvberg 2001).

Little 2003: 1–32; Hulme 2006.

1. Conceptualizing poverty

The standard economists' conception of poverty in terms of deprivation is in practice concerned with those aspects of deprivation that are most readily measured—flows of income and consumption. It is important to have an understanding of these measures and of how they are constructed in order to read the mainstream literature about poverty critically. At the same time it is important to consider other understandings and dimensions of poverty and ways of studying them. This also means considering problems in the methodology of social research and the relationships of quantitative and qualitative work.

Chambers 1988; Harriss 2007; Reddy & Pogge 2002; Saith 2005: 4601–10.

2. Trends in poverty and inequality

It has been widely claimed that both inequality and poverty are being reduced in the context of and as a result of the economic processes and trends associated with globalization. Here we examine both the logic and the evidence drawn on to support these claims and compare them with the findings of ethnographic research on the impacts of economic liberalism and of globalization. We further consider why the significance of inequality should not be dismissed, as it often is, when it is claimed that 'the living standards of the poor are getting better.'

Breman 2001: 4804–21; Cornia 2003; Thompson 2004; Chronic Poverty Research Centre 2004; Deaton & Kozel 2005; Ravallion 2003: 739–53; Thorbecke & Nissanke 2006.

3. Poverty dynamics: Why some people escape and others do not

A great deal of research is concerned with the determinants of poverty and with how and why people become poor(er) or alternatively 'climb out of poverty.' Here we compare some of the research, focused on individuals and households, with the findings of gendered agrarian political economy that illuminate the structural conditions that produce and reproduce poverty.

Harriss 2006 [1980]: 33–64; Whitehead 1981.

4. The dynamics of poverty: Critical perspectives

In the early twentieth century 'poverty knowledge' in the U.S. linked poverty with processes of the development of capitalism and with the ways in which labour markets functioned. Through the century, however, knowledge about poverty, often funded by major private research foundations, became increasingly technically sophisticated and, in the process, increasingly depoliticized. Associated with particular characteristics of individuals, poverty came increasingly to be seen as the result of choices made by those individuals. Here we re-state the case for a structural view of poverty and for understanding poverty in the context of capitalism, of gender relations and labour markets, and of power more generally.

Harriss 2007; O'Connor 2001.

5. Poverty, politics and policy

In what circumstances has the reduction of poverty sometimes been achieved? What are the relationships between politics, economic growth and the reduction of poverty? A summit in Beijing on the fight against poverty and on progress made in achieving the millennium development goals (MDGS) vis-à-vis poverty (IFPRI 2007), reported considerable progress in reducing the global poverty rate. Most of this improvement, it would seem, can be explained by the sustained rates of rapid economic growth in China, raising once again a longstanding policy debate on growth (growth first) versus distribution (redistributive growth/growth with equity).

More generally it is evident that 'pro-growth' at the level of policy does not necessarily mean 'pro-poor.' The poor in many cases—in Latin America, for example but also in South Asia and Africa—have not benefited at all from most 'pro-growth policies' (code for neoliberalism). What has been learnt over the last decade is that specific policy measures are needed to ensure that 'pro-growth' translates into 'pro-poor' (Klasen 2003). This lesson has resulted in several policy shifts as well as a the elaboration of a new comprehensive development framework (CDF) and within it a new policy tool—the Poverty Reduction Strategy Paper (PRSP)—introduced by the president of the World Bank at the G8 Summit in 1999.

It is recommended of students of CDS undertake a critical assessment of this policy tool and its use as an aid conditionality—in addition to policies of stabilization and structural adjustment and a good governance regime. The literature on this issue is voluminous but see Lopez (2004) and Veltmeyer (2007). The central concern in these readings is (1) to interrogate the World Bank's CDF and PRSP and (2) to evaluate the success of poverty reduction strategies a decade into their existence.

The return of poverty reduction as the guiding principle of all World Bank operations raises a number of interrelated questions: (1) To what extent do poverty reduction strategies represent a rupture with the Washington-Consensus based neoliberal paradigm? (2) Does the post-Washington Consensus (PWC) simply ideologically legitimate neoliberalism or are there substantial differences in policy content between SAPs and PRSPs? (3) What explains the move away from poverty alleviation towards poverty reduction? (4) What have been the positive (or negative) impacts of PRSPs on the poor (particularly in Africa, Asia and Latin America)? What are the gender implications of the Bank's policy transformations? And (5) how successful have PRSPs been in addressing poverty and exclusion?

Harriss, 2003; IFPRI 2007; Johnson & Start 2001; Klasen 2003.

6. Managing poverty and disciplining the poor:
Poverty in international development policy

The mission of the World Bank, in particular, and of other international development agencies, is described as being to bring about the reduction and ultimately the elimination of poverty. This objective is now enshrined in the millennium development goals, which were agreed upon in the General Assembly of the United Nations in 2000, and achieved through such instruments as the PRSPs that poor countries are pressured to produce by the Bank. The means seen as bringing about poverty reduction now include in particular micro-finance initiatives that would turn poor people into entrepreneurs. Here we examine international development policies toward poverty reduction and show how they may also be seen as concerned with the management of poverty in the interests of capital accumulation, through a disciplining of the poor.

Cammack 2002; Craig & Porter 2006; Collier 2007; Sachs 2005: Chaps. 3, 11–13.

Note

1. For another critical analysis of the World Bank's exercise of ideological power regarding the idea of globalization, see Veltmeyer (1997a).

Section 8

Towards a New Paradigm

Economists at the World Bank in a strategic reassessment of their development thinking regarding the 'challenges of global development' in the new millennium conceptualized the evolution of development thinking and practice in the following terms:

> Sixty years ago... [d]evelopment [wa]s synonymous with aggregate economic growth... result[ing] essentially from the accumulation of productive factors—mainly capital and labour—and from technical progress, determined largely exogenously. The state ha[d] a key role in planning and controlling economic activity to take advantage of economies of scale and prevent market failures. And there [wa]s a unique model of development—the one historically followed by the then-industrialized countries.
>
> Opinions... evolved considerably on each of these views, punctuated by major events and crises. While development thinking... steadily evolved, extreme stands on development policy... tended to alternate following those events and crises. The dominant paradigm shifted in the 1960s, taking into account elements of social and economic change. Eradicating poverty emerged as a central focus of development, illustrated by the basic needs approach. And the distributional aspects of growth and development received more emphasis, as in the influential 1974 World Bank report, *Redistribution with Growth*.
>
> By the end of the 1970s the crisis triggered by higher oil prices led to severe macroeconomic imbalances throughout the world, which in the early 1980s produced major debt problems in most developing countries.... A 'neoliberal' reaction emphasized the central role of markets and the private sector, progressively shaping conditionality in the heavy structural adjustment lending offered by development agencies in an effort to reestablish macroeconomic equilibrium and growth in the countries most affected by the debt crisis. Besides monetary and fiscal rigour, that conditionality also included liberalizing trade and foreign direct investment, privatizing inefficient state-owned enterprises, eliminating price distortions, deregulating markets, and protecting property rights. Those principles were later described as the 'Washington Consensus' (Williamson 1990).
>
> The disenchantment with structural adjustment grew during the 1990s as many countries under adjustment failed to accelerate or even to renew growth, even after several years of 'adjustment.' It was recognized that markets and the private sector alone cannot guide development without a proper environment. Acknowledged particularly were the implications of weak regulation and poorly functioning land, labour and credit markets. And attention focused again on poverty and distribution. The Washington Consensus was seen as a simplistic and restrictive view of development strategy, with little space for government interventions and neglect of the policy implications of widely different circumstances across countries.
>
> Reflection on development and poverty reduction broadened in the late 1990s and early

2000s. Thinking shifted, and awareness grew that if markets are to generate shared growth, their institutional foundations cannot be overlooked. It is one thing to identify the policies to trigger growth and reduce poverty. It is another to guarantee that these policies will be well implemented by ruling governments. Governments must be well governed: they must uphold the rule of law, limit corruption, encourage competition and voice, and support entrepreneurship. Also at this time the notion of poverty was broadened to include not only standards of living but also the provision of social services—healthcare, education and some types of collective infrastructure—and the participation of poor people in decisions affecting their lives. (World Bank 2007: 39–42)

The three modules in this section elaborate on the key dimensions of this 'emerging synthesis'—what we have recognized as the 'post-Washington Consensus.' Module 24 focuses on the shift from national to local development, and the shift away from the market and the state as agencies of development towards the empowerment of the poor, to capacitate them to act for themselves on the basis of their 'social capital'—the one asset the poor are deemed to have in abundance.

In module 25 Akram-Lodhi assesses the 'sustainable livelihoods approach' (SLA), which has come to prominence in research, policy analysis and advocacy in the area of rural development. He concludes that SLA essentially is a 'method without a theory' i.e., although 'its focus on individual agency facilitates empirical research, such research is not theoretically situated.' In consequence, Akram-Lodhi argues, 'there is a generalized failure to investigate structural constraints to individual agency, let alone to the possibilities of collective action and political responses.'

In Module 26 Tharamangalam and Mukherjee Reed turn towards an alternative model of sustainable human development constructed by the UNDP. Regardless of whether it can be considered an alternative paradigm to neoliberalism this model has provided tools with which to assess the successes or failures of the market and neoliberal policies. The suggested readings deconstruct the notion of 'human development' before turning towards some Third World success stories, particularly Cuba and Kerala. These two states (one a nation-state, the other, a state within a state) stand out as exemplars of 'human development.' They also raise questions about the non-income dimensions of poverty and development and about the assumption that economic growth and social or human development are interdependent and correlated.

Module 24

Social Capital and Local Development

Henry Veltmeyer

Universidad Autónoma de Zacatecas, Mexico; Saint Mary's University, Canada

This module is concerned with issues of theory and practice that surround processes of social change and development in the current era of neoliberal globalization and that point towards alternative forms of development—'another development' in current discourse. These processes can be analyzed at different levels—international, national, regional and local. But the central focus of this module is on the dynamics of local and community-based forms of social change and development, with primary reference to Latin America.

1. Towards a new paradigm

Thinking critically about social change and development means moving beyond the dominant paradigm of capitalist development in the form of neoliberal globalization. In the 1980s, while academics and policymakers in the mainstream of development thought and practice joined the Washington Consensus and the new world order of free market capitalism and neoliberal globalization, there emerged a movement to rethink and bring about 'another development'. The aim was to promote an alternative form of development that was not initiated *from the outside* (the World Bank, etc.) and implemented *from above* (by the government) but rather originated *from within and below* (within 'civil society')—a more participatory, socially inclusive and human form of people-led development sustainable not only in terms of the environment but the livelihoods of the world's poor. In the 1990s, however, the clear and widely perceived failure of the 'new economic model' (free-market capitalism) led to a convergence between the development mainstream and various alternative sidestreams in the form of a post-Washington Consensus (PWC) on the need for a more socially inclusive, equitable and sustainable form of development—a 'new development paradigm'.

> Veltmeyer 2007a: Chap. 2; Bebbington 2001: 7–17; Atria et al. 2004;
> Boisier 2005; Gore 2000: 789–804.

2. Locality and community: Local development in a neoliberal world

Alternative community-based and participatory forms of local development were made possible on the basis of a movement in the 1980s to democratize (actually 'redemocratize') the state, particularly at the level of government service/policy formulation and in terms of the relation of the state to civil society. This institutional basis of 'democracy' and the 'participatory development' process it facilitated was a policy that was unlamented in the 1980s both in the North and the South.

On the basis of this policy and within the framework of the PWC in the 1990s, there were several attempts to construct a 'new development paradigm'. The essential feature of this paradigm was the empowerment of the poor, capacitating them to act for themselves in the search for a pathway out of poverty. Within this paradigm, the role of the government (with 'international cooperation' and assistance provided by 'nongovernmental organizations' was to establish an appropriate institutional and policy framework and a 'level playing field' (equal opportunity or 'equity') as well as socially inclusive access to essential government services. The active agent of social change and development, however, was the poor in the form of their 'operational grassroots' or community-based local organizations. This policy required both the strengthening of civil society and popular participation in decisionmaking as well as 'good governance' (engaging civil society organizations in public action—'participatory budgeting and planning').

> Palma Carvajal 1995: 39–53; Veltmeyer & O'Malley 2001: Chaps. 1–2.

3. Social capital and local development

A critical feature of the new development paradigm was an effort to bring the 'social' back into development—into the process of community-based or local development. The principal means of doing so was through 'social capital,' with reference to the capacity of the poor for cooperation and social organization on the basis of norms of reciprocity and a culture of social solidarity. This capacity was conceived of by several sociologists and economists as a 'productive force,' an asset the poor was deemed to have in abundance.

This notion of 'social capital' is the subject of close scrutiny and considerable debate. The readings in this theme are designed to critically examine the pros and cons of 'social capital' as a key element of the new development paradigm. Apart from the conceptual difficulties in defining the term, use of the concept has been heavily criticized from a CDS perspective because of its political implications: it presupposes that the poor will not challenge the structure of economic and political power, limiting its concern for social change and development (poverty alleviation, etc.) to the local spaces of the power structure; and it leads to political demobilization, undermining the efforts of the poor to bring about change by means of active mobilization and the formation of or joining social movements.

Because of its centrality in the new paradigm and the post-Washington Consensus on the need to reach beyond both the state and the market into the localities and the communities of the poor, nothing is as important for students of CDS as a careful assessment of the value and diverse uses of 'social capital' as a concept. The readings in this unit are essential to this purpose.

Harriss 2006; Veltmeyer 2007a: Chap. 3, 2008; Bebbington et al., 2006; Durston 1998, 2001; Edwards 2006: 91–107; Kliksberg 1999: 83–102; Woolcock & Narayan 2000.

4. The deficit approach to development: Social exclusion and the war on poverty

 The dominant approach to development starts with an assessment of what a community or a population lacks or needs—what we might term a 'deficit' or 'gap' approach. 'Development' in this context is essentially a matter of providing or assisting in the provision of what is missing or in short supply, be it investment capital, human resources, knowledge, technology, entrepreneurship, a disposition towards change or the capacity and disposition to pursue existing opportunities for self-advancement.

The advances, uses and limitations of this deficit or gap-filling approach to development are brought into focus in these readings, which warrant critical study. The World Bank and other bi- and multilateral financial institutions and development agencies engaged in the project of 'international cooperation' for development have constructed an extensive database of evaluative studies and project assessments, as well as published and unpublished studies that are accessible to outside readers and the scholarly community (for example, 'What has the Bank (and We) Learned?' and 'What is to be done?'). It is imperative that these institutional self-evaluations and studies not be taken at face value but carefully deconstructed and critically reviewed.

O'Malley & Veltmeyer 2006; Johnson, Craig & Daniel Start 2001; Rückert 2007.

5. The asset-based and sustainable livelihoods approaches

The failure of the dominant deficit-based approach to the practice of development—the World Bank has pursued diverse strategies in its thirty-five-year-long war on poverty without any apparent success—has led proponents of 'another development' to propose and design diverse forms of an 'asset-based' approach, i.e., to start with a mapping of the community's or particular population's existing assets, to facilitate the design of more appropriate development projects.

The conditions required to implement an asset-based approach and the 'best practices' regarding this approach also need to be critically assessed and studied. Models and concepts based on this approach include 'asset-based community development' (ABCD), 'community economic development' (CED), 'local economic development' (LED), 'the municipalization of development' ('the productive municipality') and the sustainable livelihood approach, profiled and critically assessed in Module 25 by Akrahm-Lodhi.

Bebbington 1999; Brocklesby & Fisher 2003: 185–97; Mathie & Cunningham 2004.

5. Cooperativism, the social economy and microfinance: The economics of social solidarity

There are basically three macro-level approaches to the contradictions of capitalist development. One is to renovate the system and to consolidate the ideological commitment to 'market principles' and 'an open global economy' (White House 2008). This is the position adopted and articulated by the boosters of free market capitalism and neoliberal globalization. Another is to reform the system in the direction of equity and democracy, to create a more equitable, socially inclusive and ultimately more sustainable form of capitalist development. Proponents of this reformist approach include critics of neoliberal globalization like Joseph Stiglitz (2006), concerned to 'make globalization work,' and those committed to 'global democratic governance'—the inclusion of 'global civil society' in decisionmaking and governance. The third approach is predicated on the belief that the world capitalist system is inherently flawed and unstable, unable to resolve or manage the problems that it generates, problems that threaten to reach crisis proportions.

In this contested theoretical and political space, practitioners and proponents of 'another development' have sought a pathway to change not by renovating or reforming the system, nor by mobilizing the forces of resistance in a push for systematic change but to identify spaces for action within the existing power structure of capitalist development, and to open up and exploit these spaces for local or community-based development. The aim is to create islands of quasi-socialism (cooperativism or solidarity economics, a social economy built on social capital and collectivist form of social organization) in the sea of capitalist development. One organizational form of such 'development' is cooperativism at the level of production (not just marketing).

Cooperativism has had a stormy history, with ups and downs and cases of successful practice, such as Mondragon in the Basque region of Spain. The scholarly and evaluative literature of cooperativism in relation to capitalism is voluminous but see Bowman & Stone (2005). Another more controversial non-cooperative but non-capitalist approach to local development is micro-finance or microcredit (see Bowman & Stone (2007) and Weber (2002) for a critical assessment).

Bowman & Stone 2005, 2007; Weber 2002.

6. Critical assessment of the new paradigm

The post-Washington Consensus on the need to 'bring the state back in' and create more socially inclusive form of neoliberalism ('structural adjustment with a human face,' 'productive transformation with equity,' etc.) is predicated on a new development paradigm focused on the empowerment of the poor, capacitating them to act for themselves on the basis of an asset that they are deemed to have in abundance, namely 'social capital,' within a supportive institutional framework provided by the government and a 'new policy agenda' (Ocampo 2004). For critical assessments of this paradigm, see inter alia, O'Malley & Veltmeyer (2006) and Veltmeyer (2007b).

O'Malley & Veltmeyer 2006; Veltmeyer 2007b: Chap. 4; Jomo & Fine 2006; Weber 2002.

Module 25

The Sustainable Livelihoods Approach

Haroon Akram-Lodhi
Trent University, Canada

1. A new framework

Over the course of the last ten years, rural development studies has witnessed the introduction of a new framework that has come to dominate research, policy analysis and advocacy. That framework is called the 'sustainable livelihoods approach' (SLA). This module briefly explores this approach from a critical perspective.

The term 'livelihood' started to be used in the rural development studies literature in the early 1990s (Bernstein, Crow and Johnson 1992). At that time, 'livelihood' was used as a descriptive device to show an understanding of the complex specificity of rural life, in which people and communities undertook a set of varying productive and reproductive activities, of which only one might be farming (O'Laughlin 2004). By the late 1990s, however, and particularly since the publication of *Rural Livelihoods and Diversity in Developing Countries* (2000) by Frank Ellis, the term has come to signify an overarching framework within which poverty analysis can be undertaken—in which the 'assets' of poor people are identified and then expanded as a consequence of policy interventions, in order to foster poverty reduction.

Bernstein, Crow & Johnson 1992; Chambers & Conway 1998; Ellis 2000.

2. SLA in theory

Broadly, within current discourse, 'livelihoods' are understood to encompass the capabilities, assets and activities a household can employ in order to make a living. The SLA is thus premised upon the proposition that poor people have assets, comprised of the following:

- *natural* capital, such as land and water;

- *physical* capital, such as tools and equipment, infrastructure and transport, shelter, sanitation and energy;
- *financial* capital, such as income, savings and credit;
- *human* capital, such as education, skills, knowledge and health; and
- *social* capital, such as households, networks, formal groups, institutions and information.

People employ these assets to construct a 'livelihood strategy,' designed to improve a household's means of making a living. In so doing, people must, in many cases, carry out a multiplicity of productive and reproductive activities based upon the portfolio of assets under their control. Thus, people can, at an individual level, simultaneously undertake a range of activities and seek to achieve a range of different goals, some of which may even conflict. The implication is explicit: people, and especially poor people, do not do just one activity, nor are they passively defined within social and cultural frameworks. Rather, people are active agents who can articulate the boundaries of their capabilities. At the same time, however, the range of the agency available to people to construct a living is mediated by the institutions, policies and processes of civil society and the state, which in turn affect how people can use their livelihood assets.

Several implications flow from this admittedly simplistic account of the SLA. The first implication is that all people have assets. The second implication is that different types of assets are analytically identical. The third is that the relevant unit of analysis in livelihood studies is going to be a well-defined social grouping: the individual, a household, a community, an ethnicity, a caste, an age group, gender or class. The fourth is that, given the presence of well-defined social groups, there must be forms of social division in populations or within households themselves. With regard to this last point, many feel that a particular strength of the SLA is its explicit recognition of the gendered character of much social inequality in contemporary poor countries.

A livelihood is said to be sustainable when it is capable of absorbing shocks, maintaining capabilities and enhancing available assets in a manner that does not act to the detriment of the environment within which the livelihood strategy is constructed. Sustainable livelihoods require that the following four key dimensions of sustainability be addressed:

- *environmental* sustainability is witnessed when the productivity of environmental resources is enhanced so that they can be used in the future;
- *economic* sustainability is demonstrated when a given level of spending can be maintained over time or when an acceptable level of economic welfare is continued over time;
- *social* sustainability is achieved when social exclusion is minimized and social equity maximized; and
- *institutional* sustainability occurs when dominant formal and informal institutional structures and processes can perform livelihood-enhancing functions over time.

The SLA takes the position that poverty reduction must operate in a way that is consistent with the livelihood strategies of people, the social setting within which the livelihood strategy is constructed and the capabilities of people to adapt to changes in the economic and social environment. This has clear methodological implications. Research, policy advice and advocacy using the SLA has to clearly analyze the components of people's livelihoods and how these change over time, stressing the way in which people themselves define the strengths and the weaknesses of their livelihood strategy. Thus, there is a strong relationship between the SLA and participatory research methodologies. The analysis that is undertaken must be conducted in the context of a set of institutional arrangements and policy processes that impact upon people's livelihood strategies. Thus, the analysis must seek to identify the livelihood goals of people, households and communities and create an environment within which institutions and policymaking take full account of these goals.

Bebbington 1999; Brocklesby & Fisher 2003: 185–97; Helmore & Singh 2001.

3. Strengths of SLA (from the perspective of its advocates)

For the advocates of the SLA—which includes multilateral agencies such as the Food and Agriculture Organization, bilateral agencies such as the U.K. Department for International Development, academic institutions such as the Institute of Development Studies, research institutions such as the International Food Policy Research Institute and international nongovernmental organizations such as Oxfam International—the strengths of the SLA are found in three areas.

The first strength is that the SLA is *people-centred*. The priority of research, policy and advocacy must be to support the livelihood strategies of people in a way that enhances sustainability over time, and this criterion should be the basis upon which interventions are assessed. The second strength of the SLA is that it is *holistic*. The approach is predicated upon the idea that the ability of people to construct a livelihood strategy may be constrained or enabled by a variety of interlocking factors that cannot be addressed in isolation but must rather be approached in an integrated fashion. Thus, the SLA focuses on understanding the multiple economic and social relationships that influence people and affect their livelihood strategies. This is done is while explicitly recognizing that livelihood strategies can have multiple dimensions and, as a consequence, analysis must be non-sectoral. Livelihood strategies are moreover affected by a diversity of actors, from within local communities, civil society, the private sector and local, regional and national government. In this context, people seek to achieve a diversity of livelihood outcomes, which are determined not by the state or civil society but by people themselves. The third strength of the SLA is that it is *dynamic*. Livelihood strategies adapt to iterative chains of events and cause-and-effect relationships and are, as such, complex as people seek to take advantage of supportive changes in their vulnerability context as well as to reduce the impact of external shocks and negative predictable trends in their livelihood environment.

The SLA thus analyses the livelihood strategies of people, households and communities within an institutional setting in which civil society organizations and local governments operate under constraints imposed as a consequence of the national policy framework. In so doing, the SLA clearly operates in a terrain that has been staked out by a broad set of constituents in international development. As such, it allows those who use it to seek to understand how people may or may not affect the policymaking process, as well as how the policymaking process actually affects people.

Norton & Foster 2001; Turton 2000a, 2000b; UNDP—Sustainable Livelihoods Unit 2006.

4. Weaknesses of SLA (from the perspective of its critics)

Despite its hegemonic position within the field of rural development studies, the SLA can be criticized from a number of perspectives. The first is in terms of aspiration, which, regarding a framework designed to facilitate poverty analysis, is clearly modest if not very limited. By focusing on the ways in which poor people could make better use of their available assets to improve their living standards, the emphasis is simply that the poor should help themselves (O'Laughlin 2004). The macroeconomic environment within which overarching policy frameworks are developed, in particular core fiscal and monetary policy approaches, are removed from the analysis. The second point follows from this: whereas prior approaches to rural development stressed the importance of analyzing social arrangements governing production and reproduction amongst people, the SLA stresses the importance of individuals undertaking multiple activities to minimize risk. It thus clearly falls within the maximizing logic of orthodox neoclassical economic theory, albeit a neoclassicism that has been infused with a dose of anthropological analysis. The charge of neoclassicism leads to the third point of criticism: the notion that everyone has assets and all assets are essentially equal.

This point sidesteps three important issues: first, why do some have particular assets and others do not? Second, why are some assets of relatively greater importance to certain groups and of relatively lesser importance to other groups? Third, may there be causal relationships between those who have larger quantities of relatively more important assets and those who have relatively lesser quantities of relatively more important assets? Clearly, the assumption that all assets are equal, as is asserted within the SLA, should be demonstrated rather than assumed, as proponents of SLA do. This leads to a fourth criticism, which is that the SLA does not investigate how social groupings relate to each other. Particularly in its failure to differentiate among or prioritize assets, the SLA approach fails to identify and focus on the relations of social inequality that are found within and among households, and relations of class and class divisions within communities and beyond (Veltmeyer 2007a: Chap. 5). Such relations in their totality structurally underpin poverty processes.

With its focus on people, households and community, the SLA is likely to facilitate claims for redistributive action, which can be viewed as a sort of Achilles' heel. The solution to the poverty problematic requires abandoning or moving beyond the SLA, which, by design if not intent, falls short of prescribing structural change: collective action by the poor, yes, but not action against the structure of power that sustains and reproduces their poverty.

O'Laughlin (2004: 387) cogently argues that livelihoods research 'presents itself as a method without a theory. It frames no questions.' The point is well put. Although its focus on individual agency facilitates empirical research, such research is not theoretically situated. In consequence there is a generalized failure to investigate structural constraints to individual agency, let alone to the possibilities of collective action and political responses. The result is an approach that stresses individual maximization within a set of binding constraints that give rise to a set of choices that, through research, policy and advocacy, could be reformulated so as to improve outcomes. It is thus a thoroughly neoclassical agenda that has only a limited ability to contribute to our understanding of the structural basis of inequality and conflict that is found in much of the countryside in the developing world.

Amalric 1998: 31–44; O'Laughlin 2004: 385–92; Veltmeyer 2007a: Chap. 5.

Module 26

Human Development in Theory and Practice

Joseph Tharamangalam
Mount Saint Vincent University, Canada

Ananya Mukherjee Reed
York University, Canada

Human development (HD), an alternative approach to development, has emerged as a major challenge to neoliberalism. Regardless of whether considered an alternative paradigm to neoliberalism (Jolly 2004; Kuonqui 2006), HD has provided tools and means to expose the successes or failures of the market and the neoliberal policies. It attracts immense international media attention. There were one million downloads of the UNDP's 2004 *Human Development Report* within a week of its release (Kuonqui 2006). Even the World Bank and the IMF have appropriated much of the HD discourse, perhaps cause for concern but also, and more importantly, a good reason to engage in a critical assessment of the new policy agenda established under the post-Washington Consensus (see Module 5).

This module focuses on the theory and practice of human development. In addition to exploring theoretical issues it draws on the actual experience of some Third World success stories, especially Cuba and the Indian state of Kerala. These two stand out among a handful of well-known states and states within a state that have produced high human development outcomes even with low economic growth, contradicting the theory that economic growth and social or human development go hand in hand, the second based on the first. In a world that condemns one fifth of its people to chronic poverty and endemic deprivation, these HD achievements assume world-historical significance as they evidence that such human suffering is eradicable and indeed needless.

Early observations of some of these cases were at least partially influential in the launch of UNDP's annual human development reports and other studies on this theme. Although far from non-controversial in its theoretical and methodological approach, the UNDP's first HDR (1990) highlighted the point that a country's income does not automatically lead to HD, a broader measure of human well-being that combines per capita income (an indicator of the capacity of households to access the means of material well-being) with improvements in education (literacy), health (life expectancy), indicators of the 'expansion of choice' (freedom to act) for each individual. The UNDP also introduced the now well-known human development index (HDI), which ranks the world's countries on the basis of their HD achievements. Holding up the examples of societies such as Costa Rica and Sri Lanka, the foundational HDR asked: 'What are the policies that led [and lead] to such results?'

This module focuses not only on these policies but examines the social and cultural transformations that enabled these countries to formulate and implement them. In a nutshell, the human development outcomes were produced by the transformative practice of these societies—in regard to both government and civil society.

In Cuba and Kerala, such transformative practices involved a trajectory of struggle for social justice, including organized movements for socialism and the capture of state power to implement the transformative project. It could be argued that it was the dialectic of popular struggle and state intervention (with a certain synergy between the two) that provided these societies a measure of what Amartya Sen has called 'support-led security.'

The module reviews the theory of human development, the main architects of which were scholars behind the UNDP's HDRs, most notably Amartya Sen and Mahboob ul Haq, who headed the team preparing the HDRs for the first five years and who drew heavily on Sen's capability theory, also integrating elements of the basic needs approach, which dominated development thinking and practice in the 1970s. Claiming to put people back at the centre of the development process, they defined development itself as a process of expanding human capabilities, enlarging choices and enhancing freedoms. This approach has sometimes been criticized as no more than a liberal theory about equality of opportunity and the creation of a more equitable playing ground (Lebowitz 2007).

It could also be seen as a de-politicized approach that eschews a political theory of development. However, there are several reasons why HD should form a part of any CDS program. First, it constitutes a powerful alternative to neoliberalism, with the influential HDRs acting as a two-sided tool for assessing the social impact of economic policies on the one hand, and for advocacy on behalf of the poor and the deprived on the other. Furthermore, the HD approach is more comprehensive and multidimensional than the World Bank's more limited approach focused on equity defined as equality of opportunity.

The readings on this theme critically examine the way in which the UNDP has applied the theory of HD in its reports and policies, and attempt to gauge its relevance and usefulness in the discourse and practice of development. We examine the role of social mobilization and popular participation in bringing about social development and positive HD outcomes. The readings in this module can be used to assess the extent to which these and similar models have proved to be sustainable in the face of globalization and neoliberal reforms. They can also be used to gauge if and how HD could become a foundation for further economic growth in these low-income countries.

Adelman 1986: 493–507; Lebowitz 2007; Streeten 1984.

1. The concept of human development

For practical purposes it is possible to trace the origins of the notion of human development to the Eighteenth-Century Enlightenment—to the notion of freedom and equality as defining features of the 'human condition' and as organizational principles for 'another world.' The theorists of the Enlightenment, like Marx in his *Early Works* (1842–44), were philosophical *humanists* who criticized existing society for violating the 'human essence,' creating conditions (unfreedom and social inequality) that were in conflict with people as they essentially are.

As Sen and others in the 1980s argued, development is primarily a matter of 'freedom' (the expansion of choice, the ability to act in the realization of the individual's creative human potential and capabilities). In these terms 'capabilities' have intrinsic value, and education and health, as means for individuals to realize their essential freedom (the expansion of choice, as the UNDP's 1990 WDR defined it), are not just means but ends in themselves.

The theory includes ethical (e.g., 'entitlements' as rights) and social dimensions and has also often been integrated into a theory of development as 'public action,' the engagement of both the state and civil society in the responsibility (development 'role') of bringing about the transformative change needed to realize the 'human condition' of 'freedom' (as defined by liberalism) and 'equality' (as defined by socialists).[1]

As Sen and Ul Haq point out, the notion of human development in the sense of development of the full potential of the human person has certainly had a much longer life in the history of Western social thought and can be traced back to such thinkers as Aristotle and Marx. For Marx this was certainly the central issue—providing every human being the opportunity to develop their full potential, on the one hand, and removing conditions that prevented them from reaching this potential, that is, all sources of exploitation and *alienation*. And this goal was to be reached through struggle and *transformative practice* (Lebowitz 2007).

Anand & Sen 2000: 2029–49; Ul Haq 1995; Sen 1989, 1999b: 13–34.

2. The state and popular participation as agencies of human development

The most critical issue of HD is that of agency. In the system of BW-I (1944–1980), the agency of development, understood initially as 'economic growth,' was the state in its administrative apparatus (the government). However, from a 'basic needs' and HD perspective (development as freedom, as Sen defined it), the capacity of individuals to actively participate in decisionmaking that affects them (autonomous action) is a matter of fundamental principle, raising the question of 'popular participation'—the engagement of 'civil society' in the development process. In Kerala, this was institutionalized in the form of 'public action,' a combination of actions taken by the government and civil society organizations—public policy and social mobilization.

Dreze & Sen 2002; Roman 2003; Khan 2004; O'Leary 2004.

3. Human development as paradigm change

From the outset (in the post World War II context), the idea of development and associated programs, projects and strategies were constructed within the framework of a dominant paradigm that presupposed the institutional framework of the capitalist system but debated the relative weight and role of the state and the market. In the late 1970s and early 1980s, however, there occurred two fundamental shifts in development thinking and practice (see Module 1). One was in the direction of free market capitalism, essentially a rejection of development conceived as a more equitable distribution of society's productive resources and wealth. The other was in the direction of moving beyond both the state and the market into 'civil society' and the communities and localities of 'the people'—development 'from below' and 'from within.' This change, it could be argued, like the conception of the need for systemic change (from capitalism to socialism) entailed a paradigm shift, which was reflected (theoretically represented) in the UNDP model of 'sustainable human development' (UNDP 1996, 1997a, 2006) and also in the institution of 'people's power' in the Cuban Revolution (Saney 2004) and in Venezuela's new constitution for the Bolivarian Revolution (Lebowitz 2006, 2007).

Fukuda-Parr & Kumar 2004; Jolly 2004; Kuonqui 2006; Lebowitz 2006; Stewart 2008.

4. Pathways to human development: Kerala and Cuba

There is a substantial body of literature on this issue as regards Cuba and Kerala (and other similar cases) from a variety of perspectives, ranging from Sen's work on 'public action' to Peter Roman's (2003) work on 'people's power' in Cuba. Equally important is a detailed examination of the role of the state, the other side of 'public action.' Examining the weight of empirical evidence on this is important since state action has proved to be so critical, especially in the Third World, in producing human development outcomes that are inclusive and relatively equitable. It is also important to examine the relationship between state and society, state intervention and participation by social groups since neither can lead to the desired outcome without a certain 'synergy' between the two.

We also examine the cultural forces that *moved* these societies and states to engage in 'transformative practice.' These forces may best be described in terms of a cultural revolution, a transformation in human consciousness and a paradigm change in social values and ideals—in people's commitment to social and distributive justice, human rights and entitlements, and in their aspirations for themselves and their children. Of particular importance is a deeply cherished commitment by state and society to the pursuit of the public good as a basic goal of public action—a shared commitment to the creation of a 'new society,' which, according to Che Guevara (2007), required a cultural revolution, the creation of a 'new man and woman.'

In the historical paths travelled by Kerala and Cuba it is possible to locate pivotal 'moments' that are akin to the declaration of the 'rights of man' during the European Enlightenment. Especially important here is the concept of *entitlement* as formulated by Sen. If famines can be characterized as 'entitlement failures' (as Sen has argued) then Cuba's success in avoiding famine or severe malnutrition even as it suffered and then overcame a severe economic crisis, could indeed be seen a notable case of 'entitlement success.'

Jolly & Mehrotra 2000; Lebowitz 2007; Parayil 2000; Roman 2003; Tharamangalam 2008.

5. Lessons of human development

The first HDR (1990) brought into sharp focus the point that a country's income does not automatically produce human well-being if measured by such indicators of quality of life as knowledge and a long and healthy life. Using its new measure of 'human development,' it held up the examples of such relatively poor countries as Costa Rica and Sri Lanka, which achieved high HD relative to their income. This once again highlighted a simple fact of immense human, political and ethical significance—a point emphasized by the foundational theorists of the HD approach, such as Amartya Sen and Mahbub ul Haq—that even poor countries can reduce, if not eliminate, chronic poverty and endemic deprivation and provide for their people a measure of human well-being if they bring about certain changes in their societies. The report (1990: iii) asked the question about the success stories: 'What are the policies that led to such results?'

This question is no less important. For some two decades after the so-called 'New York Consensus,' arguably there is more, not less, poverty and deprivation. The MDGs are behind target, and many other similar schemes seem to have had no better success. The global food crisis, at least partially caused by the policies of the Washington Consensus, has added a 100 million more people to the 850 million in the ranks of the world's hungry. Yet Cuba, a small country of

11 million people, plunged into an economic crisis of the scale of the Great Depression—with a 15 percent decline in GDP and 30 percent decline in food availability (Tharamangalam 2008)— was able to avert a famine or any serious malnutrition and to sustain its HD achievements and its social programs, and to do this without foreign aid and despite a U.S. embargo (Saney 2004). Similarly, the state of Kerala in India, which has been brought to the world's attention by Amartya Sen, among others, has achieved HD indicators that are at least close to those of many developed countries, and these were achieved with a per capita GDP that was below the rather dismal Indian average. Hence the all-important question of how they did this where others failed, and what lessons the world, and especially the world's poor, can learn from their experience. This is a major focus of the readings on this theme. Another is the role of the state in the achievement of human development.

The role of the state is vigorously debated by development specialists and social theorists today (see Module 1). It is seen as an obstacle by neoliberal fundamentalists and as something being superseded by global forces by some globalization theorists. Yet as Joseph Tharamangalam (2008) points out, it is an undeniable fact that every society with high HD has a history of state-led development. This is clearly the case in both Kerala and Cuba, where the state was 'captured' through popular struggle and/or revolution by underprivileged classes and reconstituted to act on their behalf. This point is important in understanding the development role of the state, particularly as regards public provisioning for education, health, food and social security for the whole population and specific policies targeted to empower and capacitate the poor. Just as important is the point that for the state to accomplish this role, it needs to be restructured to serve the interests of the whole population and not just the dominant class.

In addition, human development, whether capitalist or socialist in form, is predicated on a synergistic relationship between an interventionist state and an actively mobilized population. As argued by Pedro Stedile, leader of Latin America's most power social movement, formed on the social base of the country's rural landless workers, 'without an active mobilization of the population, and an active engagement with the 'broader class struggle' the government does not deliver [to the grassroots and the poor].'

Jolly & Mehrotra 2000; Ghai 2000; Fukuda-Parr 2003.

6. Has human development failed us?
A social power perspective on achieving human development

At a global level, despite concerted efforts in the war on global poverty, there has been a very uneven progress in regard to human development, with an appreciable number of countries (fifty-four) experiencing an 'unprecedented development reversal' (Mukherjee Reed 2008: 1). One of the most distressing aspects of the progress made in human development is the high degree of social exclusion in this progress—in terms of gender (and this despite the shared commitment of the 'international development community' to reducing the gender gap) and other categories of difference such as race, ethnicity and religion, not to mention social class. Ananya Mukherjee Reed (2008) traces this problem to an exclusion from decisionmaking processes in economic and political spheres—a matter essentially of 'social power.' In the same connection, Tharamangalam (2008) argues that every case of successful human development, even when, as in Cuba and Kerala, this success has a weak economic foundation (a relatively low rate of economic growth), involved both an interventionist state and a population that is actively mobilized to ensure that the state would serve as an instrument of a collective interest in substantive social change.

Mukherjee Reed 2008: Chaps. 1, 3, 6; Tharamangalam 2006, 2008.

Note

1. It could be argued that 'freedom' is the ethical and conceptual basis for 'sustainable human development' from a liberal standpoint while 'equality' is the foundation of a socialist model of human development. This argument is predicated on 'development' as the synthesis and outcome of actions on certain ideas—progress, freedom and equality—and that action in the direction of freedom and equality is based respectively on the ideologies of liberalism and socialism.

Section 9

Power and Development:
Class and Gender Matters

It could be argued that the dynamics of social change and development hinge on relations (and the exercise) of power, i.e., as Max Weber conceived of it, the ability of some to make decisions on behalf of a group or to 'exert their will against resistance.' The problem is that economics as a discipline is particularly unable to conceptualize economic matters in terms of power relations.[1] Political science on this score is more concerned with matters of power, understood generally in terms of the 'authoritative allocation' of society's resources by elected or self-appointed officials (as opposed to the market, which provides a non-authoritative mechanism of resource allocation). In this 'political' sense, relations of power can be identified and power can be exercised at every social level from the family to the international arena. However, most political scientists are as likely as economists to abstract from their analysis the actual dynamics of functioning power relations in regard to the process of social change and development. In this connection what is needed is a sociological perspective on power as a social relation.

The three modules in this section conceptualize power in sociological and in feminist terms as a matter of social class and gender relations. In terms of social class, individuals in society are viewed and analyzed in terms of their relationship both to the means of production and to the instruments of class power, especially the state, which is the most effective and important repository of political and economic power in capitalist societies. Economic power in these terms is based on private property in the means of social production, but the state essentially serves to both legitimate and enforce this economic power, backing it up with political power. O'Malley, in Module 27, reviews the dynamics of class power from the perspective and with the lens of what we might term 'the sociology of social change and development' ('development' being a form of social change—change in a progressive direction).

The next two modules, Module 28 by Jane Parpart and Module 29 by Fiona MacPhail, provide a feminist perspective on the gender dimension of the process of social change and development. As with the class dimension of the social change process, 'development' is predominantly a matter of power—a social relation that seems to exist between men and women in virtually all historical and social contexts, including the current one of capitalist development as neoliberal globalization. However, both Parpart and MacPhail view the gender and engendering dimensions of social change and development not so much as a matter of relative power between men and women as an issue of 'empowerment'—women capacitating themselves to organize and act collectively as women in improving their social status and in engendering a development process, converting themselves and other women in the process from victim or object into actor or subject.

Note

1   Lourdes Benería, a prominent feminist economist at Cornell University, makes this point as follows: 'Mathematics gives the impression that economics is scientific and so you cannot question it. But you

have to dig into the assumptions. For example, look at the area known as "household economics." The neoclassical assumptions used to set up... models [in this area] imply that men and women are free and equal individuals negotiating rationally what's best for the household. Some models assume that decisions are made by a benevolent patriarch who understands what is best for the household and each member. There are no emotions or love involved in decisions based on economic rationality. But the fact is, as feminists have pointed out, within a household, men and women can be [and often are] very unequal subjects, and decisions are not merely rational [and certainly not made on an the basis of equality]. Men often have had better educational opportunities—they may own land, they may control the money, they typically have more power. T[hus t]he picture of reality portrayed by these models is very male-biased. Policies based on these models can underestimate how they affect men and women differently' ("Gender, Development and Globalization: Economics as if People Mattered," 2003; quoted by Benería as a comment in Adbusters July 15, 2009 <www.adbusters.org/magazine/85/lourdes-bener%C3%ADa.html>.

Module 27

Critical Social Analysis and Development

Anthony Holland O'Malley
Saint Mary's University, Canada

1. Theoretical perspectives on society, change and development

At the heart of what C.W. Mills called the 'sociological imagination' is the need to connect individual concerns and behaviours to features of the social structure using so-called 'structural variables' and the boundary conditions of specific forms of social organization. The type of social analysis growing out of the 'sociological imagination' is scientific in the broadest sense of the word, namely thinking that pursues the advancement of knowledge through a combination of theories about social organization and empirical data. Not all social analysts look upon their endeavour as a science—e.g., there are traditions in sociology ('interpretive' traditions) that deny the empirical basis of social thought—but those that follow Mills and the scientific tradition carry out their analysis in three steps: (1) using initial baseline data, they construct a theory of the social structure in which are located individual social actors and the larger social institutions in which they act, all of which stand in specific social relations to each other; (2) conducting research, they collect empirical data relevant to validating, extending or altering the theory; and (3) constructing a dialogue between research data and theory, they attempt to connect patterns of social behaviour and action with objective structural conditions of social action, using these empirically validated connections to predict social outcomes, or more dynamically, social change. The understanding here is that although individual social action may be *experienced* as purposive and goal-oriented, subject only to the actor's free will, in fact such action must, perforce, take place within the boundary conditions and structural byways of the given social structure. In specific terms, this means that—leaving aside exceptions that prove the rule—the repertoire of individual social behaviours (social action or agency) is often predictable given the individual's (or larger group's) 'location' in the social structure. This is simply to say that individual action is predictably *bounded*, rather than completely determined, by the social structure, and it is this boundedness that allows social science analysis to be scientific.

If we use scientific social analysis with the objective of both understanding social organization and, in many cases, effecting, social change, we find that it may be grouped into three types or traditions:

Regarding Social Organization

A Marxist (historical materialist) conception of society understands the basic structural feature of society to be classes divided, at the most basic level, along the lines of an individual's *social class* or relationship to the means of producing what the society needs to survive or feels to be most valuable. The insight here is that although social relationships may not be entirely economic (material) in nature, they are overwhelmingly constrained at the structural level—action is 'bounded'—by the firm relations imposed by underlying economic relationships. This type of analysis, can give rise to some very subtle and complex understandings of class, class position and class membership, but in its most general form the analysis posits two basic classes: the owners (possessors, manipulators, proprietors) of the crucial means of production in a society, and on the other hand a class of producers which works with, by or through the means of production but which is 'dispossessed' from participating in the rights, privileges, social prerogatives and ultimately wealth, of ownership. In our time, these two classes—due to the nature of industrial capitalism—are the capitalist class and the working class. In effect, members of the working class, by virtue of their class position in society, are compelled to offer their labour to the owning capitalist class in order to survive. Marxists theoreticians do not argue that the working class can never negotiate improvements in the price of their labour (the wage)—indeed, circumstances may allow this to happen, and it has happened. Rather, Marxist would posit, on the basis of evidence, that the true structural relationships within society—the class relationships—are at their clearest, laid bare for all to see, during times of crisis. Thinkers in this tradition pay particular theoretical attention to actual or potential social conflict.

A *structural-functional* conception of society is principally concerned with social structure as a form of *social order* and is both empirically and theoretically preoccupied with discovering the functioning institutions or behaviour-sets within society that contribute to the functional continuation of the society. In its crudest form, sociologists in this tradition understand society to be a sort of social organism in which every part (institution) is interconnected with others in a social system, each part individually and collectively fulfilling the system's 'needs.' In this tradition the social structure is theorized in terms of a social division of labour that forms the structural basis of work as a social institution and an occupational class structure, in which each individual receives a 'coefficient of well-being,' that is, a reward, commensurate with his/her contribution to society. One of the classic thinkers in this tradition, Durkheim, saw class as simply one of many other 'occupational groupings' of individuals in a social structure tied together by 'organic solidarity.' The social structure formed by these occupational groups takes the form of a value hierarchy, each social group associated with a specific 'coefficient of well-being' in proportion to the value of their contribution to society. It is this that results in the aggregate a system of social stratification. If the Marxist tradition casts light on the structural basis of social power (and hence, social inequality), the structural-functionalist, or Durkheimian tradition, suggests that the functional position of class location, and its connection with proportional value within the social order, is in a fundamental sense 'natural' or 'deserved' or, in the weakest sense, at least functionally appropriate.

A *Weberian theoretical approach* understands social groupings such as class not in terms of an individual's relation to production but rather to consumption. Using consumption as the fundamental feature of social action, the Weberian spectrum of social groupings is, like the Durkheimian tradition, rather broad and includes social categories such as 'status groups.' In this tradition, an individual's 'life chances' or social location is a function of different capacities for material consumption. In Weberian terms, the Marxist political economic understanding of class is intersected, and intercepted, by other important groupings such as status groups to form the basic general class divisions of 'lower,' 'lower middle,' 'upper middle' and 'upper' class. Although Weber was an economist by training, his most lasting contribution to sociological analysis has been a theoretical approach in which the role of the material conditions of social life, especially regarding their production, are diminished to make room for other categories of social action he felt were part of the 'boundary conditions' of the social structure, within which the individual was constrained (rather than determined) to act in the process of everyday social agency.

These three theoretical traditions contain the basic understandings of social organization within social analysis, although, as one would expect, there are many variations within and among the basic tripartite schema. Many thinkers seek to combine elements of more than one tradition into their analyses since parts of each touch upon empirically verifiable aspects of social structure. Thus, an analyst concerned with exploring the basic wage–labour relationship as this is indexed to ownership of the society's productive apparatus would turn to Marxist theory and its research on capitalist–working class relationships. An analyst working on the role of the middle class and its relationship to indices of consumption and class advancement within the social structure may turn to Weberian theory for fruitful research. A researcher intent on explaining the movement of professional or occupational groups within a stratified society may wish to use a Durkheimian approach. A sociologist wishing to explain the trajectory of the middle class in a dynamically changing society in which strong capitalist-working class relations prevailed might wish to use elements of both Marxist and Weberian theory, and so on.

Such analytical or theoretical syntheses, to whatever extent they are effected, confront the usual problems of making different central concepts function in a coordinated fashion within a single analysis. However, the differences are most apparent when considering their very different approaches to the need for, and the methods for effecting, social change.

Regarding Social Change

For Marxists, the fundamental dynamic of long-term, large-scale change is class conflict and struggle. The objective (structural) and subjective (individual) conditions that arise due to historical changes in the forces of production, which tend to expand over time throughout the social structure and its corresponding social relations of production, form the tableau for social change. Since the very conflict that creates the social dynamic arises from struggles surrounding inequalities of power, wealth, and privilege associated with exclusive ownership of productive assets vital to survival, the issue of social change arises naturally within Marxist theory as both a *description* of the dynamic of social change in a time and place and as a *prescription* for social change in order to move towards a more just and egalitarian social structure.

Structural-functionalists, on the other hand, with their emphasis on the question of social order and social functionality within the larger social structure, naturally gravitate towards a conception of social change that is essentially evolutionary and adaptive. Thus, there can be successful or unsuccessful adaptations to changes in objective conditions created by the environment (natural or social), and the general emphasis in this process of social evolution and adaptation is principally one of a return to equilibrium or a new social order. This new equilibrium heralds a new system of functionality within the social structure, and it is the social analyst's mission to understand the new social functions of the structural parts and their contribution to maintaining social equilibrium at the large scale. This analytical emphasis on the central role of equilibrium and order in society has the net effect of withdrawing conflict and struggle from the main analytical spotlight, and simply relegating it the role of a necessary bridge between the old and new social orders. This, combined with the suggestion that structural inequalities are a result of the value society puts on certain forms of work-contributions, and therefore that such inequalities are—no matter how painful—in some sense natural or inevitable outcomes of social structure functional integration, diminishes to a considerable degree the felt need for deep structural change to address deep structural inequalities.

Weberians feel that the Marxist and structural-functionalist emphasis on objective conditions of social action—whether in the form of class or functional roles in the social order—pays insufficient attention to the purposive behaviour of individual social actors. Weber wrote at length about the role of ideas and 'ideal types' as the instigators of social action, ideas which could cause the individual actor to behave contrary to what Marxists would expect on the basis of class origin and to what structural-functionalists would expect from an inhabitant of a particular social role/function within society. To the extent that such ideas are able to account for social action, quite apart from class or social order function, we must ascribe to such ideas an important role as sources of change. Weber felt this social idealism could account for anomalies in the historical analysis that seemed to lie outside the dynamic consistently described theoretically by Marxists and structural-functionalists. That is, Weber posited that in some cases change does not issue directly from class struggle or from some adaptation leading to a modified social order; rather, change can appear *sui generis* as a consequence of the development of ideas by individuals when such ideas subsequently find expression in their social praxis. Weber's work on protestantism and bureaucratic rationality best exemplify this idealist theoretical turn in scientific sociological theorizing. Although Weber sought to explain the consequences of holding certain ideas for the creation of social institutions and resulting social structures—and thus account for what happened when certain ideas came to be held among social actors—he could not account for the appearance of the ideas themselves in history (as Hegel thought he had done). In the end, the appearance of an essential component of change for Weberians—ideas—remains random and therefore unexplained, unlike Marxists and structural-functionalists, whose explanation of change (positive or negative) has a major role in their analyses. The central role given to ideas—and therefore the individual's understanding—in social action and change has led some sociologists to call Weberian theoretical analysis *verstehen* ('understanding') sociology.

Regarding Development

Development is generally understood as a process of planned change over time to bring about improvements in socioeconomic and political conditions along at least three dimensions of social life: (1) improvements in the overall material conditions of society (especially through economic growth and general prosperity); (2) improvements in each individual's stake in the social enterprise producing these conditions (social equity); and (3) improvements in the individual's capacity for expression and agency in exercising this stake in the social enterprise (freedoms and entitlements). Except for theories incorporating strong elements of social Darwinism (such as rigorously market-centred, free-enterprise theories), most social analyses addressing these improvements have been shaped in such a way that the understanding of development includes a strong element of enhanced *social justice*. That is, improvement (1) above cannot really be called development unless it is accompanied by improvements (2) and (3).

Marxist, structural-functionalist, and Weberian social analysts have constructed the following three metatheories to explain the dynamics of large-scale, long-term development:

- *capitalist development*—transformation of a precapitalist society and economy into a system based on the capitalist mode of production and with it the conversion of the class of direct producers into a proletariat, a class of individuals that dispossessed of any means of production are forced into a relation of wage-labour with capital;
- *modernization*—transformation of a traditional form of society based on a relatively simple form of technology and a communalist culture into a modern culture oriented towards individualism—based on the modern values of individual freedom and achievement (the search for individual self-realization and advancement) and the expansion of choice; and
- *industrialization*—the productive transformation of an agrarian economy and society into an industrial form based on an extended division of labour and the social construction of an autonomous market.

2. Locating and grouping individuals in the social structure: Issues of class analysis

The defining feature of the above theories is to group people according to conditions that they share with others, that is, to look at and analyze 'society' not as a collection of individuals who pursue their personal ends but as members of social groups, the conditions of which influence and shape their behaviour and courses of action. We might take this 'grouping principle' of social analysis as a complement to what could be defined as a 'typing principle'—the need to identify, for the sake of social analysis, the social characteristics of the individual and relate these to a theoretically defined typology. In practice, all analysis is predicated on notions of social groups and social type, the former generally regarded as more central, i.e., as more likely to vary with social structural factors. However, there has been significant and far-reaching debate on what would be the best or most useful categories to group people.

Historically, the dominant category for social grouping has been the concept of 'class.' Although thinkers have elaborated different ways of defining and conceiving of 'class,' three approaches dominate the debate: (1) a Marxist approach based on the concept of social class defined as the totality or structure of social relationships that individuals have to production; (2) an approach based on Max Weber's theory of social and economic organization, i.e., analyzing the social relations of individuals not to production but to consumption or the market, which is to define their 'life chances' or 'class situation' (upper or positively privileged, middle and low); and (3) an approach that can be traced back to Emile Durkheim in the tradition of structural-functionalism, analyzing the relationship of individuals to others in the organization of work, i.e., the division of labour and the occupational groups formed in the process.

No matter how 'class' is defined—and it is not unusual in actual practice for social analysts to combine categories derived from different theories—there are four principal parameters in the analysis: *structural*, a matter of locating individuals in the social organization by participation in group type; *social*, a question of social composition or of the distribution of the various social characteristics or groupings, particularly regarding gender, race or ethnicity; *economic*, the extent to which an individual's 'life chances' (Weber), the socioeconomic conditions and opportunities attached to their occupational status (Durkheim) or the economic conditions of social class (Marx) determine life chances; and *political*, a question of determining the relationship of individuals to the power structure and therefore to fundamental questions of 'who gets what.'

Portes & Hoffman 2003; Veltmeyer & Petras 2005b.

3. Dynamics of social inequality and poverty

A critical sociological analysis of social change and development is concerned not as much with 'human nature' as with the manner in which social structure both creates and is reflexively supported by human *social nature*. Human beings live fundamentally in and through their forms of social organization, and so this is no small object of concern. Critical theorists avoid notions of essentialism in human nature—that is, that human nature is somehow given or fixed for all time—such as Durkheim's notion that individuals pursue essentially selfish ends, thus requiring social control or regulation by society for the sake of social order.

Rather, social theorists in the liberal or radical tradition of the Eighteenth-Century Enlightenment view human social nature as largely malleable and to a great extent a product of conditions created by the structure of society. From this perspective, social inequalities in the distribution of wealth and income, circumstance and power, is not an inevitable social condition, the reflection of an acquisitive human nature or the obsessive concern by each and all individuals for self-advancement and self-interest. On the contrary, it reflects the structured or organized power of some over others or, to put it in the current context of societies based on a capitalist mode of production, the perquisites of private property, the sanctioned power of those whose own the means of production to profit from the labour of others.

The readings in this theme, in the critical tradition in social analysis, explore and analyze the consequences of a social structure based on private property in the means of production in the context of contemporary society, particularly of societies which find themselves on the 'South' of the global developmental divide between rich and poor countries in a global capitalist system. See Modules 22 and 23 for an analysis of the development dynamics of this divide.

4. Social relations and political dynamics of power

For Marxists the defining relationship of individuals to others is that of 'social class,' taken as the determinant factor of their social existence and the fundamental patterns of social organization and change. But for thinkers in the Weberian tradition, the basic social relationship is that of 'power,' which is taken to define the capacity to exert one's will against resistance, to issue a command with the probability that it will be obeyed or make decisions on behalf of a group. In these Weberian terms, power is an attribute not of social groups or classes, as it is for Marxists and political scientists in the 'realist' tradition, but of individuals. Regardless of theoretical perspective—and it is Marx and Weber, more than any other thinkers who defined the social scientific conception of power as a social relation—that power can be exercised in many institutional contexts, from the family to the state and international relations, and it assumes a variety of forms: primarily ideological (the power of ideas and belief), economic (decisions regarding production) and political (decisions as to 'who gets what' or the 'authoritative allocation of resources in society').

From a CDS perspective, power is essentially a structural or political issue rooted in the formation of a 'transnational capitalist class' or what Pilger (2002) labels 'the new rulers of the world.' And it takes the following forms: (1) *ideological*, with reference to the power of accepted ideas and the relation of 'legitimate' knowledge to development; (2) *economic*, with particular reference to the class power of multinational corporations and financial institutions (corporate global capital) in the global economy; and *political*, with reference to the control or predominant influence of corporate and financial capital over the state apparatus and the international organizations that set the rules that govern international relations and the global economy.

Examples of the study of the power-development relation in its ideological dimension would include the collection edited by Wolfgang Sachs (1992) on the use of the idea of development as a means of ideological control, cultural domination or colonialism. A prime almost paradigmatic example of the exercise of ideological power vis-à-vis development is the World Bank's 1995 *World Development Report*, which can be viewed both as a capitalist manifesto (Veltmeyer 1997a) and an ideological tool for convincing working people across the world that 'globalization' is a form of development and the best, indeed only, way towards a future of general prosperity. Petras and Veltmeyer (2001) provide an extended study of 'globalization' as an ideology designed to legitimate and justify a neoliberal program of policy reforms, presenting it as a form of international development. Saxe-Fernández and Núñez (2001) provide a similar analysis in the Latin American context. Economic (corporate capital) and political forms of class power in the arena of the global economy and international development relevant studies are set out clearly in Pilger's *The New Rulers of the World* (2002).

Petras & Veltmeyer 2007a: 180–209; O'Malley & Veltmeyer 2006; Pilger, 2002.

5. Political economy of capitalist development in the new world order: The new rulers of the world

The economic power of the multinational corporations or transnational corporations that currently dominate the world economy—which may be considered the basic operating units of the system, especially regarding their economic power relative to the nation-state—has been a major area of concern in critical development studies. What concerns critical thinkers in the area of development is that as bearers of capital in the form of direct foreign investment (FDI) and the transfer of technology, they are conceived by some—especially multilateral agencies and governments of the 'North'—to be the prime agents of development. However, there is considerable evidence that supports alternative perspectives from which they are viewed as the vanguard of imperialism by the 'North,' creators and conduits of global capital accumulation and institutional mechanisms for surplus transfer of the resources and surplus value of the 'South.'

The empirical evidence surrounding the operation of MNCs in the developing countries needs to be critically analyzed and closely scrutinized. There are several theoretical frameworks for interpreting the relevant facts surrounding the MNCs and their global operations. Salient facts include, for example, their size: they outstrip all but the most advanced industrial economies, leading to comparative charts based on gross income in which MNCs figure prominently in a list of the world's top 100 'economies,' a list that includes many nation-states. The increase in sheer scale and the global reach of the MNCs in the 1990s is well documented. During this period, FDI, regarded by IFIs such as the IMF as the 'backbone of development finance,' grew from around $200 billion in 1990 to almost $1.2 trillion in 2000, before dropping again in 2001 to $600 million due to a slowdown in the global economy. This slowdown lasted some three years before resuming again under heightened global demand for natural resources, energy and primary commodities, much of which involved China, India and several other Asian economies (Petras & Veltmeyer 2009).

Much FDI growth in the 1990s was unproductive, i.e., it was not designed to expand production or boost productivity via investments in new technology. Rather, FDI was used to buy state enterprises put on the purchasing block in a frenzy of privatizations and to feed a process of cross-border merger and acquisition (M&A). From under $200 billion in 1990 the value of M&A increased to $1.2 trillion in 2000, 80 percent of total FDI flows.

It is estimated that the total number of MNCs today exceed 65,000 but these have almost 850,000 affiliates. The value added to world production by these MNCs in 2005 was estimated at $3.5 trillion with total sales at $18.5 trillion, which compares with world exports of $7.4 trillion. But production is highly concentrated and sales monopolized by a relatively small number of MNCs. In terms of sales, for example, the world's largest 500 MNCs *tripled* their sales from 1990 to 2000, while the top 100 increased their sales from $3.2 trillion to $4.8 trillion.

Petras & Veltmeyer 2007b.

6. Understanding social movements: The force of resistance

Political parties, as understood and defined by Max Weber, are organizations that pursue the acquisition of power rather than change. Or, to put it more exactly, they pursue change solely for the purpose of acquiring power. In this view, the energy of political parties is focused on a change of government, or regime, and only latterly (if at all) on substantial structural changes. This is because the very structure they operate within legitimizes their taking of power and, perhaps more importantly, their continuation in power for the long term.

However, in contradistinction to the political party, another form of organization that has generally been more effective in bringing about more substantive structural, and therefore 'revolutionary,' change, is the *social movement*. Social movements are generally organized to mobilize the forces of resistance to structures of economic and political power and to contest that power from the standpoint of social groups and classes that have been marginalized, disadvantaged, exploited, oppressed and dominated by structural features of society. These 'structural distortions' have resulted in extreme forms of deprivation in its many economic, political, cultural and social forms, and social movements seek structural solutions for these structural inequalities.

For example, in Latin America in the 1990s the most effective forces of social change, used to mobilize resistance against mainstream government policies dominated by neoliberal social philosophy and its associated free market, competitive capitalist prescriptions for development (known as the Washington Consensus), were social movements created and populated by indigenous communities and peasant organizations. To this day, peasant social movements remain one of the principal forces of resistance to the hegemonic power of global capital, especially with regard to land distribution and resource allocation and usage. Other social movements—formed by students, women and other non-peasant organizations—have been equally successful in drawing attention to both the power of social movements to effect real social change and to the underlying boundary conditions of electoral party politics, which severely limit the electoral system's capacity to effect the required structural solutions to problems of impoverishment, a lack of social equity and the circumscription of the most basic freedoms and rights.

McMichael 2006; Petras & Veltmeyer 2005b.

7. Critical development thinking in action

In keeping with the motto of critical development studies ('the point is not to just interpret the world differently, but to change it'), critical social analysts are concerned not only to create usable theories and explanations for observed social structure and the forms of individual agency such structures induce, but also to use their theories and explanations to effect changes in society that will impel us towards more just and equitable forms of social organization.

In this respect, Marxism and its associated analytical tools focusing on class analysis are especially useful, in that purposive change within the context of an existing capitalist system is part of the very fabric of its theoretical analysis. Moreover, although there have been many recent advances in social analysis regarding the creation of a more just society through gender and ethnicity studies, it remains true that at the structural level, class for the most part trumps other conditions of social behaviour, including behaviours influenced by conditions of gender specialization and ethnic background. In the case of critical development studies, when urban and national (or even regional) concerns and issues are merged with rural development issues, class analysis and the worker/capitalist relationship still proves to be the most fruitful focus of thinking and discussion, especially regarding social analysis for the purpose of social change.

Berberoglu 2009; Burris 1988; Petras & Veltmeyer 2010; Veltmeyer 2010.

Module 28

Gender, Empowerment and Development

Jane L. Parpart
University of the West Indies, Jamaica

Development debates are currently in flux, with important implications for the practice and analysis of gender and development, including the role of feminist theorizing and masculinity studies. Some argue for neoliberal, market driven solutions to gender inequality, while others believe change in gender relations will only come when women (and men) are empowered to understand their predicaments and to work together for home-grown solutions. This critical empowerment approach is currently very popular among certain development practitioners (Moser 1993) and feminists concerned with gender issues (Antrobus 1995; Parpart, Rai and Staudt 2002). This module critically engages these debates in the belief that theoretical understandings have important implications for policy and action and thus matter to those who are trying to reconfigure gender roles and relations in ways that will increase both women's and men's opportunities to make full use of their talents and opportunities in an increasingly insecure world.

1. Conceptualizing women's power

In the 1980s structuralism as a form of social scientific analysis came under attack from a variety of standpoints, leading to the assertion that development theory was at an impasse. These critiques drew heavily on poststructuralist epistemology and methodology, particularly in regard to discourse analysis: concerns with the need to deconstruct language to find hidden transcripts and the power of discourse to shape and control thought and practice (Escobar 1995). Armed with this critical theoretical perspective, a new generation of feminist scholars (and practitioners) in the field of development, such as Jane Parpart (1995), emphasize the centrality of 'empowerment' as a development issue. While 'power' denotes the capacity of some to make decisions on behalf of a group or to 'exert one's will against resistance,' 'empowerment' denotes knowledge-capacitation—the ability to make decisions and to act for one's self or together with others in one's social group or with which one identifies. The writings of Foucault, particularly his analytic focus on the capillary nature, pervasiveness and relational character of the knowledge-power relation also influenced these critics, who argue that a more nuanced analysis of power as a social relation will reveal the potential power of marginalized peoples and the poor, particularly women.

Rathgeber 1990: 489–502; Cleaver 2002; Parpart & Marchand 1995.

2. Women, gender and empowerment: Finding a critical edge?

Critical alternative development (i.e., alternative development that draws on critical 'postdevelopment' thinking) pays particular attention to the power of knowledge and discourse to shape and define the way people think and the idea that development discourse can make certain ways of thinking and acting impossible. Advocates of this approach emphasize the knowledge of the poor in general and women in particular, those whose voices have been silenced in a process of active disempowerment, as a resource that if mobilized—for example, as Moser (1993) suggests, in planning for women's development or, as suggested by Karl (1995), by participating in effective decisionmaking—could play a critical role in the process of social transformation and development. Krishna Ahooja-Patel (1982, 2007) explores the dynamics of this planning process from a development and feminist perspective within the United Nations.

Rowlands 1997: Chaps. 2, 7; Mosedale 2005: 243–57; Kabeer 2003; Parpart, Rai & Staudt 2002; Kabeer 1994; Sen & Grown 1988; Karl 1995.

3. How does culture affect and effect women's empowerment?

Empowerment is essentially the capacitation of individuals to act for themselves to change their subaltern situation and enter a process of social transformation. At issue in this process is the power-effect of knowledge or, as Foucault conceives of it, the knowledge-power relation—the mobilization of a resource (knowledge) that under certain conditions can be a major force for change. As to what these conditions are or might be is a major object of analysis and a critical issue in debate among feminist critics of mainstream development thinking and practice. At issue in this debate are matters of culture, knowledge and power; i.e., although empowerment has a psychological dimension in terms of capacitation, it is more generally a cultural issue, a matter of resources embedded in a society's culture and disembedding these resources, making them available for people to use in acting collectively for themselves as a social group.

Mohanty 2002: 499–536; Racioppi & O'Sullivan 2000.

4. Is economic activity or political engagement empowering of women?

Among feminist scholars of alternative critical development there is a broad consensus on the need for, and the centrality of, empowerment as an essential condition of development and social transformation. There is also a consensus as to the fundamental agency of this develop-ment, namely women themselves and the poor more generally. But there is no agreement as to the most appropriate or effective strategy for bringing about this empowerment. This is an issue for further reflection and discussion. Another issue is microcredit lending/finance—whether it is empowering of women, as argued by mainstream theorists of development or, as argued by Heloise Weber (2002), disempowering of women because of its demobilizing effect. Kabeer (2001) reviews the debate on this critical issue.

Lairap-Fonderson 2002; Mahmud 2003: 577–605; Rai 2002;
Freeman 2001: 1007–37; Kabeer 2001; Weber 2002.

5. Education and health as conditions of human development or empowerment?

Education and health are essential conditions of social development, as well as critical factors of 'human development' (see Module 26). In addition, education can be conceived of both as a form of capital, a productive resource that if capitalized can lead to an increase in economic development, and, from a feminist development perspective, an important source of empower-ment. Not only does schooling for girls and education for women radically improve the capacity of women for expanded choices in their lives but also it empowers them to act for themselves. Although the issue of health is more controversial there is no question that the lack of health, a condition of poverty, dramatically restricts the freedom of women and the range of choices available to them. In this sense, improved health is both a condition of human development (from a mainstream development perspective) and a source of empowerment (from a feminist development perspective).

Stambach 1998; Longwe 1998: 19–26; Heward & Bunwaree 1998.

6. Can NGOs be a source of empowerment?

The post-Washington Consensus (see Modules 5) is that for development to be sustainable it needs to be participatory as well as empowering of the poor, converting them into the active agents of their own development. The government in this context is assigned the responsibility of creating an appropriate (i.e., facilitating) policy and institutional framework. As for the nongovernmental organizations of 'civil society' in the North and the South, their assigned role (in the new paradigm of alternative development) is to mediate between the overseas development associations, the donors of development aid and the local or community-based grassroots organizations of the poor by assisting them, capacitating them to act for themselves. In this sense NGOs can be viewed as sources of empowerment. But see Petras and Veltmeyer (2001) for a very different and much more critical perspective on the role of NGOs in the development process.

Shehabuddin 1999: 1011–44; Mindry 2001: 1187–211; Parpart 2002.

Module 29

Gendering the Economy
Implications for Critical Development Thinking and Practice

Fiona MacPhail
University of British Columbia, Canada

Feminist economics is a relatively new field of inquiry that draws upon and extends critical views and questions from earlier research in economics and other disciplines, along with feminist theory. This module demonstrates the contribution of feminist economics to critical development studies. It promotes an understanding of the biases and limitations of mainstream development economic theories and advances in feminist economic theory at both the household and macroeconomy levels, and its transformative potential in terms of methodology, approach to development and the position of women.

1. What is feminist economics? Gender and development theory

Feminist economics emerged in the 1970s and research accelerated in the 1990s. Feminist economics draws upon earlier research on gender wage discrimination in neoclassical economics, domestic labour in Marxist economics and gender roles in economic development, along with feminist theory and insights from other disciplines. Feminist economics provides critiques of neoclassical, Marxist and institutional economic theories and provides alternative ways of thinking about material conditions, economies and well-being, with priority given to understanding and addressing women's subordinate position.

One of the main features of feminist economics is the view of gender as a social construct that varies over time and across regions. The notion of gender varies within feminist economics from the perspective of social roles to one of gender relations situated within social relations of race and class. Likewise, analyses of sources of gender inequality include a focus on the lack of integration into the market economy and an examination of the interaction of patriarchy and capitalism. Other features of feminist economics include a broader methodology, in which the

149

influence of the prevailing social order on the nature of intellectual thought is recognized, questions of inquiry beyond the market and the transformative potential of feminist investigations.

Bería 2003; Kabeer 1994; Parpart, Connelly & Barriteau 2000.

2. Dynamics of the gendered household

The key question examined in this second theme is whether women's improved access to resources facilitates their empowerment. Moving beyond the static and harmonious view of the household in neoclassical economics, feminist economists recognize that access to resources may be valued by women but not necessarily empowering. As Bina Agarwal (1997: 15) states, norms can limit what can be bargained over, constrain bargaining power, be the 'subject of negotiation' and influence 'how the process of bargaining is conducted.' The empirical work in this area is particularly rich and informative. This and similar questions have been examined across a variety of locations and in contexts such as export processing zones, credit, migration and gender bias in the population ratios.

A potential mechanism for assisting students to engage with the available material in this area is for students themselves to take responsibility for assessing the nature of the household gender relations as analyzed in a given paper. A set of illustrative papers for this student-oriented activity include those by Kabeer (2001) and MacPhail & Dong (2007). These papers provide analyses of the dynamics of gender relations in the household in many different contexts. With this background, students will be able to debate the usefulness of the various feminist approaches to the household and the impact on empowerment of women's access to economic resources.

Agarwal 1997: 1–51; Kandiyoti 1998; Elson & Pearson 1981: 87–108.

3. Dynamics of gender and the macroeconomy

Economic liberalization has been taking place in Sub-Saharan Africa (ssa) since the early 1980s, when many countries undertook stabilization and restructuring measures of unprecedented scope as conditions for further loans from the World Bank and the IFIs. Throughout the 1990s and into the new millennium (at least until the 2008 global financial crisis), individual countries in the Global South continued to liberalize their trade regimes, encourage private investment and maintain fiscal discipline. As of 1999, IFI loans have been closely tied to the World Bank's Poverty Reduction Strategy Papers (PRSP) approach—a tacit recognition that structural adjustment has not brought ordinary people out of poverty.

The structural adjustment decades have been marked as much by contestation over the policies and their effects as they have been by the policies themselves. The minority critical stance of the late 1980s and early 1990s has become more mainstream. There is a widespread recognition that anticipated growth rates have not occurred and that the sought stimulus to production, technological change and a restructured composition of the economy has been muted at best. Nowhere are these debates more important than with respect to the agricultural sector and Africa's rural populations. In most ssa countries, a high proportion of the population lives in rural areas, is dependent on agriculture for its livelihood and is poor. One of the further characteristics of this rural population is that the family—or more properly the household—is a key institution within the rural economy (Whitehead 2005). Divisions of labour based on gender and generation have an impact on the effects of liberalization. Conversely, the gender and generations are affected in different ways by the impact of changes in the macroeconomic environment for agricultural production and in the institutions that deliver inputs and distribute outputs. Whitehead (2005) provides an overview of these gendered impacts.

Notwithstanding the obvious gendered impacts of macroeconomic policies, the macro-economy as mainstream economists view it, i.e., in terms of aggregates such as consumption, investment and government expenditures, appears to be gender neutral. Thus the need for a gender-sensitive analysis from a critical development—as well as a feminist—perspective to establish the workings of the gendered economy. Diane Elson and Cagatay (2000), in this connection, identify three approaches used to theoretically reconstruct the workings of a gendered macroeconomy:

- examinations of the differential impacts on women of macroeconomic changes, including trade liberalization, financial liberalization and foreign investment;
- analyses of the relationship between gender inequalities in one sector (e.g., labour market, access to credit and land) on macroeconomic outcomes; and
- theories that provide more complex accounts of social reproduction in macroeconomic theory.

On this latter approach, Nancy Folbre analyzes motivations for caring labour in terms of responsibility, reciprocity and altruism that contrast to the neoclassical economic view of unpaid labour as only service providing. As before, one avenue for teaching the material is to present an overview of advances in feminist (macro)economic theory and have students analyze specific empirical case studies.

Elson & Cagatay 2000: 1347–64; Elson 1990; Folbre 1995: 73–92; Whitehead 2005.

4. Women and well-being: Gender biases and silences

Feminist economists have contributed to the capabilities, social exclusion and human rights approaches to poverty and well-being, all of which contrast starkly with conventional income and indicator based approaches. The capability approach to poverty and development of Amartya Sen offers many improvements over the conventional utility and resource approach. However, Martha Nussbaum (2003) argues that it is necessary to make the ideas more specific. Ingrid Robeyns (2003) takes this idea further and outlines a method for discussing what might be appropriate indicators of capabilities from a gender perspective. The social exclusion approach, illustrated by Naila Kabeer (2006), examines how the social mechanisms of class, caste and employment among others serve to impoverish women.

One CDS approach would be to have students think about and evaluate in feminist economic terms the affect on women of the World Bank's PRSPs. Two feminist papers that offer a critical assessment of the PRSPs are Whitehead (2005) and Zuckerrman (2003). Students could use these papers as background and undertake their own gender analysis of a PRSPs for a specific country.

Kabeer 2006: 64–78; Nussbaum 2003: 33–59.

5. Economic policy and tools as if gender matters

This and the following themes focus on economic policies and tools useful in analyzing gender inequalities and that potentially could be used to improve the position of women. These policies and tools are representative of actions at national and international levels, direct transfers to women and public services, and networks of women.

Gender budgets are a tool used in the development community for understanding how macroeconomic policy can affect gender inequality. Gender budgets are being used by national governments (e.g., South Africa) and by organizations outside of governments (e.g., in Mexico). However, while gender budgets are increasingly being analyzed, their potential for facilitating improvements may be weakened, as Diane Elson (2004) notes, when 'governments, especially in the South, have less and less control over public finance decisions.' Since gender budgets exist for many countries, students could potentially analyze the different features and successes of various countries' experiences with this tool.

International labour standards are advanced as a way to improve the conditions of workers in the formal sector. There are various mechanisms of enforcement, including proposals to add punitive trade measures in the WTO, along with other mechanisms such as NGO social auditing and public pressure. Some feminist economists (e.g., Kabeer) argue that international labour standards are a form of Northern protectionism that can result in employment losses and/or informalization of work, other feminist economists advocate certain types of economic policy tools and actions over others.

Public policy has responded to the problems that affect women in the development process at the level of (1) budgeting (gender budgets); (2) work conditions (international labour standards) and (3) income conditions (basic income). The readings in this section explore the dynamics of these public policies as they affect women, their relationship to men and their participation in the development process. But significantly, women themselves have taken action, taking advantage of the opportunities available to them. Empowered by their own collective actions and organization, they have mobilized for their livelihoods and their rights, primarily in the form of international and transnational networks of women (Moghadam 2005b).

Budlender 2000: 1365–78; Budlender, Elson, Hewitt & Mukhopadhyay 2002; Elson 2004: 623–42. [basic budgets]; Berik & Van der Meulen Rodgers 2007: Kabeer 2004: 3–35. [international labour standards]; Robeyns 2007: McKay 2007: 337–48. [basic incomes]; Benería & Bisnath 2003; DAWN 1995: 2001–04; Moghadam 2005b; Rowbotham & Linkogle 2001 [transnational networks].

Section 10

Culture, Knowledge and Education
for Development

In the 1960s and 1970s, 'critical' approaches to development were generally constructed within the frame of a 'radical political economy paradigm' in which 'culture' by and large and no matter how conceived was abstracted from understanding and the analysis of the development process. One of the first critical development studies to correct this deficit was Peter Worsley's *The Three Worlds* (1984), a work of extraordinary scope and unprecedented vision as well as theoretical eclecticism. Much more than a study of the contemporary Third World, *The Three Worlds* examined the constituents of development—cultural as well as political and economic—throughout the world from prehistory to the present—and for this reason warrants consideration as an essential item in a pre-reading program of CDS 'classics.'

Worsley first considers existing theories of development, synthesizing the Marxist approach with that of social anthropologists, and identifying culture—in the sense of a society's shared set of values and beliefs—as the key element missing in traditional approaches to the sociology of development. And of course, the same can be said of traditional approaches in the economics of development, where not only culture but also politics and social issues were generally excluded from consideration. Worsley, on the other hand, brings into the centre of analysis issues such as relations of ethnicity and nationalism to social class and to each other. At the same time, reflecting the dominant intellectual and political culture, Worsley, like so many Marxists at the time (as well as mainstream theorists and practitioners), tended to marginalize the issue of gender, which in the 1980s would become a critically important dimension of critical thinking and CDS, as pointed out by Jane Parpart in Module 28.

Culture, as Munck notes in his contribution to this book (Module 7), while a highly contested concept in the 1980s, became a key element in the management of development as well as a point of reference for a radical critique of mainstream thinking. Worsley's challenge, to elaborate the 'missing concept' of culture, was taken up by a number of theorists and practitioners in the context of a postdevelopment critique of both mainstream and alternative approaches (see Tucker 1997). Vincent Tucker, among others, argued that 'development thinking must be underpinned by a conceptualization of culture as a dynamic and conflictual process' (1999: 17). Munck argues that it is best to see this shift in terms of injecting cultural politics into critical development theory, i.e., as a cultural critique of development. It is at this juncture, Munck adds, that 'the cultural critique of development joins the terrain of social movement theory and its rich understanding of the "culture of politics and the politics of culture" Alvarez, Dagnino & Escobar 1998).'

Aradhana Parmar in (Module 30) notes that '[c]ulture' is understood and used in three basic ways: (1) to differentiate among diverse ways of doing things that reflect a society's dominant beliefs and values; (2) as a condition (and thus an explanation) of social and economic development; and (3) as a resource for development—a tool for mobilizing action for progressive or radical change.

On this theme—culture as resource for change and development—CDS in its analysis of culture is concerned not so much with a society's values and beliefs, and the actions taken on these beliefs and values (in an explanation of why some societies 'develop' and others do not'), but with the power of knowledge—knowledge as a source of empowerment. As Munck notes in his module, 'knowledge' became an important issue in the 1980s among critics of the development enterprise not because of its role in the development process (as a source and form of human capital) but precisely because of its subversive potential as a source of empowerment, as a resource for action, a tool for radical change.

Interestingly, towards the end of the decade, 'knowledge for development' also became an important theme in the mainstream approach to development. This was reflected in the World Bank's 1989/90 *World Development Report,* which provided an in-depth analysis of education for the 'knowledge economy' and knowledge as a productive resource, an asset for human, social and economic development. This growing interest of the Bank in the 'knowledge economy'—viewed by many sociologists in sociological terms as the 'information society'—translated in 2000 into an in-depth study of research and development (the application of scientific research to economic production) and the role of information and communications technologies (ICT) in the development process. The World Bank Institute in recent years has conducted a broad range of studies on the role of 'global information and communication technologies' in the development process, publishing the results in the form of books, numerous case study reports and a series of working papers. Module 31 reviews some of these results and the issues involved from a CDS perspective

Module 32 looks at education, which, as a means of knowledge generation and skill acquisition, has always played a significant role in the development process, both as a productive resource, a form of capital (skill acquisition) that can be exploited as a condition of both economic development and what the UNDP conceived of as 'human development'—a means of social capacitation and individual self-realization, increasing an individual's capacity to think freely and act, allowing them to position themselves better in their transition to the world of work, enhancing the choices open to them and the opportunities for self-advancement.

This approach to education as human capital accumulation was reflected both in the World Bank's 1980 *World Development Report* and the UNDP's conception of human development as well as, more generally, UNESCO's work over the years, which is reviewed and evaluated in its annual *Global Monitoring Report,* in which development is defined as 'education for all' and viewed as a key factor of economic and social development. The World Bank in its 1980 and 1990 *World Development Reports* on poverty and earlier studies shares this concern with education as a source and condition of development, particularly in relation to what the Bank views as a critical sociological factor of the development process—the 'transition to work.' At issue in this transition, as the UNDP also emphasizes, is skill acquisition and an enhancement of choice, which increases the capacity of individuals to take advantage of and act on their opportunities, with the aggregate result of economic and social development.

Module 30

The Cultural Matrix of Development and Change

Aradhana Parmar
University of Calgary, Canada

Does culture matter for development? What does cultural analysis have to offer to development studies? Can culture be used as a variable in explaining the development process? Does culture advance or obstruct development? Can it serve as a tool for change in a progressive direction? Can we develop a form of cultural analysis for development studies? Why is it being introduced now after years of neglect in development theory?

In the beginning the study of development was dominated by economic perspectives, and economists had little to no interest in 'non-economic' factors such as culture (Crush 1995). Development theory, over the past six decades, has made passing reference to diverse factors such as economic growth, colonialism, dependency, the environment and global markets to explain development or its absence. Given the failure of so many explanatory models, it is not surprising to look at culture for a correction to development discourse steeped in Eurocentrism (Pieterse 1996: 190). Increasingly, scholars and practitioners in development are turning to culture not just as an explanatory variable, a matter of values and technology (indigenous knowledge, for example), but as a resource and tool for substantive or progressive change and as a matter of 'politics' (Alvarez, Dagnino & Escobar 1998).

According to the *Concise Oxford Dictionary*, the original connotation of the word 'culture' referred to the tillage of the soil; rearing, production (of bees, oysters, fish, silk, bacteria). During the sixteenth and seventeenth centuries, this term was used metaphorically to refer to the cultivation of the mind and intellect; in the twenty-first century, culture is generally understood in the anthropological sense of an 'entire way of life of a society: its values, practices, symbols, institutions and human relationships' (Clifford Geertz).

Culture draws attention to differences—to the diversity of values and practices, beliefs and different 'ways of doing things.' In this sense, culture is neither homogeneous nor static but an evolving, shifting and multidimensional phenomenon. It can enrich and uplift, serving as a means of mobilizing action and embodying anti-hegemonic struggle. However, it can also divide people and be used as an instrument of oppression or a source of conflict, as in Samuel Huntington's 'clash of civilizations.'

According to Vincent Tucker (1997), culture is neither a thing nor a realm but rather a way of looking at things—a way of knowing. The most important task therefore is to address the methodological challenges posed by cultural analysis, with a particular concern for the production of knowledge and the construction of meaning, and the translation of knowledge into power (Pieterse 1996). It is in this sense that Amartya Sen (2004), in his distinguished essay, 'How Does Culture Matter,' refers to culture as a resource in the study and practice of development.

Alvarez, Dagnino & Escobar 1998; Crush 1995; Escobar 1995; Pieterse 1996; Sen 2004; Radcliffe 2006; Tucker 1997.

1. Culture and development: Theoretical perspectives

Culture, it has been argued, is a relatively neglected if not entirely missing dimension of development analysis. To correct this deficit and connect 'culture' to 'development,' it is important, first of all, to clarify what is meant by 'development.' Needless to say, this is a matter of theoretical perspective and context. In the 1950s and 1960s development was generally understood as a matter of economic growth, material gain and consumption. In the 1970s, however, the development enterprise was redirected towards the goal of meeting the basic needs of the population and reducing the incidence of absolute poverty in the less developed countries of the Global South, at the time grouped under the rubric the 'Third World.' Like 'culture' the meaning and use of 'development' is highly contested.

For example, 'development' means one thing to a poor peasant in Mexico or Bangladesh and it means something totally different to a Tibetan monk, a Muslim from the Middle East or an official from China (Tucker 1997: 4). From a cultural perspective, development has to do with human beings, and when people's beliefs, ideas, values, ways of doing things and feelings are not taken into consideration and respected, human development strictly speaking cannot happen (Tucker 1997; Escobar 1995). It can also be argued that development strategies are necessarily based on culture because it is not possible to operate outside culture (Pieterse 1996: 185). This is to say, development is embedded in culture.

Development theories, whether conventional or radical, are not immune from cultural relativity. Dependency theory, for example, in its application was more specific to Latin America, while the Middle East continues to resist Western norms of modernity. According to Sardar (1996), the 'development' idea is a cultural construction of Western civilization and has virtually no meaning or relevance to Muslims. Similarly, Samir Amin uses culture to extend his Marxist 'modes of production' analysis to challenge the Eurocentrism of development studies.

The cultural arrogance and Eurocentrism of the modernization paradigm begs the fundamental question of power involved in knowledge production. Escobar (1995) studied development as a cultural system and applied Foucaultian discourse analysis to the field. He argues that, like the economic process of modernization, the system of knowledge production is also divided into North and South. The dominance of the North is viewed as an expression of neocolonialism, wherein Western ideologies created a 'mechanism of control' over developments in the 'Third World,' a concept constructed to the purpose of domination within a relation of power. When culture is used as a mechanism of control, people are stripped of their identity and are no longer capable of self-determination; they become a subjects whose projects, dreams, values and meanings are supplied by others. In the eyes of the developers, their societies are stagnant, incapable of self–directed development and an obstacle to development. Moreover, given that development is a normative concept, it is inevitably constructed as 'for their own good' (Tucker 1997: 6–7).

In order to use culture as a resource and tool for change, it is first necessary to deconstruct the concept in the study and practice of development—to deconstruct not only the concept of culture when used as an explanatory variable in development theory but also to establish its presence in its apparent absence. It is essential to address epistemological and methodological concerns and not just 'add culture and stir' (Tucker 1997: 2; Pieterse 1996: 184).

Alvarez, Dagnino & Escobar 1998; Escobar 1995; Radcliffe 2006; Tucker 1997.

2. Modernization and change: From modernizing values to capitalism

Modernization, the dominant development paradigm, heavily steeped in Western capitalist hegemony, 'mesmerized poor people by abundance of wealth and offered hope' (Williams 2001). This Americanization of modernization theory wooed governments of the Global South to accept the ethnocentric package of modernization and capitalism, along with Western institutions and values.

A number of development economists in recent years have turned to the classical study of the origins of capitalism by sociologist Max Weber in the search for the cultural conditions and sources of economic development. Harrison (1985) and Harrison & Huntington's *Culture Matters: How Values Shape Human Progress* (2000) exemplify this turn back towards an emphasis on the cultural dimension of economic development. Interestingly, Harrison and his associates locate the wellspring of capitalist development not in Western culture, as did the modernization theorists of the 1950s and 1960s, but in values embedded in Asian culture. Thus does Harrison (1985) explain the relative 'success' of a number of Asian societies, as compared to Latin American societies, in generating high rates of economic growth and entering the modern world of development. Harrison and Huntington and their colleagues emphasize the working of cultural, rather than economic or political, factors in explaining why some countries develop and others do not. Culture is used as an explanatory tool, not as a resource for action as in a critical development perspective. If Latin Americans only had a mindset based on Asian culture, Harrison argues, they could have developed. What needs to change, in this view (a form of modernization theory), is the culture.

Harrison 1985; Harrison & Huntington 2000; Williams 2001: 311–24.

3. The clash of civilization and the role of cultural conflict

Even though Max Weber himself did not establish any causal relationship between Calvinism and capitalism, merely demonstrated that there was an 'elective affinity' between them, his *Protestant Ethic and the Spirit of Capitalism* is often cited in support of the argument that a specific culture is a required condition of development. However, Weber's thesis is a more subtle argument that does not reduce into the practical diagnosis, implicitly advocated by Harrison and Huntington and others, that infusing more Calvinist values into non-western cultures would improve their potential for growth. In this variant of Huntington's 'clash of civilizations' hypothesis, poverty and low rates of growth are deeply affected by adverse rules and norms that reduce incentives for mobility and investment. The challenge for development, then, is to reform culture by inculcating more growth and mobility-oriented perspectives through education or other means of transforming 'toxic cultures.' Thus, as with some modernization theorists, non-Western or 'traditional' culture is regarded as the enemy—a voice from the past that inhibits societies from functioning in the modern world. Needless to say, this entire approach needs to be deconstructed, and notwithstanding the laudable effort to bring culture back into an analysis of the development problematic, it needs to be entirely rejected.

Huntington 1993: 22–49; Williams 2001: 311–24.

4. Culture and postdevelopment:
Knowledge and power in the development process

Cultural analysis pays particular attention to the production of knowledge and construction of meanings and will incorporate local voices (Tucker 1997: 11). If the 'culture turn' opened up development as discourse to options beyond modernity, the explicit adoption of a 'postdevelopment' perspective in the 1990s took this shift one step further by arguing that the processes of structural change and transformation identified in modernist discourse are literally figments of its author's imagination, used as a means of social control.

So where do the critical social theorists of postdevelopment take us in their critique of mainstream development? There are very distinct strands in the postdevelopment literature (see Crush 2005, for an overview of various perspectives). Some versions or modalities of post-development are in many respects a reprise of classic anti-modernist or romantic critiques of modernity. It is entirely understandable that after half a century of 'development' as we know it today not delivering on its original optimistic promises, critics may well wish to turn for inspiration to a pre-development era. But apart from producing a warm glow there is very little that this perspective might add to current debates on globalization and how oppositional social networks might in practice counter its negative effects. It certainly does not offer a plausible alternative development strategy (see Pieterse 2000 for a constructive critique of postdevelopment thinking).

Crush 1995; Esteva 1992; Pieterse 2001; Tucker 1997: Introduction.

5. From postcolonial nationalism to
cultural imperialism and globalization

The worldwide events and the epoch-defining changes that have characterized the last two decades of capitalist development can be alternatively conceptualized and theorized in terms of three different concepts: 'development,' 'globalization' and 'imperialism' (Petras & Veltmeyer 2005a). According to Tucker, theories of postmodernism, postcolonialism and globalization are all manifestations of the cultural turn, challenging both conventional and radical theories of development. Each provides a different angle from which to understand the dynamics of culture.

Thomas Friedman in *The Lexus and the Olive Tree* conceptualizes 'globalization' in terms of 'the ability of a culture, when it encounters other strong cultures, to absorb influences that naturally fit into and can enrich that culture, to resist those things that are truly alien and to compartmentalize those things that, while different, can nevertheless be enjoyed and celebrated as different' (2000: 295). To wit, Friedman thinks good globalization occurs when a little Japanese girl goes to a McDonalds in Tokyo to 'enjoy the American way of life and food.' Bad globalization would be when the same little girl gets off a plane in Los Angeles and is surprised that 'they have McDonalds in America, too!' The little girl should be aware that McDonalds is not a part of the Japanese culture. Otherwise we are headed for a very bland world: all Lexus and no olive tree.

A postcolonial angle on culture is taken by Robert Balfour (2007) via an exploration of the fictional writing of V.S. Naipaul in which culture appears as a 'phenomenon of globalization,' a 'consequence of imperialism and decolonization.' Balfour argues that 'globalization differs from postcolonialism, in the interaction it brings about between marginalized classes and nations and those who by virtue of class, economic power or race are … at the centre in the twenty-first century.'

The critical issue here, represented theoretically in economic studies of globalization and sociological studies of modernization, is that education and wage-employment constitute avenues of social mobility, providing opportunities for self-advancement. In this connection, with reference to Naipaul's *Half a Life* (2001) and *Magic Seeds* (2004), Balfour observes that the people who become unemployable are educated migrants with skills, refuting a mantra of globalization that, irrespective of race, class or gender, education and employment provide the major source of opportunity in the world of postmodern postcapitalist development—pathways out of poverty or avenues of mobility. However, he argues, with reference to both Naipaul's novels but in Amin's words, that in the postcolonial world of neoliberal globalization 'exclusion/marginalization has become a permanent feature of the landscape' (Amin 1999: 17).

Culture is a critical dimension of development and globalization. However, it can also be conceptualized as a form of imperialism, that is, as power wielded by one group or class to establish cultural domination or ideological hegemony. Cultural imperialism in this context implies two important factors: effects on another culture and the coercive power used in the process. It is closely connected to postcolonialism and orientalism in the knowledge-power relation within the development problematic. 'Cultural imperialism' also occurs through market forces creating a demand for cultural commodities. Global consumption of American goods, such as music, TV shows and sports, especially by youth, clearly demonstrates the power of cultural imperialism in the development process.

Adams, Gupta & Mengisteab 1999; Agyeman 2007; Balfour 2007: 1–21;
Pieterse 2004: 41–58; Friedman 2000.

6. Indigenous knowledge as a resource for alternative development and change

The use of the term indigenous knowledge (IK) in the context of development began with Robert Chamber's University of Sussex IDS group in 1979 featuring 'indigenous technical knowledge' (Warren et al. 1989) According to D. Michael Warren et al. (1995: xv), indigenous knowledge is a 'knowledge that is unique to a given culture or society, contrasts with the international knowledge system which is generated through the global network of universities and research institutions.' Indigenous knowledge is also referred to as local knowledge, traditional environmental knowledge, folk knowledge, rural people's knowledge, popular knowledge and non-Western knowledge. Due to the failure of 'Western' development models—those of 'top-down' development or 'dependency' theory—there has been an increasing movement towards the incorporation of indigenous knowledge into development.

According to Escobar (1995), Western science, combined with the regime and discourse of development, has contributed to suppressing other forms of knowledge including people's knowledge in the 'Third World.' The interest in local knowledge and culture provides relief from the 'ethnocentrisms' of Western knowledge and a new framework in which to look at development, especially sustainable development. Fernando (2003: 54) argues that 'the use of indigenous knowledge in sustainable development [is] another example of capitalism's capacity to configure development according to its own imperatives. Rather than being an instrument of sustainable development, IK has become a means through which the diversity of knowledge systems and the embedded cultures in which they exist are disciplined and managed according to capital's need to expand.'

Indigenous knowledge is considered local in terms of its origin and applicability to local communities. There is an apparent binary between IK and universal knowledge systems, with negotiation between them required. However, as Clifford Geertz (1983) points out, 'in the solar system, the earth is local; in the galaxy, the solar system is local; and in the universe the galaxy is local.' Within transnational institutions, the state is local; within states, the region is local; within the region, the community is local and so on. Geertz (1983: 132) argues that what is local has to be construed in relation to what is not—its opposition. Thus, this opposition (and Geertz is not persuaded that an opposition is what we need) is not between local and universal knowledge, but between one form of local knowledge and another. However, Geertz adds, as all politics is necessarily local, so all understanding is necessarily so. No one knows everything—rural people's knowledge, popular knowledge in its multitudinous forms, Western or non-Western knowledge.

Briggs 2005: 99–114; Briggs & Sharp 2004: 661–76.

Module 31

Knowledge and Technology for Development

Alexander Borda-Rodriguez
Saint Mary's University, Canada

Sam Lanfranco
York University, Canada

Development knowledge is part of the global commons.... But a global partnership is required to cultivate and disseminate it. The World Bank Group's relationships with governments and organizations all over the world, and our unique reservoir of development experience across sectors and countries, position us to play a leading role in this new global knowledge partnership. We have been in the business of researching and disseminating the lessons of development for a long time. But the revolution in information technology increases the potential value of these efforts by vastly extending their reach. We need to become, in effect, the Knowledge Bank. (Wolfensohn 1996)

1. Knowledge, science and technology in the development process

Greater production is the key to prosperity and peace. And the key to greater production is a wider and more vigorous application of modern scientific and technical knowledge. —Harry Truman 1949

Scientific knowledge applied to the invention and development of new technologies for expanded production in both agriculture and industry is a critical factor of development. This is the fundamental mechanism of productivity growth—expanding production while reducing the input of labour, which is the basic source of the value of commodities on the market and of value-added production. In this sense production technology, i.e., the technological conversion of production, has a revolutionary impact on development, leading to a long-term process of productive transformation. The dynamics of technological transformation in the developing countries of the South are explored in the readings by Surendra Patel, former director of UNCTAD's Technology and Economic Development Division. The dynamics include research, productive investment, innovation, transfer, adaptation and physical conversion.

The assumption that poor countries lack scientific knowledge has been one of the major reasons behind development interventions since the 1950s. The assumption that poor countries have a 'knowledge deficit' has been a core subject in the debates about poverty eradication. This debate and others are examined in the work of Tarp (2000) and Degnbol-Martinussen and Engberg-Pedersen (2003), who compiled a historical analysis of foreign aid and development. However, their accounts do not engage in a critical analysis as to how knowledge has played a major role in development interventions; neither do they explore the critical role of knowledge within international development agendas. More recently, this role has been placed front and centre, based on the belief that technology in the form of knowledge is a critical but undertheorized factor in the development process, more critical perhaps than the factors so salient in traditional development theories, namely capital, labour and land.

Patel 2005, 2007; Smith 2002.

2. Knowledge-based development and technical assistance

Accelerating the development of countries and their people by investing resources, transferring knowledge, creating opportunities and advocating reforms—USAID's Strategic Goal, USAID 2004

International cooperation for development of 'foreign aid' is, and has been since the late 1940s, a matter of financial and technical assistance—the North-South transfer of finance and technical assistance (TA). The main objective of this so-called 'technical assistance' in the 1950s and subsequently was to transfer knowledge and technology to developing countries (Buron 1966; Bhouraskar 2007). The 'knowledge' in question was deemed to be scientific, and 'technology' was this knowledge in applied form.[1] Initially, development projects focused on transferring knowledge by experimenting with and using technology in poor countries (Degnbol-Martinussen & Engberg-Pederson 2003; Tarp 2000). Later, however, development projects emphasized knowledge transfer through the implementation of training schemes and advisory services.

Throughout the 1960s, 1970s and 1980s, knowledge was still associated with technology transfer from the developed countries to the developing countries, although it was increasingly evident that knowledge and ideas cannot be quickly or usefully transferred across cultural and scientific boundaries and that 'current understanding and use of knowledge within the development sector is generally poor… represent[ing] a major barrier to the effectiveness of development interventions' (Powell 2006: 1). In response to widespread evidence of a failure of TA to translate into sustained development and recognition that much of the transferred 'technology' or 'assistance' was inappropriate, in the 1980s thinking and practice shifted towards a participatory approach to knowledge production and incorporation of indigenous knowledge in development projects. A key dimension of a participatory approach is respect for local knowledge and awareness that knowledge for development is constructed in context rather than simply adapted to it (Chambers 1997). The vogue in recent years for capacity building similarly places knowledge at the forefront, linking development to participation (Mohan & Hickey 2004).

Even the World Bank, having repositioned itself as the 'Knowledge Bank,' now acknowledges the importance of participatory processes and therefore, implicitly at least, the importance of local knowledge alongside its own 'expert' knowledge. However, despite its apparent conversion, the World Bank still clings to the idea of knowledge as a product to be used instrumentally. Thus, more recently, it has explored ways of applying market mechanisms of supply and demand to knowledge for development. In this it has applied classical economic theories to conceptualize decades of failure in technology transfer or TA as attributable to knowledge being supply-led by donor agencies, including itself (Ramalingam 2005).

The World Bank discourages professionals interested in producing critical research about it and its developmental endeavours across the world. As Robin Broad (2007: 704) puts it, scholars who do not project the World Bank's paradigm are diminished, ostracized or deemed misfits. Broad also argues that information produced by the World Bank has played a critical role in legitimizing the neoliberal 'free-trade' paradigm over the past twenty-five years and that its Development Economic Research Department (DEC) has been vital to its role in establishing this 'regime of truth.'

Broad raises the question: Why does the work of DEC researchers who support the dominant knowledge framework—the neoliberal policy agenda—get so much attention and funding? She argues that the World Bank explicitly enforces its research agenda by promoting and encouraging authors as well as World Bank personnel to produce research that supports its political agenda. She quotes a former World Bank professional that describes how review processes are undertaken: 'It depends on what the paper is [about] and who the author is. If you are a respected neoclassical economist, then [approval] only needs one sign-off, that of your boss. If it's critical, then you go through endless reviews, until the author gives up' (Broad 2007: 703).

Given the critical importance of 'knowledge' to development (on this see Girvan 2007), the efforts of the World Bank to monopolize its production (Broad 2007) and the use of knowledge transfer as a means of advancing powerful economic interests in the North, it is imperative that alternative centres of development knowledge be created and that this knowledge be harnessed to the substantive social change needed to bring about development in the South.

To obviate the need for more radical change, i.e., to ensure that knowledge for development is tracked along a capitalist path, mainstream development thought considers communities to be important repositories of development knowledge, i.e., knowledge as a productive resource, an asset that could be capitalized and used to alleviate poverty (see Talisayon et al. 2008) if, and only if (according to the Peruvian economist Hernando de Soto, author of *The Other Path*), the poor acquire or are given the legal right to their property, legal title to their assets, converting mere possession into 'property' (De Soto 2000).

Broad 2007; Gumucio 2006; Powell 2006; Stone 2000; Wilson 2007: 183–99.

3. Knowledge, development and power

'Historically, knowledge domination has been an integral part of North-South relations....
Knowledge renovation serves to interpret contradictions and changing realities, responding to
challenges to the hegemonic discourse in ways that maintain existing hierarchies of power. The
devices used include linguistic cooptation, conceptual/theoretical innovation and revision of
policy agendas' (Girvan 2007: 6–7). Another major issue is the role of multi- or transnational
corporations in monopolizing R&D, ownership and control of production and communication
technologies—a matter, in part, of protecting and protesting intellectual property rights, an
issue at the centre of the anti-globalization movement and the corporate agenda of the WTO.
New frontiers in this field include biotechnology and nanotechnology. Much of the research and
concerns in these areas focuses on technical issues of practical application of scientific research.
However, there is also a clear political dimension to this research—a question of property and
power, a question addressed by McAfee (2003). In regard to biotechnology, Invernizzi and
Foladori (2005) also raise the question of the development implications of nanotechnology, a
new and rapidly growing area of technological research.

Surendra Patel (2005) explores a different dimension of the scientific knowledge-development relation: the role of 'social technology'—scientific knowledge applied to the development
process by the individual bearers of this knowledge. By many accounts, social technology is the
most critical factor in the development process, which is advanced by means of productive investment of capital in the generation of new knowledge—and the generation of new technologies
based on this knowledge.

Girvan 2007; McAfee 2003: 203–19; Alampay 2008.

4. Technological transformation without equity

The capitalist development process is predicated on a revolutionary process of productive
transformation based on the substitution of human labour with physical technology, the technological conversion of national or global production, which leads to a long-term trend towards
a rise in the 'organic composition of capital.' The structural outcome of this transformation is a
long-term change in the structure of production and an associated transition from a precapitalist or traditional type of labour-intensive agrarian economy, based on the direct production of
small-scale farmers, to a modern and capital-intensive industrial economy and capitalist system.
The fundamental role of technology in this process of productive transformation is to increase
the productivity of labour.

It is possible to trace out distinct phases of this technological development of production and
society, driven by what is generally conceived of as a succession of technological revolutions—
from the industrial revolution in the nineteenth century, characterized by the dramatic increase
of productive capacity and productivity growth (viz. the innovation of new manufacturing technologies such as the steam engine and the cotton engine); a second industrial revolution based
on the generation of electrical power, the production of heavy industry in diverse sectors such
as automobile production, and the scientific management of labour at the point of production
(Taylorism and Fordism); and the design of new communication and production technologies
based on the computer chip, electronics and a new form of labour regulation (Fordism) as well
as new information and communication technologies (ICTs)—constituting what some see as a

third technological revolution, others (primarily political economists in the left political economy—French regulationism) as a new form of global production, and others again (primarily sociologists, particularly Manuel Castells) as a radically new 'information society.' Each of these conceptions of technology-driven change and the emergence of a postindustrial information-rich society and a postFordist form of global production has its critics. The literature in this area is a minefield of critical debate and studies.

Lipietz 1982; Brenner & Glick 1991: 45–120; Perez 1985; Robles 1994; Veltmeyer 1999.

5. ICT as a tool for change

There exists a large question mark around the revolutionary implications of the new production technologies—whether a computer-based and -driven new technological social order or a 'third technological revolution.' Scholars continue to debate these issues. But there are no such questions about the revolutionary impact of the new information and communication technologies, creating as they have a new 'information-rich society' and drawing people across the world into a globalization process—a veritable 'global village.'

An information society is a society in which the creation, distribution, diffusion, use and manipulation of information is a significant economic, political and cultural activity. The knowledge economy is its economic counterpart, whereby wealth is created through the economic exploitation of understanding. Specific to this kind of society is the central position information technology has for production, economy and society at large. Information society is seen as the successor to industrial society. Closely related concepts are the postindustrial society (Daniel Bell), postFordism, postmodern society, knowledge society, telematic society, information revolution and network society (Castells 2000).

There is no question about the revolutionary implications of ICT in the rise of a new 'information society.' However, where questions persist and further research is called for is in regard to the development implications of these ICTs—a question of 'ICT and equity' (equality of access), a question of 'democracy' (freedom to participate), a question above all of a possible new 'development divide.' To advance research on these and other such development issues in the Latin American context—similar research is being conducted in other parts of the world—the United Nations Commission for Latin America and the Caribbean (ECLAC) has organized the Information Society Program <http://www.cepal.org/socinfo>. The focus of this research is on the social and development implications of ICT—a study of 'ICT and equity' and 'ICT, education and youth' and the monitoring of policies and projects linked to the implementation of ICT in the region (ECLAC 2010). However, the ECLAC does not seem to be raising the broader questions of the possible formation of a new global divide between those individuals, classes and societies with access to these technologies and those with no or little access. This is *the* critical issue, requiring a closer look by students of CDS. A useful source for accessing and reviewing the ongoing albeit very conventional research in this area is the World Bank's Development Gateway, itself a product of ICT.

Norris 2001; Dawson & Foster 1998: 51–67; Castells 2000, 2001; Garnham 2004; Van Dijk 2006; Cox 2001: 3–28.

6. Capitalism and knowledge for development

The World Bank (1998/99) has advocated and operationalized what might be called the mainstream perspective on the knowledge-development relation, one that merits—and requires—a critical review and analysis, particularly in terms of the relation between knowledge and development (see #1 of this module). Its concept of 'technology for development' was also advanced by the UNDP in its 2001 *Human Development Report*, 'Making New Technologies Work for Human Development,' although the UNDP is characteristically more focused on 'technology networks' and the way that they 'can expand people's horizons.' The underlying critical issue, as with the Bank's *World Development Report*, is 'power,' the power of knowledge, a power vested in intellectual property rights and the appropriation of these rights by capitalist corporations and other organizations in the North.

More generally, the *knowledge-capitalism-development* relation is extensively studied in terms of issues related not to power in the use of technology but to R&D and the development applications of new technologies. Studies in these areas are legion, creating the opportunity and need for students of CDS to identify and sort out the diverse schools of thought and elaborate a review of the literature from a CDS perspective. An excellent starting point for such a review is Girvan's (2007) paper cited above, and critical issues are also discussed in Utting (2006).

Also of importance to CDS is the turn over the past two decades towards what could now be viewed as 'knowledge-based development,' with reference to what Castells has dubbed 'the information society,' and a new economy that is seen to have emerged in the last quarter of the twentieth century on a worldwide scale based upon knowledge. The traditional view of economic development is that it depends on natural resources, labour and capital accumulation. A knowledge-based economy, however, is dependent upon its capacity to generate, process and adopt information efficiently and to manage the resulting development applications. But the evolution of technology has propelled the productive capacity of society to generate and disseminate information rapidly and on a global scale. The advancement of knowledge has, according to the World Bank and its strategic partners in the knowledge-based approach to development, contributed to the improvement of standards of living in many parts of the world (World Bank 1999). However, many societies have not been able to sufficiently benefit from the availability of information and knowledge to improve their standards of living. Hence the knowledge for poverty alleviation perspective in using information and applying knowledge (information-rich ideas) to development, designed to optimize the identification, sharing and use of knowledge by local communities as a fundamental asset—to build on and manage the 'intangible assets of communities' (Talisayon et al. 2008).

For a critique of this and other such 'asset-based approaches' to community-development (designed or have the effect of demobilizing movements for more fundamental change), see Module 24.

Girvan 2007; Broad 2007: 700–08; Kapur 2006; Utting 2006.

Module 32

Education for Development

Gary Malcolm
University of Calgary, Canada

Investigations into education issues around the globe can take a multitude of forms. From a critical perspective, education has epistemological and methodological implications depending on what is being researched: epistemological since knowledge is being shared or transferred between teachers and learners and methodological since different types of knowledge require different teaching and learning methods. Consequently, this section has the dialogic possibility of students becoming critical of their own methods of knowing the social world as well as having the tools to critically analyze and integrate education data in its myriad contexts.

Readers of the texts in this manual bring forth an element of social privilege in that they have achieved, in global terms, a high level of economic, political and cultural integration and have cognitive access to abstract knowledge. The knowledge constructed by the readers is likely to have practical implications such that real people will be impacted by the operationalization of ideas at this level. Therefore, understanding how a researcher constructs knowledge about the world has the dual function of validating the findings of research as well as providing the intellectual tools to do objective field research. From a critical perspective the researcher balances their objective position within their subjective world. Education, in this sense, is coming to understand one's place in the social world largely by analyzing and integrating the way others educate themselves about their cultural, economic, political and historical spaces and places.

What is the best approach to knowing how education policies are put into practice around the world? The combination of many types of educational situations (informal, primary, adult, transformative, etc.) with their countless social contexts suggests that a critical concept-based approach of inquiry take a more predominant role than a statistically inclined content-based approach to acquiring and constructing knowledge. Education concepts, like all concepts used to interact in the social world, are highly contested in their meaning. A critical approach lays bare the presuppositions as indicated by quantitative research as well as the interpretive use of concepts within a specified social context. This module reveals some of these general concepts of development education.

1. Historical structures

An historical investigation into education for development is broadly an inquiry into many, if not all, the concepts that have evolved through the colonial era and beyond into the epoch of 'development,' where we currently find ourselves, including the ways we (re)use these concepts in contemporary situations. Since colonial times and through the work of Jesuit missionaries, formal education programs (i.e., expansion of values derived from a European heritage) have been transposed into foreign and indigenous contexts as a part of the Enlightenment experience. While it cannot be asserted with certainty that the intentions of the colonizers were malicious, it is up to the student to determine the social consequences or radical change in the methods and content of learning. Moreover, what are the subtle structural residues of this historical colonization of the mind within contemporary globalization?

As independent states emerged out of colonial rule, creating what became known as the Third World, education programs frequently, but not necessarily universally and certainly in qualitatively different ways, engaged in state-led formal education programs. From a critical perspective formal education has been observed and interpreted to be two paradoxical programs: a project of 'nation-building' and a project of 'assimilation,' an extension of the marginalization and exclusion of the colonial past. Education as a contribution to nation-building continued to follow Western ways of thinking and used teaching philosophies derived from functionalist models of social development. Understanding the social structure of formal education is a crucial element of analysis of the historical emergence of any education program (Archer 1979). Questions that students might ask of formal education concern the nature of power within the state and the predominant cultural, economic and political ideas as state-led education came to life.

On the other side of the dialogic formal education coin is the concept of 'assimilation,' in particular the means in which peoples are socially changed to either at best contribute to nation-building or at worst be excluded from the development of national society. The social impacts are profound and diverse. What cultural, economic and political skills did the voice of the state demand and to what extent did the learning of these skills shift local cultures, whether into the mainstream of capital development or into a marginal and silenced position within society? The student is urged to consider and imagine how epistemological shifts as propagated by state-led formal education programs positively and negatively impacted traditional societies.

Archer 1979; Bennett & LeCompte 1990; Illich 1970; Said 1993.

2. Globalized education policymaking for development

Regarding more contemporary models of state-led formal education, a similar critical awareness can be brought to education models advertised by global institutions such as UNESCO, UNICEF and the World Bank. These organizations provide a reference point for all forms of continuing and emergent education programs in many different circumstances around the world. For example, Education For All and Education for the Knowledge Economy set standards for primary education and develop human capital for economic growth, respectively. Funding from global organizations for education projects is guided by the principles of these programs and often interlinked with other social needs such as health, gender equality and technological capacity. Questions students might ask are to what extent have these programs supported or subverted social (economic, political and cultural) development in locales where these principles are applied? What socioeconomic discourses can be identified in the policies of international organizations toward education? Can we make comparisons or find contradictions in implementation and impact of education programs between locales?

Ashton & Green 1996; Stiglitz 1999.

3. Non-formal and informal education

A critical analysis of education programs implies investigating what traditional research often excludes. Formal education programs are the natural and easily identifiable points of research. However, informal and non-formal learning methods precede and coexist with formal education plans. To what extent does informal and non-formal learning affect broader learning in a given context?

Non-formal education is structured learning for adults or children that takes place outside of the state-led system (Coombs and Ahmed 1974). The goals of non-formal education are at once practical and culturally specific; furthermore, non-formal education projects are community endeavours where participation is not limited to a small administration catering to the objectives of external stakeholders.

Three types of non-formal education have been identified. The first acts as a *complement* to the formal system and is for those for whom formal education has not been able to deliver its educational purposes, e.g., school dropouts and illiterate adults. The second form acts as an *alternative* to formal education. It emerges when colonial education administrators fail to accept that there are pre-existing learning structures and processes that contribute to the social stability of indigenous cultures. Therefore, the objective is to establish, or re-establish, a link between learning and culture. The third extant of non-formal education consists of programs that *supplement* formal education. The need for supplemental education arises in times of rapid change where the formal education system is either too slow to respond or cut due to structural adjustment. Examples include English as a second language schools, which are ubiquitous around the world, and NGO-sponsored and community-based programs into specific issues such as health or technology.

Popular education is a common non-formal education strategy employed by groups of people who consider themselves to be on the margins of society. It is frequently used as a tool for establishing ethnic or class identities. As a form of *alternative* learning, popular education programs have arisen in diverse locales as a means of education by and for the people, organized at the community level outside of the control of the official education system. Learning materials derived from the real lives of people exude a political attitude and embody a community spirit (Hammond 1999).

Informal education is an anthropological concept that deals with processes of enculturation. The cultural, economic and political locales of learning provide the context in which informal learning takes place and can be analyzed as the spaces and places of learning, such as the home, community, school, workplace and Internet. This broader perspective breaks down restrictive assumptions about the traditional institutional view of education and the hegemonic limitations propagated by institutions. Moreover, taking an informal perspective encourages the researcher to examine alternative sources of learning, such as social movements, NGOs and tight-knit communities, and the target of learning whether they be primary, secondary or adult learners.

Coombs & Ahmed 1974: Hammond 1999: 69–94.

4. Critical pedagogies (Part 1)

Critical pedagogies are teaching and learning methods that bring multiple perspectives to the meaning of social concepts. Exposing social structures to a critique of power relations delineates the lived experiences of peoples able to take advantage of their privilege and those marginalized from the benefits of the social production. The notion of critical pedagogy was brought to the fore of the discourse on education by Paolo Freire, largely through his book, *Pedagogy of the*

Oppressed. Freire's pedagogy had the explicit intention of helping oppressed peoples become aware of their social exploitation as well as develop skills to take political action.

Freire's theories began as method of adult learning particularly through basic literacy. Essentially, Freiren pedagogy is the core of most popular education programs and has been applied in formal settings around the world. The philosophical tenet of this pedagogy is that through the extreme cultural, economic and political exploitation experienced by many generations of peoples on all the continents, people everywhere are dehumanized—and most people are unaware of the level of this dehumanization in both marginalized communities as well as communities of social privilege. Consequently, the first step toward finding a remedy for this broad-based dehumanization is to create a social space where historically oppressed peoples can understand their social position, learn the use of tools such as literacy and share their narrative-based knowledge with advocates outside of their communities. This is the essence of a critical pedagogy where peoples challenged with a lack of social resources create literacy skills to be heard on a broader scale and develop political skills to address these challenges. What are the narratives of peoples using a critical pedagogy as a strategy to alleviate poverty? As Thiong'o (1993) asks, what texts do people access to learn about their social place in the world? Also, what types of knowledge do learners have to share with peoples in like situations, albeit in different social and development contexts?

Freire 1984; Freire & Shor 1987; Thiong'o 1993.

5. Critical pedagogies (Part 2)

An alternative context and extension of the critical pedagogy experience in historically marginalized communities is the use of critical pedagogies in the education institutions in historically dominant countries as well as the schools of the social elite in nations with high rates of poverty and social exclusion. The growth in IDS programs in Western universities and the expansion and deepening of global education curricula in primary and secondary schools indicates that critical pedagogies have taken shape in the new context of Western education. School administrations and jurisdictions are concerned with finding a place for their students in the contemporary era of globalization, and a significant response has emerged in the form of critical pedagogy.

Global education programs and the awakening of global citizenship point to a transformative approach to education. The hub of analysis lies in why and how schools and the programs within the schools form with the possibility of reforming curricula that regulate local education programs. By focusing on the roles of teachers, students and community advocates such as NGOs in carrying out education programs, curricula can be tailored toward knowing and empathizing with the reality of diverse groups of people while placing learning in a local context and opening spaces for action in social justice. A transformative approach overhauls technocratic education methods and outlines a synthesis of the values needed for effective education development (Mezirow 1996).

Questions that students might ask of critical pedagogies in spaces of social privilege are what is the nature of social justice within these programs? What types of knowledge inform the curricula and resources used in these programs? What aspects of the culture and structure of education diminish the possibilities of the programs to critically address global social issues as well as questions of local social justice.

Kincheloe 2004; Mezirow 1996: 158–72; White 2005.

6. Democratization of knowledge

It is likely that the readers of the texts in this manual are teachers as well as learners and therefore have the privilege of being an agent of knowledge transfer. From the dialogic balance of a critical perspective, it is crucial that the knowledge itself is not prioritized over the methods used to share and (re)construct knowledge. CDS is a concept-based endeavour. This does not mean that content-based knowledge should be excluded from teaching and learning. Yet, theorizing about global phenomena is necessarily conceptual and based on narrative accounts of experience and our ability to imagine and emotionally connect with broader experiences. Working in critical development studies requires the naming of conditions that cause benefit and/or immiseration across political boundaries (Apple 1995).

Studying education requires us to understand how education programs in historically marginalized communities create knowledge, how this knowledge is shared and transferred, and how methods of teaching and learning are used in places of social privilege both in the West and countries of the South. The 'back to basics' of education also has a hermeneutic or an imaginative element largely ignored by Western thinkers. Knowledge for critical development studies is vast and is presented in different forms. Imaginative skills and participation in knowledge construction are an essential part of a critical approach to development education.

Apple 1995; Giroux 1997.

Note

1. Knowledge, if and when produced by developed countries, tends to be regarded as scientific: 'Science—the scientific method, the libraries of scientific knowledge, the sophisticated theories that guide us to the inside of the atom and to outer reaches of the universe—is the glory of Western culture.' In this sense, scientific knowledge means that it has been 'discovered' as a generalized truth that is applicable everywhere (hence the alternative title 'universal'). This leads to the further idea that developed countries have 'best practices' (because they are 'scientific') and developing countries should copy them. This provides the justification to distribute such knowledge through development assistance to poor countries. The ways in which knowledge is distributed are variously described as 'communities of practice,' 'knowledge partnerships' (e.g., World Bank's Development Gateway), 'technical assistance' and through development projects.

Section 11

Agrarian Transformation and Rural Development

Broadly conceived, 'development' denotes progressive change—improvements in the human condition based on changes needed to bring about this improvement. Under capitalism, the entire process is driven by the development of the forces of production. The improvements brought about by this 'development' are seen in two ways. From a neoliberal perspective, progress in the form of general prosperity results from letting the market operate freely in allocating returns on diverse factors of production. Thus, 'development' is seen as the inevitable result of expanded production; i.e., a bigger pie automatically or inevitably benefits an increasingly larger part of the population as the benefits of economic growth generated by the forces of economic freedom trickle down to the poor. From a structuralist perspective, however, development of the forces of production or economic growth do not automatically lead to an improvement in the human condition. This requires the active intervention of governments in the regulation of markets and in equitable distribution of the social product. There is also the perspective of radical political economy, which is that capitalism is a useful systemic device for expanding production—i.e., developing the forces of production—but that progress in terms of improvements in the human condition necessitates the supersession of capitalism. Human or social development from this perspective necessitates a system in which production is geared to the satisfaction of the population's basic material and spiritual needs and the realization of human potential—the capabilities of each and every individual as a social being.

This section focuses on the process of productive and social transformation at the heart of the capital accumulation or economic growth process—capitalist development as we see it, the 'agrarian question' as conceived by other scholars—namely, the transformation of a traditional agrarian society at a relatively low level in the development of society's forces of production into a modern industrial society with a considerably enhanced level of economic growth and development. The following three modules focus on some of the most critical dimensions of this process.

First, in Module 33, Haroon Akram-Lodhi focuses on global food production and the many local systems that make it up, arguably the foundation of the economic development process, creating as it does the economic and social conditions that allow people to meet one of their most basic needs—for nutritious food. Akram-Lodhi explores what she sees as the six most critical dimensions of the global food production system in a process of capitalist development.

Second, Cristóbal Kay, a specialist in rural development issues and the 'agrarian question' in the Latin America context and currently editor of the *Journal of Agrarian Change*, conceptualizes and briefly explores the most important dimensions of six critical issues of rural development from a Latin American perspective. He includes in his purview an analysis of the *agrarian question* in the current era of neoliberal globalization (paths of transition, the land and land reform, the

171

peasantry—is it disappearing or not?) and an analysis of critical dimensions of rural develop-ment (paradigms, rural poverty—conditions, pathways out of poverty, struggles of the poor and strategies for change and development).

Third, Jun Borras, a scholar activist with Vía Campesina and currently editor of the *Journal of Peasant Studies*, looks more closely at the land question, which has always been at the centre of the capitalist development process. This question revolves around the land policies of the state and the struggle of small-scale peasant farmers against the forces of change (moderniza-tion, industrialization, proletarianization) that beset their communities and that threaten to undermine the sustainability of their livelihoods. In this struggle, the peasant is brought into a complex relationship with the state, the fundamental repository of political power—the capacity to formulate policies and make decisions that directly affect the masses and large groups of the world population seeking to sustain their livelihoods on the basis of agriculture and farming. From Borras's CDS perspective, the land question is now a matter of government policy, the development dynamics of this policy and the struggle against it.

Module 33

Critical Rural Development Studies

A. Haroon Akram-Lodhi
Trent University, Canada

For much of period since the end of World War II the weight of food and agriculture in national and international circuits of capital accumulation diminished, and agriculture lost much of its relevance to national and global accumulation. That may now be changing. Over the past few years, in the context of an emerging global crisis in food production and consumption, the importance of food and agricultural production within global circuits of accumulation has been of increasing concern to the actors and agents of international capitalism (Bello 2006).

Climate and other environmental change, particularly in Australia but also elsewhere, such as the Gangetic Plain, have led to plummeting world supplies of wheat and, as a consequence, rising wheat prices—at one point in 2008 world wheat prices rose 25 percent in one day. At the same time, rising world demand for corn as a potential alternative source of energy (ethanol) and the resulting emergence and growth of a heavily subsidized U.S. agro-fuels sector (up to 40 percent of corn producers' production costs are met by government subsidies) has reduced world supplies of corn and driven up the price. Finally, bad harvests in Latin America and crop diversification amongst other producers have left huge shortages in world soya markets. As these three crops are essential inputs in the corporate agro-food complex, which rose to dominance during the 1990s, changing agricultural supply and price dynamics have been witnessed throughout the world food system: in staple crops, in cash crops, in livestock and in agro-industrial inputs.

Reinforced by changing dietary patterns amongst elite consumers in China and India, with an attendant rise in meat consumption and processed foods, as well as by the increased transport costs incubated by oil that witnessed its price spike to nearly $150 a barrel in 2008, agriculturally driven inflationary processes have increasingly become global: in China and India, to be sure, where food prices constitute 35 percent and 45 percent of the consumer price index, respectively, but also throughout the South. Moreover, global finance capital is increasingly concerned about whether stagflation is becoming a structural feature of the world economy. Finally, and critically, these recent trends in the global agro-food complex are having political ramifications, with consumer and peasant protests being witnessed in Afghanistan, Bangladesh, India, China, Indonesia, Italy, Mexico, Vietnam and Yemen, among others, and the U.N.'s Food and Agriculture Organization (FAO) warning of serious threats to social and economic stability.

Against this backdrop of an emerging global capitalist production and food crisis (see Bello 2006), CDS must focus upon the ways in which the operation of global capital is generating the incessant restructuring of rural livelihoods in the contemporary South. Neoliberal agrarian restructuring has altered the configuration of land, labour and capital in the production process and in the process undermined the capacity of small-scale producers to sustain their communities and livelihoods.

In some cases an expansion of agro-exports has further shifted the purpose of production away from use to exchange, deepening the commodification of labour. In other cases peasant-based petty commodity production remains significant in rural life. In a third set of cases deepening processes of semi-proletarianization have forced the rural poor to engage in a multiplicity of waged labour activities of a precarious and highly seasonal kind, even as they continue to cling to their land for reasons of security and even though land no longer provides a subsistence guarantee, in part because increasingly casualized wage labour similarly fails to provide for subsistence. These changes effect and reflect deeper transformations in the relationship between people and rural production and have thus profoundly altered the political terrain upon which rural struggles for social justice and economic democracy are played out.

Two critical variables that affect the impact of neoliberal agrarian restructuring are the distribution of assets within the countryside and the extent of the linkages that exist between agro-export and peasant production. Most commonly, but not universally, a maldistribution of assets and weak linkages between agro-export and peasant production has resulted in the buyer-driven corporate food regime tightening the operation of the law of value on a global scale. This has deepened the crisis in the agrarian economy in much of the South, simultaneously enhancing agro-exports from the South to the North and pushing increasingly marginalized petty commodity producers and semi-proletarians to migrate, thus shifting poverty from the countryside to the city and the megacity, generating what Mike Davis (2006) has memorably called a 'planet of slums.'

Critical rural development studies must capture and explain these processes. On a global scale, poverty overwhelmingly retains a rural face and thus poverty elimination must address the crisis of the agrarian economy in the South. This module is designed to facilitate a critical understanding of the impact of neoliberal agrarian restructuring on the rural economies of the South.

Bello 2008b; McMichael 2005, 2007, 2010.

1. The world food system

The module begins with an examination of the historical origins and contemporary characteristics of the world food system. It has evolved in a long-term process of capitalist development of the forces of production and an associated process of social transformation or 'capitalist moderniza-tion,' conceptualized by economists at the World Bank (see the 2008 *World Development Report: Agriculture for Development*) as the transformation of a precapitalist 'agriculture-based' society' into a capitalist 'urbanized' society based on the production relations of wage labour.

McMichael 2005; Friedmann 2004.

2. The agrarian question and rural livelihoods

This theme discusses the 'agrarian question' under capitalism. At issue here is (1) the persistence of precapitalist peasant agricultural production in poor countries on the periphery of global capitalism; (2) the characteristics and dynamics of this production system; and (3) the ways in which global capital may or may not be reconfiguring rural livelihoods.

Akram-Lodhi & Kay 2007, 2008a, 2008b; Bernstein 2008.

3. Commodity chains and the agro-food complex

An important dimension of the ongoing and accelerated transformation of agriculture-based economies and societies is the internationalization of agricultural and food production—the formation of a global agro-food complex and global commodity chains in the marketing of agriculture and food production. In sociological and economic terms this 'development' raises serious questions about the complex and changing relationship between transnational corpora-tions, agribusiness, capitalist entrepreneurs and rich and middle peasants, and the masses of small-scale peasant producers that still dominate agriculture and local food production in parts of the Global South.

Bernstein & Campling 2006: 414–47; Akram-Lodhi & Kay 2008a, 2008b.

4. Agrarian productivity and agrarian structure

Having located the place of the peasantry in the global food economy, this module continues with an exploration of the relationship between agrarian structure and agrarian productivity as well as the relationship between agrarian productivity and biotechnological change.

Akram-Lodhi, Kay & Borras 2008; Johnston & Le Roux 2007: 355–71; Bernstein 2004: 190–225.

5. Agrarian productivity and biotechnological change

The driving force underpinning the productive and social transformation of precapitalist agriculture-based economies and societies into advanced capitalism is technology, which is the principal mechanism ensuring the increased productivity of agricultural labour. The technological transformation of agriculture and food production has taken complex and changing forms over the years. This theme explores the dynamics of the biotechnological change that is driving productiv-ity growth and structural transformation in the current neoliberal era of capitalist development.

McGiffen 2005; Buckland 2004.

6. Situating food sovereignty: Enclosure, rights and the rebuilding of local food systems

This module concludes with an examination of the way in which the continual character of enclosures under contemporary capitalism (what some conceptualize as another form of 'primitive accumulation') has fostered the emergence of movements of counter-enclosure, which seek to build agro-ecological local food systems that are predicated upon food sovereignty and which seek, to some degree, to protect communities from the vicissitudes of capital and the capitalist market.

Akram-Lodhi 2007: 1437–56; Patel 2007: 87–93.

Module 34

Rural Development from a Latin American Perspective

Cristóbal Kay
Institute of Social Studies, The Netherlands

This module discusses some of the key interpretations for explaining the main processes of transformation of the rural sector in Latin America, arguing that a political economy and critical approach offers the best way to understand the dynamics of rural transformations. A key reference point is the largely Marxist debate on the agrarian question. The Latin American processes of agrarian change are analyzed from a long-term perspective and within a comparative context with other regions of the world. The various roads of transition to agrarian capitalism and their implications for the livelihoods of peasants and rural workers are examined. The module highlights the uneven and unequal character of Latin America's rural transformation as well as the persistence of rural poverty and social exclusion. Finally, the module discusses the possibilities offered by some alternative development policies and strategies for achieving a more equitable and inclusive rural development, which may lead to the eradication of poverty in the countryside.

1. The 'agrarian question' and 'paths of transition' to agrarian capitalism

At the centre of the process of capitalist development since at least the second half of the nineteenth century was what has become known as the 'agrarian question.' This question makes reference to the process of productive and social transformation involved in the transition from a precapitalist agrarian society into a modern industrial capitalist system. What this agrarian transformation meant in essence was the proletarianization of the peasantry—the transformation of a society of small-scale 'peasant' farmers into an urban and industrial working class. The debate on this 'agrarian question' has taken different forms over the years. The readings in this section explore the evolution of this debate in changing historical contexts, past and present. The focus of this debate is on the different 'roads of transition'—what economists at the World Bank, in their 2008 *World Development Report: Agriculture for Development* conceive as 'pathways out of rural poverty' (see Veltmeyer 2009 for a critical review of this report).

After exploring shifts in the debate on the agrarian question and the different roads of transition, this theme turns to the agrarian question in the form that it is currently taking in Latin America. A CDS approach to the study of this question calls for a comparative perspective on changes in the agrarian structure and transition.

Byres 2004a: 54–83; De Janvry 1981: 61–93, 141–81; Akram-Lodhi & Kay 2008a: Chap. 1.

2. The land question and agrarian reform: Past and present

The agrarian question in Latin America revolves around the land tenure system, implanted in history of the 'conquest,' in which the indigenous population—i.e., the small part of it that was not wiped out or succumbed to disease—was dispossessed of their communal landholdings. This land tenure system remains the most unequal in the world. The formation of this system, if not the dynamics of class struggle associated with it, can be traced out in the classical CIDA studies.

In addition to the land tenure issue, the agrarian question in Latin America has revolved around the issue of class struggle over the land (see Veltmeyer 2005b and Module 35) and that of land reform—instituted by governments in the context of the post World War II 'development project' and concern to avoid 'another Cuba.'

In the 1980s the state-led land reform programs of the previous two 'development' decades were drawn to a halt, put to death by the governments that sought entry into the new world order of free market capitalism. Subsequently, in the wake of direct actions by rural landless workers' movements, such as Brazil's MST, 'market-assisted' land reform programs were advocated and instituted by the World Bank. The theoretical and policy debates that have surrounded these developments (land reform by means of direct action from the grassroots, the state-led reforms of the 1960s and 1970s and the market-assisted land reform programs of the 1990s) are reviewed and critically analyzed in the readings. The arguments for agrarian reform, its achievements, limitations and contradictions are brought into focus. For example, is land redistribution a sufficient condition for achieving growth with equity? What should the agency for this distribution be? How radical or far-reaching should these reforms be? The 'agrarian reform' law implemented by the Bolivian government under the presidency of Evo Morales revived this last question, which was highly debated in the 1960s in the context of the emergence of revolutionary social movements.

Borras Jr., Kay & Akram-Lodhi 2007: 1–40; Kay 2001: 191–235; Byres 2004b: 1–16; Lahiff, Borras Jr. & Kay 2007: 1417–36; Teubal 2008: Chap 6.

3. Dynamics of the peasant economy and rural labour

A central aspect of the agrarian question both in Latin America and elsewhere relates to the changes in the rural social class structure wrought by the process of productive and social transformation. These changes have generated lively debate on debate on the future of the peasantry: '*campesinistas*' versus '*descampesinistas*' (peasant capitalized farmers, proletarianization, semi-proletarianization and peasantization). At issue on this debate are questions about the transformations in the social relations of production and the nature of the peasantry: Who are the peasants in this context? Are they disappearing into the dustbins of history, transformed out of existence (having either migrated or been proletarianized)? Or are they reproduced in a different form? Or, as in the times of Lenin and the years leading up to the Russian Revolution, are they subject to a process of differentiation and polarization—into small, medium-sized or large producers?

Bryceson 2000: Chap. 1; Feder 1979: 3–41; Barkin 2004: 270–81; Bartra 1993: 127–43, 144–67; Heynig 1982: 113–39; Kay 2008a: 24–48; Otero 1999b: 11–32.

4. Rural development paradigms

In the post World War II context of state-led development, diverse theories of rural change and development were constructed, mostly within the framework of three 'paradigms' or schools of thought: the 'expanding capitalist nucleus' (growth and modernization theory, the Green Revolution); 'Latin American structuralism' (Cepalismo); and neoclassical theory and the neoliberal counter-revolution: privatization, decollectivization, liberalization and the imperative of the global market.

Within the framework of the post-Washington Consensus), two other perspectives have emerged: one based on 'sustainable rural livelihoods' (see Module 25 for a critical assessment) and the other on a 'new rurality' perspective that has emerged over the last decade. The interpretations and ambiguities of this approach as well as the ensuing debates are at issue and discussed in these readings, especially Kay (2008b). Analysis of these issues focuses on four major transformations in the rural economy and society that are highlighted by the 'new ruralists.' These changes are interpreted as arising from the region's neoliberal shift and its closer insertion into the global system. A novel distinction is made between reformist and communitarian proposals for a new rurality. Both the merits and the limitations of this new approach to rural studies (see Barkin 2001) need to be critically examined.

Bebbington 2004: 173–92; Kay 2008b: 915–43; Barkin 2001: 21–40; Bartra 2006: 177–323.

5. Rural poverty dynamics

What are the causes and consequences of rural poverty? Who are the poor? What are the ethnic, gender and class dimensions of rural poverty? The readings in this theme provide an analysis of several, at times competing, interpretations on rural poverty. At issue in these interpretations are the relationships between poverty and marginality, social exclusion and social capital (on these issues also see Module 24). Other critical issues include the policies that have been advanced and used to reduce rural poverty—from state (developmental) to market (neoliberal) proposals; the contrast between different country experiences in Latin America; and the persistence of rural poverty in the face of diverse strategies and efforts.

Kay 2006a: 29–76; Berdegué & Schejtman 2004: 45–74.

6. Development strategies and rural development: Exploring alternatives

In this theme, the focus is on the alternative rural development strategies that have been advanced in recent years. Issues include the relationship between national development strategies and rural development; the dynamics of transnational agribusiness, neoliberalism, food security and the future of the peasantry; and the challenge of globalization for rural development and the peasantry. Also, what lessons (if any) can Latin Americans learn from (relatively) successful development strategies and experiences of rural development in the region and elsewhere? The theme concludes with an assessment of future perspectives on rural transformations and critical rural development studies.

Kay 2006a: 21–52; Kay 2009; Akram-Lodhi & Kay 2008a: Chap. 13.

Module 35

Contemporary Land Policies and Land Struggles

Saturnino M. Borras Jr.
Saint Mary's University, Canada

Land policies and land struggles are critical components of contemporary international development policies and discourses. Yet there remain important under-explored analytic issues around these themes. This can be seen from two perspectives: (1) the need for a more systematic and consistent critical understanding of the mainstream thinking on these topics, and (2) the need for alternative ways of thinking on these topics.

1. Land and land policies, rural livelihoods and development

Mainstream thinking about land is based on the fundamental consideration that land is a scarce economic resource. Policy consideration of land should thus be oriented towards its most economically efficient allocation and use. Market mechanisms are considered the principal ways through which this goal can be achieved. Such a framework informs most of the contemporary national and international land policy thinking.

This topic offers a systematic alternative critical perspective. It starts by examining the mainstream framework. It then offers a multidimensional perspective on land, including economic, social, political, cultural and geographic dimensions. This perspective captures better the actually existing realities that are founded in social relations between groups and social classes in societies. Finally, the land question is explicitly linked to the broader questions of agrarian transformation and development dynamics.

Deininger & Binswanger 1999: 247–76; Bernstein 2004: 190–225; Akram-Lodhi, Borras Jr. & Kay 2007; Kay 2002: 1073–02.

2. Theory and practice of redistributive land reform

Contemporary mainstream scholars use the term 'land reform' to refer to straightforward land sales transactions between private sellers and private buyers. This thinking, launched in the early 1990s, is referred to as market-led agrarian reform. This policy model is pushed jointly with another mainstream policy advocacy—for land rental and share tenancy promotion. With the entry of these thoughts into the current policy discourse, discussions around land reform have become complicated, especially since conventional land reform *a priori* rejects land redistribution in public lands. This has become even more complicated with the recent aggressive mainstream policy advocacy for the massive privatization of remaining public lands worldwide.

This topic puts into perspective the various competing meanings of land reform. It offers a critical discussion about the neoliberal, market-led land reform approaches as well as conventional land reform theory and practice. It also offers discussions on some analytic flaws in the existing literature on cross-national comparative political-economy studies in land reform.

Deininger 1999: 651–72; Borras 2007: Chaps. 1–2; Bernstein 2002: 433–63; Borras, Kay & Lahiff 2008: Chap. 1; Sadoulet, Murgai & De Janvry 2001: 196–229.

3. Towards truly 'pro-poor' land policies and 'democratic' land governance

Two features of contemporary mainstream thinking about land policy today are: (1) that these policies are framed and carried out supposedly to serve the interest primarily of the rural poor, and so these land policies are usually labelled as 'pro-poor' and (2) that there is a great interest among mainstream agencies today about the question of having 'good policies' and 'making it work,' and thus, the recent concern about governance, and more particularly, 'land governance.' It is worth noting that in recent years, mainstream agencies and scholars prefer to use the more 'neutral' term, 'land policy'—and not the conventional 'land reform.' Governance also implies technical efficiency, which is assumed to be a policy process devoid of power and political influences and discussions. It is important to note that all major multilateral and bilateral agencies have, during the past few years, formed and passed their own land policies.

This topic offers an alternative critical perspective to this set of important and current land policy issues. One can easily be lost in the complex discussions about land policies, land governance and so on. It is time to take a pause, and ask the question: What are we actually talking about when we say 'land policy' and 'land governance'? This topic thus offers an alternative analytic handle, having in mind the perspective of poor peasants and rural labourers.

Borras & Franco 2008; World Bank 2003.

4. Contemporary land-oriented movements and land struggles

In the context of land policymaking today, mainstream advocacy takes peasant groups and their NGO allies as important actors in the process. However, they view peasant groups and NGOs not as completely independent social movement actors, but as administrative adjuncts and business conduits in the implementation of their market-oriented land policies. Some important peasant movements and NGOs have taken advantage of such opportunities.

This topic puts into a critical perspective this mainstream view on the role of peasant movements and NGOs in (neoliberal) land policymaking. It then maps contemporary land-oriented movements and groups that are outside of, or in opposition to, the mainstream network. Key empirical examples from Africa, Asia and Latin America are examined with a view towards a better understanding of the nature and character, agendas, political strategies, forms of collective actions, accountability, alliance work and so on of these movements.

Deininger 1999: 651–72; Greenberg 2004; Kerkvliet 2009; Franco 2008.

5. Understanding contemporary transnational agrarian movements struggling for land and citizenship rights

This topic offers sympathetic discussion about transnational agrarian movements, but raises critical issues that are relevant to both activists and academics (for example, a discussion about when a transnational agrarian movement fails). Rural citizens have increasingly begun to invoke perceived citizenship rights at the transnational level, such that rural citizen engagements today have the potential to generate new meanings of global citizenship. La Vía Campesina has advocated for, created and occupied a new citizenship space that did not exist before at the global governance terrain—a distinct public space for poor peasants and small farmers from the Global South and North. La Vía Campesina's transnational campaign in protest against neoliberal land policies is a good illustration of this in that rural citizens of different countries collectively invoke their rights to define what land and land reform mean to them, struggle for their rights in reframing the terms of land policymaking and demand accountability from international development institutions whose land policies impact on peasants' everyday lives and livelihoods.

The share of space of each key civil society actor in the global governance terrain did not shrink as a result of La Vía Campesina's entry into the global governance scene; the public space created and occupied by various civil society groups expanded. Such space has also been rendered more complex with the creation of layers of sub-spaces of interactions: between movements of poor peasants/small farmers and NGOs, movements of poor peasants and intergovernmental institutions, movements of poor peasants and donor agencies. These sub-spaces of dynamic interactions that did not exist in the global scene before the entry of La Vía Campesina have important implications for the struggles of the rural poor for citizenship rights in a transnational context.

Desmarais 2002: 91–124; Borras, Edelman & Kay 2008; Borras & Franco 2009.

Section 12

Capitalism, Labour and Development

In recent years the World Bank and the Organisation for Economic Co-operation and Development (OECD), among other intergovernmental organizations, policymakers and academics perceived the need for labour to adjust to the requirements of the new economic order and to become more flexible. The rationale for this policy agenda was that labour either adjusts to these requirements or confronts a worsening of its problems—unemployment, economic insecurity, bad jobs and low income. In this context, these and many other organizations have taken up the banner of labour and labour-market reform—a mandated or legislated restructuring of 'industrial relations' and associated labour markets.

It is evident, from a CDS perspective, that this entire process of labour reform, together with the political process of convincing labour to go along with it, is part of an offensive waged by capital against labour. As such it is based on an agenda to restructure the global economy and secure the integration of economies throughout the world into the 'new world order' of neoliberal globalization. This agenda was laid out by the World Bank in its 1995 *World Development Report*: *Workers in an Integrating World*. This report provides what we might well view as a 'capitalist manifesto' on the need for neoliberal globalization.

To deconstruct this agenda from a critical development studies perspective and to review the critical dimensions of the capital-labour relation at the level of the world capitalist system, this course section provides three modules: (1) Labour, Class and Capitalism; (2) Migration and Development; and (3) Urban Development in the Global South.

Latin American Labour in a Global Context

According to the World Bank, about 99 percent of the workers projected to join the world's labour market over the next thirty years will live and work in what it labels the 'low- and middle-income' countries of Africa, Asia, the Caribbean and Latin America (the latter currently constituting about 8.4 percent of the world's economically active population; 6.1 of production; and 3.9 percent of exports and 3.2 percent of imports, down from 12 percent and 10.1 percent in 1950). As the World Bank saw it, there was—with the support and on the basis of a concerted program of structural adjustment policies—a global trend towards increasing integration into and the interdependence of countries within a global economy. However, to date there is no discernible trend towards greater equality (or even equity) in the form and conditions of such integration among countries or between the rich, the larger number of relatively well-off workers, and the much larger number of poor workers across the world. Indeed, the Bank argues, there were serious 'risks that the workers in [the] poorer countries will fall further behind' and that some national groups of workers, especially in Sub-Saharan Africa, could become increasingly marginalized in a global process of 'the general prosperity in countries that are enjoying growth' (World Bank 1995b: 6).

The only preventative remedy, from the Bank's perspective, was for all countries to pursue the right domestic policies—sound labour policies that promote labour-demanding growth. Such policies, the Bank notes, fundamentally involve 'the use of markets to create opportunities' and specifically include legislation designed to create more flexible forms of labour and labour markets. Conditions of such flexibility include, on the part of workers, greater mobility—the capacity to relocate if necessary—and a willingness to accept whatever jobs are on offer, with possibly lower levels of remuneration; and, on the part of employers, increased capacity to participate in the production process, able to hire, fire, locate and use workers as required at the point of production and to pay them on the basis of market conditions.

With reference to this idea, of a labour market in which the forces of supply and demand can reach equilibrium, providing an optimum allocation of resources (returns to factors of production)—World Bank officials stalked the corridors of power all over Latin America in the search of policymakers with the political will to introduce a program of legislative (and, if necessary, constitutional) labour reforms.

Associated with this idea was the notion that in general wages were too high, the result of government interference in the labour market (particularly in the legislation of minimum wages) as well as the supposed monopoly power of the unions. As the Bank saw it—and it was argued with as much technical support and data it could muster—high wage rates, excessive benefits accorded workers in the social programs introduced by earlier populist governments and the general inflexibility of workers lead private sector entrepreneurs to withdraw from the production process, contributing thus to the problems of high unemployment, informalization and poverty.

How did Latin American policymakers respond to such advice and associated pressures? First, virtually all governments instituted a program of structural adjustment that established an appropriate institutional framework for the new labour reform policy, the conditions of which were formed with an ongoing process of technological conversion and productive transformation.

Governments that had not done so came around in the 1990s. On the institutional basis of this structural adjustment and its associated reforms, the entrepreneurs and employers of labour in many cases have joined the financiers—and the World Bank—in demanding reforms of labour legislation and, where required (as in Brazil), the constitutional amendments to allow and secure greater flexibility of labour markets. In some cases, the new labour regime was established within the export enclave of an expanding *maquilladora* industry. In other cases (Chile, for example) the new labour regime was introduced as part of a productive transformation process. In each case, the process of structural adjustment and productive transformation has been accompanied by a political struggle to introduce through legislative reform, administrative fiat or, increasingly, executive decree, a more flexible form of production and a corresponding labour regime.

Module 36

Labour, Class and Capitalism

Rosalind Boyd
McGill University, Canada

> The profoundly dialectical concept of labour… viewed as a process that is simultaneously creative and alienating, liberating and enslaving links it directly with the concept of development. —Paresh Chattopadhyay in Boyd, Cohen and Gutkind 1987: 48–69

This unit places the struggles of labouring people at the centre of critical development studies in the current phase of global capitalism, which is characterized by a worldwide crisis of poverty and obscene inequalities, mainly in the regions of the South. Over the past two to three decades, we have witnessed the restructuring of global capitalism propelled primarily by the neoliberal agenda of transnational corporations and international financial organizations, tied to unprecedented militarism within U.S. hegemonic power, which has resulted in catastrophic changes worldwide, particularly for labouring people. The complexity of these changes is difficult to capture accurately and clearly. Setting the context in which they occur is paramount if we are going to bring about a real transformation of this dominant system and its institutions.

There have been profound changes in the labour process and in the world of work, under-mining any gains that labouring people may have made in earlier times through trade union organizations. Workers and their organizations are struggling to resist, to seek alternatives and to establish new forms of democratic organizations in order to confront the indisputable adverse effects of the current moment of global capitalist power.

This module begins with a critical review of theories and concepts related to the labour-capital relation. These are contextualized within the social realities of our contemporary societies. The issues addressed in each theme question paradigms that do not often accurately reflect the socio-economic realities faced by working people but simply echo a narrow 'capitalist' view of labour from the limited perspective of economics. Emphasis is given to critically engaged scholarship (see Saul 2006) that seeks to open up creative thinking and to analyze these social realities with the goal of organizing not only to eradicate poverty but to transform the global system towards an egalitarian and humane world order.

1. Theorizing and contesting concepts of labour and capital

Critical issues addressed in the reading include the nature of work under capitalism and the social dynamics of the capital-labour relation in the global economy; the productive and social transformation of labour in a process of capital accumulation, i.e. the 'multiplication of the proletariat'—the conversion of peasant agricultural labour into diverse forms of wage labour. This 'proletarianization' is endemic to capitalism but since the 1980s, in what Harvey (2005) conceptualized as a 'short history of neoliberalism,' it has taken new and different forms that need to be closely studied from a critical development perspective.

Bernstein 2000: 25–51; Chattopadhyay 1987: 27–60; Pillay 2007; Munck 2002.

2. Informalization of labour and deindustrialization

Critical issues include conditions for the working poor; forms and conditions of un- and under-employment; the 'living wage'; conditions of child labour; the 'informal sector', precarious labour and the global informal working class; and issues of social exclusion, marginalization, outsourcing, etc.

The term 'informal sector' is of relatively recent vintage. It was coined with reference to conditions of work that were materializing under conditions of a supposed transition from a traditional to modern form of society. The optimism of the modernization theory school of development led many scholars in the 1950s and 1960s to believe that traditional forms of work and production would disappear as a result of economic progress. As this optimism proved to be unfounded, scholars turned to study more closely what was then called the traditional sector. They found that the sector had not only persisted but also in fact expanded to encompass new developments. In accepting that these forms of production and labour were there to stay, scholars started using the term 'informal sector', which is credited to the British anthropologist Keith Hart in a study on Ghana in 1973 but also alluded to by the International Labour Organization (ILO) in a widely read study on Kenya in 1972.

The informal sector became an increasingly popular subject of investigation, not just by economists but also in sociology and anthropology. With the turn towards postFordist forms of production and labour regulation in the advanced developing countries (on this see Lipietz 1982) many workers were forced out of their formal sector and into self-employment under conditions of informalization. In a seminal collection of articles, *The Informal Economy: Studies in Advanced and Less Developed Countries*, sociologist Alejandro Portes and his collaborators emphasized the existence of an informal economy in all countries. Their case studies ranged from New York and Madrid to Uruguay and Colombia. The term 'informal sector' gave way to studies of the 'informal economy'.

Arguably the most influential book on the informal economy is Hernando de Soto's *El Otro Sendero* (1986), published in English in 1989 as *The Other Path*. De Soto argued that excessive regulation in the Peruvian (and other Latin American) economies forced many producers and workers into relations of informality, thus inhibiting economic development. While accusing the ruling class of twentieth-century mercantilism, De Soto admired the entrepreneurial spirit of individuals in the informal economy, arguing that the lack of government regulation in the sector was a virtue, allowing this spirit to flourish and creating conditions that could be harnessed for development.

However, while De Soto's work is popular with policymakers and champions of free market policies, many scholars of the informal economy have criticized it for both methodological flaws and ideological bias. A much more useful and valid approach to understanding the dynamics of the informal economy in developing societies is provided by Mike Davis (2004), who connects the informal economy and the associated 'planet of slums' to the process of proletarianization endemic to capitalist development.

Boyd 2006: 487–502; Davis 2004: 5–34; Koo 2001; Lipietz 1982; Munck 2005.

3. The gender dimension of labour

Critical issues addressed in these readings include the feminization of labour; the interrelationship of 'capitalism' and 'patriarchy' in the subordination of women; and the value-producing dynamics of household labour, unwaged work and reproductive labour, and productive agricultural labour.

The expansion of trade, capital flows and technological advances in a process of capitalist development and globalization have led to what sociologists term the 'feminization of labour.' From a mainstream development perspective this feminization generally has been liberating for women, weakening the chains of oppressive traditions and practices, reducing the relations of dependence of women on men and expanding their opportunities for self-advancement. However, the changes associated with the feminization of labour have also had dire consequences for women, e.g., gender discrimination, violence, sweatshops and sexual harassment.

As the global economy expands, multinational companies seek to recruit women in both the developing and developed world because they generally are disposed to work for lower wages and less likely to organize. Women are expected to, and often do, work for low wages, little job security and no autonomy. They are, in effect, more 'flexible' and thus more likely to successfully make the 'adjustment' to the labour force requirements of the new world order.

Mies 1988: 67–95; Moghadam 2005b: 50–77; Young 2000: 315–28; Bakker 1994; Sparr 1994.

4. Manifestations of 'raw' global capitalism

Issues in this area and addressed in the readings include the nature and dimensions of the underground economy, the dynamics of cross-border labour and labour migration and undocumented workers and their contribution to the economy (especially in the U.S.).

The underground economy is a bustling and shadowy world where jobs, services and business transactions are conducted by word of mouth and paid for in cash to avoid scrutiny by government officials and payment of taxes. It covers a vast array of activities but must be distinguished from the criminal activities of the underworld. Government officials are all too eager to lump together organized crime and drug traffickers with the producers and self-employed workers in the 'informal economy.' Both groups knowingly violate laws and government regulations and defy political authority, but they differ radically in the role they play in the development process. The social and developmental dynamics of labour in the informal sector or underground economy constitute important topics for CDS.

Migrant labour has always existed but it assumes different forms in diverse development contexts. It generally comprises of members of a peasant rural community or traditional society who, due to the pressures of capitalist development, are forced off the land to sell their labour in an urban environment—which some scholars term 'forced migration' but that the World Bank in its 2008 World *Development Report* defines as a 'pathway out of rural poverty.' Both the internal and the international dynamics of this labour migration process need to be studied from a CDS perspective.

Shelley 2007; Cohen 2004.

5. Institutions of global capital and labour

From a liberal economics perspective, *capital*[1] and *labour*[2] are viewed, together with *land*[3] and *technology*,[4] as *factors of production*. From a political economy and sociological perspective, however, capital and labour are viewed not as things but as specifying *social relations of production*[5]—the totality of these relations as constituting the economic base of the social structure, a structure that in its objective and subjective conditions can best be represented via the concept of *social class*,[6] and in its dynamics analyzed in terms of this concept. On the theory and methodology of *class analysis*, see Modules 17 and 27.

Critical issues addressed in this theme include a review of the labour policies of major global financial institutions (WTO, IMF, World Bank) and various ILO conventions, especially those related to the ILO's Decent Work program. Relevant trade agreements (APEC, NAFTA, MERCOSUR) are also examined for their effect on labour, as is the U.N. code of corporate social responsibility (CCR), implemented in 1989 as part of a strategy designed to incorporate the private sector into the development process. The potential contributions and limitations of this code in regard to sustainable development, the environment and labour are highly debated. The arguments can be organized as falling into one of four general categories: bad and good development and bad and good capitalism. The effect of this code of conduct on the actual 'behaviour' of TNCs and MNCs vis-à-vis labour is examined in selected representative cases.

Another issue of possibly transcendental significance for labour is the formation in Latin America of a new model for intra-regional trade: ALBA (Bolivarian Alternative for the Americas), based on socialist rather than capitalist principles. Originally proposed by Venezuela (Hugo Chávez), ALBA now is an alternative regional trade alliance that includes Venezuela, Cuba, Bolivia and Ecuador as well as several Central American countries (including Honduras, Nicaragua).

Munck 2001: 8–25; Veltmeyer 1997a: 226–59; Boyd 1998.

6. Organizing by working people and the forces of resistance

Critical issues here include the need to reinvigorate trade unions and the labour movement; new forms of resistance and 'social movement unionism'; the debate on basic guaranteed income; recent (as well as earlier) experiences of workers with self-management and factory takeovers; and also new forms of organization related to transnational worker solidarity.

Bieler, Lundberg & Pillay 2008; Lambert & Webster 2001: 337–62;
Eade & Leather 2005; Waterman 1999.

Module 37

Migration and Development

Labour in the Global Economy

Raúl Delgado Wise and Humberto Márquez Covarrubias
Universidad Autónoma de Zacatecas, Mexico

Led by the World Bank and the Inter-American Development Bank, some international organizations have been pursuing an international political agenda in the area of migration and development. They posit that remittances sent home by migrants can promote local, regional and national development in the countries of origin. By extension, remittances are seen as an indispensable source of foreign exchange, which provides macroeconomic stability and alleviates the ravages caused by insidious problems such as poverty. This view is supported by the growing importance of remittances as a source of subsistence income for many households in underdeveloped countries.

It has been estimated that 500 million people (8 percent of the world's population) receive remittances. According to World Bank figures, remittances sent home by emigrants from underdeveloped countries rose from U.S.$85 billion in 2000 to U.S.$199 billion in 2006. Unrecorded flows through informal channels may increase these figures by 50 percent or more (World Bank 2006). Taking unrecorded flows into account, the overall amount of remittances surpassed foreign direct investment flows and more than doubled the figures for official aid received by Third World countries. In many cases remittances have become the largest and best volatile source of foreign exchange earnings.

Although the World Bank's position vis-à-vis the relationship between remittances and migration has lately become more cautious, it is evident that the impact of structural adjustment programs, promoted by the World Bank and the IMF, is the root cause of the upsurge in South-North migration and remittance flows. Moreover, far from contributing to the development of migrant-sending countries, the World Bank's SAPs have reinforced the dynamics of underdevelopment through three major movements: the dismantling and re-articulation of the productive apparatus to the capital restructuring processes commanded by Northern countries; the creation of vast amounts of surplus population, well beyond the conventional formulation of the *reserve army of the unemployed*; and the acceleration of migration flows.

The great paradox of the migration-development agenda is that it leaves intact the principles that underpin the current process of global capital restructuring and does not affect the specific way in which neoliberal policies are applied in migrant-sending countries. At most, it offers superficial strategies involving migration, such as lowering the cost of transferring remittances and supporting financial infrastructures that enable the use of remittances in micro-projects (which, ultimately, have very limited impact in terms of development). Dominant policies regarding migration and development are neither coherent nor properly contextualized and could not serve as part of an alternative development model or a new form of regional economic integration capable of reducing the socioeconomic asymmetries that exist between sending and receiving countries. They are also unlikely to contain—or reduce—the current and burgeoning migratory flows.

Notwithstanding a recent boom in migration and development research, there is a clear dissociation between theories of development and theories of migration. This results in restricted studies that do not capture the context within which migrations—and the fundamental connections involving processes of global, national, regional and local development—are inscribed. Conceptual and theoretical research has been lagging behind the discourse and migration and development policies promoted by international organizations. Consequently, academic debate has been largely limited to a conceptual reproduction of said discourse or, at best, establishing critical distance from it.

The analytical complexity of the relationship between migration and development requires an alternative approach that does not centre on the migratory phenomenon but has a focus on the broader processes of development and social transformation. This standpoint implies comprehending international migration from a CDS perspective. In order to achieve this, it is crucial to shape theoretical objectives through interdisciplinary exercise, that is, formulate outlines and propositions based on the context, agents and processes of a multi-spatial environment.

Additionally, it is necessary to problematize and contextualize the notion of development to break through normative frameworks that, failing to consider the need for structural and institutional change, limit the formulation of any socioeconomic improvement to abstract terms. Moreover, in a context of large migration flows, the problem of development involves additional challenges, such as the asymmetric relations between countries, the reconfiguration of productive chains and concomitant restructuring and precarization of labour markets, transterritorial social inequalities and, more specifically, the decline of the material and subjective foundations that propitiate a given population's emigration, along with issues involving their integration into receiving societies under unfavourable social and labour conditions and preservation of their ties with their societies of origin.

In order to comprehend this complex phenomenon outlined and examine specific aspects in the dialectic interaction between development and migration, the following issues must be addressed:

1. *Strategic practices.* This refers to the confrontation between different projects that espouse diverging interests, which in turn underlie the structures of contemporary capitalism and its inherent development problems. There are currently two major projects. The one that has achieved a virtual hegemony is promoted by the large transnational corporations, the governments of developed countries led by the U.S. and its allied elites in the underdeveloped nations, all under the umbrella of diverse international organizations and financial institutions. The loss of legitimacy for this project under the aegis of neoliberal globalization means that nowadays rather than speaking (or writing) of hegemony we can use the term 'domination': implementation of this project is not the result of a consensus but rather military force and the imposition by Washington of an appropriate macroeconomic policy. The second project, the alternative one, consists of the socio-political actions of a range of social classes and movements as well as collective subjects and agents who endorse a political project designed to transform the structural dynamics and political and institutional environments that bar the implementation of alternative development strategies on the global, regional, national and local levels.

2. *Structural dynamics.* This refers to the asymmetric articulation of contemporary capitalism on several planes and levels. It includes the financial, commercial, productive and labour market spheres, as well as technological innovation (a strategic form of control) and the use and allotment of natural resources and environmental impacts. These factors condition the ways in which (1) developed, (2) developed and underdeveloped, and (3) underdeveloped countries relate to each other. They also determine the fields in which interactions between sectors, groups, movements and social classes take place. All of this is manifest in different ways on global, regional, nation and local levels.

This module offers an assessment of migration and development studies from a CDS perspective, where the current explosion of migration is viewed as part of the intricate machinery of the current capital restructuring process. To understand this process a redefinition of the boundaries of studies that address migration and development is required: expand the field of research and invert the terms of the present migration-development equation in order to situate the complex issues of development and social transformation at the centre of the frame. This entails an alternative way of understanding international migration. Migrants should not be held responsible for the promotion of development in their places of origin. At the same time, it is important to highlight their direct contributions to the development of receiving countries and their impact in their places of origin, as part the current global capital restructuring processes. This enterprise, as part of CDS curricula, requires new theoretical and methodological tools that can result in the production of new knowledge, research agendas, concepts, analytical categories and information systems.

1. A critical overview of migration and development theories

Modernization theory: neoclassicisism, new economics, neoMalthusian, migration hump; historical-Structural approaches: Marxist, dependency theory, world systems, cumulative causation, segmented labour markets; neostructuralism: social capital, social networks, transnationalism; general assessment of the field: nature and limitations of the relationship between migration and development.

Theories on migration tend to belong within either one of two main paradigms. The positivist outlook encompasses a modernizing approach centred on individuals' rational behaviour in the economic milieu and a social context that tends toward convergence and the reduction of asymmetries. The second paradigm is based on a more critical outlook and, unlike positivism, emphasizes social transformation and social contradictions. Neostructuralist approaches take a middle stance and attempt to explain migration dynamics by focusing on the agency of migrants. In spite of their common paradigmatic roots, theories on migration have developed somewhat separately from theories of development. Consequently, their analytical horizon has been limited and they have failed to consider central aspects of the current capitalist context.

A political economy approach based on a critical, historical/structural outlook can provide the theoretical and methodological apparatus with which to examine the important link between migration and development. It can also contribute, among other things, basic tools for the analysis of contemporary capitalism, its role in labour migration and related historical, structural and strategic aspects. A number of topics can be approached from this perspective: the depth of the systemic crisis and capitalist restructuring (i.e., so-called neoliberal globalization); the creation of economic regional blocs; the transformation of labour processes under a postFordist production system; the political and military hegemony of the United States; the increasing gap between developed and underdeveloped nations; the internationalization of production; the transnationalization, differentiation and precarization of labour markets; the global increase in social inequalities and the generation of a surplus population that must engage in forced South-North migration.

Massey et al. 1998; Massey et al. 1993: 431–66; De Hass 2007; Herrera 2006.

⁎2. Neoliberal globalization and migration: The capitalist restructuring of labour

Contemporary capitalism: globalization, neoliberalism, imperialism, capital restructuring; neoliberalism and migration: structural adjustment programs, regional integration, internation-alization of production, transnationalization and precarization of labour markets; new migratory dynamics: emerging modalities of forced migration and migration patterns, new modalities of innovation and skilled migration, labour precarization and social exclusion.

The accumulation crisis and resulting loss of profitability experienced by the global capitalist system during the 1970s led the developed countries to implement a global strategy of capital-ist restructuring. This was based on a set of three complementary mechanisms: globalization, neoliberalization, and financialization. In underdeveloped nations, the implementation of these strategies leads to three crucial problems. The first is the destruction of national patterns of accumulation and the country's reinsertion into the dynamics of capitalist restructuring led by large corporations; this effectively dismantles the production apparatus and its internal market, devastates subsistence systems and social security, and increases the gap between rich and poor. The second is the production of surplus population: this is the result of the liberaliza-tion of vast contingents from their means of production and subsistence, which increases the amount of unemployment and sub-employment, poverty and marginalization and has led to an unprecedented expansion of the so-called informal sector. This climate of social instability is also conducive to state repression, violence, illicit activities and lack of social security. The third problem is the explosion of forced migration, which is the consequence of the destruc-tion of modes of production and subsistence. Millions of workers and their families are forced to leave the countryside in order to work in urban centres—either in their own country or in a developed nation.

Bello 2006; Harvey 2007: 21–44; Castles & Miller 2008; Sassen 1990.

3. The new development mantra: Remittances, migration and public policies

Issues in these readings include the notion, measurement and typology of remittances; the international agenda on remittances and development; and a critique of the remittance-based development model in theory and practice: the macro and micro impacts and limitations, so-cioeconomic dependency on remittances and unsustainability.

Instead of promoting structural, political and institutional changes that address the root causes of forced migration and, ultimately, the problems of underdevelopment and related dependency, international organizations and the governments of migrant-sending and -receiving countries have promoted a development agenda based on remittances and their impact in regions of origin. This outlook maintains that migration is a source of development while remittances are the vehicle and migrants the agents.

Implemented in migrant-sending countries, this model of 'development' is based on the export of cheap labour. This results in regressive patterns in the accumulation process and asymmetric and subordinated relationships within the regional integration system of receiving countries.

GCIM 2005; BID-FOMI 2006; Fajnzylber & López 2007; Ratha 2003; World Bank 2006; Terry & Wilson 2005; Nyberg-Sorensen, Van Hear & Engberg-Pedersen 2002: 3–48; Delgado-Wise & Márquez 2008.

4. Migrant organizations and political participation, human and labour rights and citizenship

The critical issues in these readings include the social organization of migration; social networks and migrant organizations; the political and social participation of migrants; transnational citizenship; trends towards a transnational civil society; modes of integration and asylum policies; intergenerational incorporation and the trends and challenges related to transnationalism and development.

Despite their valuable contribution to the economies of developed, labour-importing nations, migrants are subject to labour precarization, social exclusion and political marginalization. The policies implemented by the governments of receiving countries to regulate the entry, residence and expulsion of migrants tend to violate labour and human rights and criminalize migration while responding to the needs of capitalist enterprises that benefit from an abundance of disorganized, vulnerable, flexible and precarized labour force. On the other hand, migrants themselves show little proclivity to unionize or engage in political participation in order to defend their own interests. There are growing attempts at organization and mobilization, but these have yet to produce an organized political front that influences migrants' living and working conditions. Most migrant organizations are split into identity-based groups built around a common nationality or, in extreme cases, a given place of origin. They are also split into different aspects of social practice: religion, social interaction and solidarity with their places of origin.

In contrast, the governments of migrant-sending nations do not intercede on behalf of their migrants and are, at best, only interested in establishing diplomatic ties in order to 'seduce the diaspora' and guarantee the flow of remittances into the country of origin. This allows them to reduce external pressure on national accounts while ensuring the subsistence of millions of poor families.

Schierup, Hansen & Castles 2006; Fox & Brooks 2003; Fox 2005; Goldring, Henders & Vandergeest 2003.

5. Migration and development: perspectives from the South

The readings in this theme provide a set of perspectives from the South on the migration-development nexus, including a comprehensive view of this nexus; a comparative analysis of the major migrant-sending countries in regional integration contexts; migration flows and the 'modern diaspora,' including remittances, public policies regarding incorporation into the receiving country; and the development implications as well as 'best practice' forms of migrant agency.

The first challenge facing the study of the relationship between migration and development is the lack of a proper theoretical basis. Additionally, the subject of migration has not been adequately incorporated into the field of development studies. A more integral approach necessitates a more comprehensive analytical framework—one that without bypassing the contributions of numerous researchers also addresses the context of socioeconomic regional integration and the problematic issue of development in migrant-sending nations. This will establish a specific and theoretical practical connection between migration and development.

This critical reconstruction of both migration and development studies must also overcome the partial outlook of migrant-importing developed countries, which is based on concepts such as the regulation of migration flows, security agendas, co-development and the criminalization of migrants. It is essential that we incorporate the points of view of underdeveloped, migrant-exporting nations; this requires a comprehensive understanding of current capitalist development and its context, as well as the type of asymmetric relationships established between migrant-sending and -receiving countries. Theorizing from an underdeveloped perspective is not a new endeavour. From the 1950s to the 1970s, structuralist economics and dependency theory developed a solid theoretical basis and anticipated the subsequent emergence of transnationalism when they went beyond methodological nationalism. Generally speaking, theorists and analysts from developed nations still exhibit a considerable lack of knowledge in regard to the theoretical contributions of authors from Latin American and other underdeveloped regions or actively omit them from their own work.

Castles & Delgado Wise 2008; Rapoport & Docquier 2004; UNESCO 1999.

6. Towards a CDS perspective on migration and development

What form should or does a CDS perspective on migration and development take? What kind of dialectic between migration and development emerges in the context of neoliberal globalization? What are the basic analytical dimensions and concepts to be considered?

Given that the preponderant views on migration characterize it as a source of development for places of origin, it is necessary to adopt an alternative outlook within the framework of critical development studies. Political economy allows us to critically reconstruct the links between development, migration and remittances from a historical, structural and strategic perspective:

1. Capitalist restructuring increases underdevelopment and forced migration.
2. Migrants directly contribute to the accumulation process in developed countries.
3. Through the sending of remittances, migrants contribute to the precarious, neoliberal macroeconomic stability of their countries of origin, the subsistence of their families and the undertaking of basic social infrastructure projects.

The dependence on remittances in places of origin is associated to processes of social degradation: social unsustainability, productive dismantling, environmental degradation and depopulation.

It is crucial that we critically define our key concepts. Instead of viewing migration as a population movement based on individual and family decisions we must address the prevailing context of underdevelopment and dependency. This way we can examine the current mechanisms of capitalist restructuring and the role they play in the creation of forced migration, both through the accelerated decline of working and living conditions and the demand for cheap, flexible and unorganized labour. It is important to shed light on the social nature of remittances: they evidence the social relations of a transnational production system characterized by superexploitation, social exclusion and the resulting decrease in workers' quality of life. The production of remittances also entails a transfer of resources (i.e., the transfer of productive human resources without involved costs) and invisible social costs such as depopulation, the abandonment of productive activities and family separation.

Delgado-Wise & Márquez 2008; Petras 2007; Schierup 1990; Munck 2008; Castles 2008.

Module 38

Urban Development in the Global South

Charmain Levy
Université du Québec en Outaouais, Canada

In post World War II classical modernization development theory, urbanization was considered a critical feature of the transition from traditional agrarian to modern industrial society. Labour was required for urban industrial complexes and capitalist development in the countryside pushed the peasant population off the land to the cities. Rapid urbanization took place in most developing countries, especially in Latin America and Asia, where a large part of the rural population migrated to the cities from the 1960s through to the 1980s. Despite the importance of urbanization to modernization, practically no state-supported infrastructure was provided to this population in urban centres.

As the low-income population were left to their own devices to survive in the city, in many countries and regions we find a collective 'self-help' reaction to the problems around the lack of urban infrastructure (transportation, housing, sanitation, electricity, streets, health centres, schools, daycare, etc.) and tenure regulation of the state. Neighbourhood associations became the basis of urban popular movements and nongovernmental organizations; a burgeoning 'civil society' formed to contest the urban space and demand action as well as public services from governments.

In many large cities, one way for the working classes to survive has been to illegally squat on land. This has led to the formation of slums and shantytowns, which have become part of the urban landscape in the Global South. This modern urban phenomenon is in fact a solution for the state as well as a reason not to provide low-income housing on a universal scale. Structural adjustment programs and neoliberal macroeconomic policies since the mid 1980s have exacerbated this spread of shantytowns and led to what geographers term 'spatial segregation.' However, if the golden years of economic industrial development meant stable jobs for semi-skilled workers, from the 1980s on, we have witnessed what can be called urbanization without industrialization and in many cases urbanization without development. New generations of workers and migrants now feed the informal (legal and illegal) economy, much of which takes place in large shantytowns (Davis 2006).

In order to understand the dynamics of diverse urbanization processes in the South we must, first of all, place and study them in the context of the global economy based on a new international division of labour and new forms of governance. We also need to take account of diverse but relevant development theories, the macroeconomic and social policies implemented by governments, the political regimes and changing forms of the state in terms of how open they are to urban popular movements and their claims. We also need to understand the dynamics of a growing civil society of nongovernmental organizations, an uncivil society and the role played by multilateral agencies and their policies aimed at the urban poor.

The readings in this module are intended to deepen the reflection of students on the historical, economic, social and political factors that condition the different forms and patterns of urbanization in the South. Special attention is given to three key issues: (1) urban production in terms of capital and labour; (2) urban development in terms of the dynamics involved in reproducing the workforce and the social conditions of these dynamics—social exclusion, inequality and poverty; and (3) forms of urban governance and politics. Studying these issues involves identifying at different periods of contemporary history social and political structures, social actors, their interaction and the results of their interaction in terms of social and political continuity and change. Students need to analyze how different levels of government as well as international organizations (World Bank, U.N. Habitat) deal with issues around unequal urban development and poverty. They need to study local urban governance as a form of social control and urban management in terms of maintaining order through social reform and the selective inclusion of civil society actors in governance and through the repression of what is considered uncivil society. Attention is also given to social movements, political contention and collective action around urban issues such as access to public goods and services as well as to decisions involving urban governance.

1. Neoliberal globalization and urbanization: Theoretical perspectives on the city and urban development

Urban development in the Global South over the past two decades has taken place in the context of what can be viewed as epoch-defining changes in social and economic organization and a process of 'globalization' impelled by neoliberalism, a program of 'structural reforms' in macroeconomic policy that includes the privatization of economic enterprises, financial and trade liberalization, deregulation of markets and the decentralization of government administration (Harvey 2005).

Studies differ sharply as to how they theoretically represent the dynamics of neoliberal policies, but they more or less agree that they relate to various cycles of 'structural' market-friendly 'reforms' designed under the Washington Consensus and then, in the 1990s (1) a new set of policies based on an emerging PWC to establish a 'better balance' between the state and market (Ocampo 2007); (2) a 'new social policy' protective of the most vulnerable groups of the poor; (3) a decentralized form of local governance and development; (4) a decentralized form of local governance and development; and (5) an overarching comprehensive development framework (CDF), and within it a new policy tool—the Poverty Reduction Strategy Paper (PRSP).

Within the frame of this agreement theoretical perspectives and policy action prescriptions diverge. Salient among these are permutations of 'structural Marxism' (Davis, Harvey), structural and poststructural forms of urban sociology (Castells), 'international political economy' and 'urban development economics,' a largely undertheorized approach shared by the economists at the World Bank and related organizations in the United Nations system. The open global gateway of development studies set up by the World Bank <www.developmentgateway.org> provides access to an enormous body of studies in this tradition of urban development theory and practice. What defines these studies is an approach that is supportive rather than critical of the neoliberal policy and institutional framework elaborated on the basis of the post-Washington Consensus.

Smith 1996; 9–28; Dunford 2007: 1–14; Douglass 2000: 2315–35; Gugler 2004; Harvey 1988; Jones & Visaria 1997; McKeown 1987.

2. The urban revolution, the informal sector and the urban labour market

This theme focuses on the question of how economic factors are tied to production conditions in the cities, as well as how changes in the world economy impact on capital and labour as well as the social-spatial organization of cities. A major aspect of capitalist development is a process of productive and social transformation in which a traditional, precapitalist and agrarian society is converted into a modern industrial capitalist society. Typically, on the periphery of the world capitalist system under conditions that prevailed from the 1950s to the 1970s, this process of structural change and urbanization took a different form than it did in countries at the centre of the system. The most notable feature of peripheral capitalist development regarding rural-urban migration, urbanization and the growth of cities is the emergence of a dual-sector economy, each with its own labour market: a formal sector in which economic activities are 'structured' and the capital-labour relation is regulated by government; and an unstructured 'informal sector,' in which economic activities revolve around self-employment and family-based micro-enterprise rather than the capital-labour relation. In other words, in the developed capitalist economies, rural migrants, dispossessed of land or otherwise forced to abandon the countryside, were absorbed into the urban economy at the level of modern industry as an industrial proletariat or working class. In the Global South, the social transformation (from peasant to wage worker) and productive transformation (from agriculture to industry) stalled and remains incomplete.

Becker, Hamer & Morrison 1994: 53–86; Davis 2004: 5–34; Roberts 1989: 665–91; Douglass 2000: 2315–35.

3. Urban poverty in the context of structural adjustment: Social and class dynamics of income distribution and urban poverty

In all the cities in the South, despite the diversity of the workforce, ethnic and racial differences, what the working class has in common are the living conditions of social exclusion and socio-spatial segregation. 'Poverty' in most cities is conditioned by a relative access to collective social goods and services. The distribution and concentration of these goods and services affect the level of urban inequality and poverty as well as individual and collective behaviour and attitudes towards urban development.

In most cities in the South the new economic model of pro-growth neoliberal policies, even when modified by pro-poor policies in the 1990s, resulted in increased social inequalities in the distribution of income, socioeconomic conditions and access to essential services. The social inequalities have been to the extreme of wealth at one social pole and the growth of poverty on the other—even, in some contexts (Argentina), among sectors of the middle class. The result is what some sociologists term a 'new dualism' and others (for example, Moser, Herbert & Makonnen 1993) 'urban poverty in a context of structural adjustment.'

Harvey 1997: Ravallion 2007: 5–34; Moser, Herbert & Makonnen 1993;
Petras & Veltmeyer 2007a: 180–209.

4. Social and spatial dimensions of exclusion and urban poverty

Despite the increase in the number of democratically elected regimes and the strengthening of civil society in Asia, Africa and Latin America, the urban masses have not experienced better material living conditions. In fact, in many countries, the opposite is true. It is evident that the neoliberal 'pro-growth' policies promoted by international organizations under the 'new economic model' have not been 'pro-poor.' The overall result appears to be increasing social inequalities and associated socioeconomic conditions. While some groups among the poor as well as the middle class benefit from these pro-growth policies, a larger number have born the brunt of the social costs—urban poverty is evidently on the increase in most development contexts.

Conditions of this poverty include inadequate marginal housing, precarious low wage employment, informal labour markets, high levels of unemployment, violence, crime and insecurity, affecting the middle class as well as the urban under-class and the working poor. Most sociological studies into these conditions point to the need for more socially inclusive policies as well as specific policies designed to protect the most vulnerable groups from the competitive environment of pro-growth government policies (Lopez 2004). Studies suggest that the vast majority of the urban poor rely on self-help for housing and access to food and water; they do not have 'decent jobs' with adequate working conditions and suffer from a high incidence of social exclusion. In many of the large super-cities, especially in Latin America and South Asia, they engage in poorly remunerated economic activities in the informal sector (Portes 1989) and live in what Davis (2006) terms a 'planet of slums.' Davis' study provides both a sociological portrait of the urban poor and an indictment of government policy—and of the economic model used by governments to make policy.

Aldrich & Sandhu 1995; Caldeira 2001; Davis 2006;
Durand-Lasserve & Royston 2002; Portes 1989.

5. Forms of urban governance, development policy and politics in the South

In the last thirty years, economic growth has led to economic and social inequalities as well as urban violence affecting the middle and working classes. In most countries the reaction of the state to this problem is to strengthen law enforcement or to offer palliative social programs in certain areas of the city. The readings in this theme discuss other strategies and policies designed to alleviate and reduce the incidence of urban poverty—to bring about a development process in the urban areas of the Global South. While there are a number of studies that provide a critical development perspective on the problems of urban poverty and underdevelopment (for example, Davis 2006), there is a dearth or absence of such studies regarding these diverse policy responses within the mainstream of development thought which is most clearly represented by the World Bank.

Moser 1998; Remenyi 2000; Baud & Post 2002; Leftwich 1993; Rakodi 1997.

6. Urban social movements:
Grassroots, civil society and popular responses

Until the 1980s the most important social movements were based on organized labour in the urban centres or the struggle for land waged in the countryside. But in the 1980s the urban centres in Latin America were the staging ground of a new type of urban social movements, which gave rise to a debate about 'new social movements' that were not class-based and that were more heterogeneous in their protests and demands—including, for example, issues such as environmental degradation, gender inequality, the violation of human rights and social exclusions of all sorts. In the 1990s this wave of new social movements ebbed, with the flow of another wave based on the agency of indigenous communities and landless and near-landless peasants.

Burgwal 1990: 163–76; Miller 2006: 207–11; Castells 2006: 219–23.

Notes

1. 'Capital' can be understood and is normally used to mean the 'sum total of a society's wealth' or, more specifically the source and means of generating this wealth, an investment in society's productive resources: income-or wealth-generating assets. In these terms capital can take different forms: basically *financial* (money invested in production), *physical* (technology embodied in machinery, equipment, computers, etc.), *natural* (land and its resources), *human* (education, knowledge) and *social* (norms of reciprocity embodied in a culture of social solidarity). Most theories of economic development emphasize the role of financial capital in the development process. However, proponents of the SLA and other forms of 'asset-based' approaches to development view capital as a matrix of five types of productive assets. More recently, in the context of a 'new development paradigm,' analysis and practice have highlighted the importance of social capital in a people-led and -centred approach to development designed to empower the poor to act for themselves.

2. 'Labour' is understood in abstract terms as 'labour power,' or the capacity to labour, and more concretely as the act of producing something, transforming a natural resource into a product for use or exchange. In the context of capitalist development, labour power is viewed as a commodity, what the worker exchanges against capital for a living wage.

3. Land' is understood in development analysis to denote not only 'land' as such but the stock of natural resources on and below the surface that can be extracted and processed into commodities or products for use.

4. 'Technology,' whether understood in physical and social terms, is a major factor of production. Where labour expanded in production adds value to the product, technology determines the productivity of this labour—the output relative to inputs of labour and capital.

5. According to Marx, in the process of production individuals necessarily enter into relations 'beyond their will,' 'relations of production' that specify the class position of individuals in the social structure, i.e., property in the means of production. In societies based on the capitalist mode of production there

are two basic social classes: the capitalist class, defined by its ownership of the means of production, which, under capitalism take the form of capital; and the working class, a proletariat defined by its lack of ownership or state of dispossession, which compels those in this position to exchange their labour with capital or work for wages.

6. We have here a Marxist conception of class that defines an individual's relation to production. This concept of social class can be distinguished from a structural functionalist concept of class as defining an individual's relationship to work, used to identify occupational groupings. It is also distinguished from a concept introduced by Max Weber, who uses social class to define an individual's 'life chances,' determined by an individual's relationship to the market (capacity to consume) rather than production. The categories of analysis in this conception are: upper, upper middle, middle, lower middle, lower.

Section 13

Nature, Energy and Development

Political ecology is the study of how political, economic and social factors affect the environment and how in turn the environment conditions the process of economic development. Most studies in this area of critical development studies analyze the dynamics of the nature-society-development relation in the context of the capitalist development of society and the economy. There are different approaches to an analysis of the dynamics of this relation and to the weight that should be given to the role that access to, and the exploitation of, natural resources plays in sustaining the development process. For example, the establishment of national parks in Kenya and East Africa to ensure the conservation of the environment and the natural habitat of animal life have had the effect of worsening, if not creating, poverty for the Maasai herders by excluding them from their traditional grazing routes. Therefore, international wildlife policies have a local social and developmental impact, not just an environmental one. More subtle variants of political ecology include the influence of non-human actors in environmental governance and decisionmaking, accounting for what might be called nature's agency.

The origins of the terms 'political ecology' and 'eco-socialism' can be traced to the early work of anthropologist Eric Wolf (1974) and in certain other writers like H.M. Enzensberger (1974). Some but not all political ecologists use a 'political economy' framework for analyzing the development dynamics of the nature-society-economy nexus. A widely read account in this area was *The Political Economy of Soil Erosion* by Piers Blaikie (1985), which traced land degradation in Africa to colonial policies of land appropriation rather than over-exploitation by African farmers.

Political ecology can be used to understand the decisions that communities make about the natural environment in the context of their political environment, economic pressure and societal regulations; look at how unequal relations among societies affect the natural environment; examine how relations of class and social inequality affect the environment; inform policymakers and organizations of the complexities surrounding environment and development, contributing thereby to better environmental management; and inform the development practice and politics of grassroots organizations and the social movements in the popular sector of 'civil society' with useful ideas and information.

As for eco-socialism (or green socialism, socialist ecology) it is an approach to an analysis of the nature-society-development nexus that merges aspects of Marxism, socialism, green politics, ecology and the anti-globalization movement. Eco-socialists believe that the expansion of capitalism, globalization and imperialism is the root cause of social exclusion, poverty and environmental degradation. They advocate the non-violent abolition of private property in the means of social production and the expansion of the global commons—collective ownership of the means of global production by freely associated producers and local decentralized management of both natural and human resources.

There are four modules in this area of critical development studies. Darcy Tetreault's

Module 39 provides a critical survey of mainstream thinking in this field (nature and society, natural resource and environmental management, sustainable development, energy-capitalist development). It is an excellent starting point for exploring and probing diverse perspectives on the most critical issues in this field. The following module, prepared by David Barkin, provides a critical political economy perspective on what he conceives of as the key issues. The basis of this perspective is a critique of the mainstream thinking reviewed by Tetreault and reference to a distinct philosophical and epistemological framework that affirms and makes explicit three fundamental ethical principles: intergenerational equity, social justice and sustainability. These principles guide Barkin's conceptualization and analysis of the nature-development nexus within the framework of an approach that might be dubbed 'popular sustainable development.' Module 41 identifies various alternative permutations of a 'critical' approach to the conceptualization and analysis of the issues in this field — major schools of thinking on the nature-society-development-politics nexus. The module explores the diverse ecological and development dimensions of this nexus, as well as its social and political dynamics. As for these political dynamics, they have to do with the environmental movement in its forms. This movement is formed to the purpose of mobilizing many different forms of resistance to the capitalist development of the planet's natural resources and the resulting degradation of nature, regarded by many, including the activists in the environmental movement, as the common heritage of humankind to be preserved for future generations. This section ends with a conceptualization of the energy-development nexus, with specific reference to issues that surround the extraction and capitalist development of oil, a key sector of the global economy and the not-so-hidden 'secret' of the development process unleashed by the capitalist 'development' of the forces of global production.

Module 39

Mainstream Sustainable Development

Darcy Victor Tetreault
University of Guadalajara (Ocotlán), Mexico

Environmental issues were only on the periphery of international development studies until the early 1970s. At that time, in the context of a nascent environmental movement in the North, neo-Malthusian concerns about overpopulation, resource depletion and industrial contamination gave rise to debates about the limits to economic growth, the seriousness of ecological problems and the relationship between poverty and environmental degradation. These debates have yet to be resolved, partly because of scientific uncertainty but also because of their political implications. At the same time, over the past four decades, several schools of ecological thought have emerged within the social sciences. These include mainstream sustainable development (MSD), environmental economics, ecological economics, political ecology and agroecology. This module critically analyzes the MSD discourse, competing (economic) paradigms are juxtaposed and major environmental debates are explored.

Harris, Wise, Gallagher & Goodwin 2001; Robbins 2004.

1. Deconstructing the mainstream discourse on sustainable development

Mainstream sustainable development has been defined in the international arena over the course of the past thirty-five years, marked by three major conferences on the environment: Stockholm (1972), Rio de Janeiro (1992) and Johannesburg (2002). Its main points of reference include the Brundtland Report (1987) and Agenda 21.

MSD is essentially a reformist agenda that seeks to reconcile the tension between development and escalating concerns over the deterioration of the natural environment. In this context, it indorses the principle of free trade as a means of maximizing economic growth, which is seen as necessary for overcoming poverty, in turn seen as the underlying cause of environmental degradation. Along these lines, the Brundtland Report has been highly criticized for placing emphasis on the reciprocal causal relationship between poverty and environmental destruction, while glossing over the destruction caused by the production and consumption practices of the rich and the middle classes.

To be sure, the principal objective of MSD is to achieve high rates of economic growth—not just in developing countries, where the incidence of poverty is high, but also in developed ones, supposedly to help bolster the world economy. Technological innovation and better management of natural resources are considered key ingredients in alleviating the pressure that economic growth puts on the environment. At the same time, the implementation of these measures on the international and national levels requires huge sums of money, which further justifies the need for realizing worldwide economic growth.

Technology transfer is generally conceived as being one-way: from North to South. This implies a lead role for developed countries, reinforcing their hegemony in the international arena. Although the MSD discourse pays lip service to the need for fostering the participation of NGOs and marginalized groups, the essence of the strategy implies that the main actors are to be the current power holders, such as international development agencies, national governments (especially of developed countries) and transnational corporations. On this point, the mainstream sustainable development agenda has been criticized as a strategy that 'puts the foxes in charge of the chickens' (Hildyard 1993). In other words, the main actors are the very culprits who brought about the environmental crisis in the first place. By dominating the conferences mentioned above, these actors have been able to distance themselves from past destructive policies and paint themselves as ecological saviours. In this vein, Vandana Shiva observes the following:

> Global environmental problems have been so constructed as to conceal the fact that globalization of the local is responsible for destroying the environment which supports the subjugated local peoples. The construction becomes a political tool not only to free the dominant destructive forces operating worldwide from all responsibility, but also to shift the blame and responsibility for all destruction on the communities that have no global reach. (1993: 151)

As an alternative to MSD, Shiva and other critics of a poststructuralist bent emphasize the need to reassert local control over local natural resources and to revive and build upon traditional knowledge and resource management systems. To a large extent, these principles have been enshrined in the social ecological movements that have emerged in the South over the past four decades. These movements are analyzed in detail in 41 by David Barkin.

Wackernagel & Rees 1996b: 31–40; Hildyard 1993: 22–35; Shiva 1993: 149–156.

2. Ecological economics: A critique of environmental economics

Although the terms 'ecological economics' and 'environmental economics' appear to be synonymous, they actually represent two schools of thought that are at loggerheads. Environmental economics is an area of study that analyzes environmental issues through neoclassical economic lenses. In essence, it is an effort to incorporate environmental considerations into the economic decisionmaking process. As such, it is closely linked to MSD.

Within the field of environmental economics, methods have been developed for estimating the monetary value of environmental services (usually referred to as 'environmental externalities'); market mechanisms have been invented in an effort to 'internalize' these 'externalities'; and the market itself has been assigned a primary role in controlling levels of contamination and rates of natural-resource exploitation.

On the other hand, ecological economics is largely a critique of neoclassical economic theory and its extension, environmental economics. Instead of treating environmental services as 'externalities,' it sees the human economy as a subsystem of the global ecosystem, limited in size by the earth's ability to assimilate wastes and provide natural resources. From this perspective, there are absolute limits to the size of the human economy, defined by the second law of thermodynamics.

From the same perspective, it is impossible to convincingly internalize environmental externalities; there are too many uncertainties associated with the methods used to assign monetary values to environmental services; existing markets do not and cannot include negotiations with future generations; and market signals are unable to detect breaking points at which environmental damage becomes irreversible. In the words of Mathis Wackernagel and William Rees:

> Market prices generally say nothing about the size of remaining natural capital stocks or whether there is some critical minimal stock size below which recovery is impossible. In short, prices do not monitor stock size or systems fragility, but only the commodity's short-term scarcity on the market. (1996a: 44)

In accordance with this critique, ecological economics points towards the following ways in which free trade exacerbates environmental problems: (1) international competition encourages businesses to lower their ecological standards; (2) free trade allows highly contaminating industries to relocate to countries where environmental legislation or its enforcement is weak; (3) international trade extends the distance between production and consumption, making it less probable that consumers are aware of the ecological damage caused by the production of the goods that they buy; and (4) the transportation of goods around the world consumes large quantities of energy. Finally, as Michael Redclift (1987) and several other authors have pointed out, the neoliberal structural adjustments carried out in the 1980s and 1990s have created a situation in which developing countries are encouraged to intensify the exploitation of their natural resource base in order to make debt payments.

As an alternative to 'free trade,' ecological economists suggest the need to achieve higher levels of self-sufficiency on all levels (national, regional and local), without going to the extreme of autarky. This implies economic and ecosystem reorganization. Other guiding principles include autonomy, participation, equity, productive diversification, fair trade and participatory decision-making. Along these lines, ecological economists point towards social environmental movements as the real driving force behind the so-called 'internalization of environmental externalities.' It is also bears mentioning that women have often played a lead role in these movements.

Daly 1996: 45–60; Pearce, Markandya & Barbier 1989: 51–81.

3. The relationship between poverty and environmental degradation

As already mentioned, MSD tends to emphasize the environmental destruction caused by the poor in order to justify the need for achieving high economic growth rates, supposedly best achieved through free trade. From a critical perspective, it is absurd to blame the poor for the environmental crisis. Although they undoubtedly contribute to different forms of environmental degradation, their contribution can hardly compare to the ecological destruction associated with overconsumption in the North.

In the 1990s, the Environmental Kuznets Curve (EKC) emerged within the MSD paradigm as a hypothesis for explaining the relationship between poverty and environmental degradation on the national and international level. According to this hypothesis, the quality of the natural environment tends to deteriorate during the first stages of economic development, only to improve during latter stages. Several environmental economists have attempted to demonstrate this with empirical evidence. However, their analysis has been highly criticized for the following and other reasons: first, proponents of the EKC tend to selectively choose a subset of environmental problems that have been overcome to a certain extent in developed countries (for example, certain types of air pollution), while ignoring problems that have worsened in the same countries (for example, CO^2 emissions and nuclear wastes); second, the EKC does not take into account the effects of international trade, in particular the relocation of highly contaminating industries from rich to poor countries, as well as the growing demand that consumerism in the North puts on the natural resource base in the South. Along these lines, the EKC curve suffers from the same defect as the original Kuznets Curve, that is, it assumes that poor countries can and will follow the same path as rich ones.

An alternative model for analyzing the relationship between wealth and environmental degradation on the macro-level has been put forth by Wackernagel & Rees (1996a) in the form of the Ecological Footprint. This tool helps to estimate the land area required to supply all of the goods and services of a given population, as well as assimilate all of its wastes, using existing technology. In this way, it has been demonstrated that developed countries put far more pressure on the environment than poor ones. In other words, it is not the poor who are to blame for today's environmental problems—as MSD discourse would have it—but rather the minority of the world's population that enjoys the high material standards associated with Western society.

Ekins 2000: 182–214; Wackernagel & Rees 1996a: 7–29.

4. The 'limits to growth' debate

The 'limits to growth' debate has its roots in the work of Thomas Malthus, who postulated in 1798 that the human population—left unchecked—tends to grow exponentially; while food production can only grow linearly, mostly because of the limited amount of productive land available. Based on this analysis, Malthus concluded that food production will limit demographic growth, that large segments of the human population must necessarily live on the brink of starvation and that any attempt at alleviating extreme poverty will ultimately have a detrimental effect on the poor.

In hindsight, we can now see that Malthus greatly underestimated the power of technological innovation to increase global food production. Over the past 200 years, the human population has increased sixfold and there is now more food per capita available than ever. The problem, of course, is that food and other resources are inequitably distributed. Furthermore, although the Green Revolution has been extremely successful in increasing aggregate agricultural output, it has led to a host of environmental problems that threaten food security. In light of these and other environmental problems, the Malthusian argument was taken up again in the late 1960s and early 1970s, with fears of industrial contamination and depletion of non-renewable resources added to the concerns of high population growth and limited food production. Bestsellers such as *The Population Bomb* (Ehrlich 1968) and *The Limits to Growth* (Club of Rome 1972) helped to diffuse these ideas and raise public awareness about environmental issues. However, as several critics have pointed out, they also tended to be sensational and lacked rigorous scientific analysis.

A more sophisticated argument for the existence of absolute limits to economic growth was published in 1971 by Nicholas Georgescu-Roegen, in *The Entropy Law and the Economic Process*. According this argument, human society has become increasingly dependent on the stocks of low entropy energy available on the Earth's surface; these stocks are finite; and due to the Second Law of Thermodynamics, there is no way to replace them. Goergescu-Roegen's argument has been reiterated by Herman Daly (1996) and other analysts who contend that absolute limits do in fact exist. At the same time, there have been growing concerns about the overexploitation of renewal resources such as water, fisheries, forests and soils, which according to the Ecological Footprint analysis are being exploited at a rate 30 percent higher than the Earth's ability to renew them (Wackernagel & Rees 1996b).

In spite of this evidence, MSD does not recognize absolute limits to the size of the human economy—only temporary limits imposed by the state of technology and social organization (WCED 1987: 43). Proponents of MSD point to the ways in which scarcity in the past has been overcome through technological innovation, discovery of new reserves of non-renewable resources and substitution of inputs. However, as Richard Lecomber observed over thirty years ago, this 'establishes the *logical* conceivability, not the certainty, probability or even the possibility in practice, of growth continuing indefinitely' (cited in Ekins 2000: 41). Accordingly, it seems imprudent—to say the least—to bet on the possibility of realizing exponential economic growth indefinitely.

As an alternative, Herman Daly (1996) suggests striving towards a steady-state economy, defined as one in which qualitative improvements in human welfare are constantly achieved, without quantitative increases in production and consumption. Of course, this implies the need to eventually stabilize the world population, as well as to redistribute wealth between North and South.

Daly 1996: 31–44; Ekins 2000: 40–45; Goodland 1996: 207–17.

5. Scientific uncertainty and political agendas in environmental analysis

In 2001 Bjorn Lomborg published the international best seller *The Skeptical Environmentalist*, which argues that environmental problems are not as serious as environmentalists suggest, that things are getting better in the developed world, and that we can expect the same in the developing world. Based on statistics garnered from a host of international development agencies, Lomborg argues that net forest cover has increased over the past fifty years, that pollution is not in the process of undermining our well-being, that species extinction is not a problem, that global warming will not bring about a global catastrophe and so on. This vision is, of course, in stark contrast to the one conveyed by most international environmental organizations, including Worldwatch Institute, the World Wide Fund for Nature, Greenpeace and others. How is it possible that so-called scientists can arrive at such divergent conclusions?

The answer to this question is twofold: on the one hand, there is much scientific uncertainty associated with different forms of environmental degradation; on the other, environmental discourses are constructed around political agendas. Along these lines, in a classic text on land degradation, Piers Blakie & Harold Brookfield observe the following:

> Much of the literature on land degradation is beset by a fundamental theoretical confusion. Discussants address each others' work but often appear not to discuss the same underlying issues at all. Implicit assumptions about the significance and importance of land degradations remain unexamined. 'Facts,' ideologies and beliefs are not identified, and the relevance and accuracy of much of the database remains in doubt. (1987: xvii)

There are different degrees of scientific uncertainty depending on the specific environmental issue. However, even when the threshold of uncertainty is very low, political agendas come into play in such a way as to create confusion and galvanize popular opinion. Perhaps this is best illustrated by the case of global warming. In spite of overwhelming evidence to the contrary, there are those who deny that average global temperatures are rising. More common is the admission that temperatures are rising but that human activity is not to blame; or even if it is to blame, that the best course of action is to simply adapt to a hotter climate. Finally, amongst those who advocate corrective actions in order to curb global warming, there are diverse positions: while MSD representatives like Al Gore emphasize the need to conserve energy and develop new technologies; radical political ecologists emphasize the need to restructure the global economy, placing hope in environmental movements such as agroecology.

Escobar 1996: 325–43; Forsyth 2003.

6. The tragedy of the commons vs. the tragedy of the enclosures

In 1968, Garret Hardin published his famous metaphor, the 'tragedy of the commons,' giving credence to the idea that common property is intrinsically inclined towards environmental degradation. According to Hardin and his followers, there are basically only two ways to prevent the so-called tragedy of the commons: state control or privatization. Although this metaphor has since been debunked through conceptual clarification and empirical studies, it continues to influence MSD policy prescriptions, such as privatization of water resources, liberalization of land markets and establishment of state-run biosphere reserves in indigenous territories.

One problem with the 'tragedy of the commons' metaphor is that it confuses common property regimes with situations of open access. As Bromley and Cernea (1989: ii) point out:

> Common property regimes are not the free-for-all that they have been described to be, but are structured ownership arrangements within which management rules are developed, group size is known and enforced, incentives exist for co-owners to follow the accepted institutional arrangements, and sanctions work to insure compliance.

Elinor Ostrom (1990) examined hundreds of common property regimes that have functioned effectively for long periods of time without degrading their natural resource base. On the other hand, extensive environmental degradation can be observed all over the world in both private and common property regimes.

In light of this evidence, Raymond Bryant and Sinead Bailey (1997) offer an alternative metaphor for the environmental destruction that frequents traditional common property regimes: the 'tragedy of the enclosures.' It suggests that common property is not intrinsically inclined to dissolve but is often undermined by state and/or private actors who usurp the community's natural resources for large-scale commercial exploitation.

Critics of the 'tragedy of the commons' metaphor reject simplistic solutions based on privatization and state control, suggesting the need to revive and build upon traditional common property regimes where they still exist, and where they do not, to construct new institutions on the local level. At the same time, however, they warn against romanticizing about traditional common property regimes, suggesting the need to build complementary institutions at the national and international levels (Bromley & Cernea 1989: Bryant & Bailey 1997; Ostrom 1990).

Bromley & Cernea 1989: 1–25; Bryant & Bailey 1997: 159–68.

Module 40

Sustainability in the Social Sciences
A Critical Development Perspective

David Barkin
Universidad Autónoma Metropolitana, Mexico

Development theory describes numerous forms for the interpenetration of societies/economies, assuming the historical superiority of capitalism and an inevitable progression of stages of economic growth, even while most analysts reject the Manichean view offered by Water Rostow. This hegemonic vision in political, economic and social thought—never considers it necessary to pose questions such as: What was the world like before colonial expansion? What was the nature of societies before conquest? What are the structural features of the capitalist system that produce underdevelopment?

Yet, careful study demonstrates starkly that complex and powerful forces are involved in the *deliberate construction of underdevelopment*, with severe consequences for people's standard of living, the natural resources base and societies' political and cultural fabric. Obviously, this 'discovery' is not new—honest thinkers and political actors have insisted on these truths for decades, or perhaps for more than a century. This module does not review this now classic literature but rather briefly discusses both the unspoken heritages and the egregious costs of development (Davis 2002b; SPEDC 2003) before moving on to the implications of this history for developing new tools for analyzing the present state of affairs of countries in the 'Global South' and the prospects for future changes.

To begin to broach these themes, a new approach to social science is required. We must start with a distinct philosophical and epistemological framework, one that makes explicit some important ethical matters that are generally given short shrift in such discussions. Thus, we begin by reaffirming three fundamental principles guiding our teaching and our activities: intergenerational equity, social justice and sustainability.

Methodologically this involves a commitment to conduct our teaching and research by integrating the tools of various social and natural sciences (multidisciplinarity), while also informing our work with the assumptions and instruments of several paradigms and assuring a respect for the wisdom generated by peoples of past generations as well as respecting the needs of future generations.

To implement this approach, students and practitioners must recognize the profound contradictions generated by decades, if not centuries, of a destructive pattern of development that has wreaked havoc on ecosystems and impoverished peoples throughout the world in the name of freedom and progress. This module offers a complement to the historical analysis offered in other parts of this Handbook to define mechanisms for moving forward in a constructive way in societies willing to adopt the strategic approach of 'sustainable regional resource management,' which proposes to improve people's quality of life while also contributing to rehabilitating and protecting their ecosystems.

This module faces this challenge by (1) examining the underlying ethical and methodological principles briefly outlined above; (2) exploring the fundamental tenets of a strategy of 'sustainable regional resource management'; (3) discussing the social and political characteristics that are required for its implementation; (4) describing the nature of the productive proposals that would contribute to advancing material welfare, improving infrastructures, and assuring ecosystem balance; (5) analyzing the importance of insuring the generation of surpluses in these processes and the ways in which these surpluses be allocated among individuals and communities to promote regional welfare; and (6) tracing the way in which this approach might be used to examine one of the most pressing problems facing societies around the world: sustainable water management.

Davis 2002b; SPEDC 2003.

1. Introduction: Ethics and methodology

Perhaps a useful way of beginning this discussion is by introducing a basic principle for scientific enquiry and public policy formulation: the precautionary principle. It is a moral and political principle that states that if an action or policy might cause severe or irreversible harm to the public, in the absence of a scientific consensus that harm would not ensue, the burden of proof falls on those who would advocate taking the action. It aims to provide guidance for protecting public health and the environment in the face of uncertain risks, stating that the absence of full scientific certainty shall not be used as a reason to postpone taking measures to avert the risk of serious or irreversible harm to public health or the environment. In more prosaic terms, it has been explained as follows: 'if one is embarking on something new, one should think very carefully about whether it is safe or not, and should not go ahead until reasonably convinced it is' (P. Saunders from *Wikipedia*).

There are numerous ways of studying this approach, but perhaps one of the most accessible is a set of case studies published by the European Environment Agency, which presents accounts of cases where early warnings of impending or environmental harm were ignored, representing an argument for use of the precautionary principle in environmental regulation. Cases considered include destruction of the Californian sardine industry through overfishing, the mesothelioma epidemic resulting from asbestos exposure, groundwater contamination with the gasoline additive MTBE, 'mad cow disease' and carcinogenic risks from benzene exposure.

These case studies highlight the underlying difficulty of present-day political debate: the highly charged participation of stakeholders with substantial financial interests in the current (destructive) state of affairs. Orthodox economists argue that it is simply a question of 'getting the prices right,' but this assumes we can place monetary values on natural processes and resources; they suggest using the market to fix these prices and punish transgressors by forcing them to pay for the damages they occasion. The problem with this approach is that it assumes that all processes are reversible and that pecuniary fines can be appropriately used to correct errors. The erroneous nature of this conflict is evident in policy suggestions like the one offered by the then president of the World Bank to move polluting industries to southern Africa (Foster 1993).

These debates involve a thorough challenge to the current ways of formulating and evaluating policy measures. Once the precautionary principle is accepted the typical tool of benefit-cost analysis becomes unacceptable, because it formulates the problem of one of least risk and accepts the possibility of winners compensating losers (although in reality this process rarely becomes operational). Economists also typically discount (punish) the future, on the assumption that economic growth will always make future generations better off than at present, a position that is patently untenable given the process of global environmental crisis that we are currently experiencing. This same line of reasoning leads traditional analysts to ignore the constant of social conflict in our societies and the value-laden nature of market relations, be they local, national or international. Finally, in their quest to defend the accumulation process controlled by small but powerful groups, economists must be criticized for the unstoppable optimism that leads them to believe that social production can produce goods and technologies that will compensate for the degradation of energy posited by the second law of thermodynamics and the consumption of reserves of non-renewable natural resources along with the contamination of our ecosystems (Burkett 2005; Burkett and Aguiar 2007).

Burkett 2005: 117–52; Burkett & Aguiar 2007; Foster 1993.

2. The tenets of sustainability:
Sustainable regional resource management

From the discussion above it is clear that an alternative organization of production involves locally controlled systems in which non-proletarian social relations predominate; this means that the people organizing production must be scrupulous in developing mechanisms to ensure efficient and saleable production without generating processes in which the participants are being exploited by others. This also places great responsibility on the collectivity to ensure that the production process is carried out with due respect for the environment and that great care is taken to enable the community to generate surpluses that can be used for material gains while also ensuring the continuing enrichment of the political and cultural institutions and ecosystems on which they all depend.

In this regard, the underlying principles guiding the design of the production process and the mechanisms for social control may be defined as: autonomy (regional) self-sufficiency, productive diversification and sustainable management of ecosystems.

Barkin 1998; Barkin & Rosas 2006.

3. Participation, equity, alliances

To be successful, the model of sustainability discussed in the previous theme requires a broad participation of the community in the design of their supervisory functions and consensus about the mechanism for using surplus, both as a reward for the direct producers and as a resource for improving collective infrastructures, be they physical, ecosystem, social or political (this involves an explicit reconsideration of the nature of infrastructures). A corollary to this mechanism is the question of the distribution of income (or material standards of living) among the population and the internal mechanisms for the collective determination of a suitable model of social distribution and conflict resolution.

This model of social organization implicit in this model involves an explicit collective rejection of the model of international economic integration with a dynamic of impoverishing proletarianization. This political model involves a strong role for regional government on the basis of advanced concepts of autonomy; important questions of the geographic and political scope of the organizational forms become central parts of the discussion, involving important debates about responsibilities and rights: how to guarantee basic rights and generate opportunities for a broad segment of the community. This also requires a serious new commitment on the conceptual plane: developing a multi-criteria analysis that brings the political decisionmaking process and participatory trade-offs into the academic framework and avoiding the kind of models that reduce this democratic approach to one of systems analysis. An excellent point of departure for this work are the materials available at <www.latautonomy.org>.

4. Economic and ecosystem reorganization

This theme offers an opportunity to explore the different models of building real-world alternatives, ranging from the rural production models of agroecology (Altieri and Hecht 1990), fair trade and solidarity economies, to differing frameworks of 'the other Zapatistas' and the approach of 'strengthening tradition through innovation' (Barkin and Levins 1998). These models all involve the notion of diversifying the economic base, from a presumption of local self sufficiency and moving on to strengthening and innovating in traditional productive systems while diversifying production for protected and solidarity markets. As mentioned above this requires a continual process of relating ecosystem management to economic reorganization. The readings describe the nature of the productive proposals contributing to advancing material welfare, improving infrastructures and assuring ecosystem balance.

Altieri & Hecht 1990; Barkin 2006; Barkin & Levins 1998: 53–61; Barkin & Paillés 2000: 71–79.

5. Local control and surplus allocation

The implementation of these programs involves a radical agenda of popular participation and gender balance, with clear mechanisms for the exercise of power and the ratification of authority. In order to do this, a discussion of the problems of individual rights and collective appropriation becomes a potential magnet for conflict or a solid basis for collective advancement: the secret of many experiences is the way in which both the community and the leadership anticipate these problems and bring them out into the open. This process of conflict resolution is essential because one of the features that would distinguish this organizational system from traditional peasant societies is its ability (and need) to generate surplus to ensure continuing improvements in the standard of living and the capability of protecting and rehabilitating ecosystems that have suffered from centuries of abuse.

The process of generating surplus and allocating it among community needs and individual demands is perhaps one of the most sensitive and demanding functions of this kind of society (Burkett 2006). The readings in this theme provide a rich assortment of experiences; it might be best to have student share the readings and discuss the merits of the variety of sites and approaches offered here (Allard, Davidson and Matthaei 2008; Swinton and Quiroz 2003).

Allard, Davidson & Matthaei 2008; Burkett 2006: 3–28; Swinton & Quiroz 2003: 1903–19.

6. Water management: Conflict and control

Water management can be a source of conflict, marginality and sickness or a mechanism for enriching communities, generating opportunities and collective action. The literature is replete with examples of growing scarcities, ecological devastation and social exclusion. This theme offers a view of how public control and a new paradigm for resource management—the New Culture of Water (Arrojo 2008)—can move a community/region/people ahead in taking control of their resources without denying access to legitimate users that are willing to respect the rights and needs of people and their environment. This involves a radical rethinking of the constructive ways in which market mechanisms can contribute to facilitating and strengthening social control of the stakeholders and responsibility for the environment.

Balanyá, Brennan, Hoedeman, Krishimoto & Terhorst 2005;
Johnston, Gismondi & Goodman 2006.

Module 41

Political Ecology

Environmentalism for a Change

Anthony O'Malley
Saint Mary's University, Canada

Michael Clow
Saint Thomas University, Canada

To explore the relationship between the environment and development, and between environmental and development issues, we must first define 'the environment' and 'development' and the physical and social links between them.

Development has many definitions. For liberal economists the core meaning is the expansion of production (the GNP) within the capitalist economy, which their theoretical tradition pictures as a market. For many concerned with poverty in the Global South, development means change that improves people's standards of living. Capitalist development is understood in the Marxist tradition as the expansion of production and of the ability to produce under the direction of, and for the primary benefit of, employers and investors. Their single-minded pursuit is to amass more and more and more capital for themselves in one round of investment—production, profit and reinvestment—after another, world without end, and not for any direct benefit to workers or society as a whole. Marxists and others on the left have traditionally sought to define and seek the social basis for an alternative form of economic development that will serve a broader set of more useful goals, for more people, in a more egalitarian fashion and under a more democratic direction than capitalist development permits. Whatever the differences in these understandings of development, however, they all connect directly to economic activity—the production of goods and services that can create capital under some social relations and broader human benefit under others. And for most analysts, development has included the expansion of economic activity. The connection between the environment and development is mediated through the role of the environment in economic activity and through the consequences of economic activity for the environment.

The environment, or more accurately the 'natural environment,' is what biologists call the *biosphere*. The biosphere is the complex network of living plant and animal communities and the non-living cycles of the air, water and land that connect and sustain them. An *ecosystem* is one of the constituent interdependent communities of the biosphere—a symbiotic combination of specific species of plants and animals which form a particular biotic community, along with the air, water and/or soil conditions in which they live—for example, a meadow, a tropical rainforest forest, a corral reef or a marsh. Environmental degradation is any disruption of an ecosystem or of the ocean, atmospheric and land cycles of the biosphere caused by human activities (Raskin and Bernow 1991; WCED 1987; Daly, Cobb & Cobb 1989.

The standard model of the relationship of economic activity and the environment points out that the biosphere, the Earth's crust and the Sun together provide the materials and energy necessary for economic activity to be conducted. Economic activity produces both products and services, and wastes—and in the end, all of the things produced by the economy end up as wastes. These wastes are dumped into the biosphere—into the air and the water and onto the land. The economy depends on the biosphere to produce key material inputs to production and to provide a natural 'recycling' of the economy's wastes back into the materials, energy and planetary conditions needed for production. The economy cannot be sustained without the resources and recycling capacity of the biosphere. And neither can human life; as animals who evolved in this biosphere we are dependent on the conditions created by a healthy biosphere.

Unfortunately, economic activity can be very destructive of the biosphere. The scale of our drawing of materials and energy out of the biosphere can easily exceed what local ecosystems or the biosphere as a whole can sustain; this overdrawing of nature's resources damages the ecosystems that produce these resources and harms surrounding ecosystems. Disposing of wastes in quantities and kinds that cannot be recycled by the biosphere's natural processes also disrupts and damages the environment. 'Overharvesting' and befouling the biosphere impairs the its processes—the very thing that produces what we want to appropriate as resources and the natural capacity to 'recycle' our wastes. Environmental degradation reduces the regeneration of *potentially* renewable resources and shrinks the natural waste reprocessing capacity of the biosphere. 'Renewable' resources are only renewed if the habitats of the planet and its ocean, atmosphere and other physical and chemical cycles are operating normally. The natural recycling of biodegradable materials will occur only if the habitats and physical cycles of the biosphere are working to 'reprocess' them back into the elements of the biosphere. In effect, economic activity of the wrong scale or conducted improperly can kill the 'golden goose' of the biosphere upon which production depends.

Environmental issues become development issues when environmental degradation threatens the sustainability of human economic activities and human health. And since development has always been associated with economic growth, the ability of the environment to provide the resources for economic expansion and to recycle the expanding waste of economic activity is a crucial question about the biophysical sustainability of economic growth. Development issues become environmental issues when patterns of development or proposed development projects threaten to disrupt ecosystems or the global air, water and soil systems upon which the normal functioning of the biosphere depend. The central question of the relationship between environment and development is, then, how much economic activity, of which kinds and how conducted, can be sustained and tolerated by local ecosystems and by the biosphere as a whole?

Not surprisingly, fierce debates have arisen about the compatibility of further development and preserving the natural environment. Concerns have centred on the effects of environmental degradation on human populations and the activities that sustain them, on the constraints and limits environmental degradation may pose to development and economic expansion, and on the forms of development most compatible with the need to maintain the health of ecosystems and natural cycles of the atmosphere, oceans, freshwater systems and the soil.

While environmentalists have generally focused on the symptoms of environmental degradation and the biophysical aspects of resolving environmental problems, environmental problems are also social, political and economic, and so is there solution. Environmental degradation is caused by human activities, and only changes in our activities and how we conduct them can solve the problems we have created. Inevitably, then, the linked questions of environment and development lead back to questions about the social processes that are creating environmental and development problems and preventing the achievement of their solutions. Why have environmental measures not been taken? Why are pressing problems like global warming, which will cause widespread disruption to existing agricultural, forestry and fishing patterns ignored by business and governments? Why do we recklessly pursue economic growth beyond or in disregard of its ecological limits? Why does business overwhelmingly oppose environmentally prudent measures and constraints? What measure of political and economic change is required to generate solutions that will sustain the biosphere and an ecologically sustainable pattern of economic activity that enhance people's well-being? What are the forms of social and economic life that would be compatible with ecological sustainability? In practice this requires an analysis of the processes of capitalist development and its alternatives.

Clow 1992; Daly, Cobb & Cobb 1989; Raskin & Bernow 1991: 87–103.

1. The environment, society and development: Critical theoretical perspectives

The mainstream view of the environment and development is encapsulated in the notion of 'sustainable development' introduced in the Brundtland Report (WCED 1987). This notion is predicated on the possibility of combining economic growth with environmental security through careful resource conservation and management and a technological fix (adoption of green technology) on the basis of scientific research. Within the framework of this concept of 'sustainable development' there is some scope for debate, mainly among environmentalists, sociologists and economists, as to the role of the state (environmental policy) and local communities regarding more effective resource management, but there is a shared belief in the utility and importance of technology and conservation practices.

From a CDS perspective the issues are very different; they have to do with system dynamics, i.e., industrial capitalism, and the negative impact of excessive industrialization under conditions brought about by the inexorable forces of capital accumulation—placing profits ahead of people's needs and the environment. The most important schools of thought that take this critical or radical perspective are (1) political ecology, broadly defined and conceived, and (2) Marxist ecology, in the writings of O'Connor, Redclift and Foster, but we can also include ecofeminism (Mies and Shiva 1983) and more marginal approaches such as 'left biocentrism,' a form of deep ecology (Orton).

Political ecology originated in the 1970s, but its real expansion occurred in the 1980s and 1990s. Today, political ecology is a leading source of innovative research on issues linked to poverty and the environment. The analysis in political ecology is centred on the idea of a 'politicized environment.' It explores the main actors involved in this management and their interests, aims, norms and narratives. This again leads into an investigation of power and power relations in environmental management.

Marxist ecology or eco-Marxism (Benton; O'Connor; Foster) is more concerned with the political economy or class dynamics of capitalist development and the environmental impact of this development. Among the factors fomenting tensions between ecology and Marxism, perhaps the most important is the widespread view that Marx's vision of postcapitalist society not only treats natural conditions as effectively limitless but also embraces an anti-ecological ethic of technological optimism and human domination over nature. This interpretation (see Foster 2002 for a different interpretation) is in part a product of facile identification of Marx's projection with the historical experience of environmental havoc in the U.S.S.R. and other state-run 'socialist' societies and in part a reading of Marx's theory of communism. For example, Nove (1990: 230, 237) argues that Marx presumes that 'natural resources [are] inexhaustible,' and that there is no need for 'an environment-preserving, ecologically conscious... socialism.'

The critical feature of eco-Marxism is what Foster dubs 'ecology against capitalism,' essentially an attempt to reclaim a lost tradition of ecological thinking in Marxism (Foster 2002). The environmental dynamics of capitalist development are described and theorized in Foster's *The Vulnerable Planet*. Like most Marxists he views environmental degradation as the inevitable result of these dynamics brought about by the insatiable search for profit in the process of capital accumulation.

Another critical perspective regarding the environment and development departs from a feminist rather than a Marxist perspective. Ecofeminism, in the form given it by Mies and Shiva (1993), makes a connection between nature, the capitalist production system and society, and the gender dimensions of this connection, such as women's health.

As for 'deep ecology,' which provides the most radical critique of the arranged marriage between development and the environment, the issue is not capitalism or profit-making but industrialism, materialism and consumerism, and the obsession with economic growth. However, rooted as it is (at least in part) in a Buddhist or anti-western philosophy in the form that it has taken in Norway (the Gaia principle), it is focused on the need not for systemic change (socialism) but rather a radical reorientation of thinking and practice regarding 'development.' Most deep ecological theorists are critical or sceptical about socialism as a solution to the environmental crisis of 'western civilization' but yet sympathetic towards socialism in regard to its commitment to equality, the abolition of class and political activism. Arne Naess, for example, an important Norwegian exponent of deep ecology, notes in *Wisdom in the Open Air* that green politics supports the elimination of class differences locally, regionally, nationally and globally' (Reed & Rothenberg 1993). Naess brings a class perspective into his writing. Yet, David Orton, a Canadian deep-ecologist or 'left-biocentric' who is strongly influenced by if not oriented towards Marxism, notes that this 'revolutionary' perspective is rarely seen in mainstream North American deep ecology writing. Bill Devall, for example, in a published essay called 'Deep Ecology and Political Activism,' argues that 'Political revolution is not part of the vocabulary of supporters of the deep, long-range ecology movement.'

Foladori & Pierri 2005; Shiva 2005.

2. Capitalism and the environment: Nature under siege

The concept of sustainable development placed on the development agenda by the U.N. Conference on the Environment and the resulting Brundtland Commission Report (WCED 1987) focused on the relation between economic development and the environment, specifically on the question of whether it is possible for nations to continue to pursue a path of economic growth without threatening the carrying capacity of the global environment—exceeding the limits to growth—and thus jeopardizing the development prospects and livelihood of future generations, not to mention the very survival of the human species.

The notion of 'limits to growth,' or more accurately limits on the scale and kinds of production that can be sustained in the biosphere, has been widely held from early in the contemporary environmental debate (editors of the *Ecologist* 1972). The idea of such constraints on production were rejected not just by capitalists but many others who put their faith in technological innovation to increase nature's bounty of renewable resources, create new sources of energy, increase the efficiency of production and recycling efforts, and contain pollution in an expanding economy. But can efforts to 'get more from less,' 'cleaner technology' and 'wiser' resource management prevent further degradation of the biosphere as production rises? Many argue that belief in the indefinite expansion of production is unreasonable. Magic is what is required to conjure up ever more product from the same amount of materials, ever more effort from the same quantity of energy, ever more renewable resources from the Earth, ever less wastes from industrial processes, and wastes ever more integrated into the natural flows of energy and materials in the biosphere. These proponents of environmental constraints argue indefinite improvement in technological efficiency and an indefinite ability to tailor ecosystems to deliver more resources and absorb more wastes is excluded by the laws of thermodynamics.

A critical issue arising from the limits to economic activity is the nature of the operating economic system, capitalism, and the question of whether the dynamics of this system, the laws of capitalist development—geared as they are to the logic of accumulation, profit-making and economic growth—are in fundamental conflict with nature. These readings explore critical dimensions of this issue: the connection between capitalism, development and the global environment. Most studies in this connection attribute the environmental crisis to the dynamics of economic development—rapid industrialization, use of environmentally damaging technologies and hydrocarbon-based fossil fuels, the profit-making dynamics of capitalism or economic globalization (Clow 1994; Foster 2002).

Clow 1994; Foladori 2001; O'Connor 1998.

3. The ecological crisis and neoliberal environmental governance

Sustainable development was intended to save global capitalist society from the unintended consequences of its own success at expanding production. But ecological problems and environmental degradation have continued to worsen during the more than twenty years since the promulgation of the sustainable development formula (WCED 1987). The forest industry continues to destroy the remaining stands of natural forest; industrial agricultural practices are destroying the fertility of the soil; overfishing and ocean pollution are wiping out the world's fish stocks; massive new hydro projects continue in sensitive areas; there is renewed government support for the nuclear industry. There is no move towards the systematic reduction of energy demand through conservation and increased efficiency. Planned obsolescence and rapid turnover in consumer durables is still a cornerstone of the economy. Climate change is now a contemporary problems wreaking havoc in the Arctic and bringing droughts here, floods there—not a problem for the remote future.

The message of the sustainable development formula that environmental problems could be solved and economic growth could be made ecologically sustainable is deeply attractive to the minority of capitalists and government officials, who could see the rising tide of environmental degradation overwhelming capitalist society. But sustainable development advocates have failed to 'sign-on' the major corporations that dominate the world economy or the governments that set international economic policies. Sustainable development requires that governments create policies and modify the operations of markets so as to create the conditions within which corporations will change their practices and production to meet environmental goals.

The 'sustainable development' program is directly opposed to the whole thrust of neoliberalism, whose 'market fundamentalism' serves to free corporations to globally pursue profit and growth without let, hindrance or regulation (McCarthy and Prudham 2004). Environmental regulation, environmental taxes and even environmental incentives all represent unacceptable 'interference' with the business environment in the minds of neoliberals; most corporations and their political servants have no time for 'Cassandras' trying to save them from the longer term consequences of global 'free-enterprise.' International trade agreements have been designed precisely to prevent the state from such activities (McCarthy and Prudham 2004). Environmental assets like water have been or are being privatized (Shiva 2005; Barlow 2007).

Environmentalism has proven to be one of the more resilient bases for opposition to neoliberal policies and nostrums; conversely, environmentalism has tossed up attempts to reconcile corporate interests and environmental imperatives (McCarthy & Prudham 2004). The transfer of governmental authority to corporate and transnational governance that has marked neoliberalism has limited the effectiveness of demands for both social justice and environmental priorities (Wolford 2005) in opposition to business interests.

Agrawal 2005; Altvater 1990: 10–34; Clapp & Dauverge 2005; Grove 1995: 1–15, 474–86; McCarthy & Prudham 2004: 275–83; Roberts & Thanos 2003.

4. Living with nature and surviving capitalism: Poverty, livelihoods and social movements

'What is the connection between poverty and environmental practice—between this practice and the staggering poverty and social inequalities found in Latin America and other parts of the Global South' (Roberts and Thanos 2003); in this connection, Roberts argues that 'poor people are much more affected by bad environmental practices and have far fewer resources to protect themselves. Some of the most maladaptive interactions with the environment are done as a result of desperate economic situations, too.' He adds, from a sociological perspective, that the relationship of humans to nature and the economy is mediated by the structure of social relations—by the organization of society into different sorts of social groups: 'These nations must address poverty and inequality at the same time they address environmental issues. We can't solve environmental issues without solving poverty and inequality.'

Anderson 1994: Chap. 1; Cederlöf & Sivaramakrishnan 2005: 1–40; Foladori 2007; Peet & Watts 2004.

5. Environmental conflict, forced migration and development

Much concern is being expressed about the effects on society of increasing environmental disruption. Visions of environmental refugees—people finding themselves without the environmental resource to make a living, fleeing rising sea levels or long-lasting droughts—haunts the future. But such situations are already upon us. Shortages of vital environmental assets, insistent demands for neighbouring countries' water and determination to obtain petroleum resources from those who have them all bode ill for international peace and security. As environmental degradation bites and shortages of non-renewable resources upon which we have built the global economy develop, domestic and international conflicts could well mount and add their own dimension to a spiral of ecologically related human development problems.

Homer-Dixon 1999: 3–27, 133–68; Le Billon 2006: 778–801; Watts 2005: 373–407

6. What is to be done?
Environmental politics for development and change

> If many 'reds' have landed among the 'greens,' it's first of all because they had left the red movements, had broken with 'socialism,' even in its ideal form. It's also because they found in the political ecology movements something of a 'family resemblance' with their past experience, a similarity of paradigms. Schematically, the elements they rediscovered there are: materialism, the dialectic historicism, and a 'progressive' orientation. (Lipietz 2000: 1)

The weakest dimension of environmental scholarship is an analysis of *who* will be at the forefront of change toward environmental sustainability and how they will create the real societal change required to move beyond continuing 'business-as-usual.' Those concerned with the solution to environmental degradation have often tended to put their faith in environmental education as their primary means of action—making people aware of the facts and need for change, calling on consumers to act responsibly and pleading to business and governmental leaders to address the environmental crisis. Forty and more years of such efforts by the environmental movement have had little concrete results. The question of who will be the social basis of an effective movement to challenge capitalist development and move society off the road to the exhaustion of our ecological resources is the analytic elephant in the room to which we have been paying too little attention.

Joel Kovel, in *The Enemy of Nature* (2008), speaks to this new environmental awareness and the way it plays into a possible solution to the environmental crisis. He also points to a radical way forward, as do contributors to the volume edited by Peet and Watts (2004).

Bello 2007b; Castree 2006; Harter 2004; Kovel 2008; Lipietz 2000;
Peet & Watts 2004; Sachs 1999.

Module 42

Energy and Development
Oil on Troubled Waters

John Saxe-Fernández
Universidad Nacional Autónoma de Mexico, Mexico

1. The economic and strategic importance of hydrocarbon-based forms of energy

The global capitalist economy depends on non-renewable fossil fuels or hydrocarbon resources such as oil, natural gas and coal for 80 percent of the world's energy supply. Fossil fuels fuel the modern industrial economy. Oil accounts for one-third of the total energy supply and 90 percent of the energy used in the transportation sector. Oil is the essential input for the production of fertilizers, plastics, modern medicine and other chemicals. Modern militaries cannot operate without oil. Consequently, in the post World War II period, assuring reliable supplies of crude oil and other fossil fuels, a matter of energy security, is not only an important source of capital accumulation; it has been a critically important foreign policy objective of the U.S., dictating the dynamics of the U.S.'s international relations and its imperial ambitions. The rapid depletion of fossil fuels is more than an environmental problem: it has helped to generate imperial war. It has been argued that the war in Iraq can be explained in terms of these foreign policy dynamics, as well as U.S. interests in the Gulf region and Eurasia, where the 'big game' in oil and gas can be found.

Given the strategic problems in ensuring a steady supply of non-renewable fossil fuels (oil, natural gas, coal) and the immense environmental problems associated with its global production, an important development dynamic is the search for strategic alternatives in renewable and more socially and environmentally friendly and less damaging forms of energy. One currently popular alternative is the production of agro-fuel out of corn and other sources of biomass. Biomass is the only renewable energy source that can be used as a substitute for the declining world supply of fossil fuels. In the U.S., for example, the government is currently subsidizing corn producers to 40 percent of their production costs to convert corn into biomass.

This strategy, however, is ride with problems. Apart from the fact that it is a very inefficient source of energy production and limited by the available quantity of productive land and fresh water, the conversion of a food source into energy (ethanol production) is leading directly into an emerging food scarcity crisis, resulting in even more hunger in the Global South. In addition, large-scale production of biomass is likely to lead to other serious environmental problems and accelerate the relentless move of global capitalism towards global environmental catastrophe.

Barnes, Hayes, Jaffe & Victor 2006; Christensen 2006: 81–126;
Jorgenson & Kick 2006; Yergin 2003.

2. The geopolitics of global energy production

The insatiable demand of China for resources and energy is currently a driving force of the global economy, as well as the fuel for a major global resource war as well as an impending global environmental catastrophe. The dynamics of this development process is an important subject of critical development studies. The readings on this theme explore these dynamics from a theoretical and empirical research perspective.

Bunker & Ciccantell 2005: Chaps. 2–3; Jorgenson & Kick 2003: 195–203.

3. Corporations, governments and consumers: Markets and politics

Critical issues in this area include: (1) the dynamics of global supply and demand for strategic resources such as oil and gas; (2) the nature and development of policy frameworks regulating the production and marketing of oil and natural gas; (3) the global operations of the multinational corporations in the sector, including some of the biggest; (4) the operations of governments in support of these operations and in support of foreign policy energy security objectives; (5) the 'dangers and consequences of America's growing dependency on imported petroleum' (6) the behaviour and actions of consumers in response to the dynamics of the market; and (7) the politics of these dynamics. In this area the major individual and collective consumer response is to adjust to these dynamics the best or only way they can, by cutting back on the use of these resources—to conserve the resource and cut back consumption of high demand and environmentally damaging fossil fuels 'market.' Needless to say, there are also 'supply side' issues—a matter of increasing production and consumer demand for a highly lucrative trade in a precious commodity. This is not just a matter of production but high-stakes politics—imperialism, not too put too fine a point on it.

Crandall 2006; Klare 2004.

4. Resource nationalism and market power

Critical issues in this area include the study of international political economy—primarily collective action and international cooperation; OPEC's historical experience in trying to coordinate production decisions among major oil producers; resource nationalism (and market power) in Iran and Iraq and the future of hydrocarbon production in the Persian Gulf, Russia and Asia (China, India, Japan) and Latin America (Venezuela); alternative analytical frameworks for understanding the international behaviour of national energy companies from emerging market states in Asia and their relations with national governments; state control and the re-statification (reversion of privatization) of hydrocarbon energy resources.

Cordesman & al-Rodhan 2006; Marcel 2006: 106–223.

5. U.S. imperialism, neoliberal globalization and the political economy of energy development

The major issue for CDS in this area relates to the political dynamics of global war, conflict and U.S.-led imperialism in relation to the production and supply of oil and gas, and the impact of these resource wars on economic and political developments in the South.

The most important battleground in the mounting natural resource wars is part of what might be termed 'oil imperialism.' Michael Klare's *Resource Wars* provides a landmark assessment of the critical role of oil in U.S. foreign policy and the state's actions abroad, as well as more generally the role of resources in much of the conflict in the post Cold War world. In *Blood and Oil,* Klare elaborates on this theme, delineating the dynamics of oil imperialism and warning Americans of the need for the government to change its energy policies before it is too late—before several generations of Americans, and countless others, are forced to spend the coming decades paying for oil with blood.

Other issues in this area include the political dynamics of energy and resource wars and the policy dynamics of 'structural reform,' especially regarding the neoliberal policy of privatization in the strategic energy sector. This issue relates to efforts of the neoliberal state (for example, Mexico) to bring about the privatization of the country's energy resources in the mistaken or professed belief that this would be the key to the financing and production crisis in the area. Saxe-Fernandez (2002), for one, believes that this is not only willfully mistaken but masking a hidden agenda. In any case, he argues, privatization, under conditions in Mexico and elsewhere, means the de facto denationalization of the country's energy resources. In Bolivia, this issue has entailed a series of 'gas wars,' which provided conditions, including a highly mobilized indigenous population, that brought Morales, an Amayran indigenous leader of the 'Movement towards Socialism,' to state power. Saxe-Fernandez (2002, 2008) elaborates on this issue in the case of Pemex in Mexico, where the current neoliberal administration is committed to 'structural reform' (read 'privatization') in the strategic oil sector.

Some scholars have noted that the neoliberal reform agenda not only was initiated in Latin America but that the region has provided the most effective laboratory for diverse experiments with neoliberal policies. However, after two decades of these experiments, it is evident that neoliberalism, since the 1980s the dominant economic ideology of global capitalism, is dysfunctional in economic terms and unsustainable socially and politically. Since 2000, a number of governments in the region, partly in response to popular pressures but also because of the widely held belief in the need for change, have moved away from neoliberalism, reversing key policies such as privatization in a reorientation of national policy towards radical populism or socialism. Venezuela under the presidency of Hugo Chávez and Bolivia under the presidency of Evo Morales, the first indigenous politician anywhere in the modern or postmodern world to have achieved state power, provide important case studies of the policy dynamics involved and of the role of the state in turning oil and gas into development.

Federici 2002; Federici 1992; Klare 2004; Livergood 2001;
Petras & Veltmeyer 2005b: Chaps. 8–9.

6. Natural resource wars and energy battlegrounds: The dynamics of oil imperialism and the 'battle to come' (for the right to water)

Energy battlegrounds are places where competitive interests and conflicting agendas of major producer states and corporations intersect with efforts by indigenous communities, workers and consumers to protect their interests. Major energy battlegrounds include East Asia, Eurasia (Central Asia, the Caspian sea, Iran) and the Americas (the Western Hemisphere), where the

U.S. in particular is challenged by increasingly assertive energy producers such as Venezuela under Chavez.

Regarding developments in the Global South, issues in this area include the policy dynamics of 'structural reform,' especially in regard to the policy of privatization in the energy sector. A major issue is the de facto denationalization of strategic resources and the inability of governments to design policy and protect the national interest. Efforts of the neoliberal state, in Bolivia, Ecuador, Mexico and elsewhere to implement the neoliberal agenda of 'structural reform' has generated, and continues to generate, the most diverse and virulent forms of resistance, creating a major locus of struggle in many developing countries. Bolivia in the 'gas wars' of recent years (2003, 2005) provides the most eloquent case study of the dynamics and forces involved (Kohl & Farthing 2006).

Klare 2002; Dangl 2007; Barlow 2007; Kohl & Farthing 2006.

Section 14

Development on the Margins

The world in the late 1960s, several decades into 'development with international cooperation,' was constituted by (1) a small number (twenty, to be exact) of advanced capitalist countries ('founding states'), which as of 1961 were grouped into the Organisation for Economic Co-operation and Development (OECD), essentially a club of rich countries in the capitalist 'West' with a relatively high level of GNP and per capita income; also (2) a smaller group of medium-income countries in the 'East' (the U.S.S.R. and East Europe), which shared a commitment to socialism or centralized planning as a form of economic organization; and (3) a considerably larger group of countries in a 'Third World' of relatively economic backward or 'developing' countries, with a much lower level of GNP and per capita income, most of which formed a bloc of developing countries within the U.N. (the 'Group of 77' at the time; some 120 today) and were part of the 'non-aligned movement' vis-à-vis the East-West ideological split.

Today, another four decades into the development process, the world is more complicated, much more heterogeneous—and more difficult to categorize. Even so, in terms of different development indicators, both structural and conditional, it is still possible to group and rank countries by their level of economic or human development. Both the World Bank and the UNDP in their annual reports—the *World Development Report* or WDR and the *Human Development Report* or HDR—categorize countries across the three worlds of development into three categories: high, medium and low in terms of per capita income (WDR) and levels of 'human development,' a composite of three sets of economic and social development indicators (HDR). In 2008 (projected from 2006 data) there were some 34/63 countries in the high income/HD category; 96/82 in the medium income/human development category; and 53/33 in the low income/human development category.[1]

As evident in the range of difference in the number of countries in each category (34/63; 96/82; 55/33), the grouping and ranking of countries by the World Bank and the UNDP do not coincide, even though most theorists still assume a tendency for correlation between levels of economic and social development, and at the extremes, countries in the OECD[2] score high on both measures while many of the countries in the Sub-Saharan Africa share the status of low per capita income/human development. Despite the overlap in the two rankings of countries into three worlds of development (high, intermediate, low) the average level of annual growth and annually recorded improvements in 'human development' tend to vary as much by country as by region; nevertheless, it is still possible to identity and group countries into major 'regions' (West Europe, Latin America and the Caribbean, Asia—South, Southeast, East, North Africa and the Middle East, Sub-Saharan Africa. And within this regional grouping, as in the 1960s, it is still possible to group countries and identify regions along a North-South development divide.

A major and continuing controversy among development theorists is whether or not the North-South divide is deepening: is there is a trend towards convergence or not between countries and regions along this divide? On this issue the evidence is mixed or mired in ideology, with some theorists and analysts (mostly in the mainstream of development theory and practice) seeing a trend towards income convergence and a decrease in the global development gap, and many others (mostly critics of mainstream development), arguing to the contrary—that even with the extraordinarily rapid rate of sustained economic growth in China and the apparent advances made in recent years towards the U.N. Millennium Development Goal of reducing by 50 percent the level of extreme poverty, and even without consideration of the impact of the current global crisis on the real economy, global inequalities are in fact increasing, resulting in a further deepening of the development divide, both in structural terms of a centre and periphery and in conditional terms of the 'physical quality of life.'

For the sake of a regional analysis of the development problematic in recent history and in the current conjuncture of capitalist development, this section of the book is composed of four modules, one of which is focused on Sub-Saharan Africa as a region within the Global South (mostly composed of countries in the low income/HD category); a second module concerns Latin America (and the Caribbean), a heterogeneous grouping of some thirty-three countries, most in the medium income/HD 'developing country' category; and a third module focused on Asia, a broad grouping of countries comprised of the two most populous—and fastest growing in economic development terms—countries in the world (China, India), several countries in the South in the 'least developed' category and a more heterogeneous group of developing countries (mostly in the World Bank's medium income category) in the southeast of the continent grouped into the ASEAN regional bloc, and Japan, the second biggest economy in the world and most definitely not in the 'Global South.'

Because of its weight in the global economy and its emergence as a world power in the global arena, with the fastest growing economy in the world, Module 46 focuses on China and its role in the global development process.

UNDP 2003b; World Bank 1978–2008.

Module 43

Developing Africa

Dennis Canterbury
Eastern Connecticut State University, United States

This module tackles a big problem—development and change in Africa—whose complexities defy most people's understanding, and scholars are definitely no exception. We propose to tackle this problem by first exposing the mistaken view that development as a subject for study and a goal for nation-states originated after World War II with the collapse of colonialism, the emergence of newly independent states in Africa, Asia and the Caribbean, and President Truman's 'point four' in his inauguration address in 1949. The module purposely explores via historical analysis an alternative view, that development is the single vision of progress of nation-states through wealth accumulation in their own right or by the individuals or classes in them. The mercantilist/

classical political economist launched wealth accumulation as the goal of nation-states and as a subject for study. Development theory from the 1940s merely attempted to achieve that identical goal rather than to transform it and, as such, only expanded on the mercantilist/classical political economist debate. As long as nation-states exist, the development problem will remain that of wealth accumulation in these political and economic units.

Alternative development and change in Africa must seek to transition from the development framework laid down by the mercantilist/classical political economist and extended by the development 'pioneers.' In essence, this means the transformation of the arbitrarily created nation-state in Africa as the principal form of economic and political organization on the continent. It also means a different way of understanding the past and future history of African development. It is common to attribute the lack of development on the continent to a failure of leadership and lack of 'good governance,' the proliferation of 'failed states' beset with corruption, rentierism and ethnic/tribal conflict over the continent's natural resources. Hence the focus of the international 'community' of development associations, of both scholars and policymakers, on the issue of 'governance.' With the assistance of the Kennedy School of Government and an advisory council of eminent African academics, and with reference to the World Bank's work in the area, the Mo Ibrahim Foundation has devised an index of governance with which to assess all Sub-Saharan African countries against fifty-eight 'objective' measures that together define 'good governance.'

However, a critical development studies perspective on African development suggests that the solution to the problems that beset the continent require a different approach and a different tool: a critical understanding of Africa's past, its colonial and neocolonial legacy, and a critical assessment of the changes in the existing 'structures' of society, resources, policies and actions needed to escape this legacy.

> African economies are making progress. This positive economic news marks a watershed in Africa's history and dispels the prevailing view of the continent as a region of undifferentiated hardship and despair. It is also evidence that Africa is set on a new era—one that could, if the necessary conditions are put in place, deliver lasting change … a change that is much needed. Some 300 million people on the continent live in poverty, with little to no access to the most basic resources. In the past quarter-century—during which 500 million people managed to escape from poverty worldwide—the number of the poor in Sub-Saharan Africa nearly doubled. —Joaquim Chissano, president of Mozambique from 1986 to 2005, awarded the first Mo Ibrahim Prize for Achievement in African Leadership in 2007

1. Theorizing development and change in Africa

Africa is a complex continent in itself in terms of its geography and cultural traditions, which became even more complicated by its conquest by Arab Muslims and European Christians, and the uneven development between North Africa and Sub-Saharan Africa, and other bright spots such as Kenya, South Africa, Nigeria and Ghana. Theorizing about development and change in Africa is all the more complex because of these and other difficulties. It could be undertaken from various vantage points such as the Muslim North, Southern Africa, East Africa, West Africa or Sub-Saharan Africa, which includes all the African countries South of the Sahara excluding the Muslim North. This module focuses on Sub-Saharan Africa, characterized by countries that were essentially the product of European conquest.

At the time of its conquest by the European powers development theory did not apply to Africa. Development theory was merely a concern for Europe, which was just beginning to create nation-states of its own. The most rudimentary development theory that emerged involved the mercantilist perspective that the nation-state must accumulate as much precious metals (such as gold and silver) as possible in order to become rich. The mercantilist perspective held sway until the classical political economists came up with the idea that a better way for countries to become rich was for them to engage in free trade. In essence, therefore, development concerns the activities or struggles of a country to become better off; development is only a problem for countries or nation-states. Colonies do not have a development problem; they are sites that nation-states use to secure riches, either through mercantilist or free trade policies. When colonies are transformed into nation-states, only then are they faced with the development problem because they must enter into the arena with other nation-states to amass wealth for themselves.

Theorizing about development in Africa is therefore only a recent phenomenon, associated with the creation of nation-states on the continent. This theorizing has taken place within the development problematic bequeathed to present generations by the mercantilist and classical political economists and falls under the general rubric of modernization.

Kendie & Martens 2008: Chap. 1; Leys 1975; Rodney 1973: Chaps. 2–6; Todd 2007.

2. The development trajectory in Africa

The development trajectory in Africa and the development problem in Africa are two separate issues. Whereas the development problem came to the fore with political independence, the development trajectory has to be understood in terms of the social, political and economic conditions in Africa in three distinct historical periods—Africa before its conquest by the Arab Muslims and European Christians, the post-conquest period up until political independence and the post-independence period. The first period was characterized by uneven development within African empires, among African empires and between African empires and hunter-gatherer groups on the continent. In these contexts, issues concerning the emergence of state forms and possible imperialist relations came to the fore.

The post-conquest period up until political independence is also characterized by uneven development, imperialism, colonialism and nationalism. Africa became a geographical site from which emerging and well-formulated European nation-states extracted riches through mercantilist and free trade policies. Dependency, development and underdevelopment, socialism and other such theoretical propositions became prevalent. The advent of nationalism in Africa had two broad effects. On the one hand, it stimulated Africans to put pressure on the European powers to dismantle the colonial system by granting political independence to the colonies, which would allow them to enter into the development fray to accumulate wealth for themselves. On the other hand, it pushed the European colonial powers to consider the improvement of the social and economic conditions in their colonies and to implement programs to help to achieve those improvements.

In the post independence period, those two tendencies combined in a practical sense, and development emerged in Africa focused explicitly on wealth accumulation in the African nation-states. The materialization of nation-states in Africa in pursuit of development poses a major contradiction for development. The contradiction is that the European powers must continue to develop, that is, to accumulate wealth, while Africa, a site from which the European nation-states enrich themselves, now also seeks to develop. The European nation-states want to continue to use the resources of Africa to develop Europe, and Africa wants to use its resources to develop Africa. This is the real development dilemma facing both Europe and Africa. The post-independence period is characterized *inter alia* by neocolonialism and experiments with socialism, radicalism, and neoliberalism—economic liberalization, democratization and governance, all seeking to address that contradiction.

Amin 1973; Davidson 1969; Arrighi & Saul 1973; Hochschild 1998; Harris 1998; Kendie & Martens 2008: Chap. 1; Nkrumah 1969; Rodney 1973: Chap. 2; Sender & Smith 1986.

3. Disengagement or delinking Africa from capitalism: Radical perspectives

The lack of development as wealth accumulation in Africa has led some scholars to argue that Africa needs to disengage from capitalism. Located within the post-independence debate on development as wealth accumulation, the disengagement argument that subsequently became known as 'delinking' has taken on different dimensions. Much of the debate on disengagement from capitalism went on at the University of Dar es Salaam in Tanzania among a small Marxist group organized around *Cheche*, the official organ of the radical student movement, University Students' African Revolutionary Front. *Cheche* took its name from the *Spark* of Kwame Nkrumah and *Iskra* of Lenin. The Tanzanian government banned *Cheche* on the grounds that it was under the influence of foreign communist ideas. The authors of *Cheche* regrouped, and their ideas reappeared in the *Maji Maji*, the official journal of the Youth League of the Tanganyika African National Union, the ruling party in Tanzania. Walter Rodney's work, 'Some Implications of the Question of the Disengagement from Imperialism' (1971), outlined the position of the proponents of disengagement from global capitalism (and this imperialism), as argued by the editors of *Cheche*. Their position was that disengagement was not the same as isolation but involved the 'reduction of economic dependence, elimination of surplus outflow, utilization of this surplus for construction of nationally integrated economies, equitable cooperation with friendly socialist countries and mobilization of the masses for rapid development and defence.'

We may locate Amilcar Cabral's work in the framework of disengagement in the sense that he admonished the African countries to return to the history of Africa, arguing that there was a break in the history of the continent when it encountered Europe, which halted the African traditional indigenous historical economic, political and social processes. The return of Africa to its history implies that the African countries have to disengage from imperialism.

Samir Amin, the foremost proponent of developing countries delinking from global capitalism argues that Africa has to delink from the world capitalist system in order to set the stage for socialism. Delinking was clarified as an idea that does not suggest autarkic development but is merely urging the African countries not to blindly follow to the logic of the world capitalist system but rather try to create an economic system based on their own values.

Critics of the dependency/world system perspective on delinking from capitalism argue nonetheless that the idea is unfeasible, unrealistic and utopian. The critics conflate disengagement and delinking under the general rubric of delinking, which they condemned to the dustbin of history.

Amin 1990; Cabral 1974; Gordon 1996: Chap 3; Rodney, 1971, 1973; Mahjoub 1990; Nkrumah 2001; Sandbrook, Edelman, Heller & Teichman 2006: 53, 276–83.

4. African socialism in theory and practice

The post-independence period in Africa was also characterized by what became known as African socialism, which was a part of the struggle for national liberation from the yoke of European colonialism in the Sub-Saharan African states. The history of these experiences is an important object of study for CDS—particularly in regard to understanding the ultimate failure of African socialism in its diverse forms, and drawing lessons from it.

Two different perspectives on African socialism have emerged. In the first, it is a blend of Marxism and ideas about modernizing Africa and bringing about its social transformation. In this viewpoint, African socialism was a philosophical and practical guide for African leaders, who presented their ideas on the subject as a possible solution to the problem of Africa's political and spiritual identity. The adherents of African socialism ranged from pro-Moscow and pro-Beijing communists to pro-Western humanistic socialists and 'Afro-Marxists' (Klinghoffer 1969). The African socialists were not themselves proletarians but they attempted to carry out various aspects of the program set out by Marx and Engels in *The Communist Manifesto*. They opposed private property in land, created national banks that controlled all credit, established state control over transportation and communication, extended state control over the means of production, attempted to provide free public education, believed in the equal obligation of all to work, and established agricultural labour armies (Klinghoffer 1969). Arguably, for these reasons, African socialism shared many similarities with Marxism and Soviet communism. Their difference, however, is that African socialism was not considered as a step towards communism. It was merely a programmatic response to the needs of the African peoples. It was viewed as a return to the supposed socialist structure of Africa that existed before Europeans colonized the continent. African socialism was not subject to any universal laws of development as in the Marxist historical method. Thus, Africa socialism did not espouse socialism in the Marxist-Leninist tradition, which subscribes to the existence of universal objective laws of history and believes that socialism to be true must be scientific.

In the second perspective, there is no precise definition of African socialism, only vague reference to African tradition. Even the African leaders who met in Dakar Senegal to consider the subject in 1962 failed to provide a clear definition of the concept (Friedland & Rosberg Jr. 1964). African socialism does not have a single author; it is more of a conglomeration of ideas about socialism advanced by different African political leaders. As a consequence, African socialism does not represent a precisely unified, singularly reasoned ideological direction or guide to action. Whereas individual thinkers linked to ideological movements are essential historical characteristics of socialism, no such situation existed with respect to African socialism. Arguably, African socialism represented an attempt to formulate an ideology that catered to the specific context of economic and political decolonization in particular African states. However, several themes are identifiable within the framework of African socialism, including 'the problem of continental identity; the crisis of economic development; and the dilemmas of control and class formation' (Friedland & Rosberg Jr. 1964).

The possible reasons for the failure of African socialism reside in the fact that it was not founded on scientific socialist principles but merely selectively embraced aspects of Marxism. In other words, African socialism perhaps lacked a coherent guiding ideology of proletarian liberation. Also, possibly Africa lacked developed classes including the working class and a bourgeois class to create the conditions for effective class conflict. The African peasantry nonetheless, lacked the leadership with a clear-cut socialist ideology to stage a peasant-led revolution, as was the case in Chinese Revolution.

Clapham 1992: 13–25; Cliffe & Saul 1972; Drew 1969: 53–92; Fitzgerald 1985: 5–14; Friedland & Rosberg, Jr. 1964; Klinghoffer 1969; Zeilig 2009; Mohiddin 1981; Nkrumah, Senghor, Kilson 1966; Nyerere 1968; Senghor & Cook 1964; Shivji 1976; Ottaway & Ottaway 1981.

5. Africa in the era of neoliberal globalization: Current policies and initiatives on African development

The drive to develop Africa, that is, the accumulation and distribution of capital in Africa through radical views about disengagement from imperialism, African socialism and other forms of African nationalism was severely thwarted by the neoliberal turn at the global level. The African states were forced to abandon their nationalist positions on disengagement and socialism and embrace neoliberal structural adjustment. There was a new push towards a European-influenced top-down Africa Union and economic programs such as the New Economic Partnership for Africa's Development and other economic partnership agreements (EPAs), which signal a resurgence of European imperialism in Africa. The collapse of the neoliberal model evidenced by the current global financial and economic crisis raises the possibilities of alternatives including socialism and state-led approaches.

In the context of the failure of neoliberalism and the current crises—food, fuel, financial and economic—the concrete evidence suggests that the Chinese model of development in Africa promises to bring fundamental change both for better and worse—better in the sense that China engages the African countries in much more favourable economic relations compared with neoliberalism, but worse in the sense that China's labour and environmental records in Africa, as well as its true intentions, are questionable. Despite its shortcomings, the Chinese model in Africa is concretely different to those that currently exist and represents a viable alternative.

Adésínà, Graham & Olukoshi 2006; Bond 2006; Ferguson 2006: 69–88; Kinyanjui & Kiruthu 2007; Obi 2007; Pomerantz 2004; Tandon 2008; Todd 2007.

6. The future development of Africa

There is a strong sentiment among the current political leaders of Africa that the future development of the continent lies in the African countries coming together economically and politically in the proposed Africa Union. The problem however is how the union should be conceptualized and implemented. The current Africa Union is top-down, embraces the discredited neoliberal approach and represents a visible attempt to copy the European Union model. However, the idea about unifying the African continent is not new since previous generations of African leaders had recognized the significance of African unity in the development of the continent. The bottom-up all-Africa approach to Africa's development adopted by Kwame Nkrumah was perhaps the most radical espousing a practical and less doctrinaire Marxist position. The unifying of Africa as a condition for its development nonetheless raises the issue of the transformation of the European-constructed nation-states in Africa, the dismantling of borders on the continent, and places on the development agenda for Africa issues such as the role of African traditional institutions, alternative development models and class analysis.

Ayittey 2004; Brown 1995; Ferguson 2006: 69–88; Guerrero & Manji 2008; Lewis 1998; Munck & O'Hearn 1999; Yansané 1996.

Module 44

Development and Change in Latin America and the Caribbean

Fernando I. Leiva
State University of New York at Albany, United States

1. Introduction: The need for a critical political economy framework

How are we to assess the current and future trajectory of Latin America's development in the aftermath of more than three-decades of neoliberal-led restructuring in the region? Building on earlier modules, this module answers this question by arguing that the fundamental dynamics of contemporary Latin American development can best be grasped through a critical political economy perspective. Such a perspective, still in the midst of being renewed and forged, entails a framework that among other traits (1) does not eschew power relations from the analysis of economies and social formations; (2) reintroduces class and questions about the production, appropriation and distribution of the economic surplus as a key analytic entry point; (3) historicizes economic and social analysis within the context of the overall development of capitalism; and, finally, (4) examines power relations both in the realm of production as well as that of social reproduction and their interaction in a concrete moment of history.

Six decades of wax and wane of different development theories (i.e., modernization theory, structuralism, dependency theory, neoliberalism and more recently neostructuralism, to name the most significant ones), suggests that a revitalized critical political economy perspective must also be theoretically self-conscious of how development discourses interact with existing social power. Thus more than an iron clad prescripted narrative, this module offers a dependable compass with which to explore and navigate the rapidly changing political-economic landscape in the Latin American periphery. Two reasons justify such open-ended exploratory spirit. First, the scope and pace of structural transformations in class relations is still unfolding and each country's experience is sufficiently diverse to warrant flexibility. Second, like in the past, the critical political economy perspective advocated herein has to be brought to life through 'analysis of the concrete.' Nonetheless, salient common elements in the historical experience of countries in the Latin American periphery are underscored.

Leiva 2008: Chaps. 1–2; Girvan 2006: 327–50; Petras & Veltmeyer 2003; St Cyr 2005.

2. The structure and restructuring of Latin American capitalism

Operating in tandem, neoliberal policies wielded by the state, untrammelled market forces and capitalist strategies at the firm level to ensure the expanded self-valorization of capital, destroyed the economic and institutional foundations of the 'inwardly-oriented' model of development that had predominated in the region since the late 1930s. Neoliberal policies of liberalization, deregulation and privatization, along with state intervention, initially violent, radically realigned the correlation of class forces in the region. From the late 1970s to the end of the 1990s, almost all countries of the region were force-marched through a transition from an import-substitution industrialization to an export-oriented model of capitalist accumulation. This passage was conceived by the World Bank as entailing three stages: (1) stabilization ('shock therapy,' i.e., eliminate government intervention in markets); (2) deep structural reforms (i.e., inject the logic of the market into all institutions through privatization of social security, education, health, etc.); and (3) consolidation of reforms. Not all countries coherently followed this sequence, but in all of them neoliberal ideas and policies sought to relaunch capitalist accumulation on new foundations.

Green 2003; Kay & Gwynne 2004; Harris & Nef 2008; Leiva 2008: Chaps. 3–4;
Petras & Veltmeyer 2001: Chap. 1.

3. The deep structure of contemporary Latin American capitalism

Transformations carried out by neoliberalism and global capital have profoundly restructured Latin American capitalism, giving it a distinct physiognomy and dynamics. The following five central characteristics must be explored to grasp the current structural traits of contemporary Latin American societies: (1) Latin America's changing participation in the new international division of labour; (2) the accelerated transnationalization of the economy, the state and social classes; (3) the growing financialization of Latin American economies (i.e., the rising accrual of profits through financial channels); (4) the precarization and informalization of labour-capital relations; and (5) the reorganization of arrangements for the social reproduction of individuals and social classes by redrawing state, capitalist and household responsibilities and the gendered division of labour. Although each of these may be separately analyzed, one can lose sight of the fact that each of these transformations mutually support one another, profoundly changing power relations between capital and labour, transnational and local capitals, as well as those constituting the gendered division of labour at macro-societal level as well as micro-sites such as workplaces, households and communities.

Abassi & Lutjens 2002; Leiva 2006: 337–59; Bose & Acosta-Belén 1995; Cravey 1998.

4. Dynamics of globalization and anti-globalization in Latin America and the Caribbean

In the 1980s, under conditions of a region-wide external debt, a redemocratization process and the Washington Consensus on macroeconomic policy reform (Williamson 1990), Latin America led the way into the 'new world order' of neoliberal globalization. The theoretical foundations of this ideology (neoliberal globalization) were provided by the 'new development model' (Bulmer-Thomas 1986). As for the dynamics of political and economic adjustment to this new world, in which the 'agents of economic freedom' (the 'private sector' viz., capitalist enterprise, multinational corporations, the free market) are liberated from the regulatory constraints of the welfare-developmental state, their critical dimensions are analyzed from different theoretical perspectives in the readings below.

Bowles, Veltmeyer et al. 2007 (essays by Dierckxsens & Vizentini, De Oliveira & Leda Paulani, Cypher & Delgado Wise); ECLAC 2006; Grandin 2007; Petras & Veltmeyer 2005b: 89–106; Saxe-Fernandez, Petras, Nuñez & Veltmeyer 2001.

5. Resistance, social movements and the reconstruction of popular power

Diverse forms of popular resistance have arisen to counter neoliberal restructuring of Latin American capitalism. From initially localized defensive mobilizations to neoliberal shock policies, to city-wide and sectoral uprisings, Latin America's popular classes have shown a remarkable resilience and capacity to challenge the project of transnational capital. Despite deep processes of restructuring of occupational structures, spatial and sectoral relations of production and decomposition/recomposition of social classes, politics and cultural identities, with different degrees, Latin America's popular sectors have been able to reconstruct the power to challenge the current order.

That the Latin American left has been leading the struggle against neoliberalism and beginning the process to define a twenty-first century socialism is by now hardly a discovery. In April 2009, in the wake of the fifth Summit of the Americas (a meeting of the heads of state in the OAS), two remarkable documents in this political process were released. Both serve as an important counterpoint to the summit, where President Obama of the U.S. and Prime Minister Harper of Canada did their best to sustain North American hegemony over the region and the neoliberal project for the hemisphere.

The first statement was signed by six of the seven members of the Bolivarian ALBA alliance before the summit (Ecuador was absent but it gave a blistering critique of neoliberal financial policies at the summit itself) and lays out a remarkably different approach to the economic crisis and development in a wide-ranging critique of capitalism. Such a statement from an alliance of elected governments has not been seen in a very long time. It may well take on historical importance.

The second statement comes from the Fourth People's Summit of the Americas. It too rejects the neoliberal model of development and identifies the financial crisis with the social extremes that neoliberalism has generated. And it also places a wide range of alternatives to neoliberal policies that would build a new egalitarian sustainable model of development.

These radical documents illustrate the growing and broad opposition within civil society, and indeed people and some states across the world, to the current world order. They insist that alternatives are not only possible but also must be tried in the present and not in the distant future.

Almeida 2007: 123–39; Dangl 2007; Petras & Veltmeyer 2005b, 2009; Della Buono & Bell Lara 2007; Harris 2003: 365–426; Kohl & Farthing 2006; Spronk & Webber 2007: 31–47.

6. Postneoliberal paths? Searching for alternatives

In the wake of neoliberal meltdown, persistent poverty and increased popular unrest, the following four different development paths to transcend neoliberalism have emerged: (1) local and community based development; (2) the defence of the status-quo through the more 'holistic' 'globalization with a human face' proposed by ECLAC and Latin American neostructuralism and embraced by centre-left governments in Chile, Brazil and Uruguay; (3) neo-developmentalist status-quo transformative paths such as those by Venezuela's 'twenty-first-century socialism' and Bolivia's 'Andean capitalism' that aim to channel the economic surplus towards national development by relying on the state; and (4) the revolutionary transformation of society and the construction of socialism. Each of these 'postneoliberal' alternatives embodies different social interests and has reached different levels of expression. Analyzing their strengths and weaknesses, the contradictions and prospects, is essential to gauge the future directions that development will take in the Latin American periphery.

Borón 2007; Petras & Veltmeyer 2003, 2009; Chávez 2005; Chibber 2005: 226–46;
García Linera 2006; Leiva 2008: Chaps. 10–11.

Module 45

Development and Change in Asia

Jos Mooij
Institute of Social Studies, The Netherlands

Asia is by far the largest continent, not only in terms of its size but also in terms of its population. More importantly, it is extremely diverse. One can find countries with persistent high growth rates but also pockets of extreme poverty and deprivation; major global cities as well as tribal societies; examples of both capitalist and socialist development trajectories. Given its size and diversity, it is not possible to give a systematic overview of Asia's development in just six themes. As a result, this module focuses on just a few major topics and relevant debates—in the understanding that there are other modules in this collection that cover other aspects of Asia's development (for instance, Module 46 on China).

The starting point is that critical development studies distinguishes itself from other/mainstream development studies by examining and scrutinizing explicitly the received wisdoms and truths that dominate the common understanding of the world. This module therefore seeks to challenge a number of myths in the understanding of Asia and to provide alternative interpretations. Critical development studies, however, is not only concerned with understanding the world but also with changing it. The last theme of the module focuses explicitly on resistance and progressive movements.

Currently, the world's attention for Asia has a lot to do with economic growth in the region and its increasing role in the global economy. The 2008/09 financial crisis may only further enhance this role. Asia remains, however, also the continent with more than a billion people living in extreme poverty. In a way, the Asian Drama, as Myrdal described it in 1968, continues to evolve: 'The lofty aspirations of the leading actors are separated by a wide gap from the abysmal reality—including the unreadiness of leaders, followers and the more inert masses to accept the consequences of attempting to attain those aspirations. And that gap is widening' (Myrdal 1968: 34). The gap is still widening. Although the proportion of people living in poverty has come down in almost all Asian countries, inequality continues to increase.

1. East and West: The long history of Asia's relations with the rest of the world

Globalization in Asia did not start with the arrival of European traders in the sixteenth century. Already during the early Roman Empire, there was extensive sea-borne trade between India and Europe. When these relations with the West ceased to exist, many other long-distance economic routes and relations continued to exist. In these precolonial centuries, large parts of Asia had achieved a much higher level of wealth and development than medieval Europe. The extensive and detailed study of Chinese science and civilization undertaken by Needham (1954) shows just how technologically advanced China was compared to Europe. Elaborate social, ideological and political structures emerged in many early peasant societies. In Japan, India and China, there existed powerful dynasties with large empires, highly developed court cultures and elaborate systems of surplus appropriation.

Between 1400 and 1800, there was already a worldwide trading system and division of labour, as Frank (1998) argues. While European and Asian historical trajectories are often seen in isolation, i.e., till the sixteenth or seventeenth century, Frank claims that they were interconnected. For a long time, Asia was the stronger, Europe the weaker party in this global system. The rise of the West in the eighteenth century could happen exactly because Europe could use 'Asian shoulders'; it was much less the result of an internally generated development effort, as the Euro-centric interpretation holds. The more recent renewed rise of Asia is also part of the same global development process, which is characterized more by continuities than discontinuities. Ghosh's *In an Antique Land* illustrates some of these long-distance economic and cultural relationships in a text that is fact, fiction, history, autobiography, anthropology and travel book all at the same time.

For a long time, the dominant Western perception of the East was favourable. Europeans wanted to learn and regarded the Orient as more advanced in many respects than Europe itself. In the course of the eighteenth and nineteenth centuries, however, a form of scholarship emerged that emphasized not only difference but also European superiority and Asian stagnation. This interpretation served, of course, as a useful ideology to legitimize colonial relations of power. Frank's *ReOrient* analyzes this rather abrupt reinvention of history. Said's *Orientalism* is a classical text about the way in which 'the West' looks at 'the East' and how orientalist conceptions were part and parcel of the expansion of Europe.

Frank 1998; Ghosh 1992; Said 1978.

2. Land and labour: Development and underdevelopment in colonial and postcolonial Asia

As a continent, Asia is still predominantly rural, with two-thirds of the population living in rural areas and a majority employed in agriculture. A large part of this agricultural production is done by peasants, whose labour power or products are appropriated by landlords, the state, traders, priests or others. Peasant cultivation had existed already for millennia, so when the European colonialists arrived, they found peasantries that had already been subjugated and integrated into wider networks of production and surplus appropriation. In the early phases of colonialism, the European powers collaborated with local rulers, making agreements regarding the commodities (mainly spices) they wanted to 'buy.' Later, they became more directly involved with production relations. In South Asia, for instance, the British colonial government imposed a new system of land ownership. It converted the existing *zamindars*, chiefs of lineages who held a right to receive tribute, into owners of the land. Generally, *zamindars*-turned-landlords did not cultivate the land themselves but extracted revenue from the tenants. In Indonesia, the Dutch colonial government introduced a system of forced cultivation. As Breman (2000) describes, these policies intensi-fied social differentiation, leading to a concentration of wealth on the one hand and growth of landlessness and deprivation on the other.

In the second half of the twentieth century, following the withdrawal or expulsion of the colonial powers, Asian countries have followed different paths of rural development. Some coun-tries have benefited enormously from land reforms. As Putzel (2000) argues, the rapid economic growth in South Korea, Taiwan, China and Vietnam is very much related to the redistributive land reform that had taken place in these countries. In South Asia, however, no redistributive land reform took place, contributing to a footloose proletariat that is almost permanently on the move in search of temporary employment (Breman 2000). The Green Revolution was important in many parts of Asia. This involved the implementation of a package of new, high-yielding rice and wheat seeds, irrigation, cheap credit, chemical fertilizer and pesticides to boost agricultural production. At the time of its introduction, it was seen by many as a technological solution to the problems of large-scale food insecurity, poverty and deprivation of the peasantry. In South Asia and Indonesia, where there had been no redistributive land reform, it was a strategy that transformed 'traditional' agriculture without addressing the problem of unequal land distribu-tion and tenancy relations. It resulted nevertheless in major shifts in class and gender relations (Agarwal 1985; Breman 2000).

Agarwal 1985: 67–114; Breman 2000: 231–46; Putzel 2000.

3. Dynamics of U.S. Imperialism in Asia

Briefly after World War II, the colonial era ended and European powers lost much of their influ-ence in Asia. The United States, however, emerged as a major superpower with a considerable influence in Asia. It has aggressively defended this, and fought several wars, first in Korea and later in Vietnam.

Tariq Ali 2008.

4. The East Asian miracle and the Asian crisis

The 'East Asian Miracle' refers to a period of sustained growth that several Southeast and East Asian countries went through between 1960 and the 1990s. Since the countries involved—the four tigers (Hong Kong, South Korea, Singapore and Taiwan) plus Japan, Indonesia, Malaysia and Thailand—experienced the fastest economic growth and social transformation that has even taken place in human history, they are at the centre of many debates in development economics.

The so-called 'East Asian Miracle' is also the title of a policy research report that was published by the World Bank in 1993, in which it tried to explain this economic success. According to the World Bank, government interventions were important—particularly subsidies to specific industries, strategic public investments, selective industrial protection and institutional support for export. But when Page (1994, the leader of the research team) summarizes the main lessons, the message is reduced to the Washington Consensus doctrine: getting the basics right. The alternative interpretation of the miracle focuses much more on the strategic and developmental role that governments have played. An influential example is Wade's *Governing the Market*.

The 1990s, however, brought first a recession in Japan and then a financial crisis in several East and Southeast Asian economies. This prompted a debate on alleged institutional inefficiencies, corruption, excessive state interventions, government bail-outs, etc. as the cause of the crisis. This view is challenged by Chang (2003a), who argues that the more market-oriented economies were hit harder by the crisis than the countries that have practised 'the East Asian Model.'

Chang 2003a: 107–21; Page 1994: 615–25; Wade 1990.

5. Religion, identity and development

In several Asian countries, religion and politics are intimately connected. A major historical example, and human catastrophe, was the partition of British India—a partition that went together with enormous violence between Hindus and Muslims, resulting in about half a million deaths and a much larger number of refugees, and that led to the birth of independent (and secular) India and the Islamic republic of Pakistan.

Also, and unfortunately, after the colonial era, religion has remained a major force in politics. Several new nation-states have not been able to promote or impose lasting, national and inclusive new identities; to the contrary, in some of these countries political parties or political leaders have used religion to appeal to particular population groups, to create a common denominator and often, at the same time, to suggest a simple framework for who are ' the bad guys.'

The readings focus on a few important cases illustrating these phenomena. India has witnessed the rise of Hindutva, a form of aggressive Hindu nationalism. As a result, secularism, as Sen (2005) describes, is under threat. In Sri Lanka, Sinhala Buddhist nationalism has played a major role in the ongoing Sinhala-Tamil ethnic conflict. Finally, radical Islamism has emerged in several parts of Asia, often in the context of failed developmentalism and corrupt and authoritarian regimes (Rahnema 2008).

Rahnema 2008: 483–96; Sen 2005: 294–316; Tambiah 1992.

6. Social movements and resistance:
Struggles for a more inclusive development

In many parts of Asia, there is consistent opposition and protest against the unequal distribution of resources and lack of democratic rights. Generally, industrial workers or trade unions have not been very important in these struggles. This is not surprising, given the authoritarian nature of some Asian regimes and the low proportion of workers in the formal sector. Peasant movements or other rural-based movements, on the other hand, have been more prominent, for instance, in the Philippines.

In some of the democratically governed countries, dissatisfactions and protests express themselves through political parties and other organized social movements. A well-known example from India is the social movement against the Narmada project, which involved the construction of a set of dams in West India. The project was based on a particular conception of development that privileges large capital-intensive and centrally planned interventions over smaller decentralized ones. The tribal population that lived in the Narmada Valley resisted the dams as they threatened their livelihood. Their struggles have been taken up and supported subsequently by others, including urban-based activists, and have been reformulated into a much larger movement, in which the 'tribal way of life' was presented as a more ecologically sustainable alternative to state-led development. Although the movement became world-famous and 'left its imprints on the future of large dams everywhere' (Baviskar 2006: 259), it lost the battle, and the project could not be stopped.

NGOs have become important factors or agents of change in many Asian countries. Although some of them are still oppositional, many have become 'partners in development' that work together with the government, often with the help of international donors. Although they are often seen as a positive force, the question is to what extent they contribute progressive social change. Feldman (2003) investigates this in the case of Bangladesh and concludes that NGOs have become buffers between citizens and the state, and as such they tend to diffuse political action rather than help people to mobilize.

Baviskar 2006; Feldman 2003: 5–26.

Module 46

China's Re-emergence
A Critical Development Perspective

Paul Bowles
University of Northern British Columbia, Canada

In 1800, China produced one-third of the world's manufactured output, approximately the same share as the combined amount produced by the now developed core countries. Over the course of the nineteenth century, the industrial revolution spread throughout the core countries so that by the eve of World War I, China's share of world manufacturing output had fallen to a mere 3.6 percent while that of the developed core had risen to 92.5 percent. Following three decades of 'economic reform' at the end of the twentieth century, China has now re-emerged as a major world economy, routinely predicted to become the world's largest economy by mid-twenty-first century.

From a critical development studies perspective, a central question is how to interpret China's re-emergence. The emergence of a dynamic developing country economy, continuing to grow at breakneck speed even while the world's leading capitalist economy and major market, the U.S., stands on the brink of recession amid the sub-prime financial crisis, is a new phenomenon. Certainly, this phenomenon challenges conventional dependency theory. The experience of the newly industrializing countries in the 1970s and 1980s could be reconciled with dependency theory once their special place in, and privileges arising from, Cold War geopolitics are recognized. But China provides a sterner test to theory in this regard. Furthermore, China's leadership claims that it is simultaneously following a path that involves participating in the process of 'globalization' and yet still maintaining its own 'national autonomy.' This claim to both global integration and the preservation of national policy autonomy strikes at the heart of dependency theory. It also strikes at the heart of neoliberal globalization's supporters too; for them, convergence to the Anglo-American model of market liberalization is required for successful participation in the global economy. China's path challenges both interpretations. For this reason, some have seen China as best fitting the 'late industrialization' theories advanced by Liste and Gershenkron. Understanding the dynamics of China's capitalist development experience is therefore critical to an understanding of the dynamics of global capitalism in the twenty-first century and the possibilities for, and limits of, developing countries within it.

The implications of China's re-emergence for other developing countries are, however, complex. Are the central elements of the 'Chinese model' replicable elsewhere? And, if so, is it a desirable model to emulate? Does it provide the basis for a new configuration of policies that could emerge as an alternative development consensus? Will a coalition of developing or Southern countries coalesce around such a consensus, which will become a new basis for world order? Or, does China appear as a threat to the development aspirations of other developing countries? A competitor of immense proportions able to rival them in the production of goods at all rungs on the technological ladder? These are the central questions of both theory and practice that this module addresses.

1. Theorizing China's re-emergence I:
Authoritarian neoliberal/crony capitalism

The first two themes analyze, at the systemic level, debates over the characteristics and dynamics of China's post-1978 development. All authors share the basic assumption that China is in important ways capitalist and that its capitalism is characterized by a leading role for the Chinese Communist Party. Beyond this, however, there are differing emphases and assessments. In the first set of readings, those who take, from a variety of perspectives, a predominantly negative view are examined. For some, the focus is on China as an authoritarian state engaged in the process of primitive accumulation, the beneficiaries of which are state officials, private entrepreneurs and foreign capital. The dismantling of state socialism since 1978 has led to new class configurations and the emergence of new classes and conflicts (Hart-Landsberg & Burkett).

The 'red capitalists,' who have shaped and benefited from the present system, have done so at the expense of a new proletariat forged by urban workers subject to a loss of state privileges (the 'iron rice bowl') and the 100 million plus rural migrants who have streamed into China's export-oriented coastal cities. On this reading, China's re-emergence replicates the experience of nineteenth-century capitalism in the core: the deliberate creation of a proletariat, processes of class formation and organic links between state and capital, domestic and international. The new elite includes state cadres, technocrats and enterprise managers both public and private (Blecher 2005). The dividing lines between public and private are, however, blurred and state-business alliances rely upon a network of ties and mutual obligations leading to widespread corruption. The losers in this political economy have been the new proletariat and the environment.

The Chinese experience, on this reading, illustrates that countries willing and able to enter global capitalism's orbit by exploiting their unlimited labour supplies can do so. China is unique in the sheer size of its unlimited labour supply although not necessarily in its suppression of labour rights and in the distributional consequences of such a (mal)development path.

Hart-Landsberg & Burkett 2005; Blecher 2005.

2. Theorizing China's re-emergence II: East Asian development state

For others, the historical reference point for comparison is not nineteenth-century capitalist industrialization in the core but post 1945 development in China's East Asian neighbours. On this reading, China's elite bears comparison with that in other East Asian countries: nationalist and developmentalist. Seen in this light, China most noticeably bears comparison with the early path taken by Japan and South Korea. China is similarly characterized as a 'developmental state,' intervening consciously in guiding the market in the key areas of technology, finance, trade and labour. The historical outcome, rapid industrialization and widespread increased incomes, are regarded as the proof of developmental success. China has also achieved this outcome along with reductions in poverty. The main issues that are addressed by those who interpret China in this way are the forms which the developmental state has taken and the extent to which it replicates or diverges from other East Asian countries. That is, the extent to which a common model explains common developmental successes is analyzed.

The extent of commonalities and the ability of the central state in China to play the same role as the state in other East Asian late developers are subject to debate. Perkins argues that there is no single 'East Asian model' but rather variations on a theme. Pearson's analyses supports this general thesis and cautions against viewing China's evolving reforms as converging to a 'global model'; instead she argues that there are distinct Chinese variations based on the ability of the central party-state to control the 'commanding heights' of the economy. The central government's success in this respect is questioned by Howell, who regards the preconditions for an effective developmental state to be absent in China due to the pervasive power of local governments and the intensity of external competition.

Pearson 2005: 296–322; Howell 2006: 273–97.

3. Contours of Chinese development: Labour and migration

The first two themes in this module set out in broad terms some of the debates over the nature of the Chinese development strategy. Critical areas for further analysis arise from them, particularly with respect to the implications for labour and the ability of the state to implement an effective industrial policy.

This theme analyzes the conditions of labour and the ways in which it has been incorporated into China's development strategy. The broad trends in income levels, income inequality and poverty reduction were outlined in the first two themes. Here, the focus is upon the working conditions of the workers who underpin China's manufacturing miracle. Here, of course, gender plays an important role as production in the export-manufacturing coastal cities has relied heavily on the use of young female migrant labour from the rural areas. Pun Ngai draws upon her experience of working in one such factory for eight months in her book *Made in China,* which documents the lives and perspectives of these young women workers.

One of the questions that arises out of this discussion is whether change is possible and who its agents might be. Ngai considers whether migrant workers themselves might be agents of change. Blecher (2005) among other Chinese and China scholars considers whether China's official (and only legal) trade union, the All China Federation of Trade Union, might be an agent of change. Capitalist transitions over the past three centuries have all spawned resistance from workers, both organized and unorganized, but considerable variation exists in the extent to which this has been successful. This theme examines where China might fit in this range.

Blecher, 2005; Ngai 2005.

4. Contours of Chinese development: Trade, FDI and technology

This theme examines the argument that China is an example of a successful 'late industrializer,' following in the footsteps of other East Asian industrializers. The terms of China's insertion into the global economy are critical here. While China's reliance on foreign direct investment, a substantial re-processing trade based on low wages and reliance on external markets for growth point to a typical export-oriented, enclave development path, other indicators suggest a more autonomous approach. Here, Zeng and Williamson (2007) argue that China has been able to build its own global corporations at a much earlier stage of development than its East Asian neighbours managed. This points to a level of technological sophistication indicative of an emerging industrial power. This sophistication, and the policies that have led it, are seen in China's overall export composition (Rodrik) as well as in specific sectors such as telecommunications (Harwit). Important to appreciate here is that many of China's new global companies are state owned and were built up during the state socialist period. In the 1990s, China adopted a policy of 'grasping the large, letting go of the small,' and the large enterprises remained within the orbit of the state and were encouraged to 'go global.' The continued involvement through both ownership and 'guidance' of the state in these large enterprises illustrates the path dependence of China's current position.

Rodrik 2006: Harwit 2007: 311–32; Zeng & Williamson 2007.

5. Implications for development in the South I: A model?

The final two themes of the module bring the preceding discussions and debates to bear on the question of the implications of China's development strategy for other countries in the South. For some, the specific policies adopted by China at the macroeconomic and sectoral levels provide a guide to the contours of a workable 'heterodox' policy framework. The appeal of this framework has led to discussion of whether there might be an emerging policy consensus—a 'Beijing Consensus'—in opposition to the increasingly discredited but still dominant 'Washington Consensus.' This raises the possibility of a new Southern pole of power able to use its influence to refashion the international economic and financial architecture in ways that allow greater policy space. This possibility reasserts the importance of national policy space within the global economy and, as such, offers a variant of globalization that is not premised on the Anglo-American model and that even has some broad parallels with proposals for 'deglobalization' (Bello 2004).

Flassbeck 2005; Ramo 2004.

6. Implications for development in the South II: Menace?

China's re-emergence has also appeared as a 'China threat' to the development aspirations of countries in the South. The threat of a 'race to the bottom' in labour standards is one aspect of this threat for labour elsewhere in the South. Beyond this, there are also other complexities arising from China's global economic significance. Thus, Kaplinsky argues that China's growth has played an important role in reversing the long-term tendency of the terms of trade to decline against (some) primary commodity producers. China, by producing low cost manufactured goods and demanding primary products (such as minerals and oil), has led to a reversal in historical long run price trends. This bodes well for some developing primary commodity exporting countries as the prices of their exports are stabilized or increase but poses a severe test for more industrial-ized countries of the South. Latin American countries face particular challenges in this regard. ASEAN countries perhaps face the 'opportunity or challenge' dichotomy most starkly given their geographical proximity to China and their similar export markets. Analysis focuses on whether the advantages offered by China's growth, demand for primary products and supply chains outweigh the competition it constitutes for investment and third country markets.

Kaplinsky 2006; Gallagher & Porzecanski 2008.

Notes

1. The World Bank's regional grouping and categorization by per capita income results in the following distribution. In addition to this income distribution/regional grouping, the World Bank identifies thirty-four countries in the 'other (non-OECD) high income' category. This categorization includes five small island Caribbean economies, the only high income countries in the LAC region and the three Asian NICs (Hong Kong, South Korea, Singapore), which are also in the World Bank's 'high

income' category. Thus in the World Bank's typology, there are no 'high income' countries grouped under the regional categories of 'Latin America and the Caribbean,' 'East Asia' or 'South Asia.' In this categorization, 'upper income' (N = 34) equates with 'developed,' 'middle income' (N = 96) means 'developing' and 'low income' (N = 53) is coterminous with 'least developed.' In this development divide, thirty-four countries are in the 'Global North' while 149 are in what might be viewed as the 'Global South.' However, development discourse on /analysis of 'rich' vs. 'poor' countries generally relates to the two extremes of global income distribution (34 high, 53 low).

	High	Upper Middle	Lower Middle	Low
E Asia	0	4	11	9
S Asia	0	0	3	5
LAC	0	14	14	1
OECD	25	0	0	0
E.Eu/C.Asia	0	13	10	3
SSA	0	7	7	34
	34	41	55	53

2. The OECD in this categorization is composed of all the countries in Western Europe (21), North America (U.S. and Canada) and Australia/New Zealand as well as Japan and two Asian NICs (Singapore and South Korea). In the World Bank's regional grouping (World Bank, *World Development Report 2008*), Mexico, technically a member of the OECD, is grouped within Latin America and the Caribbean; similarly Eastern European members are grouped with the countries of Central Asia as Eurasia; Japan is placed in the 'high income OECD' category, while Singapore and South Korea are categorized as 'other (non-OECD) high income,' which means that in the World Bank's regional groupings 'East/ South Asia' there are no countries in the 'high income' category.

Section 15

Looking Behind and Moving Forward

Neoliberalism is in serious decline if not dead in the political waters and on the scene of public policy. As for capitalism it is in the throes of a multiple crisis that reaches beyond the financial system into the depths of global production to threaten the very foundations of the world system. With the deepening of social inequalities and global divide in wealth and income, the entire development project is in jeopardy.

The only signs of hope in the miserable landscape of crisis, uneven development and gross inequalities and inequities, a global ruling class concerned with self-enrichment as well as power and the oppressive weight of imperialism are the resilience of the poor and the refusal of working people all over the world to lie down and passively absorb or 'adjust' to the forces of capitalism development unleashed against them. One of the key lessons of history is that every offence and advance in class power are matched by a strategic and political response of those subordinated to this power. History, as noted in the *Communist Manifesto*, is the history of class struggle, the motor force of social change. Change is not just the result of the workings of the economic system on people. Real history is made by people actively resisting the forces unleashed against them. As Marx observed, 'it is men [people] who make history albeit not under conditions of their choosing.' People make history under conditions that they themselves help bring about in the course of collective action. Social change, in effect, implicates a dialectic of objective and subjective conditions, structure and agency.

As for 'development' or 'progressive change,' in terms of this dialectic it can be understood and analyzed in two ways: in *structural* terms as the working of the operative economic and social system on people and countries according to their location; or, in *strategic* terms, as the result of socially oriented and subjectively meaningful or goal-oriented activity, actions consciously directed towards a specified goal. It is possible of course to overemphasize the structural or the strategic, to view development as the outcome of one or the other. But in practice development is both a process and a project, both structural and strategic in form, both subjective and objective in its conditions. And development theory should specify both the structural forces and the strategic factors at work—actions taken in particular conjunctures of objective and subjective conditions. In these terms questions for analysis include: What are the driving forces of social change? Who are the agents and what is the agency of development or progressive change? What is the particular or effective strategy pursued by these agents and agencies? What strategy do these agencies and agents pursue? Within this strategy what actions are taken as means for achieving the desired or projected goal of their activities? Under what conditions and in what context and conjuncture are these actions taken? What are the structural forces operating on the development agencies and change agents, limiting or impeding their capacity to achieve their goal? Can these limiting conditions or obstacles be overcome? How and by what means and what agency?

This concluding set of modules addresses in different ways these questions and the underlying development problematic. Module 47 reviews emerging and new forms of regionalism as a strategic response to the dynamics of neoliberal globalization by 'progressive' governments in the developing countries concerned to bring about 'another world'—a more equitable, socially inclusive and sustainable form of national development. Module 48 reviews the issues involved in the socialist option or development path based on more radical or systemic change. In this connection, it might be argued that the entire 'development project' assumes the institutionality of capitalism, is predicated on capitalism as the operating system. The key issue then is: how to reform the system—what changes need to be made to the system to bring about the desired improvements in socioeconomic conditions? However, this fundamental premise and ideological foundation of the development project is questioned in Module 49. It assumes rather the necessity and possibility of systemic change—that capitalism is 'the problem' and thus not part of the solution; that 'development' requires not just progressive change or reforms to the capitalism system but a fundamental overhaul ('social transformation') of the system, or socialism (the abolition of private property in the means of production). Socialism in the form that it took and actually existed in the East (the U.S.S.R. and Eastern Europe) collapsed towards the end of the 1980s in the last millennium. In Africa it was explored as an idea but the conditions for bringing it about, instituting it in some (African) form never materialized. Only in Cuba did twentieth-century socialism survive and then only after the introduction of policy reforms that placed socialism itself at risk. However, the new millennium opened with a serious crisis in the world capitalist system and the economic model used to direct policy in this system over the past two and a half decades. Under these conditions, the impulse towards socialism was resuscitated, revived by actions taken in Venezuela towards 'socialism of the twenty-first century.' The dynamics of this project are included within the purview of this course module and its readings.

The concluding module reviews the options for change and development available under current conditions. These options are conceived of and placed into four categories: (1) state-led reforms to the capitalist system under the post-Washington Consensus on the need for a more socially inclusive form of neoliberalism and a more humane and sustainable form of development based on achieving a 'better balance between the market and the state'; (2) a change of government in a progressive or centre-left direction, pressuring officials to move back to some sort of welfare-development state and a policy of national sovereignty over natural resources; (3) mobilization of the popular forces of resistance in the form of social movements in order to either take over the state apparatus or force the government of the day to implement a policy program of radical change; (4) local development based on administrative decentralization and a culture of solidarity and relations of reciprocal exchange; (5) ALBA, an alternative regional trade mechanism, a bottom-up integration of the people based on 'living well' and the principles of the Bolivarian Revolution; and (6) socialism in one form or the other—nationalizing and socializing the means of social production; control by workers over their workplaces and by communities over their communities; and a socialist mechanism for distributing the social product—socializing consumption.

Module 47

Changing Regional Dynamics

Alternatives to Neoliberal Globalization?

Paul Bowles
University of Northern British Columbia, Canada

Regionalism is a chameleon. It is a political arrangement that has been used for different purposes and at different times. It was used in the 1930s as part of defensive 'imperial preferences' as the international trading system collapsed. It has been used since the 1950s as part of European integration initiatives. During the 1950s and 1960s, it was popular among many developing countries keen on fostering South-South linkages as way of facilitating import substitution industrialization strategies. In the 1990s, a 'new regionalism' emerged parallel with, and largely supportive of, the intensification of neoliberal globalization. This module analyzes whether regionalism—defined here at the macro-regional level—might have already, or could in the future, change again to provide an alternative to neoliberal globalization in the early decades of the twenty-first century.

The 'new regionalism' of the 1990s was characterized at the economic level by a rapid expansion in the number of regional trade agreements being signed, resulting in a so-called 'spaghetti bowl' of rules often fitting uncomfortably with multilateral rules and agreements. But this new economic regionalism was also considered to be an 'open regionalism,' i.e., comprising regional agreements intended to enhance integration into the global economy. Terms such as 'global regions' and 'continental globalization' tried to capture the idea that regionalism and globalization were proceeding along complementary lines. As evidence of this, regional agreements were implemented that crossed the traditional North-South divide with the intention being to free not only the flow of goods but also of capital, typically in the form of foreign direct investment (FDI), across national borders. Notwithstanding these commonalities, it also the case that free trade agreements showed considerable variation in their forms, aims and content.

These economic agreements, implemented by states, were accompanied by renewed and new forms of non-state regional interactions (also known as regionalization). This included integration based on the regional division of labour embodied in the supply chains of major multinational companies. At the same time the diaspora resulted in increased financial flows through remittances, and states often actively encouraged greater linkages with 'overseas' nationals.

The results of the 'new regionalism' are now being to be called into question. Social movements have formed at regional levels to oppose regionalism and globalization in their neoliberal forms and to advocate alternative regional projects. This call has been taken up by some states, most obviously in the recently established ALBA involving Bolivia, Cuba, Venezuela and other countries. But there is also evidence from elsewhere that regionalism is providing a site for resistance to neoliberal globalization. This can be found in East and Southeast Asia, for example, where IMF orthodoxy has been rejected in the wake of the Asian financial crisis and where regional monetary cooperation is now occurring. This module examines the extent to which regionalism is being, or could be, harnessed to a new (non-neoliberal) alternative framework for development.

1. Regionalism in historical perspective

Charting the historical dynamics of regionalism is no easy task; in fact, even defining regionalism is a sub-field in itself. Nevertheless, it is an institutional form worth studying. It has been used as both a means of integrating into global changes as well as a form of resistance to them. States, multinational firms and civil society groups have used it as part of their broader strategies. Understanding regionalism's multi-layered and multidimensional character in historical perspective is a useful way of starting to analyze the potentials and pitfalls for current and future regionalisms.

Hettne 2005: 543–71; Väyrynen 2003: 25–51.

2. The new regionalism in the context of contemporary globalization

The 'new regionalism' of the 1990s resulted in a dramatic increase in the number of regional trade agreements. These were partly a reflection of the increasing regionalization of production under the auspices of multinational corporations as supply chains became increasingly regional in scope. State-centric approaches complemented this as countries, both North and South, entered into trade agreements that sought to provide capital with greater mobility to compete globally. This form of 'open regionalism' was accompanied by increasing regional links between NGOs, many proposing alternative forms of regionalism which could provide a defence against, rather than integration into, neoliberal globalization.

Soderbaum 2004; Breslin et al. 2002; Hettne, Inotai & Sunkel 1999
(especially chaps. by Mittelman, Amin & Mistry).

3. Regionalism and development: Potential and pitfalls

The premise of much of the 'new regionalism'—that regional agreements would provide a vehicle for countries in the South to compete more effectively on the global scale and thereby improve their development performance—has gradually come under increasing scrutiny. Shadlen (2005), for example, argues that regional trade agreements with the U.S. have imposed development straightjackets that are even more binding than those faced under the WTO regime. The benefits of the North-South 'new regionalism' of the 1990s are therefore seen as very limited. In addition, the rationale for many of these agreements—the attraction of greater inflows of FDI—by developing countries has also become more problematic. Despite record FDI flows during the mid 2000s, there have been increasing restrictions placed by states on the conditions for FDI usage. This has been the case in both North and South. In the South, the scale of tax benefits and exemptions (including labour laws) to multinational companies to attract FDI have been reduced (Sumner 2008). The benefits of a neoliberal regionalism are now increasingly questioned. These changes form the basis for analyzing regional developments in three distinct regions to see the extent to which new regional projects offer an alternative to neoliberal globalization.

Sumner 2008: 239–53; UNCTAD 2007: Chaps. 3–5; Shadlen 2005.

4. Regional experiences I: A new regional path for East Asia?

In East Asia, the fallout from the Asian financial crisis of 1997–98 has been the establishment of new forms of regional monetary cooperation. The ASEAN+3 framework (the ten ASEAN countries plus China, Japan and South Korea) has been established to allow closer monetary cooperation and bilateral swap arrangements so that the economies of the region are never forced to rely on the IMF in the event of any future regional financial crises. In the monetary sphere, East Asia has spurned the IMF and rejected the Washington Consensus policy package that the IMF used in the crisis years (Bowles 2002). Beyond this, however, wider regional structures are embryonic and contested as the implications of deeper economic integration with China are debated. China has signed a number of bilateral trade agreements but these differ from each other in significant ways. The implications of the China-ASEAN free trade agreement remain contested, and whether a wider regionalism can be built upon it, and what character it would have, remain open questions (Bello 2007a; Focus on the Global South 2006).

Bello 2007a: 169–88; Focus on the Global South 2006; Bowles 2002: 230–56.

5. Regional experiences II: Contradictions in Southern Africa

In southern Africa, the prospects for an alternative form regionalism at present are limited. The main regional initiative, the South African Development Community, formed in 1992, is neoliberal in orientation (Thompson 2007). Furthermore, the political dynamics of the region, in particular, South Africa's role, make regional agreements problematic. Nevertheless, it is still possible that the unfolding dynamics will lead to counter-reactions that may point to new regional possibilities (Taylor 2003).

Thompson 2007: 18–134; Taylor 2003: 310–30.

6. Regional experiences III:
Alternatives to neoliberalism in Latin America

In Latin America, a wide range of regional integration initiatives can be found. They include Mercosur and UNASUR, both of which provide alternatives to the U.S.-led FTAA and rely on regional cooperation in matters of technology transfer and industrial policy (Harris 2005). However, in their organizational principles and associated agreements they do not depart from or challenge the normal rules of trade in the neoliberal world order. This, however is not the case in regard to ALBA, a new set of regional trade arrangements initially proposed by Hugo Chávez, the president of Venezuela, but now encompassing nine countries including Cuba, Bolivia, Ecuador, Nicaragua and several CARICOM countries. ALBA represents a major challenge and alternative to regional integration within the neoliberal world order. It constitutes an entirely new model for schemes of regional integration. Unlike the WTO model based on a simple reciprocity in which each party agrees to exactly the same rules of trade, ALBA involves a series of bilateral trade arrangements that are differentiated to take into account the development status and needs of each country. Thus, Venezuela in its agreement under ALBA with Bolivia or Cuba does not require reciprocity in the removal of all trade barriers. Nor do the regional agreements between governments seek trade liberalization or base trade on world market prices (Kellogg 2007). Moreover, regional integration under ALBA is explicitly designed to advance the specific and different national development agenda of each country, and any bilateral or multilateral agreement is tailored to the development requirements of each country, recognizing the asymmetry of economic and social development (Girvan 2009).

In effect, ALBA is based on an entirely new model or regional integration that reflects the thinking and worldview of the indigenous communities in the region as well as a shared commitment to the values and principles of the Bolivarian Revolution.

Girvan 2009; Kellogg 2007: 187–209; Harris 2005: 403–28.

Module 48

Socialism and Development

Jeffery R. Webber
University of Toronto, Canada

When the 'actually existing' system of socialism collapsed in the Soviet Union and Eastern Europe at the turn into the 1990s, mainstream media and academic commentary proclaimed the triumphant defeat of socialism by capitalism. The end of history, a new liberal order, was said to have been installed or in the offing. Socialism was cast derisively into the dustbin of the twentieth century. But there have long been vibrant socialist traditions fundamentally at odds with Stalinism and the 'model' of bureaucratic, authoritarian, one-party states. For many socialist theorists and activists, then, socialism did not die with the collapse of the Soviet Union and the Eastern bloc. Indeed, the advance of imperialist wars, ecological crisis, famine, poverty, inequality, exploitation and oppression since the beginning of 'the end of history' has made the renewal of socialism on a world scale more of an urgent necessity than ever before. More than merely an intellectual exercise, the pursuit of socialist alternatives today must be grounded in the renewal of anti-capitalist ideas and informed by the experiences of popular social movements over the last two decades.

Beginning with the Zapatista rebellion in southern Mexico and stretching into the street protests of Seattle, Quebec City and Genoa, anti-capitalism gained a new credibility over the 1990s as part of the incipient global justice (or 'anti-globalization') movement. More recently, the last decade has witnessed the resurgence of radical rural and urban mass movements in Latin America, as well as a 'pink tide' of self-described 'centre-left' and 'left' governments coming to office in the region.

This context allowed Venezuelan president Hugo Chávez to call for a new 'socialism for the twenty-first century' at the 2005 World Social Forum, helping to bring 'socialism,' 'anti-capitalism' and 'revolution' back into the lexicon of Latin American political and social struggle. Today, the eyes of the international left are trained on the unfolding struggles for transformative structural change to the states, economies and societies of Venezuela, Bolivia, Ecuador and Argentina, among other countries.

This module provides graduate students with a firm grounding in some of the key debates that will undoubtedly play an important part in the search for twenty-first-century socialism. While raising theoretical issues relevant to both the Global North and Global South, this module focuses primarily on the problems and prospects of advancing socialist politics in the latter. It identifies six themes fundamental to 'socialism and development' in the contemporary world.

1. Socialism and democracy

Twenty-first century socialism will be radically democratic or it will not be socialism. This first theme explores the ways in which conceptions of socialist democracy seek to extend democratic practices from the limited political sphere of liberalism into all of the social and economic spheres of life. Socialist democracy is rooted in the notion of free, active and direct popular self-government, rather than merely passive representation, in workplaces and communities.

Foster 2007: 2–18; Roman & Arregui 2007; Saul 1997: 219–36; Wood 1995.

2. Socialism and the market in the Global South

After the collapse of Stalinist regimes in the late 1980s, certain sectors of the socialist left began advocating various forms of 'market socialism' as a 'realistic' response to the problems of economic planning in any future socialist society. Others on the socialist left saw this as an indefensible concession to capitalism. Theorists of the latter type suggested that market socialists were really giving up on any authentic alternative to capitalism and that the transition to socialism would have to be a persistent struggle *against* the market.

This dispute has gained new currency in recent debates in development theory, especially as regards China's remarkably expansive growth over the last number of decades. Some sectors of the left in development circles have embraced China's turn to the market as an example of the economic development possible for developing countries that adopt similar policies of 'market socialism.' Others see China's development model as a contemptible example of the depravities and contradictions of the uneven and combined development of capitalism. They highlight the social costs of authoritarian China's market turn since the late 1970s, especially in relation to the conditions of the working class, the peasantry and the environment.

Through an exploration of contemporary Chinese economic development as well as central theoretical issues concerning the debate on market socialism more generally, the essential readings ask: Can a socialist economy be grounded in the principles of the market?

Hart-Landsberg & Burkett 2005: Chaps. 1, 5; Lebowitz 2006: Chap. 1; McNally 1993: Chap. 6; Colburn & Rahmato 1992: 159–73; Leftwich 1992: 27–42; Clapham 1992: 13–25.

3. Socialism, workers' control and democratic social coordination

A transition away from capitalism and toward socialism requires the replacement of private ownership of economic resources by communal ownership. Un-alienated labour demands workers' self-management and control of their workplaces and work processes. Outside of the workplace, in local communities and the wider society, a radically democratic socialism requires that production be democratically planned through participatory processes so that it responds to human needs rather than the profit motive of private capitalists.

Workers' control and self-management in the workplace is thus at the heart of the socialist project. And yet major theoretical and practical problems arise as workers struggle to assert control and self-management in concrete situations in which the logic of market competition still prevails in society at large. Worker occupations of factories and the establishment of workers' cooperatives can help build new social values and foster new organizational forms within working-class struggles. Experimentations in workers' control can lead to positive alterations in workers' subjectivity and unveil the fact that capital is not needed for social production.

At the same time, it is also clear that workers' cooperatives, operating within a system that remains capitalist, will ultimately reproduce the structural characteristics of the market logic that defines that system. Many of the complexities of these issues are at the centre of concrete historical processes unfolding in contemporary Argentina, as workers occupy and assert their control over factories in various sectors of the economy. Earlier this century, Bolivian miners made similar attempts to establish workers' control and self-management, without ultimately being able to push the Bolivian National Revolution of 1952 toward socialism. Exploring the cases of Argentine workers today and Bolivian miners in the 1950s, alongside theoretical explorations of the connection between workers' control and revolutionary theory, will help to elucidate the key components of this defining theme in socialist theory and praxis.

Atzeni & Ghigliani 2007: 653–71; Boeger 1997; Brown 1997; Hyman 1974; Mandel 1970: 3–9.

4. Socialism and ecology

Ecosocialist theorist Joel Kovel points to one overriding tendency in capitalism that puts it at the centre of the causes of today's ecological crisis and that, in turn, suggests that any viable movement for a sustainable future must be anti-capitalist:

> Capitalism requires continual growth of the economic product and since this growth is for the sake of capital and not real human need, the result is the continual destabilization of an integral relationship to nature. The essential reason for this lies in capitalism's distinctive difference from all other modes of production, that is, that it is organized around the production of capital itself—a purely abstract, numerical entity with no internal limit. Hence it drags the material natural world, which very definitely has limits, along with it on its mad quest for value and surplus value, and can do nothing else. (Kovel 2007)

The current ecological crisis facing the world today threatens human civilization as we know it. The devastation and suffering that will be increasingly unleashed if current trends of global warming and climate change are not reversed, while not entirely predictable in their character, will surely strike the poorest sectors of the population in the Global South most ferociously.

The readings in this theme develop an analysis of the ecological crisis within the context of contemporary global capitalism. They raise critical issues about China's 'hyper-development' and its environmental implications; environmental struggles in Zimbabwe's eastern highlands; the state of agriculture and the food crisis on a global scale and their relationship to development and ecology; and the complexities of building a revolutionary response to the ecological crisis that incorporates the principles of eco-socialism and democratic planning.

Foster 2005; Li & Wen 1996; Löwy 1996; McMichael 2007; Moore 1996.

5. Socialism, religion, national liberation and anti-oppression politics

The capitalist system since its origin has been defined by gender, sexual, national, racial and religious oppressions alongside and interconnected to class exploitation. Meaningful socialist theory and praxis therefore cannot be reducible to class alone. The essential readings in this theme take up questions of religion and socialist emancipation; sexual liberation politics in the Third World and their relationship to socialism; national liberation struggles in southern Africa and the necessity of a 'next liberation struggle' to bring back the struggle for socialism in that region; and the subject of women's self-emancipation in the context of Latin America's most recent turn to the left.

Achcar 2007; Saul 2005: Chaps. 2, 12; Fernandes 2007: 97–127.

6. Socialism, strategy and the state: Views from Latin America

John Holloway's (2002) ideas on changing the world without taking power have gained a certain level of notoriety in theoretical debates occurring within and about the Latin American left in the early twenty-first century. Holloway emphasizes the notion of 'anti-power' and denies the state as a pivotal focus for popular contention. Increasingly, however, this view is being called into question by socialist and left-populist theorists, who see anti-power as a dead-end for socialist strategy. Refocusing on the state, new Marxist literature on the Latin American context raises critical issues for the future of revolutionary strategy in the region, which is also relevant for the Global South more generally. The essential readings reflect the perspectives of theorists working in all of these traditions, providing the tools for a well-rounded grasp of the central debates facing Latin American popular movements today.

Dinerstein 2002: 5–38; Ellner 2005: 160–90; Katz 2007; Petras & Veltmeyer 2005b, 2009.

Module 49

Pathways of Progressive Change and Alternative Development

Henry Veltmeyer
Universidad Autónoma de Zacatecas, Mexico; Saint Mary's University, Canada

The philosophers have only *interpreted* the world in various ways; the point is to *change* it. —Marx, 11th Thesis on Feuerbach.

He [Marx] wants to insist that we can use our everyday experiences as the medium for understanding the world's unseen complexities, and, furthermore, that world revolutions happen when we transform these experiences, rather than simply inventing new abstract… concepts in isolation from what we perceive. *Capital* is a revolutionary text not because Marx has realized something before anyone else; its power results from how Marx gives us a critical language to describe what we already know, even if in a vague and incoherent fashion, and then redirect this new-found understanding through social and political action. —Shapiro 2008: 5

The crisis of Western capitalist civilization requires us to rebuild and reinvent new and different options of coexistence between nature and society, democracy, the state and patterns of consumption. It points to the adoption new ways of living and in this context, it is not just that 'other worlds are possible.' They are urgent, indeed they are being and have been built from the time of the first victims of the most barbaric forms of capitalist violence in the colonial, modern and contemporary eras.

> We, the Indigenous Peoples and Communities, Originarios, Campesinos, Ribereños, Quilombolas, Afrodescendents, Garífunas, Caboclos, Dalits, and others, and their children who migrated to the ghettoes of the cities, and all the other excluded, invisible and 'untouchables' of the planet who continue to resist, to strengthen and to update alternative forms of social, technological, ethical, political, economic, cultural and spiritual organization of the human existence. — Declaration of Indigenous People at the World Social Forum held in 2009 in Belém

1. Envisioning the future

The first step towards substantive change and genuine progress is to envision the principal features of an alternative future and then to propose the ways and means of constructing that future—that is, to embark on what John Saul (2006) called 'development after globalization.' This will involve serious thinking about agency, strategies and objectively given conditions. What *is* clear is that there is little possibility of a genuine forward movement—genuine progress planted on a permanent foundation for systemic improvement—on the basis of repeated adjustments, adaptations and other coping strategies when confronted with the changes generated by the dynamic workings of the current system, which in our time is capitalism.

The real-world conditions of current system dynamics are indeed 'objective' in their effects, as has been argued by generations of theorists and analysts with a 'structuralist' bent or, like many practitioners of CDS, a 'political economy' perspective and analytical framework. Although ideas by themselves cannot change the world (as idealists would like to believe), neither are they the mere reflection of underlying 'more real' structural forces (as some purely reductionist historical materialists would like to believe). Rather, development is a dialectical—and dialogic, we might add—process growing out of the connection between subjective (imagined and willed) and objective (given and determined) conditions. Thus, an alternative development requires not only structural analysis but also action on ideas, a political imaginary or ideology, the socially conscious agency of individuals able to imagine an alternative future and organized collectively in the directed pursuit of a strategy designed to achieve a desired and ideologically defined goal.

Amin 2008; Saul 2006: Chaps. 3–6.

2. Pathways out of poverty in the new millennium

The World Bank's 2008 *World Development Report* focuses on agriculture and chose as its theme 'pathways out of poverty.' In keeping with its classical modernization heritage, the World Bank views the principal location of the poverty problematic to be a rural society based on 'traditional' or pre-modern production systems. According to the report, in the context of a long-term process of productive and social transformation (capitalist development), 'development' is conceived of in terms of three 'pathways out of rural poverty,' namely *farming* (under conditions of capitalist modernization), *migration* (relocation to the urban centres in the country or abroad) and *labour* (wage-labour in one form or another). However, each of these pathways in reality entails an adjustment to the existing production and social system without any substantive or structural change. In essence, these pathways have the net effect of leaving the systemic structure intact, which is pointless if the basic, underlying sources of rural poverty are actually structural in nature.

From a CDS perspective, however, true forward movement will never be generated by *adjustment* but rather by various forms of *resistance*—that is, mobilizing the forces of resistance, which in most development contexts means the construction of social movements. In the context of neoliberal globalization, anti-systemic social movements of one form or another, based in the popular sector or 'civil society' (indigenous communities, peasant organizations, etc.), dominate the political landscape in the South and have done so for the past two decades.

In a number of accounts (for example, Petras & Veltmeyer 2005b), these movements represent the most dynamic forces of resistance to global capitalism and therefore resistance to the structures that support it. Whether they also represent the forces of real social transformation and real alternative development is less clear to contemporary analysts. It would seem—at least according to the theoretical accounts of some political sociologists—that the key issue is control over, or capture of, state power, still deemed by most as the most important repository or instrument of political power. However, there remains the question of what is the best or politically the most practical path to state power—reform (progressive adaptation) or revolution (deep structural change). That is, the choice appears to be between 'buy-in' to the political forms of the current capitalist structure through activities centred on the electoral mechanism of democratic politics or, on the other hand, social mobilization of the forces of resistance and insurgency that see such 'buy-in' as ultimately providing a false sense of power while keeping the underlying structure essentially preserved (Petras & Veltmeyer 2005b; Veltmeyer 2007a).

Petras & Veltmeyer 2005b; Veltmeyer 2007a: 100–18.

3. Agents of social change and alternative development

At issue in the study of social change and alternative development is the question of agency in regard to (a) the state, the fundamental repository of political power in the institution of public policy, (b) 'civil society' in the form of diverse social and non-political organizations, (c) class-based anti-systemic social movements, a form of organization used to mobilize the forces of resistance against government policy and the system and social forces behind it, and (d) a global civil society and anti-globalization movement to mobilize for a fundamental or progressive change in the structure of the global economy and international relations.

A point of fundamental agreement among scholar activists and grassroots organizations for change is the need for an alternative to neoliberal globalization and imperialism in its different manifestations. The forces of progressive change are divided on the matters of globalization or capitalism per se (some want to abolish them, others argue for reform), but there is widespread agreement on the need for an alternative to the current driving force behind both globalization and capitalism, the structured perspective of neoliberalism. On this point John Saul (2006) argues for an intellectual activism that combines class-based struggle with support of progressive movements rooted in the demands of gender equality, progressive identity politics, social democratic anti-neoliberal globalization, anti-capitalism and anti-imperialism. Some progressive scholars have promoted environmental activism vis-à-vis protection of the environment and the need for greener technologies, the harnessing of the corporate agenda of profit-making, market regulation and more sustainable environmental and development practices. Walden Bello (2007b) argues the pivotal importance of environmental activism in the South. Trenchant critics of neoliberal globalization, including Bello, stress the importance of an anti-globalization movement that combines the diverse forms of resistance in the South and North. In spite of the broad consensus on change, thinkers are divided as to the nature, political dynamics and prospects of such a global movement—as divided as the movement itself.

Chuck Morris (2003), arguing from an anarchist perspective, sees considerable potential for radical change in the anti-globalization movement. However, Petras (2007), among other Marxist analysts, makes a sharp distinction between the North and the South in this movement, viewing the former as middle class and concerned solely, or primarily, with creating a more ethical and humane form of globalization within the framework of the actually existing capitalist system (basically the goal of thinkers such as Jeffery Sachs). From this perspective the anti-globalization movement in the South is seen as having greater potential for substantive change precisely because it is rooted not in an emergent 'global civil society' (a favourite preoccupation of the North) but in the popular sector of anti-systemic social movements. In between these perspectives can be found a range of views on the way forward—from progressive social movements and alternative forms of capitalist development (social welfarism, social liberalism, etc.) to deglobalization and socialism.

Berberoglu 2003; Bond 2004; Morris 2003; Anheier, Glasius & Kaldor 2001–2007; Peet & Watts 2004.

4. Models of progressive or radical change and genuine progress

Some public intellectuals within the establishment of the current world order—after more than two decades of neoliberalism it can hardly be called 'new' anymore—such as Joseph Stiglitz, have formulated alternative solutions to the problems of neoliberal globalization that are system supportive, that is, designed to save capitalism by changing it. The proposed solutions are generally in the direction of humanizing capitalism or development, designing a more sustainable, equitable and ethical form of globalization, a more democratic system, but one that would have the net effect of preserving neoliberal-based structures and policies at the level of macroeconomic policy. But from a more critical development perspective, many scholars argue the need for more radical change: minimally a tight regulation on the capacity and freedom of the capitalist class to exploit labour, create profit at the expense of others and appropriate an undue share of the social product.

Some argue that what is needed is a mixed system, a radical transformation of the system in a socialist direction, which may result in the abandonment of capitalism. Along these lines, a number of development scholars advance alternative proposals for the design of a better form of society, an alternative future in another world that would be based on the following:

1. A more radical form of social democracy and Keynesian planning, a regime that combines a regulated market with state-led, public-sector financed social development; a strong albeit decentralized state that is democratized in its relation to a vibrant and actively participating civil society (Sandbrook et al. 2007);

2. Radical reform or transformation of the capitalist system by means of mobilizing the forces of resistance in the popular sector, mobilizing them in a progressive direction and opening up local and regional spaces within the existing capitalist system for alternative autonomous forms of local or community-based development. This solution would include the proposals of La Vía Campesina for a production system and rural livelihoods based on small-scale agriculture and production for local markets (Desmarais 2007);

3. Socialism, understood as socialization of the means of production through and by means of the organized power of the working class, mobilized against the capitalist system and the power of private property under conditions of crisis and in quest of state power; and the agency of the state in bringing about a social transformation in the economic structure of society in the direction of freedom and equality, a society in which private property as the institutional means of permitting one class to exploit the labour of others for private profit and personal enrichment is abolished (Berberoglu, 2007); and

4. A systemic alternative *within* socialism, that is, to the socialism as actually practised in the Soviet Union and Eastern Europe in the twentieth century, what we might term, following Venezuelan president Hugo Chávez, 'socialism for the twenty-first century' or, after John Saul, a reimagined 'developmental socialism' put into practice with the active participation of popular sector organizations. Socialism in this form, that is, as 'human development' (Lebowitz 2006), would be based on 'the judgement that people can resolve economic and political tensions and potential contradictions collectively and democratically rather than having to build centrally on competition and the entrepreneurial greed of the few as the ultimate central keys to the welfare of everybody else' (Saul 2007: 14). It would take form through 'public action'—people-led actions from within and below, within civil society as well as the state, that is, popular power oriented towards and taking the form of control by workers and communities of their workplaces and communities (Lebowitz 2006).

> Berberoglu 2007; Lebowitz 2006; Desmarais 2007;
> Sandbrook, Edelman, Heller & Teichman 2007; Saul 2007.

5. A 'minga of resistance': Policymaking from below

On February 29, 2009, the ACIN, a Bolivia-based regional alliance of indigenous, peasant, rural landless and other social movements, convoked a '*minga* of resistance' in association with 'other peoples and processes' in the region (Abya Yala 2009).[1] *Minga* is a Quechua word meaning 'collective action' or 'collective project,' having wide currency among the indigenous and mestizo poor in the Andes. The ACIN's call to join in a *minga* that is at once local and global gains force from both its cultural and historical references to a shared experience of subjugation. By naming their movement a *minga*, the indigenous participants call attention to both the work that must go into politics and the need for collective action.

Thought and action in this direction—in the search for an alternative to capitalist development and its current underlying philosophy of neoliberalism, the undoubted source of the current global crisis—is underway in the popular sector of different countries in the region. See for example the Convocation (January 20, 2009) of the Social Movements of America at the World Social Forum in Belém. Based on a diagnosis of the 'profound crisis' of capitalism in the current conjuncture—a crisis the agents and agencies of capitalism and imperialism are seeking to foist onto 'our people'—the representation of a broad regional coalition of American social movements announced the need for, and its intention to create, a popular form of 'regional integration from below' (subsequently termed ALBA), a form of 'social solidarity in the face of imperialism' <www.alianzabolivariana.org>.

From this popular perspective, the global crisis is not a matter of financial markets but is rather a production and social issue, a matter of sustainable livelihoods, jobs or employment and the price of food, which is rapidly escalating under the conditions of the global and local crisis. In this connection, ECLAC executive secretary José Luis Machinea has noted that the steep and persistent rise in international food prices is hitting the poorest particularly hard in Latin America and the Caribbean and is worsening income distribution. Poverty and indigence will rise if urgent measures are not taken to reduce the effects of these price increases; nearly ten million people would become indigent, causing a similar increase in the ranks of the poor. This does not even take into consideration the aggravating social situation of those who were already poor or indigent prior to the price rises and the global crisis.

Another example of popular action against the global production, financial and food crisis—a crisis of capital—is the peasant-worker alliance formed in Mexico to make affordable food available to workers in the cities (*La Jornada* On Line, February 24, 2009). For example, in regard to the staple corn-based 'tortilla,' the price of which has skyrocketed (see the analysis of the price dynamics by Bello 2008a), spokespersons for the alliance announced that the producers in the alliance would deliver goods to workers and their families at cost or prices at least 20 percent below those at commercial enterprises—and there would be no taxes charged. Efraín García Bello, director of the Confederación Nacional de Productores Agrícolas de Maíz de México, a signatory to the production alliance, noted that actions of this sort would support the economy of both the workers in the urban areas and the inhabitants in the countryside.

Along the same line and supportive of this popular action against the crisis, different organizations in Mexico's peasant movement, including those set up by or close to the government, proposed to the government that its anti-crisis plan include a policy of local production in corn and rice, milk, vegetable oil, pork products, etc., ending the policy of free agricultural imports under NAFTA, which has, as the EZLN (the Zapatista movement) predicted, been the cause of a major production crisis in Mexican agriculture. In regard to the local production and imports of vegetable oil, the president of the Mexican Senate's Rural Development Commission pointed out that in just this one case the government's policy on the elimination of import duties has put at risk the livelihoods and direct employment of up to 10,000 jobs in the sector plus an additional 30,000 indirect jobs.

At issue in this and other such actions within the popular sector (see the Actions profiled in the insert below) is whether the political and intellectual left is up to the challenge announced by Abya Yala, that is, whether the left is willing and able actively to support, if not lead, the forces of revolutionary change that are being formed in the popular sector—forces at work on the ground, behind the lines of an ongoing class war, all over the world.

Abya Yala 2009; Petras & Veltmeyer 2005, 2009.

6. Some lessons of history: Yes we can!

A critical review of the recent history of social change and development discloses or allows us to draw a number of lessons regarding the way forward and building a better future and another, more just, world. One lesson is that the way forward is paved with state power: bringing about a new world requires the agency of the state, in our time the fundamental repository of political power and instrument for public action regarding development. No significant improvements in the quality of life and the dynamics of development have been made outside the state. In Latin America, for example, none of the social movements that were formed in the 1980s to mobilize the resistance against neoliberalism, imperialism and class rule were able to endure and sustain the forces of change, or leave a legacy of substantive change, unless—as in the case of Bolivia—they combined a strategy of social mobilization with a bid for state power. In Ecuador, a cautionary tale in this regard is the failure of the Confederation of Indigenous Nationalities of Ecuador (CONAIE). CONAIE was a powerful anti-systemic social movement of poor indigenous peasants who led a successful mobilization of resistance and succeeded in halting the neoliberal agenda of the government. It subsequently secured the removal of several presidential representatives who were strong partisans of the neoliberal agenda. But it ultimately failed in bringing about any fundamental change, this being left to Rafael Correa, a 'socialist' political leader who emerged in the wake of the retreat of CONAIE from state power. CONAIE—demoralized, divided and defeated in its attempt to secure substantive change from outside the system—retreated. In Venezuela, the country presently leading the search in the region for an alternative to neoliberalism, the social movement used to mobilize the forces of resistance in the popular sector in a progressive direction was in fact an artifact of the state, an instrument of state power used to mobilize popular support for the so-called Bolivarian Revolution.

Another lesson of history is that there are two main roads to state power: democratic elections, via the political party mechanism, and social mobilizations via the agency of anti-systemic social movements. Of these two roads to state power, history has shown that the first is less likely to lead to genuine progress. This is because it is difficult to bring about change from within the system, i.e., via the agency of the existing political class. The system is likely to either corrupt or absorb those who seek to bring about substantive change from within, or present them with structurally given alternatives neither of which serves the purpose of deep structural change. This point is amply illustrated by the experience of the centre-left regimes in the region that came to power over the last six years on the wave of anti-neoliberal sentiment (Petras & Veltmeyer 2009). All but one—Chávez's Bolivarian regime, which was formed earlier and under other conditions—failed to take advantage of exceptionally favourable economic and political conditions by instituting genuine change. Despite policy and political elements of neo- or radical populism, all of these regimes can best be described as having adopted pragmatic neoliberalism in political practice and public action.

The third lesson that can be drawn from the recent history of economic and political developments in Latin America is that there are two systemic alternatives for substantive change: development from within via the radical reform (social transformation) of capitalism at the level of the state, society and the economy; and socialist development on the basis of a radical restructuring of the operating economic system, moving away from private property in the means of production in the direction of socializing both production and consumption, nationalizing the country's reservoir of natural resources and reversing the privatization policy of the neoliberal model.

Currently, there are only two countries in the region pursuing national development along this socialist path: Cuba and Venezuela. Despite serious difficulties and constraints, and what some have termed a 'democratic deficit' (lack of popular participation in public action), Cuba has led all countries in the region in the achievement of a relatively high level of 'human development' and the integration of economic growth with genuine progress through policies and perspectives designed to fulfill the basic needs of the entire population through a substantive degree of equality and equity in the distribution of the social product. Several countries in the region score higher than Cuba on the HDI, but this is primarily because of the weight given to per capita income in the HDI index algorithm.

The other country pursuing a socialist path to development is Venezuela, although in all probability the end result will be a mixed economy, a combination of the best (and likely the worst) of both capitalism and socialism. This is perhaps our last lesson of history—our final conclusion: there is no genuine development on the extremes of thought and practice. Just as development necessitates and means both action and a facilitative institutional framework (agency and structure) and both state power and the active social mobilization of grassroots participation, genuine progress towards another world may require a combination of capitalism and socialism—a mixed system in one form or the other.

However, the possible necessity of such a combination in no way entails that social revolution is off the political agenda. The crucial need in our epoch for an 'alternative development' will no doubt necessitate radical change and a class-based, far-reaching social and societal transformation, in effect, a social revolution. To imagine the form of this revolutionary change and to bring the necessary conditions into being will require a closer look and further study from a critical development perspective on struggles such as those profiled in the insert, 'Yes We Can.' It will also require a theoretically informed, ideologically determined and class-based form of collective action. Although 'public action' in this direction and in this form (combining government policy with grassroots action) will have to be thought about critically and worked through politically we can nevertheless establish certain guiding principles in this regard:

• People and governments need to (1) orient their policies toward 'human development'— creating a society of free and equal human beings in which each individual can develop his or her potential to the maximum; (2) acknowledge human beings as productive forces but at the same time recognize that these 'productive forces' should be mobilized in the direction of meeting the material and spiritual needs of the human collective rather than creating profit for the few; and (3) mobilize the progressive forces in society against the inevitable reaction by those that benefit from the current arrangements in the social order, a mobilization that would act on behalf of policies that develop the capacities of people and meet their needs rather than serving as a vehicle for accumulating capital for private profit.

• The state needs to undergo a process of profound transformation. It needs to be (1) truly democratic and fully representative, an economic and social (i.e., substantive) democracy not just a political or formal democracy, not just structured and acting in the interests of 'the people' (humanity as a whole) but controlled by people in their communities and workplaces and through their political representation within the state; (2) free itself from the ideological domination of capital—from the culture of possessive individualism and self-interest, the belief that the market knows best, free from a personal and political dependence on capital; (3) break ideologically and politically with the forces of capital, from the perquisites (real or imagined) of private property in the means of production; and (4) move forward with the people, with the world community actively mobilized in support of genuine progress, toward another more just, more equitable and ultimately more humane world.

• Progressive change in the direction of 'another world' is both necessary and possible. The greatest resource for this 'development' of the forces of change is the resilience and collective action at the grassroots of society (see the insert "Yes We Can!"). The intellectual and political left—as well as students and practitioners of critical development studies— should, and it is hoped will, stand on the side of these forces of change.

Notes

1. This alliance includes the Coordinadora Andina de Organizaciones Indígenas, the Coordinadora de Organizaciones Indígenas de la Cuenca Amazónica, the Consejo Indígena de Centro América, the Movimiento Sin Tierra del Brasil, La Vía Campesina; the organizations of the Unity Pact (Pacto de Unidad) of Bolivia; and diverse indigenous organizations of Colombia, Ecuador and Peru—meeting together most recently on February, 26, 2009, in the locality of the Unity Pact in La Paz.

Yes We Can! Amazon villagers celebrate victory over agro-fuels (but the oil barons loom)

It took a moment for the news to sink in. The villagers, indigenous Kichwa farmers deep in Peru's Amazon jungle, looked at each other in silence. Was this really true? A few hesitant smiles, then laughter, then cheering. They had won.

The victory was there in black and white, in newspapers chugged up the Napo river to their village, Copal Urco. 'Government revokes decrees,' said one banner headline. 'García humbled,' said another, referring to President Alan García. 'Is this not a great day?' shouted Roger Yume, the village *apu*, or chief. Dozens of voices answered as one. 'Yes!'

Peru's indigenous Amazon population, a marginalized, impoverished, tiny minority, had defeated the state in a battle over economic exploitation of the rain forest. The government had parcelled out 70 percent of the jungle to oil, gas, mining and agro-fuel projects. The revenues would benefit 28 million Peruvians, said President García, and 'ignorant' Indian agitators who claimed the Amazon as their ancestral home would not be able to stop it. But from April until June indigenous groups blocked roads, waterways and pipelines. When police in the town of Bagua tried to lift the blockades, all hell broke loose. Officially 23 police and 11 protestors died. Indigenous leaders say dozens more protestors died.

The shaken government retreated and last month revoked decrees 1090 and 1064, which would have opened the forest to agro-fuel plantations, especially palm oil. The prime minister, Yehude Simón, said he would quit and García admitted mistakes were made.

Indigenous groups celebrated across the Amazon and in the capital, Lima, delegations with face paint and feathers swept in triumph through the corridors of congress. They suspended the protests.

But the battle is not over. Other decrees, still in force, keep hydrocarbon exploration on track. The government and oil and gas companies are determined to press ahead.

Oil has been drilled in the Amazon for 35 years, but on a minute scale compared to what is coming. From 27 concessions in 2003 there are now more than 100. The concern is that the pollution that disfigured the Corrientes River, for example, will be replicated across the rainforest.

'The biggest fear is that the most remote, and therefore most intact, sections of the Peruvian Amazon will soon be inhabited with islands of drilling platforms and, even worse, new roads and pipelines,' said Matt Finer, coauthor of a study by Duke University of Amazon oil and gas projects.

The forest has been divided into 'lots' among Peruvian companies as well as multinationals from Argentina, Brazil, North America and Europe. Seismic tests have been completed and barges await the first barrels of crude later this year.

Can indigenous leaders build on their victory and curb the oil rush? 'The tide has turned. They're energized; they've seen what they can do,' said Paul McAuley, 61, a British Catholic lay missionary who campaigns for indigenous rights through a civil association, Red Ambiental Loretana.

Wagner Musoline Acho, 23, a student leader in the jungle town of Iquitos, said activists were mobilizing for more action. 'We have learned to trust in ourselves. We are ready for the next steps.' He said his generation, better educated than its parents, would influence the Amazon's destiny. With the help of advocacy groups, aid agencies and wider cellphone coverage, Peru's indigenous communities are catching up with their better-organized brethren in Brazil and Ecuador.

Whether that will be enough to slow the oil rush is doubtful. There is powerful pressure, not least the steady recovery in oil prices, to convert the black ooze beneath the Amazon into fuel for western and Asian economies—and revenue for Peru.

The government is impatient for the windfall from $13bn in investments. For the Lima elite, revoking two decrees over agro-fuels was more a hiccup than a u-turn. 'We think all these [oil] projects will go ahead,' said the foreign minister, José Antonio García Belaúnde. If he is right, the questions are to what extent drilling will affect the villagers and the Amazon ecosystem and whether the revenues will be spent to ease Peru's crushing poverty or be pocketed by Lima.

In Copal Urco there was anxiety that their victory may be a one-off. 'The government wants to sell us out.' Said Heyner Tangoa, forty, a barefoot farmer. 'We want the oil left in the ground. We want to be left in peace.' The fight was just starting.
—Rory Carrol, Peru Diary, *The Guardian*, July 7, 2009

References

Abassi, Jennifer, and Sheryl Lutjens. 2002. *Rereading Women in Latin America and the Caribbean: The Political Economy of Gender*. Lanham, MD: Rowan and Littlefield.

Abya Yala—Movimientos Indígenas, Campesinos y Sociales. 2009. "Diálogo de Alternativas y Alianzas," *Minga Informativa de Movimientos Sociales*, La Paz, 26 de Febrero.

Achcar, Gilbert. 2007. "Religion and Politics Today from a Marxian Perspective." In Leo Panitch and Colin Leys (eds.), *Socialist Register 2008: Global Flashpoints, Reactions to Imperialism and Neoliberalism*. New York: Monthly Review Press.

Adams, F., S.D. Gupta and K. Mengisteab (eds.). 1999. *Globalization and the Dilemmas of the State in the South*. Basingstoke: Macmillan.

Adams, W. 1990. *Green Development: Environment and Sustainability in the Third World*. London and New York: Routledge.

Adebajo, Adekeye. 2002. *Liberia's Civil War: Nigeria, Ecomog and Regional Security in West Africa*. Boulder, CO: Lynne Rienner.

Adelman, I. 1986. "A Poverty Focused Approach to Development Policy." In J.P. Lewis and V. Kallab (eds.), *Development Strategies Reconsidered*. New Brunswick, NJ: Transaction Books. Reprinted in C.K. Wilber (ed.), *The Political Economy of Underdevelopment*. Fourth edition. New York: Random House.

Adésínà, J.O., Y. Graham, and A. Olukoshi (eds.). 2006. *Africa and Development Challenges in the New Millennium: The NEPAD Debate*. London: Zed Books.

Agarwal, Bina. 1985. "Women and Technological Change in Agriculture: The Asian and African Experience." In I. Ahmed (ed.), *Technology and Rural Women: Conceptual and Empirical Issues*. London: Allen and Unwin.

_____. 1997. "'Bargaining' and Gender Relations: Within and Beyond the Household." *Feminist Economics* 3 (1): 1–51.

Agarwala, R., and P.N. Schwartz. 1994. "Sub-Saharan Africa: A Long-Term Perspective Study." World Bank, Learning Process on Participatory Development, May, pp. 1–32.

Aglietta, M. 1976. *A Theory of Capitalist Regulation: The US Experience*. London: New Left Books.

Agrawal, Arun. 2005. *Environmentality: Technologies of Government and the Making of Subjects*. Durham: Duke University Press.

Agyeman, Opoku. 2007. "Pan-Africanism vs. Pan-Arabism." *Nigerian Village Square* 2, June.

Ahooja-Patel, Krishna. 1982. "Another Development With Women." *Development Dialogue* 1, 2.

_____. 2007. *Development Has a Woman's Face: Insights from Within the United Nations*. New Delhi: APH Publishers.

Akram-Lodhi, A.H. 2007. "Land, Markets and Neoliberal Enclosure: An Agrarian Political Economy Perspective." *Third World Quarterly* 28 (8): 1437–56.

Akram-Lodhi, Haroon, Saturnino Borras Jr., and Cristóbal Kay (eds.). 2007. *Land, Poverty and Livelihoods in an Era of Neoliberal Globalization: Perspectives from Developing and Transition Countries*. London: Routledge.

Akram-Lodhi, A.H., and C. Kay. 2008a. "The Agrarian Question: Peasants and Rural Change." In A.H. Akram-Lodhi and C. Kay (eds.), *Peasants and Globalization: Political Economy, Rural Transformation and the Agrarian Question*. London/New York: Routledge.

_____. 2008b. "Neoliberal Globalization, the Character of Rural Accumulation and Rural Politics: The Agrarian Question in the 21st Century." In A.H. Akram-Lodhi and C. Kay (eds.), *Peasants and Globalization: Political Economy, Rural Transformation and the Agrarian Question*. London and New York: Routledge.

_____. 2008c. "Neoliberal Globalization, Traits of Accumulation and Rural Politics: The Agrarian Question in the 21st Century." In A.H. Akram-Lodhi and C. Kay (ed.), *Peasants and Globalization: Political Economy, Rural Transformation and the Agrarian Question*. London: Routledge.

Akram-Lodhi, A.H., C. Kay, and S.M. Borras. 2008. "The Political Economy of Land and the Agrarian

Question in an Era of Neoliberal Globalization." In A.H. Akram-Lodhi and C. Kay (eds.), *Peasants and Globalization: Political Economy, Rural Transformation and the Agrarian Question*. London and New York: Routledge.

Alampay, Erwin. 2008. "Technology, Information and Development." In P. Haslam, J. Schafer, P. Beaudet (eds.), *Introduction to International Development: Approaches, Actors and Issues*. Oxford: Oxford University Press.

Alavi, Hamza. 1982. "State and Class Under Peripheral Capitalism." In Hamza Alavi and Teodor Shanin (eds.), *Sociology of Developing Societies*. New York: Monthly Review Press.

Aldrich, Brian C., and Ravinder S. Sandhu. 1995. *Housing the Urban Poor*. London: Zed Books.

Allard, J., Carl Davidson, and J. Matthaei. 2008. *Solidarity Economy: Building an Economy for People and Planet*. Papers and Reports from the U.S. Social Forum 2007. Amherst, MA: Centre for Popular Economics.

Almeida, Paul. 2007. "Defensive Mobilization: Popular Movements against Economic Adjustment Policies in Latin America." *Latin American Perspectives* 34 (3): 123–39.

Altieri, Miguel A., and Susanna Hecht. 1990. *Agroecology and Small Farm Development*. Boca Raton: CRC Press.

Altvater, Elmar. 1990. "The Foundations of Life (Nature) and the Maintenance of Life (Work): The Relations between Ecology and Economics in the Crisis." *International Journal of Political Economy* 20: 10–34.

Alvarez, S., E. Dagnino, and A. Escobar (eds.). 1998. *Cultures of Politics, Politics of Cultures: Re-visioning Latin American Social Movements*. Boulder, CO: Westview Press.

Amalric, Frank. 1998. "Sustainable Livelihoods, Entrepreneurship, Political Strategies and Governance." *Development* 41 (3): 31–44.

Amin, Samir. 1972. *Unequal Development*. New York: Monthly Review Press.

_____. 1973. *Neo-Colonialism in West Africa*. Harmondsworth: Penguin Books.

_____. 1990. *Delinking: Towards a Polycentric World*. London and New Jersey: Zed Books.

_____. 1997. *Capitalism in the Age of Globalization*. London: Zed Books.

_____. 1999. "For a Progressive and Democratic New World Order." In Adams et al. (eds.), *Globalization and the Dilemmas of the State in the South*. Basingstoke: Macmillan.

_____. 2008. *The World We Wish to See: Revolutionary Objectives in the 21st Century*. New York: Monthly Review Press.

Amsden, Alice. 2005. "Promoting Industry under WTO Law." In Kevin Gallagher (ed.), *Putting Development First*. London: Zed Books.

_____. 2007. "Gift of the Gods and The Light of the Moon." In *Escape From Empire*. Cambridge, MA: MIT Press.

Anand, S., and A.K. Sen. 2000. "Human Development and Economic Sustainability." *World Development* 28 (12): 2029–49.

Andersen, Regine. 2000. "How Multilateral Development Assistance Triggered the Conflict in Rwanda." *Third World Quarterly* 21 (3).

Anderson, Leslie. 1994. *The Political Ecology of the Modern Peasant: Calculation and Commodity*. Baltimore: Johns Hopkins University Press.

Anheier, Helmut, Marlies Glasius and Mary Kaldor. 2001–2007 *Global Civil Society* Yearbook series.

Annan, Kofi A. 2000. *We the People: The Role of the United Nations in the 21st Century*, New York: United Nations.

Antrobus, Peggy. 1995. "Third World Women Challenge the Given." *PCD Forum*, 75, March 6.

Apple, Michael. 1995. *Education and Power*. New York: Routledge.

Arce, A., and N. Long. 1992. "The Dynamics of Knowledge: Interfaces between Bureaucrats and Peasants." In N. Long and A. Long (eds.), *Battlefields of Knowledge: The Interlocking of Theory and Practice in Social Research and Development*. London: Routledge.

Archer, M. 1979. *Social Origins of Educational Systems*. London: Sage Publications.

Arrighi, G., and J.S. Saul (eds.). 1973. *Essays on the Political Economy of Africa*. New York: Monthly Review Press.

Ashton, D., and F. Green. 1996. *Education, Training and the Global Economy*. Chetenham: Edward Elgan.

Atria, R., M. Siles, M. Arriagada, L. Robison and S. Whiteford (eds.). 2004. *Social Capital and Poverty Reduction in Latin America and the Caribbean: Towards a New Paradigm*. Santiago: ECLAC.

Atzeni, Maurizio, and Pablo Ghigliani. 2007. "Labour Process and Decision-Making in Factories under Workers' Self-Management: Empirical Evidence from Argentina." *Work, Employment and Society* 21 (4): 653–71.

Ayittey, G.B.N. 2004. *Africa Unchained: The Blueprint from Africa's Future*. London: Palgrave Macmillan.

Baiocchi, G. 2005. *Militants and Citizens: The Politics of Participatory Development in Porto Alegre*. Palo Alto, CA: Stanford University Press

Bakker, Isabella (ed.). 1994. *The Strategic Silence: Gender and Economic Policy*. London: Zed Books.

Balanyá, B., B. Brennan, O. Hoedeman, S. Krishimoto and P. Terhorst. 2005. *Reclaiming Public Water: Achievements, Struggles and Visions from Around the World*. Amsterdam: TNI.

Balfour, Robert. 2007. "Naipaul's *Half a Life, Magic Seeds* and Globalization." *Literator* 28(1) April: 1–21.

Baran, Paul. 1957. *The Political Economy of Growth*. New York: Monthly Review Press.

Bardhan, Pranab. 1993. *Democracy and Development: A Symposium*. (Articles by Adam Przeworski and F. Limongi; and Evelyn Huber and Dietrich Rueschmeyer.) *Journal of Economic Perspectives* 7 (3): 40–86.

_____. 2005. "History, Institutions and Underdevelopment." In *Scarcity, Conflicts and Cooperation: Essays in the Political and Institutional Economics of Development*. Cambridge/London: MIT Press.

Barkin, David. 1998. *Wealth, Poverty, and Sustainable Development*. México: Editorial Jus/Centro de Ecología y Desarrollo/Centro Lindavista.

_____. 2001. "La nueva ruralidad y la globalización." In Edelmira Pérez and María Adelaida Farah (eds.), *La Nueva Ruralidad en América Latina: Maestría de Desarrollo Rural 20 Años*. Bogotá: Pontificia Universidad Javeriana, 2.

_____. 2004. "Who are the Peasants?" *Latin American Research Review* 39 (3): 270–81.

_____. 2006. "Building a Future for Rural Mexico." *Latin American Perspectives* 33 (2).

Barkin, David, and Richard Levins. 1998. "The Eco-Social dynamics of Rural Systems." In David Rapport (ed.), *Ecosystem Health*. Malden, MA: Basil Blackwell.

Barkin, David, and Carlos Paillés. 2000. "Water and Forests as Instruments for Sustainable Regional Development." *International Journal of Water* 1 (1): 71–79.

Barkin, David, and Mara Rosas. 2006. "¿Es posible un modelo alterno de acumulación?" *Revista Polis* 5 (15). Available from <http://www.revistapolis.cl/13/bark.htm>.

Barlow, Maude. 2007. *The Global Water Crisis and the Coming Battle for the Right to Water*. Toronto: McClelland and Stewart.

Barnes, Joe, Mark Hayes, Amy Jaffe and David Victor. 2006. "Introduction to the Study." In David Victor, Amy Jaffe and Mark Hayes (eds.), *Natural Gas and Geopolitics: From 1970 to 2040*. New York: Cambridge University Press.

Bartra, Armando. 2006. "Los campesinos del capital: Su papel en la acumulación y su racionalidad inmanente." In A. Bartra, *El Capital en su Laberinto: De la Renta de la Tierra a la Renta de la Vida*. Mexico City: Universidad Autónoma de la Ciudad de México.

Bartra, Roger. 1993. "And if the Peasants Become Extinct…." and "… An Impossible, Ongoing Annihilation." In R. Bartra, *Agrarian Structure and Political Power in Mexico*. Baltimore: Johns Hopkins University Press. Available in Spanish.

Bates, Robert H. 1981. *Markets and States in Tropical Africa: The Political Basis of Agricultural Policies*. Berkeley, CA: University of California Press.

Baud, I.S.A., and J. Post (eds.). 2002. *Realigning Actors in an Urbanizing World: Governance and Institutions from a Development Perspective*. Aldershot: Ashgate Publishers.

Bauer, P.T. 1982. *Equality, The Third World and Economic Delusion*. Cambridge: Harvard University Press.

Baviskar, Amita. 2006. *In the Belly of the River: Tribal Conflicts over Development in the Narmada Valley*.

New Delhi: Oxford University Press.

Baylis, John, Steve Smith, and Patricia Owens (eds.). 2008. *The Globalization of World Politics: An Introduction to International Relations.* Oxford: Oxford University Press.

Beams, Nick. 1998. *The Significance and Implications of Globalization: A Marxist Assessment.* Southfield: Mehring Books.

Bebbington, A. 1999. "Capitals and Capabilities: A Framework for Analysing Peasant Viability, Rural Livelihoods and Poverty." *World Development* 27 (12).

_____. 2001. "Development Alternatives: Practice, Dilemmas and Theory." *Area* 33 (1): 7–17.

_____. 2004. "Livelihood Transitions, Place Transformations: Grounding Globalization and Modernity." In Robert N. Gwynne and Cristóbal Kay (eds.), *Latin America Transformed: Globalization and Modernity.* London: Arnold.

Bebbington, A., et al. 2006. *The Search for Empowerment: Social Capital as Idea and Practice at the World Bank.* Sterling, VA: Kumarian Press.

Bebbington, Anthony, Samuel Hickey and Diana C. Mitlin (eds.). 2008. *Can NGOs Make a Difference: The Challenge of Development Alternatives.* London: Zed Books.

Becker, Charles, Andrew Hamer, and Andrew Morrison. 1994. "African City Systems and Urban Growth." In Charles Becker, Andrew Hamer and Andrew Morrison, *Beyond Urban Bias in Africa.* New Hampshire: Heinemann.

Bello, Walden. 2004. *Deglobalization: Ideas for a New World Economy.* London: Zed.

_____. 2005. *Dilemmas of Domination.* New York: Metropolitan Books.

_____. 2006. "The Capitalist Conjuncture: Overaccumulation, Financial Crises, and the Retreat from Globalization." *Third World Quarterly* 27 (8): 1345–68.

_____. 2007a. "A Roller Coaster Ride: A Perspective from Southeast Asia." In P. Bowles, et al. (ed.), *Regional Perspectives on Globalization.* Basingstoke: Palgrave Macmillan.

_____. 2007b. "Environmental Movement in the Global South: The Pivotal Agent in the Fight against Global Warming." *Alternatives International* 2, November.

_____. 2008a. "Crisis and the Retreat from Globalization in Asia." In H. Veltmeyer (ed.), *Globalization/ Antiglobalization.* UK: Ashgate.

_____. 2008b. "Globalization, Development and Democracy: A Reflection on the Global Food Crisis." Keynote Address, CASID, Vancouver, June 3.

_____. 2009. "The Global Collapse: A Non-Orthodox View." *Mrzine*, February 20 <http://mrzine.monthlyreview.org/2009/bello200209.html>.

Bello, Walden, with Shea Cunningham and Bill Rau. 1994. *Dark Victory: United States, Structural Adjustment and Global Poverty.* London: Pluto Press.

Benería, Lourdes. 2003. *Gender, Development, and Globalization: Economics as If All People Mattered.* New York/London: Routledge.

Benería, Lourdes, and Savitri Bisnath (eds.). 2003. *Global Tensions: Challenges and Opportunities in World Economy.* London: Routledge.

Benn, Dennis, and Kenneth Hall (eds.). 2000. *Globalization: A Calculus of Inequality. Perspectives from the South,* Kingston: Ian Randle Publishers.

Bennett, K., and M. LeCompte. 1990. *The Way Schools Work: A Sociological Analysis of Education.* White Plains, NY: Longman.

Benton, Ted. 1989. "Marxism and Natural Limits: An Ecological Critique and Reconstruction." *New Left Review* 178: 51–86.

_____. 1996. "Marxism and Natural Limits: An Ecological Critique and Reconstruction." In Ted Benton (ed.), *The Greening of Marxism.* New York: Guilford.

Berberoglu, Berch. 1987. *The Internationalization of Capital: Imperialism and Capitalist Development on a World Scale.* New York: Praeger.

_____. 1992. *The Political Economy of Development.* Albany: State University of New York Press.

_____. 2003. *Globalization of Capital and the Nation-State: Imperialism, Class Struggle, and the State in the*

Age of Global Capitalism. Lanham, MD: Rowman and Littlefield.

_____ (ed.). 2005. *Globalization and Change: The Transformation of Global Capitalism.* Lanham. MD: Lexington Books.

_____. 2007. *The State and Revolution in the Twentieth Century: Major Social Transformations of Our Time.* Lanham, MD: Rowman and Littlefield.

_____. 2009. *Class and Class Conflict in the Age of Globalization.* Lanham, MD: Lexington Books.

Berdegué, Julio, and Alexander Schejtman. 2004. "Pobreza y desarrollo social rural." In Clarisa Hardy, *Equidad y Protección Social: Desafíos de Políticas Sociales en América Latina.* Santiago: LOM Ediciones.

Berger, Mark, and Mark Beeson. 2007. "Miracles of Modernisation and Crises of Capitalism: The World Bank, East Asian Development and Liberal Hegemony." In Moore (ed.), *The World Bank.*

Berik, Günseli, and Yana van der Meulen Rodgers. 2007. "The Debate on Labor Standards and International Trade: Lessons from Cambodia and Bangladesh." Department of Economics Working Paper No. 2007-03, University of Utah.

Bernstein, Henry. 2000. "'The Peasantry' in *Global Capitalism: Who, Where and Why?*" In L. Panitch and C. Leys (eds.), Socialist Register 37. London: Merlin Press.

_____. 2002. "Land Reform: Taking a Long(er) View." *Journal of Agrarian Change* 2(4): 433–63.

_____. 2004. "Changing before our Very Eyes: Agrarian Questions and the Politics of Land in Capitalism Today." *Journal of Agrarian Change* 4 (1–2): 190–225.

_____. 2005. "Development Studies and the Marxists." In Uma Kothari (ed.), *A Radical History of Development Studies.* London: Zed Press.

_____. 2007. "Structural Adjustment and African Agriculture." In Moore (ed.), *The World Bank,* Chap 11.

_____. 2008. "Agrarian Questions from Transition to Globalization." In A.H. Akram-Lodhi and C. Kay (ed.), *Peasants and Globalization: Political Economy, Rural Transformation and the Agrarian Question.* London/New York: Routledge.

Bernstein, H., and L. Campling. 2006. "Commodity Studies and Commodity Fetishism 2: Profits with Principle?" *Journal of Agrarian Change* 6 (3): 414–47.

Bernstein, H., B. Crow, and H. Johnson (eds.). 1992. *Rural Livelihoods: Crises And Responses.* Oxford: Oxford University Press.

Berry, Albert, and John Serioux. 2004. "World Economic Growth and Income Distribution 1980–2000." In K.S. Jomo and Jacques Baudot (eds.), *Key Issues in Development.*

Bessell, S. 2001. "Social Capital and Conflict Management: Rethinking the Issues Using a Gender-Sensitive Lens." In N. Colletta, T. Ghee Lim, and A. Kelles-Viitanen (eds.), *Social Cohesion and Conflict Prevention in Asia.* Washington, DC: World Bank.

Bhavnani, K., J. Foran, and P. Kurian (eds.). 2003. *Feminist Futures: Re-imagining Women, Culture and Development.* New York: Zed Books.

Bhouraskar, D. 2007. *United Nations Development Aid: A Study in History and Politics.* New Delhi: Academic Foundation.

BID. 2006. *Las remesas como instrumento del Desarrollo.* Washington: BID.

Biekart, Kees. 1996. "Strengthening Intermediary Roles in Civil Society: Experiences from Central America." In Andrew Clayton (ed.), *NGOs, Civil Society and the State: Building Democracy in Transitional Societies.* Oxford: International NGO Training and Research Centre (INTRAC).

Biel, R. 2000. *The New Imperialism: Crisis and Contradictions in North/South Relations.* London: Zed Books.

Bieler, A., I. Lundberg, and Devan Pillay (eds.). 2008. *Labour and the Challenges of Globalization: What Prospect for Transnational Solidarity?* London: Pluto Press.

Bienefeld, Manfred. 1988. "In Defence of 'Nationalism' from a Trade Union Perspective." In R. Southall (ed.), *Trade Unions and the New Industrialisation of the Third World.* London: Zed Books.

_____. 1991. "Karl Polanyi and the Contradictions of the 1980s." In M. Mendell and D. Salée (eds.), *The Legacy of Karl Polanyi.* New York: St.Martin's.

_____. 1993a. "Financial Liberalization: Disarming the Nation State." In M. Bienefeld, J. Jenson and R. Mahon (eds.), *Production, Space, Identity*. Toronto: Canadian Scholars Press.

_____. 1993b. "The New World Order: Echoes of a New Imperialism." *Third World Quarterly*.

_____. 1994. "Capitalism and the Nation State." In L. Panitch (ed.), *The Globalization Decade*. Halifax, NS: Fernwood Publishing

_____. 2000. "Globalization and Social Change: Drowning in the Icy Waters of Commercial Calculation." *Development Research Series Working Paper* No. 80, Aalborg University, Research Centre on Development and International Relations.

Birdsall, Nancy. 1997. "On Growth And Poverty Reduction: Distribution Matters." Remarks at the Conference on Poverty Reduction, Harvard Institute For International Development, February. Available at <http://www.famousquotes.me.uk/speeches/Nancy-Birdsall/index.htm>.

Blackburn, Robin. 1998. *The Making of New World Slavery*. London: Verso.

Blaikie, Piers. 1985. *The Political Economy of Soil Erosion*. Methuen.

Blakie, Piers, and Harold Brookfield. 1987. *Land Degradation and Society*. Boston: Methuen.

Blecher, Marc. 2005. "Inequality and Capitalism in China." Paper prepared for the American Political Science Association Task Force, Conference on Inequality and Difference in the Third World.

Boeger, Andrew. 1997. "Struggling for Emancipation: Tungsten Miners and the Bolivian Revolution." In Jonathan C. Brown (ed.), *Workers' Control in Latin America, 19301979*. Chapel Hill: University of North Carolina Press.

Boisier, Sergio. 2005. "Is There Room for Local Development in a Globalized World?" CEPAL *Review* 86, August.

Boisier, Sergio, et al. 1992. *La descentralización: el eslabón perdido de la cadena transformación productiva con equidad y sustentabilidad*. Santiago: Cuadernos de CEPAL.

Bolivia. 1994. *Ley No. 1551 de Participación Popular*. La Paz.

Bond, Patrick. 2004. "Decommodification and Deglobalization: Strategic Challenges for African Social Movements." *Afriche e Oriente* 7 (4).

_____. 2006. *Looting Africa: The Economics of Exploitation*. London: Zed Books.

_____. 2007. "Civil Society and Wolfowitz's World Bank: Reform or Rejection?" In Moore (ed.), *The World Bank*.

Borón, Atilio. 2007. "El mito del desarrollo capitalista nacional en la nueva coyuntura política de América Latina." *Rebelión* February 18.

Borras, Saturnino Jr. 2007. *Pro-Poor Land Reform: A Critique*. Ottawa: University of Ottawa Press.

Borras, Saturnino Jr., Marc Edelman, and Cristóbal Kay (eds.). 2008. "Transnational Agrarian Movements Confronting Globalization." *Journal of Agrarian Change* 8 (2–3). All the relevant articles in this special double issue.

Borras, Saturnino Jr., and Jennifer C. Franco. 2008. "Democratic Land Governance: A Framework for Analysis." Oslo: UNDP-Oslo Governance Centre.

_____. 2009. "Transnational Agrarian Movements Struggling for Land and Citizenship Rights." IDS *Working Paper Series*. Brighton: Institute of Development Studies (IDS), University of Sussex.

Borras, Saturnino M. Jr., Cristóbal Kay, and A. Haroon Akram-Lodhi. 2007. "Agrarian Reform and Rural Development: Historical Overview and Current Issues." In A.H. Akram-Lodhi, S.M. Borras Jr. and C. Kay (eds.), *Land, Poverty and Livelihoods in an Era of Globalization: Perspectives from Developing and Transition Countries*. London: Routledge.

Borras, Saturnino Jr., Cristóbal Kay, and Edward Lahiff (eds.). 2008. *Market-Led Agrarian Reform: Critical Perspectives on Neoliberal Land Policies and the Rural Poor*. London: Routledge.

Bose, Christine E., and Edna Acosta-Belén (eds.). 1995. *Women in the Latin American Development Process*. Philadelphia: Temple University Press.

Bowles, P., H. Veltmeyer, et al. (eds.). 2007. *National Perspectives on Globalization*. Vol. 1. *Regional Perspectives on Globalization*, Vol. 2. New York: Palgrave Macmillan.

Bowles, Paul. 2002. "Asia's Post-Crisis Regionalism: Bringing the State Back In, Keeping the (United)

States Out." *Review of International Political Economy* 9 (2): 230–56.

_____. 2008. "Globalization: A Taxonomy of Theoretical Approaches." In H. Veltmeyer (ed.), *New Perspectives on Globalization and Antiglobalization: Prospects for a New World Order*. Ashgate.

Bowman, Betsy, and Bob Stone. 2005. "Cooperativization as Alternative to Globalizing Capitalism." San Miguel de Allende: Global Justice Centre.

_____. 2007. "Can Grameen-Style Microcredit Eliminate Poverty?" San Miguel de Allende: Global Justice Centre.

Boyd, Rosalind (ed.). 1998. Special Issue on "Workers and Borders in the Context of Regional Blocs: NAFTA, APEC and EU." *Labour, Capital and Society* 1–2.

_____. 2006. "Labour's Response to the Informalization of Work in the Current Restructuring of Global Capitalism: China, South Korea, and South Africa." *Canadian Journal of Development Studies* 27 (4): 487–502.

Boyd, Rosalind, Robin Cohen, and Peter C.W. Gutkind (eds.). 1987. *International Labour and the Third World: The Making of a New Working Class*. Aldershot, UK: Avebury.

Boyer, R., and D. Drache. 1996. *States Against Markets: The Limits of Globalization*. London: Routledge.

Bratton, Michael, and Nicholas Can de Walle. 1997. *Democratic Experiments in Africa: Regime Transitions in Comparative Perspective*. Cambridge: Cambridge University Press.

Brecher, Jeremy, and Tim Costello. 1994. *Global Village or Global Pillage*. Boston: South End Press.

Breman, Jan. 2000. "Labour and Landlessness in South and South-East Asia." In Deborah Bryceson, Cristóbal Kay and Jos Mooij (eds.), *Disappearing Peasantries? Rural Labour in Africa, Asia and Latin America*. London: Intermediate Technology Publications.

_____. 2001. "An Informalized Labour System: End of Labour Market Dualism." *Economic and Political Weekly* 36 (52): 4804–21.

Brenner, Robert, and Mark Glick. 1991. "The Regulation School and the West's Economic Impasse." *New Left Review* 188.

Breslin, Shaun. 2007. *China and the Global Political Economy*. London: Palgrave Macmillan.

Breslin, Shaun, et al. (eds.). 2002. *New Regionalisms in the Global Political Economy*. London: Routledge.

Briggs, John. 2005. "The Use of Indigenous Knowledge in Development: Problems and Challenges." *Progress in Development Studies* 5, 2: 99–114.

Briggs, John, and Joanne Sharp. 2004. "Indigenous Knowledges and Development: A Postcolonial Caution." *Third World Quarterly* 25, 4: 661–76.

Broad, Robin. 2007. "Knowledge Management: A Case Study of the World Bank's Research Department." *Development in Practice* 17(4–5): 700–08.

_____. 2008. "Development Wars: Market Fundamentalism Meets the Alter-Globalization Movement." ISA Meeting, San Francisco.

Brocklesby, M.A., and E. Fisher. 2003. "Community Development in Sustainable Livelihoods Approaches: An Introduction." *Community Development Journal* 38 (3): 185–97.

Bromley, Daniel, and Michael Cernea. 1989. "Introduction: The Growing Interest in Common Property." *The Management of Common Property Natural Resources: Some Conceptual and Operational Fallacies*. Washington, DC: World Bank.

Brown, Jonathan C. 1997. "What is Workers' Control?" In Jonathan C. Brown (ed.), *Workers' Control in Latin America, 1930–1979*. Chapel Hill: University of North Carolina Press.

Brown, Lester. 1981. *Building a Sustainable Society*. New York: W.W. Norton.

Brown, M.B. 1995. *Africa's Choices After Thirty Years of the World Bank*. Harmondsworth: Penguin Books.

Bryant, Raymond, and Sinead Bailey. 1997. "Access, Livelihoods and Enclosure." In R. Bryant and S. Bailey, *Third World Political Ecology*. London/New York: Routledge.

Bryceson, Deborah. 2000. "Peasant Theories and Smallholder Policies: Past and Present." In D. Bryceson, Cristóbal Kay and Jos Mooij (eds.), *Disappearing Peasantries? Rural Labour in Africa, Asia and Latin America*. London: ITDG Publishing and Practical Action Publishing.

Buckland, Jerry. 2004. "The Technology Treadmill." In *Ploughing Up The Farm: Neoliberalism, Modern Technology and the State of The World's Farmers*. Black Point, NS and Winnipeg, MB: Fernwood Publishing.

Buckley, Ross P. 2002/03. "The Rich Borrow and the Poor Repay: The Fatal Flaw in International Finance." *World Policy Journal* XIX (4).

Budlender, Debbie. 2000. "The Political Economy of Women's Budgets in the South." *World Development* 28 (7): 1365–78.

Budlender, Debbie, Diane Elson, Guy Hewitt and Tanni Mukhopadhyay. 2002. *Gender Budgets Make Cents*. Ottawa: International Development Research Centre. <http://www.internationalbudget.org/resources/library/GBMC.pdf>

Bulmer-Thomas, Victor. 1986. *The New Economic Model in Latin America and its Impact on Income Distribution and Power*. New York: St. Martin's Press.

_____. 2005. "The Wider Caribbean in the 20th Century: A Long Developmental Perspective." In Dennis Pantin (ed.), *The Caribbean Economy: A Reader*. Kingston, Jamaica: Ian Randell Publishers.

Bunker, Stephen, and Paul Ciccantell. 2005. *Globalization and the Race for Resources*. Baltimore: Johns Hopkins Press.

Burgwal, Gerrit. 1990. "An Introduction to the Literature on Urban Movements in Latin America." In Willem Assies, Gerrit Burgwal and Ton Salman, *Structures of Power, Movements of Resistance*. Amsterdam: CEDLA.

Burkett, Paul. 1990. "Poverty Crisis in the Third World: The Contradictions of World Bank Policy." *Monthly Review* 42, 7 (December): 20–31.

_____. 2005. "Entropy in Ecological Economics: A Marxist Intervention." *Historical Materialism* 13 (1): 117–52.

_____. 2006. "Two Stages of Ecosocialism? Implications of Some Neglected Analyses of Ecological Conflict and Crisis." *International Journal of Political Economy* 35 (3): 3–28.

Burkett, Paul, and Joao Aguiar. 2007. "Capital and Nature: An Interview with Paul Burkett." *Monthly Review MRZine* <http://mrzine.monthlyreview.org/aguiar240407.html>.

Burkey, Stan. 1993. *People First: A Guide to Self-Reliant, Participatory Rural Development*. London: Zed Books.

Buron, R. 1966. "Some Basic Realities of Development Assistance." *International Affairs* (Royal Institute of International Affairs) 42(1): 55–60.

Burris, Val. 1988. "New Directions in Class Analysis." *Critical Sociology* 15 (1), Spring.

Byres Terence J. 2004a. "Neoclassical Neopopulism 25 Years On: Déjà Vu and Déjà Passé. Towards a Critique." *Journal of Agrarian Change* 4 (1–2): 17–44.

_____. 2004b. "Introduction: Contextualizing and Interrogating the GKI Case for Redistributive Land Reform." *Journal of Agrarian Change* 4 (1–2): 1–16.

Byrne, B. 1996. *Gender, Conflict and Development*. Vols. I-II. Report prepared for the Netherlands Ministry of Foreign Affairs, Institute of Development Studies, Brighton.

Cabral, A. 1974. *Return to the Source: Selected Speeches of Amilcar Cabral*. New York: Monthly Review Press.

Caldeira, Teresa. 2001. *City of Walls: Crime, Segregation, and Citizenship in São Paulo*. Berkeley: University of California Press.

Callinicos, Alex. 1987. *Making History: Agency, Structure and Change in Social Theory*. Cambridge: Polity Press.

Cambridge Review of International Affairs. 2000. Special issue on "Globalization." Articles by Desai, Gen, Sklair, Lal, Petras and Veltmeyer.

Cammack, Paul. 2002. "Neoliberalism, the World Bank and the New Politics of Development." In Uma Kothari and Martin Minogue (eds.), *Development Theory and Practice: Critical Perspectives*. Basingstoke: Palgrave Macmillan

_____. 2006. "UN Imperialism: Unleashing Entrepreneurship in the Developing World." In C. Mooers (ed.), *The New Imperialists: Ideologies of Empire*. Oxford, UK: Oneworld Publications.

Cardoso, F.H. 1972. "Dependency and Development in Latin America." *New Left Review* 74.

Cardoso, F.H., and E. Faletto. 1979. *Dependency and Development in Latin America*. Berkeley and Los Angeles: University of California Press.

Caringella-MacDonald, Susan, and Drew Humphries. 1991. "Battering Women and Battering Central Americans: A Peacemaking Synthesis." In Harold E. Pepinsky and Richard Quinney (eds.), *Criminology as Peacemaking*. Bloomington: Indiana University Press

Carrothers, T. 1999. *Aiding Democracy Abroad*. Washington, DC: Brookings Institution (critical assessment of U.S. democracy assistance).

Cartledge, Paul. 2006. *Thermopylae: The Battle that Changed the World*. New York: Overlook Press.

Casanova, González P. 1965. "Internal Colonialism and National Development." *Studies in Comparative International Development* 1 (4): 27–37. Available in Spanish.

Castells, Manuel. 2000. *The Rise of the Network Society. The Information Age: Economy, Society and Culture*. Vol. 1. Malden: Blackwell.

_____. 2001. *The Internet Galaxy: Reflections on the Internet Business and Society*. Oxford: Oxford University Press.

_____. 2006. "Changer la Ville: A Rejoinder." *International Journal of Urban and Regional Research* 30 (1): 219–23.

Castles, S. 2008. "Development and Migration — Migration and Development: What Comes First?' Social Science Research Council Conference: Migration and Development: Future Directions for Research and Policy, 28 February–1 March. New York City.

Castles, S., and R. Delgado Wise (eds.). 2008. *Migration and Development: Perspectives from the South*. Geneva: IOM.

Castles, S. and M. Miller. 2008. *The Age of Migration*. Fourth edition. Basingstoke: Palgrave MacMillan.

Castree, Noel. 2006. "Commentary: From Neoliberalism to Neoliberalisation: Consolations, Analytical and Political tools for Building Survivable Futures." In Noel Castree and Bruce Braun (eds.), *Remaking Reality: Nature at the Millennium*. London: Routledge.

Cavanagh, John, and Jerry Mander. 2004a. *Alternatives to Economic Globalization*. San Francisco: Brett Koehler Publishers.

_____ (eds.). 2004b. "'New International Structures' Global Governance." In *Alternatives to Economic Globalization*. San Francisco: Berrett Koehler.

Cederlöf, G., and K. Sivaramakrishnan (eds.). 2005. *Ecological Nationalisms: Nature, Livelihoods and Identities*. Florham Park, NJ: Washington Press.

Chambers, Robert. 1987. *Sustainable Rural Livelihoods: A Strategy for People, Environment and Development*. Brighton: IDS, University of Sussex.

_____. 1988. *Poverty in India: Concepts, Measurement and Reality*. IDS Working Paper No 241. Brighton: IDS

_____. 1997. *Whose Reality Counts? Putting the First Last*. London: ITDG Publishing.

Chambers, Robert, and Gordon Conway. 1998. "Sustainable Rural Livelihoods: Some Working Definitions." *Development* 41 (3).

Chan, Yu Ping. 2001. "Democracy or Bust? The Development Dilemma." *Harvard International Review* Fall.

Chandra, Bipan. 1975. "The Indian Capitalist Class and Imperialism before 1947." *Journal of Contemporary Asia* 5 (3).

Chang, Ha-Joon. 1998. "Globalization, Transnational Corporations and Economic Development." In D. Baker, G. Epstein and R. Pollin (eds.), *Globalization and Progressive Economic Policy*. Cambridge: Cambridge University Press.

_____. 2003a. "The East Asian Development Experience." In Ha-Joon Chang (ed.), *Rethinking Development Economics*. London: Anthem.

_____. 2003b. "The Market, The State and Institutions in Economic Development." In Ha-Joon Chan (ed.), *Rethinking Development Economics*. London: Anthem Press.

_____. 2006. *Kicking Away the Ladder: Development Strategy in Historical Perspective*. London: Anthem Press.

_____. 2007a. "Is Free Trade Always the Answer?" In *Bad Samaritans: Rich Nations, Poor Policies, and the Threat to the Developing World*. London: Random House.

_____. 2007b. "Man Exploits Man-Private Enterprise Good, Public Enterprise Bad?" In *Bad Samaritans: Rich Nations, Poor Policies, and the Threat to the Developing World*. London: Random House.

_____. 2008. *Bad Samaritans: The Myth of Free Trade and the Secret History of Capitalism*. New York: Bloomsbury Press.

Chang, Ha-Joon, and Ilene Grabel. 2001. *Reclaiming Development: An Alternative Policy Manual*.

Chase-Dunn, Christopher. 2007. "The World Revolution of 20xx." Institute for Research on World-Systems, University of California, Riverside, CA. <www.irows.ucr.edu>.

Chase-Dunn, Christopher, and B. Gills. 2005. "Waves of Globalization and Resistance in the Capitalist World-System." In Richard Applebaum and William Robinson (eds.), *Critical Globalization Studies*. New York and London: Routledge.

Chatterjee, Partha. 2004. *The Politics of the Governed: Reflections on Popular Politics in Most of the World*. Princeton and Oxford: Princeton University Press.

Chattopadhyay, Paresh. 1987. "Labour and Development." In Boyd et al. (eds.), *International Labour and the Third World: The Making of a New Working Class*.

Chávez, Hugo. 2005. *Understanding the Venezuelan Revolution: Hugo Chávez Talks to Marta Harnecker*. New York: Monthly Review Press.

Chibber, Vivek. 2005. "Reviving the Developmentalist State? The Myth of the National Bourgeoisie." *Socialist Register*.

Chilcote, Ronald H. (ed.). 1982. *Dependency and Marxism: Toward a Resolution of the Debate*. Boulder, CO: Westview Press.

Chomsky, Noam. 1998. *Profit over People: Neoliberalism and Global Order: Doctrine and Reality*. London: Seven Stories Press.

_____. 2003. *Hegemony or Survival: America's Quest for Global Dominance*. London: Hamish Hamilton.

Chopra, K., G. Kadekodi, and M. Murty. 1990. *Participatory Development*. London: Sage.

Chossudovsky, Michel. 1997. *The Globalization of Poverty: Impacts of IMF and World Bank Reforms*. London: Zed Books.

Christensen, Thomas. 2006. "Fostering Stability or Creating a Monster? The Rise of China and US Policy Toward East Asia." *International Security* 31, 1 (Summer): 81–126.

Chronic Poverty Research Centre. 2004. *The Chronic Poverty Report 2004/5*. University of Manchester, Chronic Poverty Research Centre <www. chronicpoverty.org>.

Clapham, C. 1992. "The Collapse of Socialist Development in the Third World." *Third World Quarterly* 13 (1): 13–25.

Clapp, J., and P. Dauverge. 2005. *Paths to a Greener World: the Political Economy of the Global Environment*. Cambridge/London: MIT Press.

Cleaver, Frances. 2002. "Men and Masculinities." In I.F. Cleaver (ed.), *Masculinities Matter: Men, Gender and Development*.

Cliffe, Lionel, and John S. Saul. 1972. *Socialism in Tanzania: An Interdisciplinary Reader*.

Clow, Michael. 1992. "Ecological Exhaustion and the Crisis of Global Capitalism." *Our Generation* 23 (1).

_____. 1994. "Making Red and Green Complementary." In Jessie Vorst, Ross Dobson and Ron Fletcher (eds.), *Green on Red: Evolving Ecological Socialism*. Halifax: Fernwood Publishing.

Club of Rome. 1972. *The Limits to Growth*. Universe Books.

Cohen, J.M., and N.T. Uphoff. 1977. *Rural Development Participation: Concepts and Measure for Project Design, Implementation and Evaluation*. Ithaca, NY: Cornell University, Centre for International Studies.

Cohen, Robin. 2004. "Chinese Cockle-pickers, the Transnational Turn and Everyday Cosmopolitanism:

Reflections on the New Global Migrants." *Labour, Capital and Society* 1–2.

Colburn, F.D., and D. Rahmato. 1992. "Rethinking socialism in the Third World." *Third World Quarterly* 13 (1): 159–73.

Collier, Paul. 2003. "Breaking the Conflict Trap: Civil War and Development Policy." *World Bank Policy Research Reports.* Washington, DC: World Bank.

_____. 2004. "Aid, Policy and Growth in Post-Conflict Situations." *European Economic Review* 48: 1125–45.

_____. 2007. *The Bottom Billion.* Oxford: Oxford University Press.

Collins, Chuck, Chris Hartman, and Holly Sklar. 1999. "Divided Decade: Economic Disparity at the Century's Turn." *United for a Fair Economy,* Economic Policy Institute Report, December 15.

Coombs, P.H., and M. Ahmed. 1974. *Attacking Rural Poverty: How Non-formal Education Can Help.* Baltimore: Johns Hopkins University Press.

Corbridge, S. 2007. "The (Im)possibility of Development Studies." *Economy and Society* 36 (2): 179–211.

Cordesman, Anthony, and Khalid al-Rodhan. 2006. *The Global Oil Market: Risks and Uncertainties.* Washington, DC: CSIS Press (Centre for Strategic and International Studies).

Cornia, A. 2003. "Globalization and the Distribution of Income Between and Within Countries." In Ha-Joon Chang (ed.), *Rethinking Development Economics.* London: Anthem Press.

Cornia, Andrea, Richard Jolly, and Frances Stewart (eds.). 1987. *Adjustment with a Human Face.* Oxford: Oxford University Press.

Cornia, Giovanni, and Sampsa Kiiski. 2001. "Trends in Income Distribution in the Post-World War II Period Evidence and Interpretation." Working Papers UNU-WIDER Research Paper, World Institute for Development Economic Research (UNU-WIDER).

Cowen, M., and R. Shenton. 1995. *Doctrines of Development.* London: Routledge.

Cox, R. 1987. *Production, Power, and World Order: Social Forces in the Making of History.* New York: Columbia University Press.

_____. 2001. "Civil Society at the Turn of the Millennium: Prospects for an Alternative World Order." *Review of International Studies* 25 (1): 3–28.

Craig, D., and D. Porter. 2006. *Development Beyond Neoliberalism? Governance, Poverty Reduction and Political Economy.* Abingdon Oxon: Routledge.

Crandall, M. 2006. *Energy, Economics, and Politics in the Caspian Region: Dreams and Realities.* Westport, CT: Praeger Security International.

Cravey, A. 1998. *Women and Work in Mexico's Maquiladoras.* Lanham, MD: Rowan and Littlefield.

Crewe, W., and E. Harrison. 2002. *Whose Development? An Ethnography of Aid.* London: Zed Books.

Crouch, C., and A. Pizzorno. 1978. *Resurgence of Class Conflict in Western Europe Since 1968.* London: Holmes and Meier.

Crush, J. (ed.). 1995. *Power of Development.* London: Routledge.

Culpeper, R. 2002. "Approaches to Globalization and Inequality within the International System." Improving Knowledge on Social Development project. Geneva, UNRISD <www.nsi-ins.ca>.

Cypher, J. 2007. "Shifting Developmental Paradigms in Latin America: Is Neoliberalism History?" In Esteban Pérez and Matías Vernengo (eds.), *Ideas, Policies and Economic Development in the Americas.* London: Routledge.

Cypher, J., and R. Delgado Wise. 2007. "Subordinate Economic Integration Through the Labour-Export Model: A Perspective from Mexico." In P. Bowles, H. Veltmeyer, et al. (eds.), *National Perspectives on Globalization.* New York: Palgrave Macmillan.

Cypher, J.M., and J. Dietz. 2008a. "Transnational Corporations and Economic Development." In *The Process of Economic Development.* Third edition. London: Routledge.

_____. 2008b. "The State as a Potential Agent of Transformation: From Neoliberalism to Embedded Autonomy." In *The Process of Economic Development.* Third edition. London: Routledge.

Daly, Herman. 1996. *Beyond Growth.* Boston: Beacon Press.

Daly, Herman E, John B. Cobb, and Clifford W. Cobb. 1989. *For the Common Good: Redirecting the Economy toward Community, the Environment, and a Sustainable Future.* Boston: Beacon Press

Dangl, Benjamin. 2007. *The Price of Fire: Resource Wars and Social Movements in Bolivia.* AK Press.

Dasgupta, Biplab. 1998. *Structural Adjustment, Trade and the New Political Economy.* London: Zed Books.

Davidson, Basil. 1969. *Africa in History: Themes and Outlines.* London: Macmillan.

Daviron, B., and S. Ponte. 2005. *The Coffee Paradox: Global Markets, Commodity Trade and the Elusive Promise of Development.* London: Zed Books.

Davis, Mike. 2002a. *The Late Victorian Holocaust.* London: Verso.

_____. 2002b. *The Origins of the Third World: Markets, states and climate.* Dorset, UK: The Corner House (Cornerhouse Briefing Papers; 27). <http://www.thecornerhouse.org.uk /pdf/briefing/ 27origins. pdf>.

_____. 2004. "Planet of Slums: Urban Involution and the Informal Proletariat." *New Left Review* 26: 5–34.

_____. 2006. *Planet of Slums.* New York: Verso.

DAWN. 1995. "Rethinking Social Development: DAWN's Vision." *World Development* 23 (11): 2001–04.

Dawson, Michael, and John Bellamy Foster. 1998. "Virtual Capitalism." In R.W. McChesney, E. Meiksins Wood and J.B. Foster (eds.), *Capitalism and the Information Age.* New York: Monthly Review Press.

De Hass, H. 2007. "Migration and Development: A Theoretical Perspective." Paper at the conference Transnationalisation and Development(s); Towards a North-South Perspective, Bielefeld University, Bielefeld, Germany, May 31–June 1.

De Janvry, Alain. 1981. *The Agrarian Question and Reformism in Latin America.* Baltimore: Johns Hopkins University Press.

De Soto, Hernando. 1989. *The Other Path: The Invisible Revolution in the Third World.* Harper Collins.

_____. 2000. *The Mystery of Capital: Why Capitalism Triumphs in the West and Fails Everywhere Else.* Basic Books.

Deaton, Angus, and Valerie Kozel (eds.). 2005. *The Great Indian Poverty Debate.* Delhi: Macmillan India. (See Abhijit Sen and Himanshu, "Poverty and Inequality in India," and Angus Deaton and Jean Dreze, "Poverty and Inequality in India: A Re-Examination.")

Degnbol-Martinussen, J., and P. Engberg-Pedersen. 2003. *Aid: Understanding International Development Cooperation.* London: Zed Books.

Deininger, J., and L. Squire. 1998. "New Ways of Looking at Old Issues: Inequality and Growth." *Journal of Development Economics* 57 (2): 259–87.

Deininger, Klaus. 1999. "Making Negotiated Land Reform Work: Initial Experience from Colombia, Brazil and South Africa." *World Development* 27 (4): 651–72.

Deininger, Klaus, and Hans Binswanger. 1999. "The Evolution of the World Bank's Land Policy: Principles, Experience and Future Challenges." *The World Bank Research Observer* 14 (2): 247–76.

Delgado-Wise, R., and H. Márquez. 2008. "Towards a New Theoretical Approach to Understanding the Relationship between Migration and Development." *Social Analysis.* Special Issue coordinated by Nina Glick-Schiller.

Della Buono, R.A., and José Bell Lara (eds.). 2007. *Imperialism, Neoliberalism and Social Struggles in Latin America.* Leiden/Boston: Brill.

Dercon, S. 2006. "Poverty Measurement." In D. Clark (ed.), *The Elgar Companion to Development Studies.* Cheltenham, UK/Northampton MA: Edward Elgar.

Desai, Meghdad. 2000. "Globalization: Neither Ideology nor Utopia." *Cambridge Review of International Affairs* Autumn-Winter, XI (1).

Desmarais, Annette. 2002. "La Vía Campesina: Consolidating an International Peasant and Farm Movement." *Journal of Peasant Studies* 29 (2): 91–124.

_____. 2007. *La Vía Campesina: Globalization and Power of Peasants.* Halifax and London: Fernwood Publishing and Pluto Books.

Detienne, Marcel. 2007. *The Greeks and Us: A Comparative Anthropology of Ancient Greece.* Cambridge:

Polity Press.

Development. Cape Coast: Marcel Hughes Publicity Group.

Dinerstein, Ana Cecelia. 2002. "The Battle of Buenos Aires: Crisis, Insurrection and the Reinvention of Politics in Argentina." *Historical Materialism* 10 (4): 5–38.

Doner, R., et al. 2005. "Systemic Vulnerability and the Origins of Developmental States: Northeast and Southeast Asia in Comparative Perspective." *International Organization* 59 (2): 327–61.

Douglass, M. 2000. "Mega-Urban Regions and World City Formation: Globalization, the Economic Crisis and Urban Policy Issues in Pacific Asia." *Urban Studies* 37(12): 2315–35.

Drew, Allison. 1969. "The Theory and Practice of the Agrarian Question in South African Socialism, 1928–1960." In Henry Bernstein (ed.), *The Agrarian Question in South Africa.* London: Frank Cass and Co.

Dreze, Jean, and Amartya Sen. 2002. *India: Development and Participation.* Oxford: Oxford University Press.

Duffield, Mark. 2001. *Governance and the New Wars: The Merging of Development and Security.* London: Zed.

Duménil, Gérard, and D. Lévy. 2002. "The Nature and Contradictions of Neoliberalism." In Panitch et al. (eds.) *The Globalization Decade.* Halifax, NS: Fernwood Publishing.

Dunford, Michael. 2007. "Structuralist Marxism, Urban Sociology and Geography: Reflections on Urban Sociology: Critical Essays." <http://www.geog.susx.ac.uk /research/ eggd/ege/pdf/URBANSOC. pdf>.

Durand-Lasserve, Alain, and Lauren Royston (eds.). 2002. *Holding their Ground: Secure Land Tenure for the Urban Poor in Developing Countries*: London: Earthscan.

Durston, J. 1998. "Building Social Capital in Rural Communities (Where it Doesn't Exist): Theoretical and Policy Implications of Peasant Empowerment in Chiquimula Guatemala." Santiago: ECLAC.

_____. 2001. "Social Capital — Part of the Problem, Part of the Solution: Its Role in the Persistence and Overcoming of Poverty in Latin America and the Caribbean." Santiago: ECLAC.

Dyer, Gwynne. 2004. *Future Tense: The Coming World Order.* Toronto: McClelland and Stewart.

Eade, Deborah, and Alan Leather (eds.). 2005. *Development, NGOs and Labor Unions: Terms of Engagement.* Bloomfield, CT: Kumarian Press.

Easterly, William. 2002. "The Failure of Economic Development." *Challenge* January-February: 88–103.

_____. 2006. *The White Man's Burden: Why the West's Efforts to Aid the Rest Have Done So Much Ill and So Little Good.* Penguin Press.

ECLAC. 1990. *Productive Transformation with Equity.* Santiago, Chile.

_____. 2006? *Globalization and Development.* Santiago: United Nations.

_____, 2010. *Public Policies for the Information Society: A Shared Vision?* Santiago: ECLAC, Programme for the Information Society in the Caribbean. March.

Edelman, M. 2003. "Transnational Peasant and Farmer Movements and Networks." In M. Kaldor, H. Anheier and M. Glasius (eds.), *Global Civil Society.* Oxford: Oxford University Press.

Edwards, Michael. 1993. "The Irrelevance of Development." In F. Schuurman (ed.), *The Development Impasse.* London: Zed Books.

_____. 2006. "Enthusiasts, Tacticians and Sceptics: Social Capital and the Structures of Power." In Bebbington, et al.

Egan, D., and L. Chorbajian (eds.). 2005. *Power: A Critical Reader.* Prentice Hall.

Ehrlich. 1968. *The Population Bomb.* New York: Sierra Club-Ballantine Book.

Ekins, Paul. 2000. "The Limits to Growth Debate." *Economic Growth and Environmental Sustainability: The Prospects for Green Growth.* London/New York: Routledge.

Ellis, F. 2000. *Rural Livelihoods and Diversity in Developing Countries.* Oxford: Oxford University Press.

Ellner, Steve. 2005. "Revolutionary and Non-Revolutionary Paths of Radical Populism: Directions of the *Chavista* Movement in Venezuela." *Science and Society* 69 (2), April: 160–90.

Ellwood. 2001. *The No-Nonsense Guide to Globalization.* New Internationalist.

Elson, Diane (ed.). 1990. *Male Bias in the Development Process.* Manchester: Manchester University Press.

_____. 2004. "Engendering Government Budgets in the Context of Globalization(s)." *International Feminist Journal of Politics* 6 (4): 623–42.

Elson, Diane, and Nilüfer Cagatay. 2000. "The Social Content of Macroeconomic Policies." *World Development* 29 (7): 1347–64.

Elson, Diane, and Ruth Pearson. 1981. "Nimble Fingers Make Cheaper Workers: An Analysis of Women's Employment in Third World Export Manufacturing." *Feminist Review* 7: 87–108.

Engdahl, William. 2004. *A Century of War: Anglo-American Politics and the New World Order.* London: Pluto Press.

_____. 2007. "Seeds of Destruction: The Hidden Agenda of Genetic Manipulation." *Global Research* July 10 <www.globalresearch.ca>.

Enzensberger, H.M. 1974. "A Critique of Political Ecology." *New Left Review* I/84/

Escobar, A. 1995. "Imagining a Postdevelopment Era." In J. Crush (ed.), *The Power of Development.* London: Routledge.

_____. 1996. "Construction Nature: Elements for a Post-Structuralist Political Ecology." *Futures* 28 (4): 325–43.

_____. 1997. "Unmasking Development." In M. Rahnema and V. Bawtree (eds.), *The Postdevelopment Reader.* London: Zed Books.

_____. 1998. "Whose Knowledge, Whose Nature? Biodiversity, Conservation, and the Political Ecology of Social Movements." *Journal of Political Ecology* (5): 53–82.

_____. Espen, Moe. 2006. "War and Development." Paper presented at the annual meeting of ISA, San Diego, March 22.

Esping-Anderson. 1994. *After the Golden Age: the Future of the Welfare State in the new Global Order.* Geneva: UNRISD.

Esteva, G. 1985. "Beware of Participation, and Development: Metaphor, Myth, and Threat." *Development: Seeds of Change* 77–79.

_____. 1987. "Regenerating People's Space." In Saul H. Mendlovitz and R.B.J. Walker (eds.), *Towards a Just World Peace.* London: Butterworths.

_____. 1992. "Development." In W. Sachs (ed.), *The Development Dictionary: A Guide to Knowledge as Power.* London: Zed Books.

Esteva, Gustavo, and Madhu Suri Prakash. 1998. *Grassroots Post-Modernism.* London: Zed Books.

Evans, P. 1992. "The State as Problem and Solution: Predation, Embedded Autonomy and Structural Change." In Stephan Haggard and Robert Kaufman (eds.), *The Politics of Economic Adjustment: International Constraints, Distributive Conflicts and the State.* Princeton, NJ: Princeton University Press.

_____. 1995. *Embedded Autonomy: States and Industrial Transformation.* Princeton University Press.

Fajnzylber, P., and H. López. 2007. *Close to Home: The Development Impact of Remittances in Latin America.* Washington: World Bank.

Faux, Jeffrey. 2005. *The Global Class War.* Wiley.

Feder, Ernest. 1979. "Regeneration and Degeneration of the Peasants: Three Views about the Destruction of the Countryside." *Social Scientist* 7 (7): 3–41.

Federici, Silvia. 1992. "The Debt Crisis, Africa and the New Enclosures." In Midnight Notes Collective (eds.), *Midnight Oil: Work, Energy, War, 1973–1992.* New York: Autonomedia. *Economic Reconstruction from the Bottom Up.* Boston: South End Press.

_____. 2002. "War, Globalization, and Reproduction." <www.nadir.org>.

Feldman, Shelley. 2003. "Paradoxes of Institutionalisation: The Depoliticization of Bangladeshi NGOs." *Development in Practice* 13 (1): 5–26.

Ferguson, James. 1991. *The Anti-Politics Machine: Development, Depoliticization, and Bureaucratic Power in Lesotho.* Minneapolis: University of Minnesota Press.

_____. 2006. *Global Shadows: Africa in the Neoliberal World Order.* Durham: Duke University Press.

Fernandes, L. 2006. "Liberalization, Democracy and Middle Class Politics." In *India's New Middle Class.* Minneapolis/London: University of Minnesota Press.

Fernandes, Sujatha. 2007. "Barrio Women and Popular Politics in Chávez's Venezuela." *Latin American Politics and Society* 49 (3) Fall: 97–127.

Fernando, Judel. 2003. "NGOs and the Production of Indigenous Knowledge Under the Condition of Post-Modernity." *The Annals of American Academy of Political and Social Science* November.

Ferreira, Francisco H.G., and Michael Walton. 2005. "The Inequality Trap: Why Equity Must be Central to Development Policy." *Finance and Development* 42 (4) December: 34–37.

Fforde, Adam. 2009. *Coping with Facts: A Skeptic's Guide to the Problem of Development.* Herndon, VA: Kumarian Press.

Fine, Ben. 2006. "The New Development Economics." In K.S. Jomo and Ben Fine (eds.), *The New Development Economics.* London: Zed Books.

_____. 2007. "The Developmental State is Dead: Long Live Social Capital?" In Moore (ed.), *The World Bank.*

Fitzgerald, E. 1985. "The Problem of Balance in the Peripheral Socialist Economy." *World Development* 13 (1): 5–14.

Flassbeck, Heiner. 2005. "China's Spectacular Growth since the Mid-1990s: Macroeconomic Conditions and Economic Policy Changes." In *China in a Globalizing World.* New York and Geneva: UNCTAD/GDS/MDPB/2005/1. <http://www.unctad.org/en/docs/gdsmdpb20051_en.pdf>.

Flyvberg, Bent. 2001. *Making Social Science Matter: Why Social Inquiry Fails and How It Can Succeed Again.* Cambridge University Press.

Focus on the Global South. 2006. "Revisiting Southeast Asia Regionalism." <http://www.focusweb.org/pdf/ASEAN%20dossier2006-full.pdf>.

Focus on the South. 2004. *The Transfer of Wealth: Debt and the Making of the Global South.* Bangkok.

Foladori, G. 2001. *Controversias sobre sustentabilidad: La coevolución sociedad-naturaleza.* México, DF: Miguel Ángel Porrúa.

_____. 2007. "Environmental Changes and the Perception of Society: The Case of Climate Change." In Pedro Leite da Silva Dias, Wagner Costa Ribeiro, and Luc Hidalgo Nunes (eds.), *A Contribution to Understanding the Regional Impacts of Global Change in South America.* São Paulo: Instituto de Estudos Avançados da Universidade de São Paulo.

Foladori, G., and N. Pierri. 2005. *¿Sustentabilidad? Desacuerdos sobre el desarrollo sustentable.* México: Miguel Ángel Porrúa.

Folbre, Nancy. 1995. "Holding Hands at Midnight: The Paradox of Caring Labor." *Feminist Economics* (1): 73–92.

Forsyth, Tim. 2003. "Political Ecology and the Politics of Environmental Science." *Critical Political Ecology: The Politics of Environmental Science.* London/New York: Routledge.

Foster, John Bellamy. 1993. "Let Them Eat Pollution: Capitalism and the World Environment." *Monthly Review* January.

_____. 1999. *The Vulnerable Planet.* New York: Monthly Review Press.

_____. 2002. *Ecology Against Capitalism.* New York: Monthly Review Press.

_____. 2005. "Organizing Ecological Revolution." *Monthly Review* 57 (5), October. <http://www.monthlyreview.org/1005jbf.htm>.

_____. 2007. "The Renewing of Socialism: An Introduction." *Monthly Review* 57 (3), July–August: 2–18.

Foster, John Bellamy, and Fred Magdoff. 2008. "The Great Financial Crisis: Causes and Consequences." *Monthly Review* December 18.

Fox, J. 2005. "Mapping Mexican Migrant Civil Society." Presented at Mexican Migrant Civic and Political Participation, Woodrow Wilson International Centre for Scholars, co-sponsored by Latin American and Latino Studies Department, University of California, Santa Cruz.

Fox, J., and D. Brooks (eds.). 2003. *Cross-Border Dialogues: Mexico-US Social Movement Networking*. La Jolla: University of California, San Diego, Centre for US-Mexican Studies.

Franco, Jennifer. 2008. "Making Land Rights Accessible: Social Movement Innovation and Political-Legal Strategies in the Philippines." *Journal of Development Studies*.

Frank, André Gunder. 1967. *Capitalism and Underdevelopment in Latin America*. New York: Monthly Review Press.

_____. 1971. *The Sociology of Development and the Underdevelopment of Sociology*. London: Pluto Press.

_____. 1998. *Reorient: Global economy in the Asian Age*. Berkeley: University of California Press.

Freedman, J. (ed.). 2000. *Transforming Development*. Toronto: University of Toronto Press.

Freeman, Carla. 2001. "Is Local: Global as Feminine: Masculine? Rethinking the Gender of Globalization." *Signs* 26 (4); 1007–37 (e-journal).

Freire, P. 1970. *The Pedagogy of the Oppressed*. New York: Continuum.

_____. 1984. *Pedagogy of the Oppressed*. New York: Seabury Press.

Freire, P., and I. Shor. 1987. *A Pedagogy for Liberation*. Massachusetts: Bergin and Garvey Publishers.

Fridell, Gavin. 2007. *Fair Trade Coffee: The Prospects and Pitfalls of Market-Driven Social Justice*. Toronto: University of Toronto Press.

Frieden, Jeffrey. 2006. *Global Capitalism: Its Fall and Rise in the 20th Century*. W.W. Norton.

Friedland, W.H., and C.G. Rosberg, Jr. 1964. *African Socialism*. Stanford: Stanford University Press.

Friedman, Milton. 1962. *Capitalism and Freedom*. Chicago: Chicago University Press.

Friedman, Thomas. 2000. *The Lexus and the Olive Tree*. New York: Random House.

Friedmann, H. 2004. "Feeding the Empire: The Pathologies of Globalized Agriculture." In L. Panitch and C. Leys (eds.), *Socialist Register 2005: The Empire Reloaded*. London: Merlin Press.

Friedmann, John. 1992. *Empowerment: The Politics of Alternative Development*. Oxford, UK: Blackwell.

Fukuda-Parr, Sakiko. 2003. "The Human Development Paradigm: Operationalizing Sen's Ideas on Capabilities." *Feminist Economics* 9 (2): 301–17.

Fukuda-Parr, Sakiko, and A.K. Shiva Kumar (eds.). 2004. *Readings in Human Development Concepts, Measures and Policies for a Development Paradigm*. Oxford: Oxford University Press.

Fung, A, and E.O. Wright. 2003. *Deepening Democracy: Institutional Innovations in Empowered Participatory Governance*. London: Verso. Chaps. by Baiocchi, Heller and Isaac.

Furtado, C. 1964. *Development and Underdevelopment: A Structural View of the Problems of Developed and Underdeveloped Countries*. Berkeley, CA: University of California Press. Portuguese and Spanish versions available.

Gallagher, Kevin P., and Roberto Porzecanski. 2008. "Climbing Up the Technology Ladder? High-Technology Exports in China and Latin America." *Berkeley Centre for LAS Working Paper*. No. 20. <http://escholarship.org/uc/item/5027r0fb?pageNum=28#page-28>.

García Linera, Alvaro. 2006. "El capitalismo andino-amazónico." *Le Monde Diplomatique* (Chile edition). <http://www.lemondediplomatique.cl/El-capitalismo-andino-amazonico.html>.

Garnham, Nicholas. 2004. "Information Society Theory as Ideology." In Frank Webster (ed.), *The Information Society Reader*. London: Routledge.

GCIM. 2005. "Migration in an Interconnected World: New Directions for Action." Report for the Global Commission on International Migration (October 2005). <http://www.gcim.org/attachements/gcim-complete-report-2005.pdf>.

Geertz, Clifford. 1983. *Local Knowledge: Further Essays in Interpretive Anthropology*. New York: Basic Books.

George, Susan. 1998. *A Fate Worse than Debt*. Penguin.

Georgescu-Roegen, Nicholas. 1999. *The Entropy Law and the Economic Process*. Universe Books.

Ghai, Dharam P. (ed.). 2000. *Social Development and Public Policy: A Study of Some Successful Experiences*. St. Martin's Press.

Ghosh, Amitav. 1992. *In an Antique Land: History in the Guise of a Traveler's Tale*. New York: Vintage.

Gill, Stephen. 1995. "Theorising the Interregnum: The Double Movement and Global Politics in the

1990s." In B. Hettne (ed.), *International Political Economy: Understanding Global Disorder*. Halifax: Fernwood Publishing.

Gills, Barry. 1999. "American Power, Neoliberal Globalization and Low Intensity Democracy: An Unstable Trinity?" In Michael Cox, Takashi Inoguchi and John Ikenberry (eds.), *US Democracy Promotion*. Oxford, Oxford University Press.

_____ (ed.). 2000. *Globalization and the Politics of Resistance*. London: Macmillan Press.

_____. (ed.). 2008. *The Global Politics of Globalization: 'Empire' versus 'Cosmopolis.'* London: Routledge. Also in a special issue of *Globalizations* 2 (1), May 2005.

Gills, Barry K., Joel Rocamora, and Richard Wilson (eds.). 1993. *Low Intensity Democracy: Political Power in the New World Order*. London: Pluto. Especially the "Introduction: Low Intensity Democracy" (also available in article form in *Third World Quarterly* 1992).

Giroux, H.A. 1997. *Pedagogy and the Politics of Hope: Theory, Culture and Schooling*. Boulder, CO: Westview Press.

Girvan Norman. 2006. "Caribbean Dependency Thought Revisited." *Canadian Journal of International Studies* XXVII (3): 327–50.

_____. 2007. "Power Imbalances and Development Knowledge." Theme Paper for the Wilton Park Conference on Southern Perspectives on Reform of the International Development Architecture, Ottawa: North-South Institute.

_____. 2009. "ALBA: A Work in Progress." Paper presented at the symposium on "Tranformations: Latin America on the Move," Halifax, October 3.

Globalization and War texts and analysis by author. <www.agp.org/www.all4all.org>.

Glynn, A, A. Hughes, A. Lipietz, and A. Singh. 1990. "The Rise and Fall of the Golden Age." In Stephen Marglin and Juliet Schor (eds.), *The Golden Age of Capitalism: Re-interpreting the Post-War Experience*. Oxford: Clarendon Press.

Goldring, L., S. Henders and P. Vandergeest. 2003. "The Politics of Transnational Ties: Implications for Policy, Research, and Communities." Report submitted to the Department of Foreign Affairs and International Trade. <http://www.yorku.ca/ycar/workshop/workshop_final_report.pdf>.

Goodland, Robert. 1996. "Growth Has Reached its Limit." In Jerry Mander and Edward Goldsmith (eds.), *The Case Against the Global Economy*. San Francisco: Sierra Club Books.

Goody, Jack. 2006. *The Theft of History*. Cambridge University Press.

Gordon, A.A. 1996. *Transforming Capitalism and Patriarchy: Gender and Development in Africa*. Boulder, CO: Lynne Rinner Publishers. Chap 3.

Gore, C. 2000. "The Rise and Fall of the Washington Consensus as a Paradigm for Developing Countries." *World Development* 28 (5): 789–804.

Goudge, P. 2003. *The Whiteness of Power: Racism in Third World Development and Aid*. London: Lawrence and Wishart.

Goulet, Denis. 1989. "Participation in Development: New Avenues." *World Development* 17 (2): 185–78

Gowan, Peter. 1999. *The Global Gamble: Washington's Faustian Bid for World Dominance*. London: Verso.

_____. 2003. "The American Campaign for Global Sovereignty." In Panitch et al.

Gramsci, A. 1971. *Selections from the Prison Notebooks*. London: Lawrence and Wishart.

Grandin, Greg. 2006. *Empire's Workshop*. New York: Metropolitan Books

_____. 2007. *Empire's Workshop: Latin America, the United States and the Rise of the New Imperialism*. American Empire Project.

Green, Duncan. 2003. *Silent Revolution: The Rise and Crisis of Market Economies in Latin America*. New York: Monthly Review Press.

Greenberg, Stephen. 2004. "The Landless People's Movement and the Failure of Post-apartheid Land Reform." Durban: University of KwaZulu-Natal.

Gresh, Alain. 2009. "The West's Selective Reading of Eastern History and Values: From Thermopylae to the Twin Towers." *The Asia-Pacific Journal: Japan Focus* January 1. <http://www.japanfocus.org>.

Grove, R. 1995. *Green Imperialism*. Cambridge: Cambridge University Press..

Guerrero, Dorothy, and Firoze Manji (ed.). 2008. *China's New Role in Africa and the South: A Search for a New Perspective.* Oxford and Nairobi: Pambazuka Press.

Guevara [Che] Ernesto. 1970. *Ernesto Che Guevara. Obras (1957–1967).* Vol. II. Havana: Casa de las Américas.

_____. 2007. "El socialismo y el hombre en Cuba." In Néstor Kohan (ed.), *Introducción al pensamiento socialista.* Bogota: Ocean Sur.

Gugler, Josef. 2004. *World Cities Beyond the West: Globalization, Development and Inequality.* Cambridge University Press.

Gulbenkian Commission. 1996. *Open the Social Sciences: Report of the Gulbenkian Commission on the Restructuring of the Social Sciences.* Stanford, CA: Stanford University Press.

Gumucio, A. 2006. "Knowledge, Communication, Development: A Perspective from Latin America." *Development in Practice* (16).

Hahnel, Robin. 2008. "Against the Market Economy: Advice to Venezuelan Friends." *Monthly Review* 59 (8) January: 11–28.

Hall, Thomas, and Christopher Chase-Dunn. 2006. "Global Social Change in the Long Run." In *Global Social Change: Historical and Comparative Perspectives.* Baltimore: Johns Hopkins University Press.

Hammond, J. 1999. "Popular Education as Community Organizing in El Salvador." *Latin American Perspectives* 26 (4): 69–94.

Han, Dongfang. 2005. "Chinese Labour Struggles." *New Left Review* 34 (July-August): 65–85.

Hanieh, Adam. 2009. "Making the World's Poor Pay: The Economic Crisis and the Global South." *The Bullet* 155. <http://www.socialistproject.ca/bullet/bullet155.html>.

Haque, Shamsul. 1999. *Restructuring Development Theories and Policies: A Critical Study.* Albany, NY: State University of New York Press.

Hallward, Peter. 2007. *Damning the Flood: Haiti, Aristide and the Politics of Containment.* London: Verso.

Hardt, Robert, and Antonio Negri. 2000. *Empire.* Cambridge: Harvard University Press.

Harman, Chris. 2008. *A People's History of the World.* London: Verso.

Harris, J., T. Wise, K. Gallagher and N. Goodwin (eds.). 2001. *A Survey of Sustainable Development: Social and Economic Dimensions.* Island Press, Washington.

Harris, Joseph. 1998. *Africans and their History.* Second edition. Meridian.

Harris, Richard. 2003. "Popular Resistance to Globalization and Neoliberalism in Latin America." *Journal of Developing Societies* 19 (2–3), September: 365–426.

_____. 2005. "Resistance and Alternatives to Washington's Agenda for the Americas." *Journal of Developing Societies* 21 (3–4): 403–28.

Harris, Richard, and Jorge Nef (eds.). 2008. *Capital, Power and Inequality in Latin America and the Caribbean.* Lanham, MD: Rowan and Littlefield.

Harrison, Graham. 2007. "The World Bank and the Construction of Governance States in Africa." In Moore (ed.), *The World Bank,* Chap 12: 369–86.

Harrison, Lawrence. 1985. *Underdevelopment is a State of Mind.* Madison.

Harrison, Lawrence, and Samuel Huntington (eds.). 2000. "Introduction." *Culture Matters: How Values Shape Human Progress.*

Harriss, John. 2003. "Do Political Regimes Matter? Poverty Reduction and Regime Differences Across India." In M. Moore and P. Houtzager (eds.), *Changing Paths: International Development and the New Politics of Inclusion.* Ann Arbor: University of Michigan Press.

_____. 2005. "Great Promise, Hubris and Recovery: A Participant's History of Development Studies." In U. Kothari (ed.), *A Radical History of Development Studies, Individuals, Institutions and Ideologies.* London: Zed Books.

_____. 2006. "Social Capital." In K.S. Jomo and Ben Fine (eds.), *The New Development Economics after the Washington Consensus.* London: Zed Books.

_____. 2007. "Antinomies of Empowerment: Civil Society, Politics and Urban Governance." *Economic and Political Weekly* 42 (26) June 30: 2716–24.

Hart-Landsberg, Martin, and Paul Burkett. 2005. *China and Socialism: Market Reforms and Class Struggle.* New York: Monthly Review Press.

Harter, John-Henry. 2004. "Environmental Justice for Whom? Class, New Social Movements, and the Environment: A Case Study of Greenpeace Canada, 1971–2000." *Labour/Le Travail* 54.

Harvey, D. 2007. "Neoliberalism as Creative Destruction." *The Annals of the American Academy of Political and Social Science* 610: 21–44.

Harvey, David. 1988. *Social Justice and the City.* Basil Blackwell.

_____. 1997. "Contested Cities: Social Process and Spatial Form." In N. Jewson and S. McGregor (eds.), *Transforming Cities: Contested Governance and New Spatial Divisions.*

_____. 2005. *A Brief History of Neoliberalism.* Oxford: Oxford University Press.

Harwit, Eric. 2007. "Building China's Telecommunications Network: Industrial Policy and the Role of State-Owned, Foreign and Private Domestic Enterprises." *The China Quarterly* 190: 311–32.

Hayek. F.A. 1944. *The Road to Serfdom.* Chicago: University of Chicago Press.

Hayter, Teresa. 1971. *Aid as Imperialism.* Harmondsmouth: Penguin Books.

Held, David. 2004. *Global Covenant.* Cambridge: Polity Press.

Held, David, and A. McGrew (eds.). 2002. *Governing Globalization: Power, Authority and Global Governance.* Cambridge, UK: Polity Press.

Helleiner, Eric. 1994. *States and the Reemergence of Global Finance.* Ithaca: Cornell.

Heller, P. 2001. "Moving the State: The Politics of Decentralisation in Kerala, South Africa and Porto Alegre." *Politics and Society* 29 (1): 131–63.

Helmore, Kristen, and Naresh Singh. 2001. *Sustainable Livelihoods: Building on the Wealth of the Poor.* West Hartford, CT: Kumarian Press.

Henderson, Hazel. 1996. "Changing Paradigms and Indicators: Implementing Equitable, Sustainable and Participatory Development." In Jo Marie Griesgaber & Bernard Gunter (eds.) *Development: New Paradigms and Principles for the 21st Century.* Pluto Press.

Herrera, R. 2006. *La Perspectiva teórica en el Estudio de las Migraciones.* Mexico: Siglo XXI.

Hettne, Björn. 1995. *Development Theory and the Three Worlds.* Second edition. London: Longman.

_____. 2005. "Beyond the 'New' Regionalism." *New Political Economy* 10 (4) December: 543–71.

Hettne, Björn, András Inotai, and Osvaldo Sunkel (eds.). 1999. *Globalism and the New Regionalism.* London: Palgrave Macmillan. Especially the chapters by Mittelman, Amin and Mistry.

Heward, C., and S. Bunwaree (eds.). 1998. *Gender, Education and Development: Beyond Access to Empowerment.*

Heynig, Klaus. 1982. "The Principal Schools of Thought on the Peasant Economy." CEPAL Review (16): 113–39. Available in Spanish in *Revista de la CEPAL* (16), 1980.

Hildyard, Nicholas. 1993. "Foxes in Charge of the Chickens." In W. Sachs (ed.), *Global Ecology.* London: Zed Books.

Hirsch, John. 2001. "Sierra Leone: Diamonds and the Struggle for Democracy." *Occasional Paper,* International Peace Academy.

Hirshman, Mitu. 1995. "Women and Development: A Critique." In Marchand and Parpart (eds.), *Feminism/ Postmodernism/Development.* London: Routledge.

Hirst, P., and G. Thompson. 1996. *Globalization in Question.* Cambridge: Polity Press.

Hobson, John M. 2004. *The Eastern Origins of Western Civilisation.* Cambridge University Press.

Hochschild, Adam. 1998. *King Leopold's Ghost: A Story of Greed, Terror and Heroism in Colonial Africa.* New York: Houghton Mifflin.

Hollnsteiner, M.R. 1977. "People Power: Community Participation in the Planning of Human Settlements." *Assignment Children* 40, October–December.

Holloway, John. 2002. "What Labour Debate?" In Dinerstein and Neary (eds.).

Homer-Dixon, T.F. 1999. *Environment, Scarcity and Violence.* Princeton and Oxford: Princeton University Press.

Hoogvelt, Ankie. 2008. "Globalization and Post-Modern Imperialism." In Barry K. Gills (ed.), *Globalization and the Global Politics of Justice*. London: Routledge.

Hounie, Adela, Lucia Pittaluga, Gabriel Porcile and Fabio Scatolin. 1999. "ECLAC and the New Growth Theory." *CEPAL Review* 68, August.

Howe, Gary Nigel. 1982. "Dependency Theory, Imperialism, and the Production of Surplus Value on a World Scale." In Ronald H. Chilcote (ed.), *Dependency and Marxism*. Boulder, CO: Westview Press.

Howell, Jude. 2006. "Reflections on the Chinese State." *Development and Change* 37 (2): 273–97.

Hulme, D. 2006. "Chronic Poverty." and M. Ramphele, 'Poverty, Characteristics of'. In D. Clark (ed.), *The Elgar Companion to Development Studies*. Cheltenham, UK/Northampton MA: Edward Elgar.

Hulme, David, and Michael Edwards. 1997. *NGOs, States and Donors: Too Close for Comfort?* New York: St. Martin's Press.

Humphrey, John, and D. Messner. 2006. "China and India as Emerging Governance Actors: Challenges for Developing and Developed Countries." *IDS Bulletin* 37(1): 107–14

Hunt, Diane. 1989. *Economic Theories of Development: An Analysis of Competing Paradigms*. Hertfordshire: Harvester Wheatsheaf.

Huntington, Samuel. 1993. "The Clash of Civilizations." *Foreign Affairs* 72 (3): 22–49.

Hyman, Richard. 1974. "Workers' Control and Revolutionary Theory." In Ralph Milliband and John Saville (eds.), *Socialist Register 1975*. London: Merlin Press.

IFPRI (International Food Policy Research Institute). 2007. "Taking Action for the World's Poor and Hungry People." Beijing, October 17–19. <http://www.ifpri.org/ 2020ChinaConference>.

Illich, Ivan. 1970. *Deschooling Society*. New York: Harper and Row.

_____. 1971. *Celebration of Awareness*. London: Calder and Boyars.

_____. 1998. "Development as Planned Poverty." In M. Rahnema, and V. Bawtree (eds.), *The Postdevelopment Reader*. London: Zed Books.

ILO. 1994. "Defending Values. Promoting Change: Social Justice on a Global Economy: An ILO Agenda." Report of the Director-General 81st session. Geneva: ILO.

_____. 2003. *A Fair Globalization: Creating Opportunities for All*. World Commission on the Social Dimension of Globalization, Geneva.

IMF (International Monetary Fund). 1994. "International Trade Policies: The Uruguay Round and Beyond." *World Economic and Financial Surveys*. Vol. I. Washington, DC: IMF.

_____. 2009. *World Economic Outlook 2009: Crisis and Recovery*. April. <http://www.imf.org/external/pubs/ft/weo/2009/01/>.

Invernizzi, Noela, and Guillermo Foladori. 2005. "Nanotechnology and the Developing World: Will Nanotechnology Overcome Poverty or Widen Disparities?" *NANOTECH. L and B* 2 (3). <http://www.nanoandsociety.com/ourlibrary/ documents/NanotechBusiness.pdf>.

Isaak, Robert. 2005. *The Globalization Gap: How the Rich Get Richer and the Poor Get Left Further Behind*. New Jersey: Prentice Hall.

Jabu-Lughod, Janet. 1991. *Before European Hegemony: The World System A.D. 1250–1350*. Oxford: Oxford University Press.

James, Paul. 2006. *Globalism, Nationalism, Tribalism: Bringing Theory Back In*. London: Sage Publications.

James, Paul, and Tom Nairn (eds.). 2006. *Globalizing Empires: Old and New*. London: Sage Publications.

Johnson, Chalmers. 1995. *Japan: Who Governs? The Rise of the Developmental State*. New York: W.W. Norton.

_____. 2001. "Blowback." *The Nation* October 15.

_____. 2004. *The Sorrows of Empire*. New York: Henry Holt & Co.

Johnson, Craig, and Daniel Start. 2001. "Rights, Claims and Capture: Understanding the Politics of Pro-Poor Policy." London: Overseas Development Institute. <http://www.odi.org.uk/rights/Publications/WP145_RightsClaimsCapture.pdf>.

Johnston, D. and H. Le Roux. 2007. "Leaving the Household out of Family Labour? The Implications for the Size-Efficiency Debate." *The European Journal of Development Research* 19 (3): 355–71.

Johnston, J., M. Gismondi, and J. Goodman. 2006. *Nature's Revenge: Reclaiming Sustainability in an Age of Corporate Globalization*. Toronto: Broadview Press.

Jolly, R. 2004. "Human Development and Neoliberalism: Paradigms Compared." In Sakiko Fukuda-Parr and A.K. Shiva Kumar (eds.), *Readings in Human Development Concepts, Measures and Policies for a Development Paradigm*. Oxford: Oxford University Press.

Jolly, R., L. Emmerij, D. Ghai, and F. Lapeire. 2004. *UN Contributions to Development Thinking and Practice*. Indiana University Press.

Jolly, R., and S. Mehrotra. 2000. *Development with a Human Face: Experiences in Social Achievement and Economic Growth*. Oxford: Oxford University Press.

Jomo, K.S., with Jacques Baudot. 2007. *Flat Worlds, Big Gaps*. Orient Longman/Zed Books/Third world Network. Especially chapters 1–5, 10–15.

Jomo, K.S., and Ben Fine (eds.). 2006. *The New Development Economics After the Washington Consensus*. London/New York: Zed Books.

Jones, Gavin, and Pravin Visaria (eds.). 1997. *Urbanization in Large Developing Countries: China, Indonesia, Brazil and India*. Oxford: Clarendon Press.

Jorgenson, Andrew, and Edward Kick (eds.). 2003. "Globalization and the Environment." *Journal of World-System Research* 9 (2): 195–203.

_____ (eds.). 2006. *Globalization and the Environment*. Leiden: Brill.

Kabeer, Naila. 1994. *Reversed Realities: Gender Hierarchies in Development Thought*. London: Verso.

_____. 1999. "Resources, Agency, Achievements: Reflections on the Measurement of Women's Empowerment." *Development and Change* 30 (3): 435–64 (e-journal).

_____. 2001. "Conflicts over Credit: Re-evaluating the Empowerment Potential of Loans to Women in Rural Bangladesh." *World Development* 29 (1).

_____. 2003. *The Power to Choose: Bangladeshi Women and Labour Market Decisions in London and Dhaka*. London: Verso.

_____. 2004. "Globalization, Labor Standards, and Women's Rights: Dilemmas of Collective (In)Action in an Interdependent World." *Feminist Economics* 10 (1): 3–35.

_____. 2006. "Poverty, Social Exclusion and the MDGs: The Challenge of 'Durable Inequalities' in the Asian Context." *IDS Bulletin* 37 (3): 64–78.

Kaldor, Mary. 1999. *New and Old Wars: Organized Violence in a Global Era*. Cambridge: Polity.

Kandiyoti, Deniz. 1998. "Gender, Power and Contestation." In Cecile Jackson and Ruth Pearson (eds.), *Feminist Visions of Development*. London/New York: Routledge.

Kaplinsky, Raphael. 2006. "Revisiting the Revisited Terms of Trade: Will China Make a Difference?" *World Development* 34 (6), June: 981–95 (Reprinted from "Asian Drivers: Opportunities and Threats." *IDS Bulletin* 37 (1), January.

Kaplinsky, Raphael, and Dirk Messner (eds.). 2008. "The Impact of Asian Drivers on the Developing World." *World Development* 36 (2), February: 197–344.

Kapstein, Ethan. 1996. "Workers and the World Economy." *Foreign Affairs* 75 (3).

Kapur, Devesh. 2006. "The 'Knowledge' Bank." In *Rescuing the World Bank*. Washington, DC: Centre for Global Development. <http://www.cgdev.org/doc/books/rescuing/Kapur_Knowledge.pdf>.

Karl, Marilee. 1995. *Women and Empowerment: Participation and Decision-making*. London: Zed Books.

Karl, T.L. 2000. "Economic Inequality and Democratic Instability." *Journal of Democracy* XI (1): 149–56.

Katz, Claudio. 2007. "Socialist Strategies in Latin America." *Monthly Review* 59 (4), September. <http://www.monthlyreview.org/0907katz.php>.

Kay, Cristóbal. 1989. *Latin American Theories of Development and Underdevelopment*. London: Routledge.

_____. 1993. "For a Renewal of Development Studies: Latin American Theories and Neoliberalism in the Era of Structural Adjustment." *Third World Quarterly* 14 (4): 691–702.

_____. 2001. "Agrarian Reform and Rural Development in Latin America: Lights and Shadows." In Horacio

R. Morales Jr. and James Putzel (eds.), *Power in the Village: Agrarian Reform, Rural Politics, Institutional Change and Globalization.* Quezon City: University of the Philippines Press. Available in Spanish.

_____. 2002. "Why East Asia Overtook Latin America: Agrarian Reform, Industrialization and Development." *Third World Quarterly* 23 (6): 1073–02.

_____. 2005. "Celso Furtado: Pioneer of Structuralist Economic Theory." *Development and Change* 26 (6): 1201–07.

_____. 2006a. "East Asia's Success and Latin America's Failure: Agrarian Reform, Industrial Policy and State Capacity." In Richard Boyd, Benno Galjart and Tak-Wing Ngo (eds.), *Political Conflict and Development in East Asia and Latin America.* London and New York: Routledge.

_____. 2006b. "Rural Poverty and Development Strategies in Latin America." *Journal of Agrarian Change* 6 (4): 455–508. For a similar version in Spanish, see C. Kay, "Una reflexión sobre los estudios de pobreza rural y estrategias de desarrollo en América Latina." ALASRU *(Nueva Época): Análisis Latinoamericano del Medio Rural* (4): 29–76.

_____. 2008a. "Latin America's Rural Transformation: Unequal Development and Persistent Poverty." In Richard L. Harris and Jorge Nef (eds.), *Capital, Power, and Inequality in Latin America and the Caribbean.* New edition. Lanham, MD: Rowman and Littlefield Publishers.

_____. 2008b. "Reflections on Latin American Rural Studies in the Neoliberal Globalization Period: A New Rurality?" *Development and Change* 39 (6): 915–43.

_____. 2009. "Development Strategies and Rural Development: Exploring Synergies, Eradicating Poverty." *Journal of Peasant Studies* 36 (1): 103–37.

Kay, Cristóbal, and Robert N. Gwynne. 2000. "Relevance of Structuralist and Dependency Theories in the Neoliberal Period: A Latin American Perspective." *Journal of Developing Societies* 16 (1): 49–69.

_____. 2004. *Latin America Transformed: Globalization and Modernity.* London: Arnold.

Kellogg, Paul. 2007. "Regional Integration in Latin America: Dawn of an Alternative to Neoliberalism?" *New Political Science* 29 (2): 187–209.

Kendie, Stephen B., and Martens, Pim (ed.). 2008. *Governance and Sustainable Development.* Cape Coast: Marcel Hughes Publicity Group.

Keping, Yu. 2007. "From Sino-West to Globalization: A Perspective from China." In P. Bowles, H. Veltmeyer et al. (eds.), *National Perspectives on Globalization.* New York: Palgrave Macmillan.

Kerkvliet, Benedict. 2009. "Everyday Politics in Peasant Societies (and Ours)." *Journal of Peasant Studies* 36 (1).

Khan, Mushtaq. 2004. "State Failure in Developing Countries and Strategies of Institutional Reform." In B. Tungodden, N. Stern, and I. Kolstad (eds.), *Annual World Bank Conference on Development Economics, Europe 2003: Toward Pro-Poor Policies—Aid, Institutions, and Globalization.* Oxford University Press/ World Bank.

_____. 2005. "Markets, States and Democracy: Patron–Client Networks and the Case for Democracy in Developing Countries." *Democratization* 12 (5): 704–24.

Kiely, Ray. 2005. *Empire in the Age of Globalization: US Hegemony and Neoliberal Disorder.* London: Pluto.

_____. 2007. *The New Political Economy of Development: Globalization, Imperialism, Hegemony.* Basingstoke: Palgrave Macmillan.

Kincheloe, J.L. 2004. *Critical Pedagogy.* New York: Peter Lang Publishing.

Kinyanjui, Mary, and Felix Kiruthu. 2007. "Super-Imperialism: A Perspective from East Africa." In P. Bowles et al. (eds.), *Regional Perspectives on Globalization: A Critical Reader.* Basingstoke: Palgrave Macmillan.

Klare, Michael. 2002. *Resource Wars: The New Landscape of Global Conflict.* New York: Owl Books.

_____. 2004. *Blood and Oil: The Dangers and Consequences of America's Growing Dependency on Imported Petroleum.* New York: Metropolitan Books.

Klasen, S. 2003. "In Search of the Holy Grail: How to Achieve Pro-Poor Growth." In L. Kolstad, B. Tungodden and N. Stern (eds.), Proceedings from the ABCDE Europe Conference. Washington, DC.

Klein, Naomi. 2007. *The Shock Doctrine: The Rise of Disaster Capitalism*. New York: Metropolitan Books/ Henry Holt.

Kliksberg, B. 1999. "Social Capital and Culture: Master Keys to Development." CEPAL *Review* 69, December: 83–102.

Klinghoffer, Arthur J. 1969. *Soviet Perspective on African Socialism*, Cranbury, NJ: Associated University Presses.

Kohl, Benjamin, and Linda Farthing. 2006. *Impasse in Bolivia: Neoliberal Hegemony and Popular Resistance*. London: Zed Books.

Kohli, Atul. 2004. *State Directed Development. Political Power and Industrialization in the Global Periphery*. Cambridge University Press.

Koo, Hagen. 2001. *Korean Workers: The Culture and Politics of Class Formation*. Ithaca: Cornell University Press.

Korten, David, and Rudi Klaus (eds.). 1984. *People-Centred Development: Contributions Toward Theory and Planning Frameworks*. West Hartford, CT: Kumarian Press.

Kothari, Uma. 2005. "From Colonial Administration to Development Studies: A Post-Colonial Critique of the History of Development Studies." In U. Kothari (ed.), *A Radical History of Development Studies*. London and New York: Zed Books.

Kothari, Uma, and Martin Minogue. 2001. *Development Theory and Practice: Critical Perspectives*. London: Macmillan.

_____ (eds.). 2002. *Development Theory in Practice: Critical Perspectives*. London: Palgrave.

Kovel, Joel. 2007. "Why Ecosocialism Today." *New Socialist*. <http://www.newsocialist .org/index. php?id=1321>.

_____. 2008. *The Enemy of Nature: The End of Capitalism or the End of the World?* Second edition. London: Zed Books.

Krasno, Jean (ed.). 2004. *The United Nations: Confronting the Challenges of a Global Society*. Boulder, CO: Lynne Rienner.

Krueger, Anne O. 1974. "The Political Economy of the Rent-Seeking Society." *The American Economic Review* 64 (3).

Kuhn, Thomas. 1970. *The Structure of Scientific Revolutions*. Chicago: Chicago University Press.

Kumar, K. 2000. *Women and Women's Organizations in Post-Conflict Societies: The Role of International Assistance*. Washington, DC: UAID.

Kuonqui, Christopher. 2006. "Is Human Development a New Paradigm for Development? Capabilities Approach, Neoliberalism and Paradigm Shifts." Paper presented at he August 2006 international conference "Freedom and Justice" of the HD and HDCA, Groningen, Netherlands. <http://www. capabilityapproach.com/pubs/6_3_Kuonqui.pdf>.

Kuznets, Simon. 1953. "Economic Growth and Income Inequality." *The American Economic Review* March.

Lahiff, Edward, Saturnino M. Borras Jr., and Cristóbal Kay. 2007. "Market-led Agrarian Reform: Policies, Performance and Prospects." *Third World Quarterly* 28 (8): 1417–36.

Lairap-Fonderson, Josephine. 2002. "The Disciplinary Power of Micro-Credit: Examples from Kenya and Cameroon." In Parpart, Rai and Staudt (eds.), *Rethinking Empowerment: Gender and Development in a Global/Local World*. London: Routledge.

Lal, Deepak. 1983. *The Poverty of Development Economics*. London: Institute of Economic Affairs.

Lambert, Rob, and Eddie Webster. 2001. "Southern Unionism and the New Labour Internationalism." *Antipode* 33 (3): 337–62.

Langdon, Steven. 1999. "Debt, Downturns and Crisis." In *Global Poverty, Democracy and the North-South Divide*. Toronto: Garamond Press.

Lawson, H., and L. Appignanesi. 1989. *Dismantling Truth: Reality in the Post-Modern World*. New York: St. Martin's Press.

Le Billon, P. 2001. "The Political Ecology of War: Natural Resources and Armed Conflicts." *Political

Geography 20 (5): 561–84.

_____. 2006. "Fatal Transactions: Conflict Diamonds and the (Anti) Terrorist Consumer." *Antipode* 38 (4): 778–801.

Lebowitz, Michael. 2006. *Build It Now: Twenty-First Century Socialism*. New York: Monthly Review Press.

_____. 2007. "Human Development and Practice." Opening comments at conference on Participation, Change and Human Development at Centro International Miranda in Caracas, Venezuela, March 27.

Le Carré, John. 2009. *A Most Wanted Man*. New York: Barnes & Noble.

Leftwich, Adrian. 1992. "Is There a Socialist Path to Socialism?" *Third World Quarterly* 13 (1): 27–42.

_____. 1993. "Governance. Democracy and Development in the Third World." *Third World Quarterly* 14 (3).

_____. 2000. "The Meanings of Development: Post-War Developments." In *States of Development: On the Primacy of Politics in Development*. Cambridge: Polity.

Leiva, Fernando Ignacio. 2006. "Neoliberal and Neostructuralist Perspectives on Labour Flexibility, Poverty and Inequality: A Critical Appraisal." *New Political Economy* 11 (3): 337–59.

_____. 2008. *Latin American Neostructuralism: The Contradictions of Post-Neoliberal Development*.

Lenin, V.I. 1969. *Imperialism: The Highest Stage of Capitalism*. London: International Publishing Co.

Levitt, Kari. 2005. "Reclaiming Economics for Development." In *Reclaiming Development: Independent Thought and Caribbean Community*. Kingston: Ian Rundle Publishers.

_____. 2009. "Mercantilist Roots of Capitalist Development and Underdevelopment." Chap. 1.

Lewis, P. (ed.). 1998. *Africa: Dilemmas of Development and Change*. Boulder, CO: Westview Press.

Lewis, W. Arthur. 1963 [1954]. "Economic Development with Unlimited Supplies of Labour." Republished in A.N. Agarwala and S.P. Singh, *Economics of Underdevelopment*. New York: Oxford.

Leys, Colin. 1975. *Underdevelopment in Kenya: The Political Economy of Neo-Colonialism 1964–1971*. Berkeley: University of California Press.

Li, Minq, and Dale Wen. 1996. "China: Hyper-Development and Environmental Crisis." In Colin Leys and Leo Panitch (eds.), *Socialist Register 2007: Coming to Terms With Nature*. New York: Monthly Review Press.

Liamzon, Tina, et al. (eds.). 1996. *Towards Sustainable Livelihoods*. Rome: Society for International Development.

Lipietz, Alain. 1982. "Towards Global Fordism." *New Left Review* 132 (March–April).

_____. 1987. *Mirages and Miracles: The Crisis in Global Fordism*. London: Verso.

_____. 2000. "Political Ecology and the Future of Marxism." *Capitalism, Nature Socialism* March.

Little, D. 2003. "Concepts of Growth, Inequality and Poverty" and "Welfare, Well-Being and Needs." *The Paradox of Wealth and Poverty: Mapping the Ethical Dilemmas of Global Development*. Boulder. CO: Westview Press.

Little, R., and M. Smith (eds.). 2005. *Perspectives on World Politics*. London/NY: Routledge.

Livergood, Norman. 2001. "The New U.S.-British Oil Imperialism." The New Enlightenment. <http://www.hermes-press.com/impintro1.htm>.

Lomborg, Bjorn. 2001. *The Skeptical Environmentalist*. Cambridge University Press.

Longwe, Sara. 1998. "Education for Women's Empowerment or Schooling for Women's Subordination?" *Gender and Development* 6 (2): 19–26.

Lopez, H. 2004. "Pro-Poor Growth, Pro-Poor: Is There a Trade-Off?" The World Bank, April 20.

Love, J. 1980. "Raúl Prebisch and the Origins of the Doctrine of Unequal Exchange." *Latin American Research Review* 15 (3): 45–72.

Löwy, Michael. 1996. "Eco-Socialism and Democratic Planning." In Colin Leys and Leo Panitch (eds.), *Socialist Register 2007: Coming to Terms With Nature*. New York: Monthly Review Press.

MacPhail, Fiona, and Xiao-Yuan Dong. 2007. "Women's Market Work and Household Status in Rural China: Evidence from Jiangsu and Shandong in the late 1990s." *Feminist Economics* 13 (3–4): 93–124.

MacWilliam, Scott. 2007. "Plenty of Poverty or the Poverty of Plenty." In Moore (ed.), *The World Bank*. Chapter 2.

Mahjoub, A. (ed.). 1990. *Adjustment or Delinking: The African Experience*. London: Zed Press.

Mahmud, Simeen. 2003. "Actually How Empowering is Microcredit?" *Development and Change* 34 (4): 577–605.

Malik, K., C. Lopes, and S. Fukuda-Parr. 2002. *Capacity for Development: New Solutions to Old Problems*. London: Earthscan Publications.

Mallon, Florencia. 1994. "The Promise and Dilemma of Subaltern Studies: Perspectives from Latin American History." *American Historical Review* 99 (5): 1491–915.

Manchanda, R. (ed.). 2001. *Women, War and Peace in South Asia: Beyond Victimhood to Agency*. New Delhi: Sage Productions.

Mandel, Ernest. 1970. "Self-Management: Dangers and Possibilities." *International* 2 (4): 3–9.

Marcel, Valerie. 2006. *Oil Titans: National Oil Companies in the Middle East*. Baltimore, MD: Brookings Institution Press.

Marchand, Marianne, and Jane Parpart (eds.). 1994. *Feminism/Postmodernism/ Development*. London and New York: Routledge.

Marglin, Stephen, and Juliet Schor. 1990. *The Golden Age of Capitalism: Reinterpreting the Post-War Experience*. Oxford: Clarendon Press.

Marx, Karl. 1976. "On Primitive Accumulation." Part VIII, Chap. 26. *Capital: A Critique of Political Economy*. Vol. 1. London: Penguin Books.

_____. 1993. "Original Accumulation of Capital." In *Grundrisse: Foundations of the Critique of Political Economy*. London: Penguin Press.

Massey, D., et al. 1993. "Theories of International Migration: A Review and Appraisal." *Population and Development Review* 19 (3): 431–66.

_____ et. al. 1998. *Worlds in Motion: Understanding International Migration at the End of the Millennium*. Oxford: Clarendon Press.

Massis, Henri. 1927. *Défense de l'Occident*. Paris: Plon.

Mathie, A., and G. Cunningham. 2004. "Who [or What] is Driving Development? Reflections on the Transformative Potential of Asset-Based Community Development." *Canadian Journal of Development Studies* XXVI (1).

Mayhew, Anne. 2000. "Review of Karl Polanyi, *The Great Transformation: The Political and Economic Origins of Our Time*." EH. Net, Economic History Services, Jun 1. <http://eh.net/bookreviews/library/polanyi>.

McAfee K. 2003. "Neoliberalism on the Molecular Scale: Economic and Genetic Reductionism in Biotechnology Battles." *Geoforum* 34: 203–19.

McCarthy, James, and Scott Prudham. 2004. "Neoliberal Nature and the Nature of Neoliberalism." *Geoforum* 35: 275–83.

McGiffen, S. 2005. *Biotechnology: Corporate Power vs. the Public Interest*. London: Pluto Press.

McKay, Ailsa. 2007. "Why a Citizens' Basic Income: A Question of Gender Equality or Gender Bias." *Work, Employment and Society* 21 (2): 3377–48.

McKeown, Kieran. 1987. *Marxist Political Economy and Marxist Urban Sociology*. London: Macmillian Press.

McMichael, Philip. 2005. "Global Development and the Corporate Food Regime." In F. H. Buttel and P. McMichael (eds.), *New Directions in the Sociology of Global Development: Research in Rural Sociology and Development*. Vol. 11. Oxford: Elsevier.

_____. 2006. "Reframing Development: Global Peasant Movements and the New Agrarian Question." Prepared for RC02 (Economy and Society) Panel—Workers, Peasants and Development. ISA World Congress, Durban, July.

_____. 2007. "Feeding the World: Agriculture, Development and Ecology." In Colin Leys and Leo Panitch (eds.), *Socialist Register: Coming to Terms With Nature*. New York: Monthly Review Press.

_____. 2010. "The Agrofuels Project at Large." In H. Veltmeyer (ed.), *The Enduring Verities of Capitalism.* Leiden/Boston: Brill.

McNally, David. 1993. *Against the Market: Political Economy, Market Socialism and the Marxist Critique.* London: Verso.

_____. 2002. *Another World is Possible: Globalization and Anti-Capitalism.* Winnipeg: Arbeiter Ring Publishing.

_____. 2008. "From Financial Crisis to World Slump: Accumulation, Financialization, and the Global Slowdown." Paper, December 2. <dmcnally@yorku.ca>

Mehta, L. 2001. "The World Bank and its Emerging Knowledge Empire." *Human Organisation* 60(2): 189–196.

Meier, Gerald, and Dudley Seers (eds.). 1984. *Pioneers in Development.* New York: Oxford University Press.

Meller, Patricio (ed.). 1991. *The Latin American Development Debate: Neo-structuralism, Neo-Monetarism and Adjustment Processes.* Boulder, CO: Westview Press.

Mezirow, J. 1996. "Contemporary Paradigms of Learning." *Adult Education Quarterly* 46, 3: 158–172.

Mies, Maria. 1988. "Social Origins of the Sexual Division of Labour." In M. Mies and V. Shiva, *Ecofeminism.* Halifax and London: Fernwood and Zed Books.

Mies, Maria, and Vandana Shiva. 1993. *Ecofeminism.* Halifax and London: Fernwood and Zed Books.

Milanovic, Branko. 2004. "Global Income Inequality: What Is It and Why It Matters?" In K.S. Jomo and Jacques Baudot (eds.), *Key Issues in Development.*

Miller, Byron. 2006. "Castell's The City and the Grassroots: 1983 and Today." *International Journal of Urban and Regional Research* 30 (1) March: 207–11.

Milward, A.S. 1984. *The Reconstruction of Western Europe 1945–1951.* London: Methuen.

Mindry, Deborah. 2001. "Nongovernmental Organizations, 'Grassroots' and the Politics of Virtue." *Signs* 26 (4): 1187–211 (e-journal).

Mirowski, P., and D. Plehwe. 2009. *The Road from Mont Pelerin: The Making of the Neoliberal Thought Collective.* Cambridge University Press.

Mittelman, James, and Norani Othman (eds.). 2000. "Special Issue: Capturing Globalization." *Third World Quarterly* 21 (6).

Moghadam, Valentine. 2005a. "Female Labor, Regional Crises and Feminist Responses." In Moghadam *Globalizing Women.*

_____. 2005b. *Globalizing Women: Transnational Feminist Networks.* Baltimore: Johns Hopkins University Press.

Mohan, G., and S. Hickey. 2004. *Participation: From Tyranny to Transformation? Exploring New Approaches to Participation in Development.* London: Zed Books.

Mohanty, Chandra T. 2002. "'Under Western Eyes' Revisited: Feminist Solidarity through Anti-Capitalist Struggles." *Signs* 28 (2): 499–536. [e-journal].

Mohiddin, Ahmed. 1981. *African Socialism in Two Countries.* London: Croom Helm.

Moore, D.S. 1996. "Marxism, Culture, and Political Ecology: Environmental Struggles in Zimbabwe's Eastern Highlands." In Richard Peet and Michael Watts (eds.), *Liberation Ecologies: Environment, Development, Social Movements.* London: Routledge.

Moore, David. 2007a. "Sail on the Ship of State: Neoliberalism, Globalization and the Governance of Africa." In Moore (ed.), *The World Bank* Chap 8.

_____ (ed.). 2007b. *The World Bank: Development, Poverty, Hegemony.* Scotsville, Capetown: The University of KwaZulu-Natal Press.

Moore, Mick. 2001. "Political Underdevelopment: What Causes 'Bad Governance'?" *Public Management Review* 3, 3: 385–418. <http://www.welpolitik.net/>.

Morris, Chuck. 2003. "The Antiglobalization Movement." *New Formulation* 3(1) February.

Morrison, David. 1998. *Aid and Ebb Tide: A History of CIDA and Canadian Development Assistance.* Ottawa: Wilfrid Laurier University Press.

Mosedale, Sarah. 2005. "Assessing Women's Empowerment: Towards a Conceptual Framework." *Journal of International Development* 17 (2): 243–57 (e-journal).

Moser, Caroline. 1993. *Gender Planning and Development: Theory, Practice and Training*. London/New York: Routledge.

_____. 1998. "The Asset Vulnerability Framework: Reassessing Urban Poverty Reduction Strategies." *World Development* 26 (1).

_____. 2001. "Gender and Social Capital in Contexts of Political Violence: Community Perceptions from Colombia and Guatemala." In C.O. Moser and F. Clark (eds.), *Victims, Perpetrators or Actors? Gender, Armed Conflict and Political Violence*. London/New York: Zed Books.

Moser, Caroline, Alicia Herbert, and Roza Makonnen. 1993. "Urban Poverty in the Context of Structural Adjustment: Recent Evidence and Policy Responses." *Discussion Paper*. Washington, DC: World Bank.

Mosse, D. 2005. *Cultivating Development: An Ethnography of Aid Policy and Practice*. London: Pluto Press.

Munck, Ronaldo. 1999a. "Deconstructing Development Discourses: of Impasses, Alternatives and Politics." In R. Munck and D.O. O'Hearn (eds.), *Critical Development Theory*. London: Zed Books.

_____. 1999b. "Dependency and Imperialism in the New Times: A Latin American Perspective." *European Journal of Development Research* 11 (1): 56–74.

_____. 2001. "Globalization, Regionalism and Labour: The Case of MERCOSUR." *Labour, Capital and Society* 34 (1): 8–25.

_____. 2002. *Globalization and Labour: The New 'Great Transformation.'* London: Zed Books.

_____. 2005. *Globalization and Social Exclusion: A Transformationalist Perspective*. Bloomfield: Kumarian Press.

_____. 2007. *Globalization and Contestation: The New Great Counter-Movement*. London: Routledge.

_____. 2008. *Globalization and Migration: New Issues, New Politics*. London: Routledge.

Munck, Ronaldo. 2008. *Globalisation and the Labour Movement: Challenges and Responses*"—Special Conference, "Trade union and social movements: What is in it for us?" Oslo, Global Labour Institute, October 16–17. <http://www.globallabour.info/en/2009/12/globalisation_and_the_labour_m.html>.

Mukherjee Reed, Ananya. 2008. *Human Development and Social Power*. London and New York: Routledge.

Munck, R., and D. O'Hearn (eds.). 1999. *Critical Development Theory: Contributions to a New Paradigm*. London: Zed Books.

Murphy, Craig. 1998. "Globalization and Governance: A Historical Perspective." In R. Axtman (ed.), *Globalization and Europe: Theoretical and Empirical Investigations*. London: Pinter.

Myrdal, Gunnar. 1968. *Asian Drama: An Inquiry into the Poverty of Nations*. New York: Twentieth Century Fund.

National Academy of Sciences. 2006. *The Fundamental Role of Science and Technology in International Development: An Imperative for the US Agency for International Development*.

Nayyar, Deepak. 2006. "Globalization and Development in the Long 20th Century." In K.S. Jomo (ed.), *Globalization Under Hegemony*. Oxford, UK: Oxford University Press.

Needham, J. 1954. *Science and Civilization in China*. Cambridge: Cambridge University Press.

Ngai, Pun. 2005. *Made in China: Women Factory Workers in a Global Workplace*. Durham, NC: Duke University Press.

Nixson, Frederick. 2006. "Rethinking the Political Economy of Development: Back to Basics and Beyond." *Journal of International Development* 18 (7): 967–81.

Nkrumah, Kwame. 1965. *Neocolonisation as the Last stage of Capitalism*.

_____. 1969. *Neocolonialism: The Highest Stage of Imperialism*. London: Thomas Nelson and Sons.

_____. 2001. *Conscienticism: Philosophy and Ideology for De-Colonization*. London: Panaf Books.

Nkrumah, Kwame, Léopold Sédar Senghor, and Martin Kilson. 1966. *African Socialism*. The American

Society of African Culture.

Noel, Alain. 1987. "Accumulation, Regulation, and Social Change: an Essay on French Political Economy." *International Organization* 41(2) Spring.

Norris, P. 2001. *Digital Divide, Civic Engagement, Information Poverty and the Internet Worldwide.* Cambridge University Press.

Norton, A., and M. Foster. 2001. "The Potential of Using Sustainable Livelihoods Approaches in Poverty Reduction." *Working Paper* 148, July. London: Overseas Development Institute (ODI).

Nove, Alec. 1990. "Socialism." In J. Eatwell, M. Milgate and P. Newman (eds.), *Problems of the Planned Economy.* New York: Norton.

Nussbaum, Martha C. 2003. "Capabilities as Fundamental Entitlements: Sen and Social Justice." *Feminist Economics* 9 (2–3): 33–59.

Nyberg-Sorensen, N., N. Van Hear, and P. Engberg-Pedersen. 2002. "The Migration Development Nexus: Evidence and Policy Options State of the Art Review." *International Migration* 40(5): 3–48.

Nyerere, Julius K. 1968. "Socialism and Rural Development." In *Freedom and Socialism.* Dar es Salaam: Oxford University Press.

O'Brien, R., A.M. Goetz, J.A. Scholte and M. Williams. 2000. *Contesting Global Governance: Multilateral Institutions and Global Social Movements.* Cambridge University Press.

O'Connor, A. 2001. *Poverty Knowledge: Social Science, Social Policy and the Poor in Twentieth Century US History.* Princeton and Oxford: Princeton University Press.

O'Connor, J. 1998. *Natural Causes: Essays in Ecological Marxism.* New York: Guilford Press.

O'Laughlin, B. 2004. "Review of Seven Livelihoods Books." *Development and Change* 35 (2): 385–92.

O'Leary, Brendan. 2004. "Building Inclusive States, Background Paper for the UNDP's HDR-04."

O'Malley, A., and H. Veltmeyer. 2006. "Banking on Poverty." *Canadian Journal of Development Studies* XXVI (3).

Oakland Institute. 2009. "The Food Crisis and Latin America: Framing a new Approach." *Policy Brief.*

Obi, Cyril. 2007. "The Struggle for Resource Control in a Petro-State: A Perspective from Nigeria." In Paul Bowles et al. (eds.), *National Perspectives on Globalization: A Critical Reader.* Vol. I. Chap. 7. Basingstoke: Palgrave Macmillan.

Ocampo, José Antonio. 1998. "Beyond the Washington Consensus: An ECLAC Perspective." *CEPAL Review* (66), December: 7–28.

_____. 2004. "Social Capital and the Development Agenda." In R. Atria et al. (eds.), *Social Capital and Poverty Reduction in Latin America and the Caribbean: Towards a New Paradigm.* Santiago: ECLAC.

_____. 2007. "Markets: Social Cohesion and Democracy." In J.A. Ocampo, K.S. Jomo and S. Kahn (eds.), *Policy Matters: Economic and Social Policies to Sustain Equitable Development.* London: Zed.

Onis, Ziya. 2006. "Varieties and Crises of Neoliberal Globalization: Argentina, Turkey, and the IMF." *Third World Quarterly* 27(2): 239–63.

Orton, David. 2002. "Deep Ecology and Political Activism." Saltsprings, NS: Green Web Publications.

Ostrom, Elinor. 1990. *Governing the Commons: The Evolution of Institutions for Collective Action.* New York: Cambridge University Press.

Ostry, Silvia. 1990. *Government and Corporations in a Shrinking World: Trade and Innovation Policies in the US, Europe and Japan.* New York: Council on Foreign Relations.

Otero, Gerardo. 1999a. "The Mexican Debate and Beyond: Class, State, and Culture." In G. Otero, *Farewell to the Peasantry?*

_____. 1999b. *Farewell to the Peasantry? Political Formation in Rural Mexico.* Boulder, CO: Westview Press.

Ottaway, Marina, and David B. Ottaway. 1981. *Afrocommunism.* Teaneck, NJ: Holmes and Meier.

Overton, John. 2000. *Development in Chaos?* Institute of Development Studies (IDS). <http://www.devnet.org.nz/conf/Papers/Overton.pdf>.

Owen, D. 1950. "The United Nations Program of Technical Assistance." *Annal of the American Academy of Political and Social Science* 270: 109–17.

Pagden, Anthony. 2008. *Worlds at War: The 2,500-Year Struggle Between East and West.* New York: Random House.

Page, John M. 1994. "The East-Asian Miracle: An Introduction." *World Development* 22 (4): 615–25.

Pakenham, Thoma. 1992. *The Scramble for Africa: White Man's Conquest of the Dark Continent from 1876 to 1912.* New York: Avon Books.

Palma Carvajal, Eduardo. 1995. "Decentralization and Democracy: The New Latin American Municipality." CEPAL *Review* 55: 39–53.

Palma, Gabriel. 1978. "Dependency: A Formal Theory of Underdevelopment or a Methodology for the Analysis of Concrete Situations of Underdevelopment?" *World Development* 6 (7–8): 881–924.

_____. 1981. "Dependency and Development: A Critical Overview." In D. Seers (ed.), *Dependency Theory: A Critical Reassessment.* London: Frances Pinter.

Panitch, Leo. 1994. "Globalization and the State." In Panitch et al. (eds.), *The Globalization Decade.* Halifax, NS: Fernwood Publishing.

Parayil, Govindan (ed.). 2000. *Kerala: The Development Experience.* London: Zed Books.

Parker, John, and Richard Rathbone. 2007. *A Very Short Introduction to African History.* Chap 1. Oxford: Oxford University Press.

Parpart, Jane. 2002. "Lessons from the Field: Rethinking Empowerment, Gender and Development from a Post-(post?) Development Perspective." In K. Saunders (ed.), *Feminist Postdevelopment Thought.*

Parpart, Jane, Patricia Connelly and Eudine Barriteau (eds.). 2000. *Theoretical Perspectives on Gender and Development.* Ottawa: IDRC.

Parpart, Jane, and M. Marchand. 1995. "Feminism/Postmodernism/Development Introduction: Exploding the Canon." In M. Marchand and J. Parpart (eds.), *Feminism/Postmodernism/Development.* London: Routledge.

Parpart, Jane, Shirin Rai and Kathleen Staudt (eds.). 2002. *Rethinking Empowerment: Gender and Development in a Global/Local World.* London: Routledge.

Parpart, Jane, and Henry Veltmeyer. 2004. "The Dynamics of Development Theory and Practice: A Review of its Shifting Dynamics." Published originally in *Canadian Journal of Development Studies* XXV (1), Special Issue.

Patel, R. 2007. "Transgressing Rights: La Vía Campesina's Call for Food Sovereignty." *Feminist Economics* 13 (1): 87–93.

Patel, Surendra. 2005. "Development and Technological Transformation: The Historic Process." *Technological Transformation of the Third World.* Vol. V. Helsinki: Wider.

_____. 2007. *Technological Transformation and Development in the South.* New Delhi: APH Publishing.

Patomäki, H., and T. Teivainen. 2004. *A Possible World: Democratic Transformation of Global Institutions.* London: Zed Books.

Paul, James, and Katarina Wahlberg. 2008. "A New Era of World Hunger? The Global Food Crisis Analyzed." *Dialogue on Globalization Briefing Paper.* New York: FES.

Pearce, David, Anil Markandya, and Edward Barbier. 1989. *Blueprint for a Green Economy.* London: Earthscan Publications.

Pearce, Jenny. 1981. *Under the Eagle: U.S. Intervention in Central America and the Caribbean.* London: Latin American Bureau.

Pearson, Margaret. 2005. "The Business of Governing Business in China: Institutions and Norms of the Emerging Regulatory State." *World Politics* 57 (2), January: 296–322.

Peet, Richard, and Michael Watts. 2004. *Liberation Ecologies: Environment, Development, Social Movements.* London: Routledge.

Perelman M. 2000. *The Invention of Capitalism: Classical Political Economy and the Secret History of Primitive Accumulation.* Durham: Duke University Press.

Perez, C. 1985. "Microelectronics, Long Waves and Structural Change: New Perspectives for Developing Countries." *World Development* 13 (1).

Petras, James. 1978. *Critical Perspectives on Imperialism and Social Class in the Third World.* New York:

Monthly Review Press.

_____. 1981. *Class, State and Power in the Third World*. Montclair, NJ: Allanheld, Osmun.

_____. 2005. "Latin American Strategies: Class-Based Direct Action Versus Populist Electoral Politics." *Science and Society* 69 (2), April: 152–59.

_____. 2007. *Rulers and Ruled in the US Empire: Bankers, Zionist, Militants*. Atlanta, GA: Clarity Press.

Petras, J., and H. Veltmeyer. 2001. *Unmasking Globalization: The New Face of Imperialism*. Halifax: Fernwood Publications/London: Zed Books.

_____. 2002. "The Age of Reverse Aid: Neoliberalism as a Catalyst of Regression." *Development and Change* 33 (2), April. Also in Jan P. Pronk (ed.), 2004. *Catalysing Development*. Blackwell Publishers

_____. 2003. *System in Crisis: The Dynamics of Free Market Capitalism*. London: Zed Books/Halifax: Fernwood Books. In Spanish as *El Sistema en Crisis* (Buenos Aires/Mexico: Editorial Lumen).

_____. 2004. "Capitalism in Latin America at the End of the Millennium." *Monthly Review* 51 (3), July–August: 31–52.

_____. 2005a. "Development and Globalization as Imperialism." *Canadian Journal of Development Studies* XXVI (1): 89–106.

_____. 2005b. *Social Movements and the State: Argentina, Bolivia, Brazil, Ecuador*. London: Pluto Press. In Spanish, *Movimientos sociales y poder estatal*. Buenos Aires: Editorial Lumen.

_____. 2005c. *Empire with Imperialism*. Halifax and London: Fernwood Publications and Zed Books. In Spanish as *Imperio con Imperialismo: la dinámica globalizadora del capitalismo neoliberal* (Havana: Editorial de Ciencias Sociales; Mexico: Siglo XXI).

_____. 2007a. "The Standard of Living Debate in Development Policy." *Critical Sociology* 3: 180–209.

_____. 2007b. *Multinationals on Trial: Foreign Investment Matters*. London: Ashgate.

_____. 2009. *What's Left in Latin America*. London: Ashgate. In Spanish as *Espejismos de la izquierda en América Latina*. Buenos Aires: Editorial Lumen.

Petras, J., and M. Zeitlin. 1968. *Reform or Revolution: Politics and Social Structure in Latin America*. New York: Fawcett.

Pieterse, Jan Nederveen. 1996. "The Cultural Turn in Development: Question of Power." *The European Journal of Development Research*.

_____. 2000. "Trends in development theory." In R. Palan (ed.), *Global Political Economy: Contemporary Theories*. London: Routledge.

_____. 2001. *Development Theory: Deconstructions/Reconstructions*. London: Sage.

_____. 2004. "Globalization and Culture: Three Paradigms." In *Globalization and Culture*. Lanham, MD: Rowman and Littlefield.

Pilger, John. 2002. *The New Rulers of the World*. London: Verso.

_____. 2005. "As the Workings of Foreign Aid in Cambodia Demonstrate, Behind the Charade of 'Loans,' 'Assistance' And 'Partnerships' Lies Systematic Western Plunder and Corruption." *New Statesman* 134 (4742): 5–30.

Pillay, Devan (ed.). 2007. Special Issue on "Globalization and the Challenges to Labour and Development." *Labour, Capital and Society* 40: 1–2.

Pincus, J., and J. Sender. 2006. "Quantifying Poverty in Vietnam: Who Counts?" Paper presented at the Annual Meeting of the Association of Asian Studies, San Francisco.

Pithouse, Richard. 2007. "Producing the Poor: The World Bank's New Discourse of Domination." In Moore (ed.), *The World Bank*. Chap 14.

Pochmann, Marcio, et al. 2004. *Atlas da exclusão no mundo*. Five volumes. Sao Paulo: Cortez Editora.

Polanyi, Karl. 1944 [1957, 1968]. *The Great Transformation: The Political and Economic Origins of Our Time*. Boston: Beacon Press, by arrangement with Rinehart and Co.

Pomerantz, Phyllis. 2004. *Aid Effectiveness in Africa: Developing Trust Between Donors and Governments*. Lexington Books.

Pomeranz, Kenneth. 2000. *The Great Divergence: China, Europe and the Making of the World Modern Economy*. Princeton University Press.

Portes, A. (ed.). 1989. *The Informal Economy: Studies in Advanced and Less Developed Countries*. Baltimore: Johns Hopkins University Press.

Portes, A., and K. Hoffman. 2003. "Latin American Class Structures: Their Composition and Change During the Neoliberal Era." *Latin American Research Review* 38 (1).

Powell, Mike. 2006. "Which Knowledge? Whose Reality? An Overview of Knowledge Used in the Development Sector." *Development in Practice* 16, 6 (November): 518–32

Putzel, James. 2000. "Land Reforms in Asia: Lessons from the Past for the 21st Century." DESTIN *Working Papers* No. 4. <http://www.lse.ac.uk/collections /DESTIN/pdf/WP04.pdf>.

Racioppi, L., and K. O'Sullivan. 2000. "Ulsterman and Loyalist Ladies on Parade." *IJFP* 2 (1).

Radcliffe, Sarah (ed.). 2006. *Culture and Development in a Globalizing World: Geographies, Actors and Paradigms*. London: Routledge.

Rahman, Anisur. 1991. "Towards an Alternative Development Paradigm." IFDA *Dossier*, (81), April–June: 17–27.

Rahnema, M. 1998. "Towards Postdevelopment: Searching for Signposts, a New Language and New Paradigms." In M. Rahnema and V. Bawtree (eds.), *The Postdevelopment Reader*.

_____. 1990. "Participatory Action Research: The Last Temptation of Saint Development." *Alternatives* XV: 199–226.

Rahnema, M., and V. Bawtree (eds.). 1998. *The Postdevelopment Reader*. London: Zed Books.

Rahnema, Saeed. 2008. "Radical Islamism and Failed Developmentalism." *Third World Quarterly* 29 (3): 483–96.

Rai, Shirin. 2002. "Political Representation, Democratic Institutions and Women's Empowerment." In Parpart, Rai and Staudt, *Rethinking Empowerment*.

_____. 2005. "Gender and Development." In J. Haynes (ed.), *Palgrave Advances in Development Studies*. Houndmills: Palgrave.

Rakodi, Carole (ed.). 1997. *The Urban Challenge in Africa: Growth and Management of Its Large Cities*. Tokyo.

Ramalingam, B. 2005. Implementing Knowledge Strategies: Lessons from International Development Agencies. ODI *Working Paper*. London, ODI.

Ramo, Joshua Cooper. 2004. "The Beijing Consensus." The Foreign Policy Centre, May. <http://fpc.org.uk/fsblob/ 244.pdf>

Ramos, Joseph, and Osvaldo Sunkel. 1993. "Towards a Neostructuralist Synthesis." In Osvaldo Sunkel (ed.), *Development from Within: Toward a Neostructuralist Approach for Latin America*. Boulder, CO: Lynne Rienner Publishers.

Ramphele, M. 2006. "Poverty, Characteristics of." In D. Clark (ed.), *The Elgar Companion to Development Studies*. Cheltenham, UK/Northampton MA: Edward Elgar.

Rapley, John. 2004. *Globalization and Inequality: Neoliberalism's Downward Spiral*. London: Lynne Reinner Publishers.

Rapoport, Hillel, and Frederic Docquier. 2004. "The Economics of Migrant Remittances." IZA *Discussion Paper* (1531), 1 (81).

Raskin, P.D., and S.S. Bernow. 1991. "Ecology and Marxism: Are Red and Green Complementary?" *Rethinking Marxism* 4 (1), Spring: 87–103.

Ratha, D. 2003. "Workers' Remittances: An Important and Stable Source of External Development Finance." In *Global Development Finance 2003: Striving for Stability in Development Finance*. Washington, DC: World Bank.

Rathgeber, Eva. 1990. "WID, WAD, GAD." *Journal of Developing Areas* July 24: 489–502.

Ravallion, Martin. 2003. "The Debate on Globalization, Poverty and Inequality: Why Measurement Matters." *International Affairs* 79 (4): 739–53.

_____. 2006. "Poverty and Growth." In D. Clark (ed.), *The Elgar Companion to Development Studies*. Cheltenham, UK/Northampton MA: Edward Elgar.

_____. 2007. "Urban Poverty." *Finance and Development* 44 (3): 15–19.

Razeto, L. 1993. *De la economia popular a la economia de solidaridad en un proyecto de desarrollo alternativo.* Santiago: Programa de Economía del Trabajo (pet).

Redclift, M. 1984. *Development and the Environmental Crisis: Red or Green Alternatives?* London and New York: Routledge.

_____. 1987. *Sustainable Development: Exploring the Contradictions.* London: Methuen.

Reddy, Sanjay, and Thomas Pogge. 2002. "How *Not* to Count the Poor." Barnard College, New York. <http://www.columbia.edu/~sr793/count.pdf>

Reed, Peter, and David Rothenberg (eds.). 1993. *Wisdom In the Open Air: The Norwegian Roots of Deep Ecology.* Minneapolis: University of Minnesota Press.

Regalado, Roberto. 2007. *América Latina Entre Siglos: Dominación, Crisis, Luchas Sociales y Alternativas Polticas.* Ocean Sur.

Remenyi, Joe. 2000. "Poverty Reduction and Urban Renewal through Urban Agriculture and Microfinance: A Case Study of Dhaka, Bangladesh." <http://www.devnet.org.nz/conf/Papers/remenyi.pdf>.

Reuveny, Rafael, and William Thompson. 2007. "The North-South Divide and International Studies: A Symposium." *International Studies Review* 9 (4), Winter: 556–64.

Rist, Gilbert. 2002. *The History of Development: From Western Origins to Global Faith.* New edition. London: Zed Books.

Robbins, Paul. 2004. *Political Ecology.* Oxford: Blackwell Publishing.

Roberts, Bryan R. 1989. "Urbanization, Migration and Development." *Sociological Forum* 4 (4), December: 665–91.

Roberts, J. Timmons, and Nikki Demetria Thanos. 2003. *Trouble in Paradise: Globalization and Environmental Crises in Latin America.* London: Routledge.

Robeyns, Ingrid. 2003. "Gender Inequality. A Capability Perspective." PhD dissertation, Faculty of Economics and Politics, Cambridge University, UK.

_____. 2007. "Some Thoughts on Basic Income From a Feminist Perspective." Paper presented at workshop at the Heinrich Böll Stifung, Berlin, July 5.

Robinson, William. 2003. "The Dialectics of Globalization and Development." In *Transnational Conflicts: Central America, Social Change and Globalization.* London: Verso.

Robles, Alfredo. 1994. *French Regulation Theories of Regulation and Conceptions of the International Division of Labour.* London and Basingstoke: Macmillan.

Rocha, Maria Geisa. 2007. "Celso Furtado and the Resumption of Construction in Brazil: Structuralism as an Alternative to Neoliberalism." *Latin American Perspectives* 34: 132–61.

Rodney, Walter. 1971. "Some Implications of the Question of the Disengagement from Imperialism." *Maji Maji*, Dar es Salaam.

_____. 1973. *How Europe Underdeveloped Africa.* London and Dar-Es-Salaam: Bogle-L'Ouverture Publications/Tanzanian Publishing House.

Rodríguez, O. 1977. "On the Conception of the Centre-Periphery System." cepal *Review* 3: 195–239. Also available in Spanish in *Revista de la* cepal, 3.

Rodrik, Dani. 1990. "How Should Structural Adjustment Programs be Designed?" *Development* 18, 7: 933–47.

_____. 1997. *Has Globalization Gone Too Far?* Washington, DC: Institute for International Economics, Harvard University.

_____. 2002. "Feasible Globalizations." Working Paper, Harvard University, July.

_____. 2006. "What's So Special about China's Exports?" nber *Working Paper Series* No. 11947, January. <www.nber.org/papers/w11947>.

_____. 2007. "Industrial Policy for the Twenty-first Century." In *One Economics, Many Recipes.* Princeton, NJ: Princeton University Press.

Rolph-Trouillot, Michel. 1995. *Silencing the Past: Power and the Production of History.*

Roman, Peter. 2003. *People's Power: Cuba's Experience with Representative Government.* Rowman and Littlefield.

Roman, Richard, and Edur Velasco Arregui. 2007. "Mexico's Oaxaca Commune." In Leo Panitch and Colin Leys (eds.), *Socialist Register 2008: Global Flashpoints, Reactions to Imperialism and Neoliberalism.*

Rondinelli, D.A. 1989. "Implementing Decentralization Programs in Asia: A Comparative Analysis." *Public Administration and Development* 3 (3): 181–207.

Rondinelli, D.A., J. McCullough and W. Johnson. 1989. "Analyzing Decentralization Policies in Developing Countries: A Political Economy Framework." *Development and Change* 20 (1): 57–87.

Rostow, Walt. 1960. *The Stages of Economic Growth.* (See self-assessment/comments in Meier and Seers (eds.), 1984, *Pioneers in Development.*)

Rowbotham, Sheila, and Stephanie Linkogle (eds.). 2001. *Women Resist Globalization: Mobilizing for Livelihood and Rights.* London: Zed Books.

Rowlands, Jo. 1997. *Questioning Empowerment.* Oxford: Oxfam Publications.

Rückert, Arne. 2007. "Producing Neoliberal Hegemony? A Neo-Gramscian Analysis of the Poverty Reduction Strategy Paper (PRSP) in Nicaragua." *Studies in Political Economy* 70, Spring.

Rueschemeyer, Dietrich, et al. 1992. *Capitalist Development and Democracy.* Cambridge: Polity Press.

Saad-Filho, Alfredo. 2003. *Anti-Capitalism: A Marxist Introduction.* London: Pluto Press.

_____. 2005. "From Washington to Post-Washington Consensus." In Alfredo Saad-Fhilo and Debora Johnston (eds.), *Neoliberalism: A Critical Reader.* London: Pluto Press.

Saad-Filho, A., and. D. Johnston (eds.). 2005. *Neoliberalism: A Critical Reader.* London: Pluto Press.

Sachs, J. 1999. "Twentieth-Century Political Economy: A Brief History of Global Capitalism." *Oxford Review of Economic Policy* 15: 90–101.

_____. 2005. *The End of Poverty.* New York: Penguin.

Sachs, Wolfgang. 1990. "The Archaeology of the Development Idea." *The Ecologist* 20 (2).

_____. 1992. *The Development Dictionary: A Guide to Knowledge as Power.* London: Zed Books.

_____. 1999a. *Planet Dialectics: Explorations in Environment and Development.* London and New York: Zed Books.

_____ (ed.). 1999b. *Global Ecology: Conflicts and Contradictions.* Zed Books.

Sadoulet, Elisabeth, Rinku Murgai and Alain de Janvry. 2001. "Access to Land Via Land Rental Markets." In A. de Janvry, G. Gordillo, J.P. Platteau and E. Sadoulet (eds.), *Access to Land, Rural Poverty, and Public Action.* Oxford: Oxford University Press.

Saguier, M. 2007. "The Hemispheric Social Alliance and the Free Trade Area of the Americas Process: The Challenges and Opportunities of Transnational Coalitions against Neo-liberalism." *Globalizations* 4 (2): 251–65.

Said, Edward W. 1978. *Orientalism: Western Conceptions of the Orient.* Penguin Books.

_____. 1993. *Culture and Imperialism.* New York: Vintage Books.

Saith, Ashwani. 2005. "Poverty Lines versus the Poor, Method versus Meaning." *Economic and Political Weekly* XL (43): 4601–10.

Salbuchi, Adrian. 2000. *El cerebro del mundo: la cara oculta de la globalización.* Córdoba: Ediciones del Copista.

Salop, Joanne. 1992. "Reducing Poverty: Spreading the Word." *Finance and Development* 29 (4), December.

Sandbrook, Richard, Marc Edelman, Patrick Heller and Judith Teichman. 2006. "Can Social Democracies Survive in the Global South?" *Dissent* Spring, 53.2: 76–83.

_____. 2007. *Social Democracy on the Periphery.* Cambridge, UK: Cambridge University Press.

Saney, Isaac. 2004. *Cuba: A Revolution in Motion.* Halifax, NS: Fernwood Publishing.

SAPRIN (Structural Adjustment Participatory Review International Network). 2001. "The Policy Roots of Economic Crisis and Poverty." Washington, DC: SAPRIN. Critical assessments include one produced by an international team of experts initially assembled by the IMF but whose work was rejected when its conclusions were deemed "too negative." <http://www.saprin.org/SAPRIN_Findings.pdf>.

Sardar, Ziauddin. 1996. *Decolonising the 21st Century.* London: Grey Seal/Kuala Lumpur: Institute for Policy Research.

Sassen, S. 1990. *The Mobility of Labour and Capital: A Study in International Investment and Labour Flow.* Cambridge University Press.

Saul, John S. 1997. "Liberal Democracy vs. Popular Democracy in Southern Africa." *Review of African Political Economy* 24 (72), June: 219–36.

_____. 2005. *The Next Liberation Struggle: Capitalism, Socialism and Democracy in Southern Africa.* New York: Monthly Review Press.

_____. 2006. *Development after Globalization: Theory and Practice for the Embattled South in a New Imperial Age.* London: Zed Books.

_____. 2007. "Development and Resistance to the Empire of Capital." *Developmental Socialism.* <http:// www.socialistproject.ca/relay/relay16_saul.pdf>.

Saxe-Fernández, John. 2002. *La Compra Venta de México.* México: Plaza James.

_____. 2008 "Denationalization of Mexico: The World Bank in Action." In H. Veltmeyer (ed.), *New Perspectives on Globalization and Antiglobalization: Prospects for a New World Order.* Ashgate Publishing,

Saxe-Fernández, John and Omar Núñez. 2001. "Globalización e Imperialismo: La transferencia de Excedentes de América Latina." In Saxe-Fernández et al. *Globalización, Imperialismo y Clase Social.* Buenos Aires/México, Editorial Lúmen.

Saxe-Fernandez, J., J. Petras, O. Núñez, and H. Veltmeyer. 2001. *Globalización, imperialismo y clase social.* Buenos Aires and Mexico City: Editorial Lumen.

Schech, Susanne, and Sanjugta vas Dev. 2007. "Governing through Participation? The World Bank's New Approach to the Poor." In Moore (ed.), *The World Bank,* Chap 2.

Schierup, C. 1990. *Migration, Socialism and the International Division of Labour.* England: Avebury.

Schierup, Carl-Ulrik, Peo Hansen, and Stephen Castles. 2006. *Migration, Citizenship and the European Welfare State: A European Dilemma.* Oxford: Oxford University Press.

Schmitz, Hubert. 2007. "The Rise of the East: What Does it Mean for Development Studies?" *IDS Bulletin* 38 (2), March: 51–58.

Schuurman, Frans (ed.). 1993. *Beyond the Impasse: New Directions in Development Theory.* London: Zed Books.

_____. 2000. "Paradigms Lost, Paradigms Regained? Development Studies in the 21st Century." *Third World Quarterly* 21 (1): 7–20.

Selassie, Bereket. 2001. "Peace, Conflict and Development." Conference on Sustainable Development, Governance and Globalization, an African Forum on Strategic Thinking and Acting Towards the Earth Summit 2002 and Beyond, Nairobi, 1September 17–20.

Sen, Amartya. 1989. "Development as Capability Expansion." *Journal of Development Expansion* 19: 41–58.

_____. 1999a. "The Importance of Democracy." In *Development as Freedom.* New York: Alfred A Knopf.

_____. 1999b. *Development as Freedom.* New York: Alfred A. Knopf.

_____. 2004. "Culture Matters." In Michael Walton (ed.), *Culture and Public Action: A Cross-Disciplinary Dialogue on Development Policy.* Washington, DC: World Bank Publications.

_____. 2005. "Secularism and Its Discontents." In Amartya Sen *The Argumentative Indian: Writings on Indian Culture, History and Identity.* Penguin Books.

Sen, G., and C.I. Grown. 1988. *Development, Crises and Alternative Visions: Third World Women's Perspectives.* London: Earthscan.

Sender, J., and S. Smith. 1986. *The Development of Capitalism in Africa.* New York: Methuen.

Senghor, Léopold Sédar, and Mercer Cook. 1964. *On African Socialism.* Westport, CT: Praeger.

Shadlen, Kenneth. 2005. "Exchanging Development for Market Access? Deep Integration and Industrial Policy under Multilateral and Regional-Bilateral Trade Agreements."

Shahnaz, Khan. 1998. "Muslim Women: Negotiations in the Third Space." *Signs* 23 (2): 463–94 (e-journal).

Shaik, Anwar. 2005. "The Economic Mythology of Neoliberalism." In Alfredo Saad-Fhilo and Debora

Johnston (eds.), *Neoliberalism: A Critical Reader*. London: Pluto Press.

Shapiro, Stephen. 2008. *Marx's Capital*. London: Pluto Press.

Shehabuddin, Elora. 1999. "Contesting the Illicit: Gender and the Politics of Fatwas in Bangladesh." *Signs* 24, 4 (1999): 1011–44 (e-journal).

Shelley, Toby. 2007. *Exploited: Migrant Labour in the New Global Economy*. London: Zed Books.

Shiva, Vandana. 1993. "The Greening of the Global Reach." In W. Sachs (ed.) *Global Ecology*. London: Zed Books.

_____. 2005. *Globalization's New Wars: Seed, Water and Life Forms*. New Delhi: Women Unlimited.

Shivji, Issa. 1976. *Class Struggles in Tanzania*. New York: Monthly Review Press.

Smart, Barry. 1983. "Genealogy, Critique and the Analytic of Power." In *Foucault, Marxism and Critique*. London: Routledge and Kegan.

Smith, David A. 1996. *Third World Cities in a Global Perspective*.

Smith, Keith. 2002. "What is the Knowledge Economy? Knowledge Intensity and Distributed Knowledge Bases." *Discussion Paper Series*. United Nations University. Maastricht: Institute for New Technologies.

So, Alvin Y. 1990. "How to Conduct Class Analysis in the World Economy?" *Sociological Perspectives* 33.

Soderbaum, Fredrik. 2004. "Introduction: Theories of the New Regionalism." In Fredrik Soderbaum and Timothy Shaw (eds.), *Theories of New Regionalism: A Palgrave Reader*. London: Palgrave Macmillan.

Solimano, Andrés, Osvaldo Sunkel, and Mario Blejer (eds.). 1993. *Rebuilding Capitalism: Alternative Roads after Socialism and Dirigisme*. Ann Arbor: University of Michigan Press.

Sparr, Pamela (ed.). 1994. *Mortgaging Women's Lives: Feminist Critiques of Structural Adjustment*. London: Zed Books.

SPEDC (Southern Peoples Ecological Debt Creditors Alliance). 2003. *No More Looting and Destruction! We the Peoples of the South Are the Ecological Creditors*. SPEDC. <http://www.deudaecologica.org/modules.php?name=Downloads anddop=viewdownloadandcid=4>.

Spronk, S., and J. Webber. 2007. "Struggles Against Accumulation by Dispossession: The Political Economy of Natural Resource Contention." *Latin American Perspectives* 34 (2): 31–47.

St Cyr, Eric. 2005. "Some Fundamentals in the Theory of Caribbean Economy." In Dennis Pantin (ed.), *The Caribbean Economy: A Reader*. Jamaica: Ian Randle Publishers.

Stambach, Amy. 1998. "Education Is my Husband: Marriage, Gender and Reproduction in Northern Tanzania." In M. Bloch, J. Beoku-Betts and R. Tabachnick (eds.), *Women and Education in Sub-Saharan Africa*.

Stavenhagen, R. 1965. "Classes, Colonialism, and Acculturation. Essay on a System of Inter-Ethnic Relations in Mesoamerica." *Studies in Comparative International Development* 1 (6): 53–77.

_____. 1968. "Seven Fallacies about Latin America." In J. Petras and M. Zeitlin (eds.), *Latin America: Reform or Revolution? A Reader*. Greenwich, CT: Fawcett.

Stehr, N., and Meja, V. 2005. *Society and Knowledge: Contemporary Perspectives in the Sociology of Knowledge and Science*. New Brunswick, NJ: Transaction Publishers.

Stewart, F., C. Huang, and M. Wang. 2001. "Internal Wars in Developing Countries: An Empirical Overview of Economic and Social Consequences." In F. Stewart and V. Fitzgerald (eds.), *War and Underdevelopment*. Vol. 1. Oxford: Oxford University Press.

Stewart, Francis. 2008. "Human Development as an Alternative Development Paradigm." UNDP. <http://hdr.undp.org/en/media/Stewart.pdf>.

Stiefel, Matthias, and Marshall Wolfe. 1994. *A Voice for the Excluded: Popular Participation in Development: Utopia or Necessity?* London and Atlantic Highlands, NJ: Zed Books and UNRISD.

Stiglitz, J.E. 1998. "More Instruments and Broader Goals: Moving Beyond the Post-Washington Consensus." *Wider Annual Lectures*. 2, WIDER, Helsinki.

_____. 1999. "Knowledge as a Global Public Good." In I. Kaul, I. Grunberg and M. Stern (eds.), *Global Public Goods: International Cooperation in the 21st Century*. New York: Oxford University Press.

_____. 2002. *Globalization and its Discontents*. New York: Norton Press.

_____. 2005. "Development Policies in a World of Globalization." In Kevin Gallagher (ed.), *Putting Development First*. London: Zed Books.

_____. 2006. *Making Globalization Work*. New York: W.W. Norton.

Stone, D. 2000. *Banking on Knowledge: The Genesis of the Global Development Network*. London.

Streeten, Paul. 1984. "Basic Needs: Some Unsettled Questions." *World Development* 12 (9).

Sumner, Andrew. 2008. "Foreign Direct Investment in Developing Countries: Have We Reached a Policy 'Tipping Point'?' *Third World Quarterly* 29 (2): 239–53.

Sunkel, Osvaldo. 1990. "Structuralism, Dependency and Institutionalism: An Exploration of Common Ground and Disparities." In James Dietz and Dilmus James (eds.), *Progress Toward Development in Latin America*. London: Lynne Reinner.

_____. 1993. *Development from Within: Toward a Neo-Structuralist Approach for Latin America*. Boulder, CO: Lynne Rienner.

_____. 2010. *Towards Inclusive Development*.

Sutcliffe, Bob. 2006. "Imperialism Old and New: A Comment on David Harvey's *The New Imperialism* and Ellen Meiksins Wood's *Empire of Capital*." *Historical Materialism* 14 (4): 59–78. <www.brill.nl>.

Swinton, Scott M., and Roberto Quiroz. 2003. "Is Poverty to Blame for Soil, Pasture and Forest Degradation in Peru's Altiplano?" *World Development* 31 (11): 1903–19.

Tabb, William K. 2004. "Neoliberalism and Anticorporate Globalization as Class Struggle." In Michael Zweig (ed.), *What's Class Got to Do With It? American Society in the Twenty-first* Century. Ithaca: ILR Press.

Talisayon, S.J. et al. 2008. *Community Wealth Rediscovered: Knowledge for Poverty Alleviation*. Center for Conscious Living Foundation and Peace Equity Access for Community Empowerment Foundation.

Tambiah, Stanley Jeyaraja. 1992. *Buddhism Betrayed: Religion, Politics and Violence in Sri Lanka*. Chicago: University of Chicago Press.

Tandon, Yash. 2008. *Ending Aid Dependence*, Oxford, UK and Geneva, Switzerland: Fahamu Books and South Centre.

Tariq, Ali. 2008. "Afghanistan: Mirage of the Good War." *New Left Review* (50).

Tarp, F. 2000. *Foreign Aid and Development, Lessons Learnt and Directions for the Future*. London: Routledge.

Taylor, Ian. 2003. "Globalization and Regionalization in Africa: Reactions to Attempts at Neoliberal Regionalism." *Review of International Political Economy* 10 (2): May: 310–30.

Tendler, J. 1997. *Good Government in the Tropics*. Baltimore and London: Johns Hopkins University Press.

Terry, D., and S. Wilson (eds.). 2005 *Remesas de inmigrantes. Moneda de cambio económico y social*. Washington: Banco Interamericano de Desarrollo.

Teubal, Miguel. 2008. "Peasant Struggles for Land and Agrarian Reform in Latin America." In A. Haroon Akram-Lodhi and Cristóbal Kay (eds.), *Peasants and Globalization: Political Economy, Rural Transformation and the Agrarian Question*. London and New York: Routledge.

Tharamangalam, Joseph (ed.). 2006. *Kerala: The Paradoxes of Pubic Action and Development*. India: Orient Longman.

_____. 2008. "Human Development as Transformative Practice: Lessons from Kerala and Cuba." presented at the annual HDCA Conference, New Delhi, September 11–14.

Thiong'o, Ngũgĩ wa. 1993. *Moving the Centre: The Struggle for Cultural Freedoms*. Nairobi: East African Educational Publishers.

Thompson, Grahame. 2004. "Global Inequality, Economic Globalization and Technological Change." [Sections 1–5]. In W. Brown, S. Bromley and S. Athreye (eds.), *Ordering the International: History, Change and Transformation*. London and Ann Arbor: Pluto Press with the Open University.

Thompson, Lisa. 2007. "The Contradictions between Globalization and Development? A Perspective from Southern Africa." In P. Bowles et al. (eds.), *Regional Perspectives on Globalization*. Basingstoke: Palgrave Macmillan.

Thorbecke, Eric, and M. Nissanke (eds.). 2006. "The Impact of Globalization on the World's Poor." *World Development* 34 (8). Special Issue.

Todd, Moss. 2007. "The Complexities and Uncertainties of Development." In *African Development: Making Sense of the Issues and Actors*. Boulder, CO: Lynne Rienner.

Todorov, Tzvetan. 1998. *On Human Diversity: Nationalism, Racism, and Exoticism in French Thought*. Cambridge: Harvard University Press.

_____. 2008. *La peur des barbares. Au-dèla du choc des civilisations*. Paris: Robert Laffont.

Torres, M. 2000. "Knowledge-Based International Aid: Do We Want it, Do We Need It?" In W. Gmelin, K. King and S. McGrath (eds.), *Development Knowledge*. National Research and International Cooperation. Scotland, Germany and Switzerland, Centre of African Studies with the German Foundation for International Development.

Toye, John. 1987. *Dilemmas of Development: Reflections on the Counter-Revolution in Development Theory and Policy*. Oxford: Basil Blackwell.

Tsjeard Bouta, Georg Frerks, and Ian Bannon. 2005. *Gender, Conflict and Development*. Washington, DC: World Bank.

Tucker, V. (ed.). 1997. *Cultural Perspectives on Development*. London: Frank Cass.

_____. 1999. "The Myth of Development: A Critique of Eurocentric Discourse." In Ronaldo Munck and Denis O'Hearn (eds.), *Critical Development Theory*. London: Zed Books.

Tulchin, Joseph, and Allison Garland (eds.). 2000. *Social Development in Latin America*. Boulder, CO: Lynne Rienner.

Turton, C. 2000a. "Sustainable Livelihoods and Project Design in India." ODI *Working Paper 127*, ODI, February.

_____. 2000b. "The Sustainable Livelihoods Approach and Programme Development in Cambodia." ODI *Working Paper 130*, ODI, February.

UK, Ministry of Defence. 2007. *Global Strategic Trends 2007–2036*. London: Development, Concepts and Doctrine Centre (DCDC).

Ul Haq, Mahbub. 1995. *Reflections on Human Development*. New York: Oxford University Press.

UNCTAD. 1998. *Trade and Development Report 1998*. Geneva: UNCTAD, Chap. 3 (83–110). <http://www.unctad.org/en/docs/tdr1998_en.pdf>.

_____. 2007. *Trade and Development Report 2007: Regional Cooperation for Development*. Chaps. 3–5. <http://www.unctad.org/en/docs/tdr2007_en.pdf>.

UNDP (United Nations Development Programme). 1990, 1993, 1995, 1996, 2002. *Human Development Report*. New York: Oxford University Press.

_____. 1997. *Capacity Development*. Management Development and Governance Division. New York: UNDP.

_____. 1997a. *Governance for Sustainable Human Development*. Policy document. New York.

_____. 1997b. *Participatory Local Governance*, Policy Document. New York.

_____. 1997c. "Report on the Third International Conference of the New and Restored Democracies on Democracy and Development, Bucharest, Romania, September 2–4 1997." New York. <http://www.undp.org.>

_____. 1997d. *The Shrinking State: Governance and Sustainable Human Development*. Policy Document. New York: UNDP.

_____. 2003a. *Gender Approaches in Conflict and Post-Conflict Situations*. New York: UNDP.

_____. 2003b. *Human Development Report. Millennium Development Goals: A Compact Among Nations to End Human Poverty*. New York: Oxford University Press.

_____. 2006a. *Governance for the Future: Democracy and Development in the Least Developed Countries*. New York: UNDP.

_____. 2006b. *Gender in Sustainable Livelihoods: Issues, Guidelines and a Strategy for Action*. New York: UNDP, Sustainable Livelihoods Unit, Social Development and Poverty Elimination Division, Bureau for Development Policy.

UNESCO (United Nations Department of Economic and Social Affairs). 1999. *Globalization and international Migration in Latin America and the Caribbean: Trends and Prospects of the 21st Century.* Migration Studies Network for Latin America and the Caribbean.

_____. 2005. *The World Social Situation: The Inequality Predicament.* New York: UNESCO.

United Nations. 1995. *World Summit for Social Development: The Copenhagen Declaration and Programme of Action,* New York.

_____. 1998. "The UN and Business: A Global Partnership." New York: United Nations Department of Public Information. <http://www.un.org/news/facts/business.htm>.

_____. 2000. *Millennium Declaration (2000). Millennium Summit.* New York: UN, September 6–8.

_____. 2005. *The Inequality Predicament.* New York: UN.

USAID (U.S. Aid for International Development). 2004. *Strategic Plan: Fiscal Years 2004–2009.* Washington DC.

UNRISD. 1995. *States in Disarray: An Overview.* Geneva.

Utting, Peter (ed.). 2006. *Reclaiming Development Agendas: Knowledge, Power and International Policy Making.* London: Palgrave Macmillan and UNRISD.

Van Dijk, Jan. 2006. *The Network Society.* Second Edition. London: Sage.

Van Waeyenberge, Elisa. 2006. "From Washington to Post-Washington Consensus." In K.S. Jomo and Ben Fine (eds.), *The New Development Economics.* London: Zed Books.

Väyrynen, Raimo. 2003. "Regionalism: Old and New." *International Studies Review* 5 (1): 25–51.

Veltmeyer, H. 1997a. "Challenging the World Bank's Agenda to Restructure Labour in Latin America." LCS 30 (2): 226–59.

_____. 1997b. "Decentralisation as the Institutional Basis for Participatory Development: The Latin American Perspective." *Canadian Journal of Development Studies* XVIII (2).

_____. 1999. "Labour and the World Economy." *Canadian Journal of Development Studies* Special Issue, December.

_____. 2002. "The Politics of Language: Deconstructing Postdevelopment Discourse." *Canadian Journal of Development Studies* XX11 (3): 597–624.

_____. 2005a. "Development and Globalization as Imperialism." *Canadian Journal of Development Studies* XXVI (1): 89–106.

_____. 2005b. "The Dynamics of Land Occupation in Latin America." In Sam Moyo and Paris Yeros (eds.), *Reclaiming the Land: The Resurgence of Rural Movements in Africa, Asia, and Latin America.* London: Zed Books.

_____. 2007a. *Illusions and Opportunities: Civil Society in the Quest for Social Change.* Halifax: Fernwood Publishing.

_____. 2007b. "Civil Society and Development." In Paul Haslam, Pierre Beaudet and Jessica Schafer (eds.), *Introduction to International Development Studies: Approaches, Actors and Issues.* Oxford University Press Canada.

_____. (ed.). 2008. *New Perspectives on Globalization and Antiglobalization: Prospects for a New World Order.* Ashgate, UK.

_____. 2009. "The World Bank on 'Agriculture for Development': A Failure of Imagination or the Power of Ideology?" *The Journal of Peasant Studies* 36 (2), April: 391–408.

_____. (ed.). 2010. *Imperialism, Crisis and Class Struggle: The Verities of Capitalism.* Leiden: Brill.

Veltmeyer, H., and A. O'Malley. 2001. *Beyond Neoliberalism: Community-Based Development in Latin America.*

Veltmeyer, H., and J. Petras. 1997. *Economic Liberalism and Class Conflict in Latin America.* London: MacMillan Press.

_____. 2005a. "Foreign Aid, Neoliberalism and Imperialism." In Alfredo Saad-Filho and Deborah Johnston (eds.), *Neoliberalism: A Critical Reader.* London: Pluto Press.

_____. 2005b. "Latin America's Social Structure and the Dynamics of Change." In Jan Kuiper Black (ed.), *Latin America: its Problems and its Promise.* Fourth edition. Boulder, CO: Westview Press.

Von Meijenfeldt, Roel. 2001. *Comprehensive Development Framework and Conflict-Affected Countries.* CDF Secretariat, The World Bank.

Wackernagel, Mathis, and William Rees. 1996a. "Ecological Footprints for Beginners." *Our Ecological Footprint: Reducing Human Impact on the Earth.* Gabriola Island, BC: New Society Publishers.

_____. 1996b. "The Sustainability Debate." In *Our Ecological Footprint: Reducing Human Impact on the Earth.* Gabriola Island, BC: New Society Publishers.

Wade, Robert. 1990. *Governing the Market: Economic Theory and the Role of Government in East Asian Industrialization.* Princeton: Princeton University Press.

_____. 2002. "Out of the Box: Rethinking the Governance of International Financial Markets." LSE DESTIN Working Paper Series No. 02-24, February (1–15) [W].

_____. 2007. "Japan, the World Bank and the Art of Paradigm Maintenance." In D. Moore (ed.) *The World Bank.*

Wallerstein, Immanuel. 1979. *The Capitalist World Economy.* Cambridge: Cambridge University Press.

_____. 2006. *European Universalism: The Rhetoric of Power.*

Wanner, Thomas. 2007. "The Bank's *Greenspeak,* the Power of Knowledge and *Sustaindevelopment.*" In Moore (ed.), *The World Bank.*

Warren, Bill. 1980. *Imperialism: Pioneer of Imperialism.* London: Verso.

Warren, D.M., et al. 1989. "Indigenous Knowledge Systems: Implications for Agriculture and International Development." *Studies in Technology and Social Change* 11. Ames, Iowa: Technology and Social Change Program, Iowa State University.

_____. 1995. *The Cultural Dimension of Development: Indigenous Knowledge Systems.* London: Intermediate Technology.

Waterman, Peter. 1999. "The New Social Unionism: A New Union Model for a New World Order." In Munck and Waterman.

Watts, M. J. 2005. "Righteous Oil? Human Rights, the Oil Complex, and Corporate Social Responsibility." *Annual Review of Environment and Resources* (30): 373–407.

WCED (World Commission on Environment and Development). 1987. *Our Common Future.*

Weber, Heloise. 2002. "Global Governance and Poverty Reduction: The Case of Microcredit." In Rorden Wilkinson and Steve Hughes (eds.), *Global Governance: Critical Perspectives.* London and New York: Routledge.

Weisbrot, M., et al. 2000. "Growth may be Good for the Poor — but are IMF and Policies Good for Growth?" Washington, DC: CEPR (Centre for Econ and Policy Research), August 7. <http://www.cepr.net/documents/publications/econ_growth_2001_05.pdf>.

Weiss, Linda. 2000. "Developmental States in Transition: Adapting, Dismantling, Innovating, not Normalising." *Pacific Review* 13(1): 21–55.

Welch, Gita, and Zahra Nuru. 2006. "Governance for the Future: Democracy and Development in the Least Developed Countries Work." New York: UNDP. <http://www.UNDP.org/governance/docs/Policy-Pub-LDCReport.pdf>.

White, C. 2005. *Democracy at the Crossroads: International Perspectives on Critical Global Citizenship.* Lanham: Lexington Books.

White House. 2008. "Declaration of the [G-20] Summit on Financial Markets and the World Economy." Press release, November 15.

Whitehead, Ann. 1981. "I'm Hungry, Mum: The Politics of Domestic Budgeting in North East Ghana." In Kate Young et al. (eds.), *Of Marriage and the Market.* London: CSE Books.

_____. 2005. "The Gendered Impacts of Liberalisation Policies on African Agricultural Economies and Rural Livelihoods." Background paper prepared for the UNRISD report "Gender Equality: Striving for Justice in an Unequal World." Geneva: UNRISD.

Wilber, Charles, and Kenneth Jameson. 1975 [1989]). "Paradigms of Economic Development and Beyond." In C. Wilber (ed.) *Political Economy of Development and Underdevelopment.* Fourth edition.

Williams, David. 2007. "Constructing the Economic Space: The World Bank and the Making of *Homo*

Economicus." In Moore (ed.), *The World Bank.*

Williams, Eric. 1944. *Capitalism and Slavery.* University of North Carolina Press.

Williams, Horatio. 2001. "Hindsight After Cold War: Samuel Huntington, the Social Sciences and Development Paradigms." *Dialectic Anthropology* 26: 311–24.

Williamson, J. (ed.). 1990. *Latin American Adjustment. How Much Has Happened?* Washington, DC: Institute for International Economics.

Wilpert, Gregory. 2007. *Changing Venezuela by Taking Power: The History and Policies of the Chávez Government.* London and New York: Verso.

Wilson, G. 2007. "Knowledge, Innovation and Re-inventing Technical Assistance for Development." *Progress in Development Studies* 7 (3): 183–99.

Wolf, Eric. 1974. *The Hidden Frontier: Ecology and Ethnicity in an Alpine Valley.* London: Academic Press.

Woo-Cumings, M. (ed.). 1999. *The Developmental State.* Ithaca, NY: Cornell University Press.

Wood, Ellen Meiksins. 1994. "From Opportunity to Imperative: The History of the Market." *Monthly Review* July–August: 14–40.

_____. 1995. *Democracy Against Capitalism: Renewing Historical Materialism.* Cambridge: Cambridge University Press.

Woods, Ngaire. 2006. *The Globalizers: The IMF, the World Bank, and Their Borrowers.* Ithaca: Cornell University Press.

Woolcock, M., and D. Narayan. 2000. "Social Capital: Implications for Development Theory, Research and Policy." *World Bank Research Observer* 15 (2).

World Bank. 1978–2008. *World Development Report.* New York: Oxford University Press.

_____. 1979. *Recognizing the "Invisible" Women in Development: The World Bank's Experience.* Washington, DC: World Bank.

_____. 1982. "Sociologists: Putting People First in Projects." *Report* March-April.

_____. 1994. *Governance and Development.* Washington, DC: World Bank;

_____. 1995. *World Development Report: Workers in an Integrating World.* Oxford: Oxford University Press.

_____. 1995b. *Policy Research Bulletin* 6, 4 (August–October).

_____. 1996. "A Stronger, More Agile and More Effective World Bank." World Bank Report, September 26. Washington DC.

_____. 1998. *Indigenous Knowledge for Development: A Framework for Action.* Knowledge and Learning Centre, Africa Region.

_____. 1999. *Knowledge for Development. World Development Report 1998/99.* Washington, DC: Oxford University Press.

_____. 2001. *Development Cooperation and Conflict: OP 2.30.* Washington, DC: World Bank.

_____. 2003. *Land Policies for Growth and Poverty Reduction.* Washington, DC: World Bank; Oxford: Oxford University Press (World Bank Policy Research Report prepared by Klaus Deininger).

_____. 2006. *Global Economic Prospects. Economic Implications of Remittances and Migration.* Washington, DC: World Bank.

_____. 2007. *Meeting the Challenges of Global Development.* Washington, DC, October 12.

Worsley, Peter. 1984. *The Three Worlds: Culture and World Development.* University of Chicago Press.

Wright, Erik Olin. 2005. *Approaches to Class Analysis.* Cambridge, UK: Cambridge University Press.

Wright, Ronald. 1993. *Stolen Continents: 500 Years of Conquest and Resistance in the Americas* Penguin Books.

www.agp.org|archives| War and Globalization.

Yansané, A.Y. (ed.). 1996. *Development Strategies in Africa: Current Economic, Socio-Political and Institutional Trends and Issues.* London: Greenwood Press.

Yergin, Daniel. 2003. *The Prize: The Epic Quest for Oil, Money, and Power.* New York: Free Press.

Young, Brigitte. 2000. "The 'Mistress' and the 'Maid' in the Globalised Economy." In Panitch and Leys.

Young, Tom, and David Williams. 2007. "The World Bank and the Liberal Project." In D. Moore (ed.), *The World Bank Development Poverty Hegemony*. Scottsville, South Africa: University of KwaZulu-Natal Press.

Zayago Lau, Edgar. 2006. "The Proposed World Bank Scientific Millennium Initiatives and Nanotechnogy in Latin America." In A. Baranon (ed.), *Research in Nanotechnology Developments.*

Zeilig, Leo (ed.). 2009. *Class Struggle and Resistance in Africa*. Chicago: Haymarket.

Zeng, Ming, and Peter Williamson. 2007. *Dragons at Your Door: How Chinese Cost Innovation Is Disrupting Global Competition*. Boston: Harvard Business School Press.

Zuckerman, Elaine. 2003. "Engendering PRSPs: The Track Record and Key Entry Points." GTZ Regional Workshop '"Engendering PRSPs in Africa." Nairobi, December.

Zweig, Michael (ed.). 2004. *What's Class Got to Do With It? American Society in the Twenty-first Century.* Ithaca: ILR Press.

Index

Africa, 18-19, 107, 150, 199, 223-230, 247-251
agriculture, 174, 235, 252
    agrarian question, 111, 171, 174-176
    agrarian reform, 176, 178
    agrarian stagnation, 32
    agri-business, 174, 177
    agro-exports, 173
    agro-food, 172-174
    agro-fuel, 63, 172, 218, 259-260
    investment in, 4, 61, 111, 252
    transformation, 142, 171-180, 195
ALBA, *see* Bolivarian Alternative for Latin America
autonomy, 185, 203, 209, 238

Boliviarian Alternative for Latin America, 37, 186, 232, 244-248, 256
Bolivarian Revolution, 37, 132, 244, 248, 257
Bolivia, 37, 49, 84, 99, 176, 186, 220-221, 233, 245, 247-250, 255, 257, 259
Brazil, 16, 20, 22-23, 37, 49, 60, 99, 102, 176, 182, 233, 260
Bretton Woods, 4, 54, 73, 77-83, 89

capital, 33, 160-161, 197
    accumulation, 4, 7-8, 19, 24-26, 36, 40-41, 43-44, 50, 51, 54, 56, 61, 63, 64, 73, 78, 89, 94, 95, 97, 105, 113, 119, 144, 154, 165, 171, 172, 183, 213, 214, 218, 229, 231, 258
    Chinese, 18, 62, 67
    corporate, 53, 106, 144
    crisis, 256
    deregulation, 52, 84
    displacement, 47, 50
    financial, 21, 51, 127, 144, 173, 197
    flows, 13, 16, 19, 20, 21, 37, 61, 64, 82, 185, 245
    foreign, 20, 144, 239
    gains, 21
    globalization of, 52, 57, 59, 61, 93, 114, 144, 146, 173, 174, 187, 232
    human, 127, 154, 167
    investment, 40, 51, 52, 95, 124, 163
    markets, 52, 62, 175
    merchant, 25
    natural, 126, 202
    physical, 13, 127
    power, 15, 53

    private, 51
    regulation, 101
    relationship with labour, 64, 113, 142, 146, 173, 181, 183, 195, 231
    restructuring, 190
    social, 7-8, 36, 98, 99, 111, 122-127, 177, 189, 197
Chávez, 38, 49, 186, 221-221, 233, 247-248, 255, 257
civil society, 7, 48, 48, 56-57, 64, 66, 69, 71, 76, 79, 80, 84, 90, 95, 98, 100-102, 112, 123, 125, 127-128, 130, 132, 149, 180, 191, 193-194, 196-197, 199, 232, 246, 253, 254, 255
class,
    analysis, 51, 66, 90-94, 142, 146, 186, 230
    capitalist, 5, 6, 11, 40, 50, 54, 57, 67, 89, 95-96, 100, 102, 107, 113, 139, 144, 198, 254
    conflict, 91, 97, 105, 140, 229
    dominant, 55, 94, 134
    middle, 71, 112, 140, 196, 254
    political, 49, 50, 90, 99, 257
    power, 90, 98, 137, 144, 243
    social, 1, 94, 101, 134, 137, 139, 142-143, 153, 176, 186, 198
    struggle, 90, 93-94, 107, 134, 141, 176, 243
    ruling, 45, 54, 67, 80, 90, 94, 184, 243
    war, 90, 97, 104-105, 107-108, 256
    working, 40, 49-53, 107, 139, 175, 184, 195, 198, 229, 249, 255
commodities, 18-19, 22, 39, 48-49, 62, 86, 145, 159, 161, 197, 235
communism, 4, 15, 27, 53, 87, 214, 228
crisis,
    Asian, 21, 23, 62, 236, 245, 246
    accumulation, 190
    capitalist, 47, 106
    debt, 16-19, 54, 69, 85, 121
    economic, 21-24, 133-134, 229, 232
    environmental, 42, 63, 201-203, 208, 214-217, 248, 250
    financial, 49, 57, 59-60, 63, 79, 150, 232-233, 236, 238
    fiscal, 54, 56
    food, 13, 32, 63, 133, 172-173, 218, 250, 256
    global, 11, 20, 64, 224, 255, 256
    political, 47
    production, 5-6, 40, 47-49, 54, 59-60, 62-63, 78-79, 220, 256